THE MAN WHO INVENTED HIMSELF

Burns: A Biography of Robert Burns
Vagabond of Verse: A Biography of Robert Service
William Wallace: Brave Heart
The Eye Who Never Slept: A Life of Allan Pinkerton
Michael Collins: A Life
Sounds Out of Silence: A Life of Alexander Graham Bell
Little Boss: A Life of Andrew Carnegie

THE MAN WHO INVENTED HIMSELF

A Life of Sir Thomas Lipton

JAMES MACKAY

MAINSTREAM
PUBLISHING

EDINBURGH AND LONDON

For Isobel and Freddy Anderson

First published in Great Britain in 1998 by
MAINSTREAM PUBLISHING COMPANY (EDINBURGH) LTD
7 Albany Street
Edinburgh EH1 3UG

ISBN 1 85158 831 0

A catalogue record for this book is available from the British Library

Typeset in Sabon
Printed and bound in Great Britain by Butler & Tanner Ltd

CONTENTS

INTRODUCTION

Growing up in Glasgow in the 1940s I remember the Lipton grocery stores vividly, with their dazzling black-and-white floor tiles and gleaming brasswork. It mattered not whether they were in Partick or Pollokshields, the decor, both inside and out, was the same. What I remember most about them were the shop assistants clad in white, and the name LIPTON which must have appeared a hundred times if it appeared once. Majolica tiles below the fronts of the counters extolled Lipton's Tea, Lipton's Butter, Lipton's Sauces, Lipton's Pickles and Lipton's Cheese. There were Lipton's Rolls and even (if you had sufficient points) boxes of Lipton's Chocolates, temptingly displayed on the confectionery counter. Everything was labelled Lipton's Price with the figures stridently inscribed underneath. 'This is the best buy in town' they seemed to shout. It seemed to me then a wonder that other grocers could survive such cut-throat competition.

Everybody in Glasgow knew that Tommy Lipton was a Glasgow man. He had built a grocery empire that encircled the world, but it had all started here. More than that, he was from the Gorbals and that seemed to make his achievements even more remarkable. Next to the boxer Benny Lynch, in fact, he was the most famous person to come out of that notorious slum district.

A stone's throw away, on the opposite side of the River Clyde, stood the People's Palace, a handsome red sandstone pile intended, as its name suggests, to be the museum of the ordinary folk of Glasgow, unlike that other red sandstone pile, the Museum and Art Galleries at Kelvingrove in the posh West End, where Old Masters rubbed shoulders with the works of the Glasgow Boys. The People's Palace was a popular school outing, but subsequently a place to be visited from time to time, to gaze in wonder at all those extravaganzas in gold and silver and enamels, the cups and trophies of the late Sir Thomas Lipton. On the walls hung huge photographs of his *Shamrocks* – six in all, for as well as the five contenders for the America's Cup (the one trophy which eluded him) there was the twenty-three-metre yacht of the same name, but without a number, which was, I think, the great yachtsman's favourite for the simple reason that it was the boat in which he himself raced, rather than leave it to another skipper. I recall the schoolmaster who introduced my class to the Lipton Room holding him up as an example. Like Bruce and his spider, Lipton and his *Shamrocks* typified Scottish pluck, grit and 'stickability' – no matter that the first was half-Norman and the other wholly Irish, though both born in Scotland.

In the 1940s there were still plenty of old folk in Glasgow who had personal memories of Tommy Lipton and his shop-window cartoons, his Orphans, his Jumbo cheeses and his funny mirrors. The publication of Alec Waugh's book *The Lipton Story* in 1950 caused quite a stir at the time, especially as it was serialised by the *Scottish Daily Express*; but even then the Glasgow which Lipton had known so well was rapidly disappearing. All the streets associated with him – where he was born and grew up, where his parents had their wee corner shop and where he opened his first market – all were swept away in the ruthless redevelopment that overwhelmed the inner districts of Glasgow in the 1950s and 1960s. Considering how rich and famous he was, it is remarkable that so little remains in Glasgow as a reminder of him. There used to be a plaque on an inside wall of the villa in Cambuslang where he lived from 1877 until 1892 but it disappeared long ago, and even the name of the house itself, Johnston Villa, has been erased from the gateposts. There is the family tombstone in the Southern Necropolis, but that is all. Even the Lipton Room is no more, his trophies having been transferred to Kelvingrove and consigned to a basement storeroom.

My interest in Lipton was rekindled for two reasons. From 1990 until 1996 I lived in a penthouse flat in Lancefield Quay, a luxury conversion of the wharf where the Irish boats tied up on the Broomielaw. It was thither that young Tommy Lipton came each week with a hand-cart to load up produce fresh from County Monaghan for his parents' little shop, and from my dining-room window I looked up Lancefield Street to the site where, a century ago, there stood the impressive buildings that were the nerve centre of the Lipton enterprise. Today little remains except a part of the foundations and one wall. Perhaps archaeologists in a future century will excavate the site and uncover the remains of artefacts associated with this colossal empire; but it is a sad place today, overgrown with weeds and rich in memories.

One thing tends to lead to another, and it was while researching my biography of Allan Pinkerton, another son of the Gorbals, that it occurred to me that Lipton was long overdue for reappraisal. Mention the name to most people and they will immediately react with the key-words 'Tea' and 'Yachting'; but the man who revolutionised the provision trade in general had sporting interests that went far beyond his epic and unprecedented challenges for the America's Cup. How many people, I wonder, are aware that, long before Jules Rimet, Lipton had organised international football championships in Europe and Latin America? Not only had he set Argentina and Uruguay on track to become two of the greatest soccer nations in the world, but, twenty years before the first contest for the FIFA trophy, Juventus and other top European teams were battling in Turin for the Lipton Cup.

To say that Sir Thomas Johnston Lipton, Baronet, KCVO, was a self-made man is a thundering understatement. He quite literally invented himself. The image which he cultivated, the persona which he created, even the middle name he gave himself, were nothing like the real person. A kenspeckle figure in the Gorbals and Anderston districts of Glasgow in the 1880s, this is a man who sprang to national fame in 1897, in the year of Queen Victoria's Diamond Jubilee. Within two years his was a household name all over the world, and so it would remain right up until his death in October 1931 at the age of eighty-three. The paradox was that, while Lipton was a name on everyone's lips, there were very few people who knew the real man. Indeed, it was often rumoured that there was no such person as Thomas J. Lipton, that the name was merely a front for a consortium of Irish Nationalist businessmen.

Lipton claimed to have been born in Crown Street in the Gorbals in May 1850. I had no reason to doubt this statement, until I checked the 1851 Census and found no trace of the Lipton family at that address. Many days were spent (and considerable eye-strain incurred) in poring over microfilms of the Gorbals census books – all 117 of them – before I came to the reluctant conclusion that the Liptons did not live in the Gorbals after all. It was then that the Glasgow Family History Society came to my rescue, and I discovered that they had actually computerised the 1851 Census. From the Census co-ordinator, Mrs Elizabeth D. Smith, I obtained a print-out which revealed that the only family of that surname in the whole of Glasgow was that of Tommy Lipton, his parents, brother and sister, living some miles away on the other side of the Clyde in Barony parish. The second shock was to discover that, at the time of the Census, Tommy was three years of age, and not the months-old babe in arms which the 'facts' had hitherto asserted.

I am afraid that it was downhill all the way after that. Far from having been born in Crown Street, it transpired that Lipton had not settled there until 1861. Instead of 1858, the family corner shop was not established till 1864, which made a nonsense of Lipton's oft-repeated claim that he left school in November 1860, at the age of nine, to get a job at half-a-crown a week to keep the family business from bankruptcy. In fact he left school in May 1863 at the age of fifteen, and thus possessed a far better general education than he later implied. His early association with the Dick Brothers and his adventures in America in the late 1860s turn out to be highly romanticised or a complete fabrication. He was a born raconteur who, with repeated telling, eventually came to believe his own stories.

Lipton was also a mass of contradictions: an Ulster Protestant who became an ardent Irish Nationalist; the world's most eligible bachelor who had, in fact, contracted a youthful but disastrous marriage; and the world's most celebrated ladies' man who was in actuality a homosexual with an extremely well-developed mother fixation. Curiously enough, that last aspect of him was often extolled as his most singular virtue. He was – at one and the same time – a very simple man and an exceptionally vain man; an ardent exponent of shorter shop hours who outrageously overworked himself (and his closest associates). This child of the Glasgow slums, offspring of poor Irish peasants, would one day rub shoulders with kings and emperors. Not only was he at his ease with them but he had an extraordinary ability to put them at ease with themselves and with each other; and his handling of such notoriously headstrong characters as the Empress Eugénie and the Kaiser was astounding. At the same time he was telling them, to their faces, that their days were numbered and that within a few years there would not be a single monarchy in Europe. He was also on the most intimate terms with notorious revolutionaries like Arabi Pasha, Colonel Arthur Lynch and Michael Davitt.

He was something of a revolutionary himself, a buccaneer and a maverick. The epithet 'Napoleon of the Provision Trade' was singularly apt for there was something of the great Bonaparte in the man who planned each move with military precision but never hesitated in taking bold decisions. He had the unenviable distinction of being blackballed by the Royal Yacht Club because he was a grocer, though he was arguably the outstanding yachtsman of his generation, and at the same time blackballed by the Grocers' Federation who heartily detested his swashbuckling techniques. The man who invented himself was also a self-publicist of quite prodigious proportions, but behind the stunts and the parades was an intensely private man who had, perhaps, more reason than most for keeping a tight lid on his domestic life.

In some respects, Lipton is the biographer's dream, for he assiduously preserved every newspaper scrap that so much as mentioned his name. Eventually these cuttings, ranging from 1878 to 1926, would fill eighty-four fat folio volumes, housed in a bookcase especially constructed for the purpose. After his death these scrapbooks, together with supplementary volumes, photograph albums and other ephemera, were bequeathed to the Mitchell Library in Glasgow. Over the past three years, whenever I had a spare hour or two, and latterly over many weeks of intensive study, I have pored over these volumes and extracted many of the nuggets which are now revealed for the first time in this book. The staff of the Mitchell Library have been unfailingly courteous and helpful at all times, but I must single out Karen Cunningham, Curator of the Lipton Collection, and David McMenemy, Unilever Research Assistant, without whose assistance this book would never have been possible.

Farther afield, I have had a great deal of help and encouragement from John Wotherspoon of the Consultative Tea Group Limited in Crawley and Jeanette Strickland of Unilever House, London. At Osidge, Lipton's London home and now the Lipton Memorial Home for Retired Nurses, I am indebted to the Matron, Joyce Pickering, for showing me round, and also to the Secretary of the Lipton Memorial Trust, Miss Marion Tickner.

Helen Dick in Largs, Alice and Ian Robertson in Southgate, Michael Coyle and James Forsyth in Cambuslang, Hamish MacLeod in Bearsden and Roderick Macpherson in Glasgow have all contributed in some way towards this project. Dr Donal Bateson of the Hunterian Museum and Ronald Breingan, President of the Glasgow and West of Scotland Numismatic Society, Peter Ramsay of the Clydesdale Bank and Daniel Keren and Sam Malamud of the Inter-Governmental Philatelic Corporation provided me with illustrations of Lipton medals, the 'pound note' and the stamps pertaining to Lipton and his challenges for the Americas Cup. Dr Arthur Shenkin gave me a fascinating psychological profile of Lipton.

Professor Colin M. Coates of Edinburgh University furnished me with illuminating details of Lipton's alleged engagement to his grandmother, Margaret Dey, one of the many ladies with whom Lipton was romantically associated. My old friend Professor G. Ross Roy of the University of South Carolina, and his colleague Dr Allen H. Stokes, University Librarian for Special Collections (and, as such, Head of the South Caroliniana Library) investigated Lipton's sojourn in Charleston. John Holman did the useful legwork in London and Peadar Murnane provided information on the family in County Monaghan.

For details of the Lipton trophies and memorabilia, formerly in the People's Palace and now at Kelvingrove, Glasgow, I must thank Henry Diamond, Elspeth Gallie, Colin Hunter-McQueen Elspeth King and Peter Searle.

Last but by no means least, I must thank my old friend Freddy Anderson, a Monaghan man himself though long domiciled in Glasgow, for his interest in this book and for furnishing me with useful background on the Lipton ancestral area around Clones. Research into Lipton – who would have been horrified if he had realised how well even the lives of ordinary people are documented – has also been conducted at Register House, Edinburgh, the National Library of Scotland, Glasgow University Library and the British Library in London; to the staff of these institutions I record my profound thanks for all their help.

James Mackay,
Glasgow,
June 1997

PROLOGUE

Ay free, aff han', your story tell,
When wi a bosom cronie;
But still keep something to yoursel
Ye scarcely tell to onie.
    Robert Burns, 'Epistle to a Young Friend', 15 May 1786

For many years, until the summer of 1930, four Scotsmen met frequently for an early-evening dinner in a sprawling, rather old-fashioned mansion in New Southgate, an unpretentious district of north London. Osidge had been occupied by one of the four since 1893. For many years he had been content merely to lease it and it was not until 1926 that he exercised the option to purchase it. Southgate was then still semi-rural, on the outskirts of the metropolis, and the house had been leased for the simple reason that it was within easy commuting distance of its owner's London office.

In the fullness of time, however, he had come to love Osidge with the sort of wholehearted affection which a man normally gives to his wife; and the wonder is that he took so long in making it his own property. This was no family home for its proprietor was, to all intents and purposes, a confirmed bachelor. He was frequently away from home, either on business trips or sporting adventures in many different parts of the world, but invariably the prospect of returning to his London home, with its gloomy, stuffy, over-furnished rooms and rather untidy gardens, filled him with pleasurable excitement. One could never describe the house as palatial; rather it was the suburban villa of the successful manager. An unpretentious house in an unfashionable suburb, it was for almost forty years the unlikely home of one of the greatest self-made multi-millionaires the British Isles has ever produced.

The old man's pleasure at returning from abroad would be complete if he knew that the three guests at his five o'clock dinner party would be Lord Dewar, Lord Inverforth and Sir Harry Lauder, three celebrated Scots who were his most intimate friends and bosom pals. Occasionally a fifth Scotsman was invited to dine with them, a much younger man, a Glasgow man who had gravitated towards Fleet Street. William Blackwood got to know his host very well from the turn of the century onwards. Blackwood heard the great man's stories many, many times, for the old boy was a brilliant raconteur, and he often urged Lipton to set them down on paper. But the mighty merchant prince was no scribe, and in the end Blackwood agreed to ghost the great man's memoirs. This 'autobiography' was published in 1931, and furnishes all that its subject chose to let the world know of himself. 'My only troubles will be in what to tell and what to leave out, where to be frank and where to be guarded.'[1]

In the last forty-five years of his long and remarkable life, his every thought and action were thoroughly documented in the world's press; and he himself assiduously collected his press-cuttings which would eventually fill eighty-four fat volumes. But of his early, formative years, extremely little has previously been published, and not much of that turns out to be truthful or correct. Blackwood, as his literary ghost, was obliged to be careful in what he put into the autobiography, but not long after his friend's death in 1931 he was commissioned to contribute a chapter on him to a volume dealing with some of the great men of the late-Victorian period. In this essay, Blackwood pulled no punches. 'The truth was that Lipton was vain, domineering, and immensely self-centred. He not infrequently referred to himself as the Great Lipton!'[2]

Blackwood recalled a conversation at one of those select little dinner parties. The conversation had drifted to a discussion of how much the element of luck had to do with any particular man's success in life. Tom Dewar, one of the greatest personalities in the world of commerce, a man of wit, learning, shrewdness, high intellect and tremendous native ability, admitted quite frankly that he had had the luck to introduce blended Scotch whisky to the English public at the correct psychological moment and soon found himself a millionaire as a consequence. Harry Lauder, never given to underrating his own abilities by one jot or tittle throughout his phenomenally successful career, was equally willing to concede that he was fortunate in coming to the fore just at the time the gramophone was perfected and helping to carry his voice to the farthest corners of the globe. What had Lipton to say about Luck? What set of circumstances had combined to help him as a young businessman? What was *his* first fortunate break? Lipton's answer was characteristically forthright: 'I never got help, or assistance, or a penny-piece from anybody,' he growled, 'and every Royalty in the world has dined

14

with me on my beautiful yacht the *Erin*!' There was no further discussion about luck or good fortune that evening.

That incident burned itself into Blackwood's soul. In a few words it encapsulated Lipton's outlook. He was the archetypal self-made man; the man who had risen from nothing to hobnob with kings and emperors. Although Blackwood got to know Sir Thomas Lipton as well as any – and a great deal better than most – there were aspects of the old man's personality which never failed to interest and puzzle him. Of course, it went without saying that Lipton, as a young man, must have possessed marked ability. That his ambition, commercial talents and drive were quite exceptional his extraordinary career demonstrated beyond any shadow of doubt. That sagacity of an outstanding nature and a spirit of enterprise little short of the colossal were thrown into the development of his worldwide empire was freely admitted by succeeding generations of businessmen. That he achieved spectacular triumphs and vast wealth while still a very young man and, later in life, a personal popularity on both sides of the Atlantic because of his yachting challenges, all this is a simple matter of record. But never once did his confidant hear Lipton 'give the slightest meed of praise or credit for his success in life to any man or any circumstance apart from himself, his own determination, his own courage, his own keen wits, his own alert, scheming brain'.[3]

He had one well-worn phrase, which he trotted out on each and every occasion when asked to indicate the inspiration behind his prodigious triumphs as a businessman: 'My mother was my guiding star!' To be fair, he always said it with the greatest sincerity. Indeed, whenever he spoke of his mother he was invariably extravagant with his praise, and characteristically he opened his autobiography with this fulsome statement:

> A good start is half the battle. I don't know who originated the phrase, but I do know that nothing more trite or true has been coined in words. I had a good start. For I had a good mother. The best, the bravest-hearted, the noblest mother God ever sent straight from heaven to be one of His angels on earth.
>
> I loved my mother dearly in life and although she has long gone back to the place she came from, I can honestly say that no single day elapses without some fragrant memory of my mother coming to me and sweetening the hour of its coming. Her photograph is never far from my hand whether I am on land or sea: I commune with that dear face many times in every twenty-four hours. Whatever I am, whatever I possess, whatever I have done – all, all is due to the

little Irish lady from Clones, in Ulster. She was my guiding star. And
by the light of that star I shall steer for the time that yet remains to
me.[4]

Guiding star she may have been, but his old Irish peasant mother
was often agitated at his ploys and strenuously opposed them, as
Lipton himself was fond of retelling, so that it is difficult to see
how she could have guided her famous son to the unparalleled
fame and fortune which he eventually attained. Despite the trite
remark, old Mrs Lipton invariably comes across as a rather
kindly but simple soul who could never grasp the magnitude of
her boy's dreams and ambitions. Nevertheless, she must have
acted as a sounding-board and he must have respected her
opinions, even if he usually chose to ignore them. All great men
have had their failings – they would not be human otherwise –
and often these failings serve as a foil to their remarkable
achievements. In Lipton's case his chief failing was that he could
never bring himself to admit that any other man, or woman, or
fortuitous fact, had played even the slightest part in assisting him
up the ladder of success. 'He was the most thorough and
complete egotist I have come across in a journalistic experience of
almost forty years,' wrote Blackwood.

> Occasionally, for the sheer amusement of seeing his certain reaction
> to a given suggestion, I have urged him to admit that at different times
> in his business life he must have had the assistance of many brilliant
> associates and employees. 'I did everything myself!' he would sternly
> remark, and brook no further encroachment on what was to him a
> distasteful and ridiculous proposition. Even in the company of men
> like Lord Dewar and Lord Inverforth, both immeasurably Lipton's
> superiors from an intellectual point of view, he had always to be top
> dog. If either of them tried to monopolise the conversation too long
> he would break in upon it without the slightest hesitation and begin
> some story or recount some experience richly to his own credit. He
> had to occupy the centre of the stage always; otherwise he wasn't
> faintly interested. I recollect picking up a photograph in his den at
> Osidge shortly before he died and pointing out that the three men in
> the picture had all attained deserved prominence in life – himself,
> Lord Camrose and the late Lord Birkenhead. Sir Thomas took the
> picture, glanced at it for a second and pitched it aside. 'Aye,' he
> remarked, 'that's true enough. But Birkenhead didn't leave any
> money, and I can beat Lord Camrose's boat every time we meet!'[5]

In mitigation it should be remembered that Blackwood only

knew Lipton in his latter years when his egocentricity may have been magnified rather than diminished by the passage of time. But it is safe to suppose that all through his long and incredibly successful life he must have exhibited many of the characteristics which became so marked in his last years.

The other side of the coin presented a picture of a character who was larger than life, and Lipton was physically above-average height to begin with. Most of the time he displayed the kindly, down-to-earth disposition which he inherited from his mother. He could be extremely affable, indeed garrulous at times, and he had a simple, unassuming manner which won the sympathies, if not the real affection, of most men and all women with whom he came in contact. He possessed immense charm and was perfectly at his ease in any company. The easy bonhomie that endeared him to his first customers would eventually captivate the Princess of Wales and give him an entrée to the highest society in the land. By the turn of the century he had become a media darling, never out of the limelight for the rest of his life. Journalists loved him; he was always ready to be interviewed, to give them a witty sound-bite, a telling *bon mot*. And millions of readers of the popular papers on both sides of the Atlantic avidly followed his exploits and the latest rumours of a romance. Blackwood could claim to have known him as intimately as any of his friends, but even Dewar and Inverforth, his most faithful and constant companions, his confidential secretary John Westwood, and his yachting mentor Colonel Duncan Neill, often admitted to Blackwood that they never seemed to reach the innermost recesses of the old man's heart. There was something which none of them could quite fathom. There was an enigmatic quality behind the ready wit and the boyish charm, a self-erected barrier which they sensed rather than realised. For a man who was constantly in the glare of publicity and appeared to revel in it, there was also a hint of an intensely private persona. The very transparent front which Lipton affected in fact concealed a very private man who had very good reasons for guarding his privacy so jealously.

He was tall, slim, handsome, with brown curly hair and penetrating blue eyes. Before he was out of his teens he had begun to grow a large Kitchener moustache, with the tiniest wisp of a beard immediately below his lip. This presented rather a startling effect, especially in his younger years, but it may have been cultivated to conceal the scars of a knife attack. As he grew older, however, and his hair turned grey and then white, the moustache and tiny beard seemed less obtrusive. He possessed

17

boundless energy and extraordinary personal magnetism, both assets which he fully exploited in pursuit of business success as well as in his epic attempts to secure the yachting world's most coveted trophy, the America's Cup.

Many other self-made men have had little or no education, yet found the time in later life to acquire an interest in, or knowledge of, the finer things in life, to cultivate the arts or at least take an intelligent interest in matters outside their business world. Lipton's formal schooling lasted seven years, supplemented by attendance at night classes, but his studies seem to have been focused entirely on acquiring the skills necessary for his chosen career. He had a quick grasp of arithmetic, which enabled him to read a balance sheet amazingly quickly, and he had the neat penmanship that would help him to make the transition from manual labourer to accounts clerk; but otherwise he had little or no learning as the word is generally understood. 'Science, the arts, politics, history, invention, interested him not at all,' concluded Blackwood:

> I never heard him discuss intelligently the daily events of the hemispheres as they were reported in the newspapers. Try to draw him into a conversation on any one of the thousand topics the usual man takes delight in discussing, be it never so superficially, and Lipton would listen for a few moments. Then suddenly he would veer right away and come out with some completely inconsequential remark about himself, his business acumen, his yacht, or one or other of the Royal personages he had had the high honour of entertaining! Any prolonged talk which did not embrace 'Sir Thomas', his amazing career, and his position as the world's most gallant sportsman was so much wasted breath in his company.[6]

In giving this very perceptive pen-portrait, Blackwood was at pains to be fair and put his conclusions into perspective. 'Had I known him for fifty years instead of twenty I might have written differently of him. I would like that to be perfectly understood.' And he summed him up succinctly:

> He was in many, many respects an astonishing and singular man. It is inconceivable to me that there can ever be quite such another. Tom Lipton made his own standards in everything. His defects were, to a great extent, his peculiar qualities; he was frigidly unique in all that he did, said, and thought.[7]

He was truly a multi-faceted personality, and this was never more true than when applied to matters of the heart. A man who could flirt easily – and sometimes outrageously – with society belles and titled ladies, who was often described in the popular press as the world's most eligible bachelor, whose name was often romantically linked with women of beauty, rank and fortune, successfully evaded matrimony. Just as his mother was invariably given as the key to his business success, so too she became the excuse for dodging matrimonial entanglements: 'I have never met any lady who measured up to my mother,' he would smile enigmatically when asked why he had never married. Whatever qualities Mother Lipton possessed, they were certainly not beauty or elegance. The only extant portraits of her, admittedly taken later in life, show a dumpy little woman, fat and rather masculine in features. Lipton assiduously cultivated the notion that he was so utterly devoted to his mother that the thought of marriage never entered his head. One might have accepted this while she was alive; after all, had not Andrew Carnegie, another self-made Scottish multi-millionaire, eschewed matrimony so long as his dour, wooden-faced mother remained alive, and only taken the plunge at the age of fifty-two? In Lipton's case, his mother died when he was fifty-one; but neither then, nor thirteen years later when he received his baronetcy, did he see any incentive to perpetuate his name and his title. It seemed odd that, by that time, when he had his baronetcy, had relinquished much of the day-to-day running of his business, was immensely rich and still very much in the prime of life, he did not take any steps towards the altar, especially when so much tempting pulchritude was thrust at him. By that time, of course, yachting had become the grand passion of his life, and all his energies were devoted to that sport.

The confirmed bachelor was not regarded with suspicion as he would be nowadays when the world is so much more knowledgeable about the byways of human sexuality and the word gay has lost its innocent, original connotation. At Osidge, Lipton lived alone, apart from servants, but there was never so much as a hint of any impropriety between him and his three Sinhalese house-boys. Instead, it was accepted that for much of his life he had just been far too busy, too preoccupied, with the whole-hearted pursuit of his business which left no time, physically or emotionally, for a wife and family. Alec Waugh, author of a centennial biography, succinctly summed this up. In a passage speculating on what short-cut Lipton might have taken to achieve his astonishing success, he concluded 'chastity may have been his short-cut'.[8] In any case, Lipton was not so mother-fixated as previous biographers, taking the man at face value, have always supposed. Much has been made of the fact that he lived with his parents until 1890 when, following the death of his surviving parent, he moved from Glasgow to London. In fact, as we shall see, for a crucial part of his life, in his twenties, he maintained his own separate establishment.

Lipton the ladies' man was also very much a man's man. For all his coquettish gallantry with the fair sex, he obviously preferred male company, whether his Scottish cronies of long-standing or the yachting fraternity. He never lost the common touch, but he became a terrible snob who went to incredible lengths to court royalty and the aristocracy and was latterly an incorrigible name-dropper. The great capitalist was also a socialist at heart. Just as he made his fortune by providing the working classes with good food at affordable prices, he never pursued profit at all costs, and was usually fair to his employees who numbered many thousands at the height of his success. He sympathised with the Irish Nationalists and the nascent Labour Party and made donations to party funds; but aside from an innate sense of justice for all, he took absolutely no interest in politics. He was on first-name terms with every American president from Rutherford Hayes onwards, yet was oblivious to party and faction.

So, too, in matters of nationality. He is, even now, frequently referred to as a great Irishman, and the fact that his yachts were all named either *Shamrock* or *Erin* bears out the supposition that Lipton regarded himself as, first and foremost, an Irishman. But he was born and raised in Scotland, and thus, later in life, would describe himself as an Irish-Scotsman or a Scottish-Irishman, or even a Glasgow Irishman, depending on the company he was in. When he came to prominence people were quick to comment on his well-modulated voice with just a hint of a regional accent that was variously interpreted as an Irish brogue or a Scots burr. Lipton himself boasted that, early in his career, he became adept at detecting the regional accents of his customers, identifying them correctly, and even imitating them to put customers at their ease and gain their goodwill and custom. This symbolises the chameleon-like character of a man who could be all things to all men. Lipton invented himself; therein lay the secret of his phenomenal success.

1. BOYHOOD
1848–63

'Tis virtue, and not birth that makes us noble;
Great actions speak great minds, and such should govern.
    Francis Beaumont and John Fletcher, *The Prophetess*

The ancestors of Thomas Johnston Lipton were of good Scottish, Presbyterian stock, settled in Ulster in the seventeenth century. To be sure, there had been a farmstead called Lipton in the Craven district of Yorkshire, mentioned in the Domesday Book, and a hamlet called Lupton in Westmorland. Lupton and Lopton as well as Lipton are surnames which were occasionally found in the north of England as well as the lowlands of Scotland. Its absence from the parish registers of Scotland from the early eighteenth century onwards suggests a migration to Ulster, where the surname in its various forms occurs in parish records from that time.

In 1607 the Earls of Tyrone and Tyrconnell, together with almost a hundred Irish chieftains, gave up the struggle against the encroachments of the hated English administration, and fled from Ulster, never to return. Ulster, the last bastion of resistance, would shortly be transformed into the most British of the provinces of Ireland. This was achieved by a policy of plantation, carried out as systematically and more ruthlessly than any comparable settlement in Virginia and the Carolinas. The Earls and their followers were found guilty of treason in their absence, and by a complex, not to say devious, legal process the six counties in the north-east of Ireland were declared to be 'escheated'. In 1609 the escheated lands were divided among undertakers, servitors and the natives. The undertakers (mainly English) were to lease land only to English or Scottish tenants and were required to take the Oath of Supremacy. Servitors (mainly Scots), might take Irish tenants, but if so their rents to the Crown were substantially increased. Native Irish grantees were to pay quit-rents to the Crown, twice as large as the undertakers, but at least they were spared the humiliation of being obliged to take the oath. Cadet branches of some of the oldest families, like the O'Neills and the Magennises, did take advantage of this and survived as large landlords, though no longer as Irish chiefs.

The colonists, of course, got the best lands; the town of Derry, for example, was given to the City of London, and the London companies received grants that gave them practically the whole of that county. The plantation of Ulster was a huge success. Not since the Anglo-Norman invasion of Ireland in 1166 had the Irish problem been so admirably solved. As a result, for the first time, a large part of Ireland was not merely owned by Saxon landlords but was tilled and farmed by Scottish Protestant farmers. Of course the native Irish, driven off the good land into the more mountainous regions, remained resentful and rebellious, ever-hopeful that their rightful chiefs would some day return, but on the surface they seemed no longer a danger. The success of the Ulster project led to plantations in other parts of Ireland where, though the native Irish were treated with more equity, the ambition of the Crown lawyers was to find that most of the Irish were not freeholders but merely tenants-at-will, a subtle distinction which would in the ensuing centuries be employed to their disadvantage.

English adventurers and speculators profited from this scheme; the new rich displaced the old aristocracy. The rank and file of the settlers, however, brought their Calvinist faith and Protestant work ethic, their skills and their enterprise. After a century of continual warfare Ireland was at peace and, economically if not politically, the island benefited from the invasion.

Fermanagh was one of the escheated counties of Ulster, planted by Scots from Strathclyde. Their ancestors had been Picts, Gaels and Cymric Celts, so that ethnically they were very similar to the Ulster Irish; indeed, a thousand years earlier Argyll and neighbouring districts had formed the kingdom of Dalriada, conquered and colonised by the Scoti of Ulster. In religion the Scottish migrants and the native Irish were at opposite ends of the spectrum but they made common cause against their mutual enemy. In view of the sectarianism of more recent times, it is sometimes hard to realise that the Presbyterians of Ulster were, throughout much of the eighteenth century, treated almost as harshly by the Episcopalian ascendancy as were the native Irish Catholics. In particular Presbyterians and Catholics shared the grievance of paying tithes to the Established Church of Ireland which they both detested. This gave them a solidarity against the Anglo-Irish ascendancy which found practical expression in the Society of United Irishmen, aiming at the establishment of an Irish

republic on the French revolutionary model. It was to counteract
this that the government of William Pitt, true to the policy of
divide and rule, encouraged the formation of the Orange Order in
1795 and thus laid the foundations of that sectarianism which has
bedevilled Irish politics ever since.

In the eighteenth century Ireland had arguably the worst land
system anywhere in Europe, provoking those embittered agrarian
movements, such as the Whiteboys and the Peep o' Day Boys, in
which Presbyterian tenant farmers as well as the Catholic
peasantry took a prominent part. The Lipton family (variously
spelled Lupton or Lopton in the earliest records) were settled in
County Fermanagh by the middle of the seventeenth century at
least. Within a couple of generations they had the management of
the corn mills at the centre of the tiny and insignificant townland
of Shannock, or Shannog Green, in the parish of Galloon in the
barony of Coole, in the extreme south-east of the county where it
marched with Monaghan. Fermanagh is a corruption of the
Gaelic *Fear-magh-Eanagh*, literally 'the mountain-valley marsh
district' from the loughs of the Erne Valley that divide it in two.
Shannock Green, at the very edge of the county, was hilly, bleak
and barren. It was a poor district, remote from Fermanagh's main
population centres, Newtown Butler, Lisnaskea and Enniskillen.
Its nearest town of any size was, in fact, across the county
boundary in Monaghan, and it was to Clones that the farmers of
Shannock Green went to market on the last Thursday of every
month. This explains the oft-repeated error that Thomas Lipton's
family hailed from County Monaghan. Though not one of the
escheated counties, Monaghan had over the centuries been
penetrated by the settlers, as the names of such villages as
Scotshouse and Scotstown testify. Lipton's maternal family, the
Johnstons (originally from Dumfriesshire), were particularly
prominent at all levels of society in Monaghan, producing both
ultramontane Unionists and ardent Irish patriots.

When County Fermanagh was surveyed in 1834 it revealed a
single road, from Rosslea to Clones, traversing the south-eastern
corner of Shannock Green. Near the western end of this rough
road, a track ran due north about 200 yards to terminate at the
corn mills. There were no towns, villages or even hamlets in the
district, only the scattered cottages of the small Presbyterian
tenants and the Catholic peasantry. Both struggled on the margins
of existence, and made common cause against their landlord,
John Madden of Springrove, whose College estates included the
townlands of Shannock and Shannock Green.

During the 1760s there had been sporadic outbreaks of unrest throughout the nine counties of Ulster, but they were usually repressed with considerable brutality on the part of the bailiffs and land agents. In 1764, for example, Charles Coote, who had only recently been made a Knight of the Bath for his services in keeping his unruly tenantry in check, overstepped the mark when he and Edward Mayne killed Alexander MacDonald at Castleblayney. This incident neatly symbolises the long-running struggle between English landlords and their Scots–Irish tenants, which had now erupted into violence. The good Sir Charles and his lieutenant were brought to trial at the Monaghan Lent Assizes, but were acquitted. A year later two of the 'Hearts of Steel', as the rebels were known, Robert Nesbitt and William Pringle, were 'tried for High Treason as being concerned in the late tumultuous risings in the Province of Ulster, and were honourably acquitted'.[1]

Significantly, the Liptons first came to prominence as the result of an armed showdown in the year 1767 involving Madden's bailiff and his assistants, aided by the military, on one side, and the small tenant farmers and their cotters on the other. It was recorded that the farmers were led by 'Lipton's Ones' – the brothers John, Robert and William, sons of William Lipton of Shannock Green Mills – along with James Moore Junior of Lisrooskey. In the ensuing fracas, the bailiff and the forces of law and order were soundly defeated; but inevitably the perpetrators of this outrage were arrested soon afterwards and brought to trial at Enniskillen. Despite the overwhelming evidence, the jury acquitted all of the defendants and seem to have left no one in any doubt as to what they thought of the landlord class.[2]

These violent agrarian troubles culminated in the incident on 23 December 1770 when the Presbyterian farmers from the border districts of Fermanagh and Monaghan joined forces with their brethren farther east. To the number of 1,200, this well-armed body of latter-day Covenanters marched on Belfast and attacked the barracks, releasing their hero David Douglas, one of the 'Hearts of Steel' who was confined there. After this the Ulster Land War gradually died away. One outcome of the troubles was the recognition of the Ulster Tenant Right Custom; but another was the emigration of more than 400,000 Ulster people to America where the bitter memory of their wrongs formed an important factor in the American Revolution a few years later.

In January 1770 Lipton's Ones were involved in an escapade of a very different character. In that year, Elizabeth Graham, the daughter of a Scottish farmer, William Graham, who had settled at Kilmore in the parish of Tydavnet (a few miles east of Clones), was courted by a young tenant farmer named George Nicholls of Mullin. The girl's father, however, disapproved of the young man and barred Nicholls from the house. In retaliation, Nicholls called upon his cousins, the Lipton brothers, to help him and Elizabeth to elope. With four others to help them, the Lipton boys raided the Kilmore farmhouse, seized the girl and carried her off to a secret rendezvous with her lover, at the home of their kinsman William Lipton of Allagesh. This violent incident caused a tremendous furore throughout the district. William Graham did not take the outrage calmly but gathered his friends and farm labourers and, armed to the teeth, set out to wreak vengeance and retrieve his beloved daughter. Graham was very well connected, and in this savage enterprise he had the tacit support of the powerful landlords, the Forsters of Tullaghan and Evatts of Mount Louise. A large party crossed the county boundary and descended on Shannock Green Mills and after a bloody affray seized many of the local men and carried them off as prisoners. Lipton's Ones were eventually brought to trial at Clones, along with George Nicholls, William Coine of Rosslea, William Mahaffy of Aghafin, Michael McCaffrey and Hugh Maguire. Graham was determined that the culprits should go to the gallows, for kidnapping was then a capital offence, and went so far as to hire the best barristers from Dublin to prepare the prosecution case. The trial of the Kilmore Eight collapsed when Elizabeth Graham went into the witness-box and smilingly stated that she loved George Nicholls and had gone with her abductors of her own free will, adding that the Lipton boys had merely convoyed her to her lover and wished her God-speed.[3] While Graham had the powerful backing of the Monaghan landlords, Nicholls and the Liptons were just as strenuously supported by the Fermanagh landlords, and the outcome of this case was a long-running feud between the gentry of the two counties.

The few documented facts about the Liptons of Shannock Green are entirely derived from those escapades which brought them into conflict with the law. Virtually nothing is known of the more mundane, everyday matters of birth, marriage and death, for the simple fact that most of the parish registers of Fermanagh and Monaghan, along with the priceless records of Ireland over a period of seven centuries, were destroyed in 1922 when Free State artillery pounded the Four Courts in Dublin in the opening round of the tragic Irish Civil War. What little information is available is fragmentary and contradictory. From census returns and death certificates, however, we may glean the meagre facts. A son of John Lipton was called Thomas, born about 1780, and unlike his uncles, he was neither a farmer nor a miller but earned his living as a weaver of fine damask linen. In the early 1800s he married Margaret Mulligan and on 22 October 1805 had a son named Thomas. This Thomas Lipton is described as a poor labourer by Herbert Grimsditch, author of the entry on Sir Thomas Lipton in the *Dictionary of National Biography*, who goes on to state that he married Frances Johnstone [*sic*], daughter of Frank Johnstone of Kilrid, Clones. Where Grimsditch got this from is not clear, for he cites as his sources Lipton's autobiography (which gives no personal details at all) and various obituaries. Perhaps this detail came under the heading of 'private information' which was also cited. Be that as it may, it conflicts with the details given on the death certificate of Frances Lipton *née* Johnston, which indicates that she was the daughter of a farmer named James Johnston and his wife Frances Blakeley. The same certificate gives Frances Lipton's age as eighty at the time of her death, which would place her birth in 1809.[4] It appears that she was in her late-twenties when she got married, her husband being three years older. No record of the marriage is now extant; but in a newspaper interview in 1930 Lipton stated that his parents were married for fifty-four years, which would have placed their marriage in 1835. Their first son, John, was born in 1838; two years later came Christopher, who died in infancy, followed by Mary Ann, born late in 1842, who died on 26 January 1844, and Frances who was born in 1844 but died on 25 November 1848.[5] John was named after his paternal great-grandfather. Christopher seems an unusual choice of name for the second son, but those records which have survived indicate that this was a popular name in the Blakeley family.

'My parents decided to leave Ireland at the time of the great potato famine,' says Sir Thomas Lipton in his autobiography.[6] By 1841 Ireland was supporting a population of over eight million, almost double what it had been forty years earlier. In that year the density of population was almost the same as that of England and Wales – 251 persons per square mile, compared with 272. There were 685,000 farms in Ireland, but of these about 300,000 were under three acres in extent and a quarter of a million between three and fifteen acres. These units were too small to be economically viable, but an iniquitous outcome of the Gavelling Act, dating from the early eighteenth century, was the sub-division of landholdings among all the sons of a tenant. By the 1840s the condition of the vast majority of those who lived on the land was miserable in the extreme. Theirs was a subsistence economy which relied very heavily on a single crop for domestic consumption.

So long as conditions were right, the potato plants yielded a good crop that would be the staple diet for most people. Potato blight, a disease that turned healthy plants overnight into a black, slimy mess, struck in North America in 1844 and spread to Europe the following year. The British Isles felt the worst effects of the blight in 1846 and 1847, with hardly any part of the United Kingdom escaping. In Ireland, where the population was so utterly dependent on the potato, destitution was common. Though the statistics show that deaths from sheer starvation in the decade between the censuses of 1841 and 1851 totalled 21,770, total Irish mortality in the same period was close to a million, and many of these deaths may be attributed directly or indirectly to hunger. In the decade that followed 1847, the worst year of the blight, more than a million and a half emigrated from Ireland. Crampsey[7] challenges Lipton's notion that his parents had been driven out of Ireland by the Great Famine, pointing out that other crops flourished during this period. In fact, the harvests of grain in the years 1845-47 were of record proportions. Both Fermanagh and Monaghan were fortunate in having a mixed agriculture and were not as reliant on the coarse lumper potato as the more southerly and western counties. Moreover, the strongly Unionist county of Fermanagh was more likely to benefit from the rather partial measures taken by the British government to relieve suffering and distress.

Of course, what Sir Thomas says does not actually imply that his parents left Ireland *because* of the potato famine, although the agricultural depression which came in its wake was clearly a factor:

> The agricultural districts of Ulster, indeed the whole of Ireland, passed through a very bad time round about this period and those emigrants who did not make up their minds to cross the western ocean to the spacious and promising lands of America cast their eyes over a much smaller stretch of water, namely, in the direction of the west of Scotland. The industrial cities and towns of this area were then growing by leaps and bounds and offering chances of labour and wages to all who were willing to work. So my father and mother decided to go to Glasgow. They sold up their little home, as thousands of Irish families did at the time, and made their way to Belfast, crossing over from there to the famous Broomielaw Quay right in the heart of the great Scottish city in which I was destined to be born a few years later.[8]

Fermanagh, one of the counties least affected by the potato famine and better served than most in terms of government relief, had had a population of 156,481 at the census of 1841, but by the census of 1851 this had fallen by a quarter, to 116,047. It would continue to fall in each successive decade, standing at only 50,000 a century later. The Lipton family became a part of the statistics, however, even before the advent of the potato blight. The move from Shannock Green to Glasgow does not appear to have been made in a single operation. The fifth of the Lipton children, Margaret, was born in 1845, but unlike the first four, she was born in Downpatrick, County Down – more than sixty miles north-east of Clones, as the crow flies.[9] This indicates that the Lipton family had already left Fermanagh, either late in 1844 after the birth of Frances or early in 1845, which certainly places the disruption well before the Great Famine took a hold. What drove the Liptons out of Shannock Green is therefore unknown, but it may have been that Thomas and Frances were displaced simply by a desire to improve their lot. Contrary to popular belief, economic refugees from Ireland were leaving in their droves for several years before the potato blight appeared on the scene.[10] It may be simply that at long last Thomas Senior realised the hopelessness of trying to make a living on the land, and he probably concluded that the only way of getting ahead was to seek unskilled work in the more industrialised north-east of Ireland. At what stage the family took the momentous decision to cross the narrow stretch of water and return to the land of their roots is likewise unknown, but by late 1847 they had arrived in the Glasgow area.

The Gorbals district, separated from the city of Glasgow proper by the River Clyde, was then, and had been for some years, the principal destination of economic migrants, from the Highlands and Islands of Scotland in the 1830s and from Ireland a decade later. What had been a pleasant little town with a population of about 5,000 at the beginning of the nineteenth century, had grown seven-fold by 1841 and over the ensuing fifteen years it would more than double again, reaching 80,000 by 1856 – which was approximately the total population of the city of Glasgow in 1800. The problem with the Gorbals, however, was that there was precious little room for lateral expansion, with the result that its already crowded tenements became grossly overpopulated.

Thomas Lipton himself is the source of the canard that he was born in Crown Street, one of the main thoroughfares of the Gorbals. Although, for some reason, his birth was never entered in any parish register,[11] we may accept the date of birth which he gives – 10 May – as people never forget their birthday; but his statement regarding the *year* and *where* he was born is not confirmed by the Census returns. 'I was born on the top storey of a humble but eminently respectable tenement house in Crown Street, Rutherglen Road, Glasgow.'[12]

His autobiography even includes an artist's impression of the tenement block, at the corner of Crown Street and Rutherglen Road, where he was allegedly born, and it may be this that led Crampsey to deduce that Lipton was born at 10 Crown Street. The 1851 Census, however, reveals that this was a two-storey private dwelling-house on the west side of the street, occupied by one family: James MacIntyre, a teacher of English, his wife Jessie, their sons James (a druggist), William (a law clerk), school-children Jane, Martha, Nathaniel and Jessie, and baby John.

In fact, the sketch about 1930, which may have been drawn especially for the autobiography, shows the block on the opposite side of the street. The Lipton family were certainly living in a four-room apartment on the top floor of 13 Crown Street by 1864, for Thomas Senior appears in the 1865 Glasgow Directory as a butter and egg merchant at 11 Crown Street, with his house next door. This is confirmed by the entry in the 1871 Census, but there is no mention of the Lipton family in Crown Street in the earlier census returns.

Twenty years earlier, however, the family was actually living several miles away, on the north side of the Clyde, in the Milton district of Barony parish in the city of Glasgow. The Liptons, in fact, were one of sixteen families (totalling eighty-one persons) living in a three-storey tenement at 99 East Milton Street. As well as their three children Mr and Mrs Lipton had a lodger, John Cameron, a twenty-eight-year-old general labourer from Argyll.[13] In a two-room apartment, it is difficult to imagine what the sleeping arrangements must have been. This street had been developed twenty years previously to accommodate workers at Port Dundas, the Glasgow terminal of the Forth and Clyde Canal; but over the intervening years numerous factories had sprung up and the dwelling-houses of Milton Street and Dobbie's Loan were now grossly overcrowded slums. The Census, taken on 7 April 1851, reveals that Thomas, aged forty, was a native of Ireland and at that time employed as a 'watchman'. This does not contradict Lipton's own comment that, shortly after settling in Glasgow, his father was employed in a factory that made cardboard boxes. The wife, Frances, gave her age as thirty-nine, an understandable discrepancy as women in middle age habitually lopped two or three years off their age, especially if, in reality, they were older than their husbands. This was a process which Frances would continue in successive decennial censuses, though there is no reason to doubt that at the time of her death in 1889 her correct age was stated.[14] During the same period, however, Thomas Senior was consistent in stating his age.

By 1851 only three of the Lipton's six children were still living. The eldest was John, aged thirteen, followed by Margaret whose age was given as ten. John's year of birth (1838) is consistent with the only other record we have of him, his death certificate (1857), but the age given for Margaret in 1851 does not accord with any other data. The entries in the 1861 and 1871 censuses, together with her death certificate in 1878, point to a birth in 1845, which means that she was only six or seven in 1851. This error is compounded by the fact that although Thomas and Frances admitted to being born in Ireland – their accents would have betrayed that fact to the census-taker – they claimed that all three children had been born in Glasgow. This error may have arisen from a desire to establish the next generation as Scottish, and in view of the widespread anti-Irish sentiment in Glasgow during this period, this is understandable. In the Census returns for 1861 and 1871, however, Margaret is clearly stated as Irish-born.

While the census-taker might have been deceived regarding the precise age of a middle-aged woman or even a girl of school years, no such mistake could have arisen in the case of the youngest child. Plain Thomas – no middle name – was listed as aged three, which would fix his date of birth as 10 May 1848. Many years later, when he had mysteriously acquired a middle name, Lipton would claim to have been born in 1850. As there is a vast difference between an eleven-month-old baby and a three-year-old boy, it has to be assumed that the census-taker got it right first time; and this is confirmed by the entries in the 1861 and 1871 Census returns. So, the plain facts are that Thomas Lipton was born on 10 May 1848, and that wherever he was born, it certainly was not in the Gorbals. Of course, he may have been born somewhere else in Glasgow other than Milton Street, but that is the earliest place for which we have a record. The congested tenements of this run-down district were swept away during massive slum-clearance projects in the 1930s. Today, only a solitary two-storey red sandstone building survives from the middle of the nineteenth century, the rest of the area having been redeveloped in more recent years as light industrial premises, factories and warehouses. Where little Tommy Lipton probably first saw the light of day is now occupied by the premises of the *Sunday Post*.

Lipton described his father as 'a big, broad-shouldered man, clean of heart and clear-eyed, with a homely, whiskered face'. An oil painting of him, executed in the last decade of his life, when he was in his seventies, shows a white-haired, balding man with a flowing beard and side-whiskers. He wore a dark high-buttoned coat that fell away to reveal a gold watch chain. The long nose, high forehead and shrewd, twinkling eyes betray a man who was noted for his native sagacity and pawky humour. 'Among strangers he was inclined to be shy and awkward,' wrote his son, 'but with his own kith and kin he was genial and boisterous enough and he had a keen sense of humour which made him a popular character with all who got to know him intimately.'[15] Tantalisingly, Lipton tells us little more about his father, other than that, 'His ruling passion was his love and admiration of my mother'. Strangely enough, there is no comparable pen-portrait of this paragon of wifely and motherly virtue, nor is she even named, and this anonymity has been dutifully followed by all other writers on the subject of Lipton's antecedents, although Crampsey alone commented on it: 'It is an oddity in the junior Lipton's recollection that he never mentions his mother by her Christian name.'[16] It is not so much an oddity as an indication that the subject of his mother was too sacred. The failure to mention her name betrays Lipton's attitude: his angelic mother was on a pedestal, and her memory must not be sullied by revealing her name to the vulgar reader.[17]

After a few years Thomas Senior became a time-keeper at the Springfield Print Works in McNeil Street, on the south bank of the Clyde opposite the east end of Glasgow Green, and it may have been in connection with this change of occupation that the family moved from Barony parish to the Gorbals. When his nineteen-year-old son, John, died on 17 August 1857, Thomas was described on the death certificate as a printfield worker. The Springfield Print Works was not a paper mill, as Sir Thomas recalled in his autobiography, but a factory for printing calico. The other occupants of the riverside of McNeil Street – dye works and silk or woollen mills – were engaged in similar textile business. Thomas continued to work there for several years, earning a pound a week which was later increased to twenty-five shillings. This would be roughly the equivalent of £150 in the depreciated currency of the present day. It represented a wage above the average, and there were thousands of families whose sole breadwinner brought home smaller sums, from fifteen to eighteen shillings.

At the time of John's death the family were living in an

apartment at 57 Rutherglen Loan (now Old Rutherglen Road).[18] As Lipton described his home at 13 Crown Street from a much later period, it is unlikely that that the rent paid for the family residence in the 1850s was as much as the twelve pounds ten shillings a year which was undoubtedly the rent of the later flat. The average rent for a small, two-room apartment in the Gorbals in the 1850s was three shillings a week, but there were plenty of families who had to share a 'single-end' whose rental was a modest shilling or eighteen pence. It seems strange that Lipton should have been so imprecise regarding the house in which he was born, though his description of it doubtless applied to all of the homes of his early childhood:

> By no stretch of imagination could our house be termed elegant or artistic, but scrupulously clean and comfortable it was. My mother saw to it that it was kept, as the saying has it, like 'a new pin'; you could have eaten your food off the floor and certainly you could have seen your face reflected in the highly-polished kitchen 'grate' or fireplace. Like the majority of Glasgow housewives, she took a tremendous interest in her humble home and no effort was too much to keep it spick and span. I well remember the scoldings I used to receive if ever I dared to come over the outside door without wiping my feet on the mat.[19]

This faulty memory enabled Lipton to embroider the tale of his boyhood in Crown Street with a piece of shameless name-dropping:

> About the same time, too, I believe that James Naysmith [sic], the inventor of the steam hammer, often walked up and down its grimy pavements while serving part of his apprenticeship at Dixon's Blast Furnaces.[20]

James Nasmyth (1808–90), the youngest son of Alexander Nasmyth who painted the celebrated portrait of Robert Burns, was born in Edinburgh and started business on his own account in Manchester in 1834, inventing the steam hammer five years later and retiring from business a very wealthy man, to spend the rest of his life at Penshurst in Kent in 1856. As William Dixon did not establish the Govan Iron Works, popularly known to generations of Glaswegians as Dixon's Blazes, until 1837, there is no way that Nasmyth was connected with it, nor indeed a contemporary of Lipton in the vicinity of Crown Street. Another story which does not stand up to close examination concerns 'two quiet working men . . . who lived next door to the house in which I was born'.

> Almost every evening and certainly every Saturday afternoon these brothers retired to a wash-house at the back of the tenement, locked themselves in and proceeded to conduct experiments of a peculiarly foul-smelling description. From the crevices in the door and window emerged smoke and fumes of, as it appeared to my wondering eyes, different colours and density. The neighbours were not slow to complain of the terrible, throat-catching effluvium which found its way into their homes and I can remember the profound impression that was caused upon me by an old, Highland wife proclaiming, from the house-tops, as it were, the curse that would befall the street if the authorities did not step in and stop these 'warlocks and their devils brew'! The young experimenters were none other than Robert and James Dick, the inventors of gutta-percha and the founders of the world-famous firm of R. & J. Dick.
>
> In spite of the awful smells and the air of mystery which hung about the little outhouse in Crown Street, Glasgow – or, more probably, because of them – I was fascinated beyond measure by the two quiet purposeful brothers and it was a joyful moment when they asked me into the shed one Saturday afternoon and invited me to assist them in their work. Naturally their plant was of the most primitive order – an old copper or two for boiling the gutta and an ancient printing-press which they used for squeezing the prepared solution down to the necessary thickness for soling boots and shoes. My task was to scrape the coppers free from the 'gutty' after it had been heated. My reward was the scrapings which I could have taken away with me had I been inclined, but I was so enthusiastic about the business of rubber-sole making that generally I insisted on the scrapings going back into the next 'brew'! People all over the world have been much interested when I have told them that I was 'closely associated with the rubber industy in its very earliest days'.[21]

It is to be hoped that Lipton refrained from recounting this boyhood experience until after the Dick brothers were dead. Robert (1820–91) and James (1823–1902) were born in Kilmarnock but settled in the Gorbals in 1828. Robert served his apprenticeship as a watchmaker but James drifted in and out of several jobs and was an unemployed upholsterer when they stumbled across something which was to change their lives dramatically. In 1843 Dr William Montgomerie, a medical missionary employed by the East India Company, brought back to Glasgow from Malaya some lumps of a strange, dirty grey material called gutta percha, the evaporated latex of the palaquium tree. Unlike india rubber latex, no practical use had been found for this substance, though the Malays used it in fashioning the handles of knives and whips. Montgomerie tried unsuccessfully to promote gutta percha as a substitute for leather in footwear, but in 1846 he sold his samples to the Dick brothers. The incident with the lumps melting in a frying-pan in the wash-house at the back of 61 Crown Street took place later that year – eighteen months before the Liptons migrated from Ireland and two years before Thomas Junior was born. Although the neighbours complained of the frightful stench, the brothers succeeded in producing 'pancakes' of gutta percha. That night James soled and heeled three pairs of shoes, and when their experiment worked Robert put his savings into the lease of a shop at 12 Gallowgate, Glasgow. By the time young Tommy Lipton was on the scene, Dick Brothers were well established in a rapidly expanding factory at Greenhead on the other side of the river from the Gorbals, and well on the way to becoming Scotland's first self-made millionaires.[22] Incidentally, the Dick brothers lived with their mother Mary who kept a little grocery shop at the corner of Crown Street and Govan Street, a block away from the corner shop later kept by Lipton's parents.

In his autobiography Lipton wrote: 'There had been two other brothers who had died in infancy,'[23] although the only one of whom we have record is Christopher (1840). Given the fact that his father and grandfather were called Thomas, it would have been reasonable to expect that the first-born son would likewise have borne this name. There might well have been such a child born to Thomas and Frances, in 1836 or 1837, but who died soon after birth. Indeed, this would have been a virtual certainty had the Liptons adhered to the usual Scottish and Scots-Irish custom of naming the first son after the father's father. This would explain the three-year gap between marriage and the birth of John in 1838. On the other hand, the Liptons broke with tradition in naming John and Christopher. By the same custom, the first daughter should have been named after the mother's mother, but Frances was the name reserved for the second daughter. It was not uncommon for a later child to be named after an elder brother or sister who had died in infancy, especially if the deceased infant had been the first-born and had inherited a cherished family Christian name. In that case it would not have been out of the ordinary for Thomas to be used for a third or even fourth son, and this might explain why it was not until 1848 that the name was thus used. But this is only speculation, and in the absence of parish records it is quite impossible to confirm or rebut this notion.

Lipton remembered his surviving siblings with affection. Like the children who had died before he was born, his surviving elder brother and sister were of delicate constitution and would eventually succumb at an early age. John, who was born in 1838 and may have been the eldest child of the family, died on 17 August 1857 at the age of nineteen:

> He was frail in body but full of grit and ambition. He was determined to be a doctor and on leaving school he worked in a chemist's shop in Virginia Street. Out of his scanty pay he managed to save enough to enter for classes at Glasgow University and had it been God's will to spare him I have no doubt he would have made a name for himself. His death was a sad blow to our father and mother and to me also who regarded Big Brother John with something akin to hero-worship.[24]

John was employed by the Glasgow Apothecaries' Company of 34 Virginia Street, across the river, and in the academic session of 1856–57 he was attending classes in anatomy and physiology at the old University a couple of hundred yards to the east at the top of Glasgow's High Street. Although he appears to have been far from robust all his life, the immediate cause of death was congestion and enlargement of the spleen and liver over a period of six months. This was confirmed by a post mortem examination carried out by Dr H.R. Hewatt who had attended the youth in his last days. He was buried in the Southern Necropolis, a large cemetery which had only recently taken over from the original Gorbals burial ground.[25]

'My sister Margaret, or Maggie as we called her at home, lived for several years after John's death, but she likewise was taken away in early womanhood.'[26] In fact she died on 11 December 1878 at the age of thirty-three. She had long been a sufferer of valvular heart disease and bronchitis; eventually the congestion of her lungs was more than her poor heart could cope with.[27] By contrast, Thomas and Frances Lipton enjoyed rude, good health and would both reach their eighties, just like their sole surviving offspring. Tom recalled that he was rarely ill in childhood, and went on to develop a strong and hardy constitution. There was one brief period, however, when he had trouble with his eyesight and had to make a series of much-dreaded visits to the old Glasgow Eye Hospital in Charlotte Steet. Whatever the problem was, it must have cleared up for even as an old man he seldom wore spectacles and then only for reading.

Young Tom was only nine when his brother died, so his recollections of John were bound to be hazy; but one might have expected that his unmarried sister would have left more of an impression. She never worked and seems to have been semi-invalid most of her life. Someone who was as closely bound to his family as Tom was, a young man who never formed a lasting relationship with anyone of the opposite sex, might have been expected to be more than usually close to his only sister; but she is dismissed in those three lines. Characteristically, much of Lipton's description of his family background revolved around his saintly mother:

> Pondering on these early days I sometimes find myself wondering how my mother succeeded in keeping a comfortable roof above our heads, feeding us and clothing us, on the scanty wages earned by my father, Even allowing that money went farther in those days than it does now it has always been a mystery to me. We had an abundance of good food, in which porridge and Scotch broth, potato soup, home-baked scones and oatcakes played an important part. My mother was clever with her needle and she made practically all my clothes. She was never idle from morning til night. And I cannot recall her without a smile on her face and a cheery word on her tongue.[28]

In 1775 the Revd John Wesley came to Clones and preached one evening at the Fort to a vast, open-air audience, the largest congregation he had anywhere in Ireland. This contrasted well with Belturbet, a town which he condemned as 'possessing neither Papists nor Presbyterians, but to supply that defect there are Sabbath-breakers, drunkards and common swearers in abundance'. In Clones, however, the message was well received. A few years later a traveller from England wrote that in Gomorrah five righteous persons could not be found to save it from destruction; but at Clones 'the inhabitants set judgments by fire and water, pillars of salt and lakes of sulphur at defiance, for they are all righteous or Methodists, which is the same thing'.[29]

Wesley's success among the people of Monaghan and Fermanagh may be partly explained by his warm espousal of their cause in the land wars; but certainly from then onwards there was a very strong element of Methodism which survives to this day. The Liptons were among those converted to this sect, described by the same traveller as 'mild and unassuming men, with short hair combed sleek behind the ears, sanctified look, an assumed English accent'. Across the water, however, the Liptons rejoined the Presbyterian faith and were regular attenders at the Church of Scotland for the Hutchesontown district, at the intersection of Hospital Street with Cleland and Greenside Streets. 'I liked going to church for one thing particularly,' wrote Lipton smugly, 'and that was to see the respect in which my parents were held by the minister and other members of the congregation.'[30] When there was a special preacher, such as the celebrated Dr Norman McLeod, the Queen's chaplain, seats were reserved for the Liptons, and they were admitted by a side door that kept them apart from the common crowd. 'On occasions like these my breast swelled with pride to think that I was a Lipton and because my people were entitled to such a privilege and honour.' There is no evidence that Lipton was much a church-goer in later life, but at the impressionable age of six or seven he recalled being sent off to church on his own one day:

> The elder at the door conducted me to a seat directly facing the minister, a good, but stern-faced Scottish divine of the old school who thundered forth a powerful and eloquent sermon from the text 'Am I my brother's keeper –'. I say 'powerful and eloquent' because I have no doubt whatever that the sermon was all this and more. The only thing I remember about it, apart from the text, was that the preacher kept glaring at me most of the time, making me more and more fidgety and self-conscious as he proceeded. Finally, after an overwhelming torrent of words the good man in the pulpit pointed straight at me, as I thought, and repeated the question three times, 'Am I my brother's keeper?' With the repetition of the momentous query for the third time his blazing eyes caught my own. Terrified, I thought it was absolutely necessary for me to reply, so I shouted out at the pitch of my voice: 'Yes, Sir!' Preacher and congregation alike were dumbfoundered and soon a titter went round the church which was with difficulty repressed, as the police court reporters say. I remember that I was painfully conscious of having, as I thought 'disgraced the Lipton family' and ran, weeping, all the way home.[31]

Someone who had known Lipton in boyhood contributed a brief sketch to one of the Glasgow newspapers half a century later, and said that he and Tommy Lipton had attended the Sabbath school 'in a portion of Hutcheson Boys' School'. This correspondent also stated that Lipton, for a time, attended the Glasgow Eye Hospital – then in David Dale's old mansion in Charlotte Street near Glasgow Green.[32] Of his schooldays, Lipton had very little to say, and that was mostly inaccurate. At the age of six he was enrolled at St Andrew's Parish School, which may in fact fix the date of the move from Milton Street to the Gorbals. Every morning, Tom would walk the two blocks north along Crown Street and cross the river by the Albert Bridge to the little school facing the west end of Glasgow Green. The schoolmaster, James Lochhead, was one of the old-fashioned Scottish dominies, with a reputation for scholarship and the knack of getting the best out of his pupils. Every Monday morning Tom would take the threepence weekly tuition fee and hand it over to Lochhead in person. Lipton described his schoolmaster as 'wise, solemn and severe, but with a kindly disposition peeping out, unwillingly almost, in many of his actions'. Lipton confessed that he was an indifferent scholar. Poor Frances came to the conclusion that he was not making sufficient progress under Lochhead, so she removed him to another school for a short period.

> Here, however, the results were definitely not what my mother had hoped for, and back again I was dispatched to St Andrew's, where I remained until the close of my school career. Mr Lochhead lived to a ripe old age and I may be pardoned for saying that throughout the latter years of his life he was very proud of his old pupil, Tommy Lipton.[33]

One of the few precise dates in Lipton's autobiography is November 1860, at which point he claims to have left school at the age of nine to take his first full-time job. In light of facts which will be made clearer in the next chapter, however, this date is impossible. Moreover, the records show that James Lochhead was headmaster of Bridgeton Parish School in Old Dalmarnock Road until his transfer to St Andrew's Parish School in 1861, so this flatly contradicts Lipton's claim to have left school the previous year. He was actually eleven years of age by November 1860, but the myth that he had left school at the age of nine to help in the family shop would gain with every retelling during countless interviews at the turn of the century, and in the autobiography become transmuted into hard fact. Besides, although the family moved to 13 Crown Street late in 1861, there was, as yet, no corner grocery store. In the Valuation Roll of that year Thomas Senior was listed merely as a labourer, paying a rent of twelve pounds a year.

Lipton's account of his boyhood is extremely sketchy. By the time he had entered his teens he had developed into a fine, strapping lad, well above average height and well set-up. On his own admission he was always ready for his fair share of mischief and devilment.

> There were lots of lads of my own age in Crown Street and round about the district and I was a ringleader in all manner of 'ploys' and escapades and adventures. Mere high spirits were responsible for us forming ourselves into what we called the 'Crown Street Clan' and going forth to find what excitement we could in attacking combinations of boys from other quarters of the town. Sometimes we lost and sometimes we won. But you may depend upon it that we thoroughly enjoyed ourselves.[34]

It is clear that even at this young age, he had those attributes which would mark him out in later life. Apart from his stature he possessed a high level of self-esteem and brimmed with confidence, the sort of boy that others, often older than himself, would rally to. As a leader in these street battles he had learned to use his fists. Indeed, the only way you could make your reputation on the streets was through 'a series of fistic encounters'. Lipton recalled his first real fight with considerable relish. His adversary was Willie Ross, the son of the local butcher and widely regarded as the leading bully in Crown Street. He was 'a great hulking lout of a boy' who demanded tribute in marbles from the smaller boys. On this occasion, however, Tom refused to hand over some of the 'bools' he had won in fair contest.

> He threatened me and although I was much younger than he was, I thereupon challenged him to fight. Most of my comrades urged me to withdraw, telling me point blank that Wullie would kill me. Others urged me to put a stop, once and for all – if I were able that is to say – to the domination of the hated bully. 'A fight! A fight!' The words ran through our street like wildfire. Off we went, principals and supporters, to a court at the back of Crown Street where there was little chance of the combat being overlooked or interfered with.[35]

According to the narrative, the fight was conducted according to strict rules, with seconds, a referee and a timekeeper (the only boy who possessed a watch). 'Round after round I came up for my medicine. But I gave Wullie a good deal more than he bargained for.' The result was a foregone conclusion, but the younger boy gamely stuck it out for five or six rounds of severe punishment before his seconds threw in the towel. 'Far from lording his success over me and my companions, I must hand it to Wullie that he left us alone for the future.' Thus, very early on in life, Lipton learned a valuable lesson: a good loser can often gain the moral victory. 'As a result of my fight with the bully, my stock soared high among all boys of the district.' Predictably, his mother was sore distressed when she saw the mess he was in but 'I fancied I saw a merry twinkle in my father's eye when I told him that I had stood up for so many rounds against Wullie Ross, the butcher's boy.'

There was the obligatory brush with the law, in this instance a constable who was determined to curb the rowdy behaviour of the Crown Street gang as they played their noisy games in the middle of the road. As in all these anecdotes, Lipton cast himself in the role of leader and hero, and so it was that the peeler swore to get even with 'that young varmint, Tommy Lipton'. On one occasion which 'I can recall as clearly as if it had happened yesterday', Lipton and his pals were rudely disturbed by this policeman 'with his coat-tails flying and holding his high hat with one hand and gripping his baton in the other'. He chased his quarry who dodged up one of the entries that ran right through the tenement block. At the top of this close was a place called Kerr's Byre where cattle were penned, and in his anxiety to escape Lipton leaped onto the midden in order to scale the wall to safety. The mound was not as solid as it appeared, and the boy sank to his armpits in manure. By now the constable had caught up with him, but instead of arresting him he merely stood at the side, laughing and jeering at the boy's predicament. 'Serves ye right, me lad!' he cried, and left him to wriggle out of the filth as best he could. The wretched boy, covered in cow shit and stinking to high heaven, hobbled to the public pump in Govan Street where he tried to clean himself up, much to the amusement of a crowd which had gathered to witness the sorry spectacle.

> My misfortune awakened the compassion of an old cobbler's wife who took me into the little kitchen behind her husband's shop, stripped off my clothes, rolled me in a blanket and put me to bed. Then she washed and dried my clothes so that, two hours later, I was able to present myself at home with little outward appearance of the disaster which had overtaken me.
>
> Looking back on these days now I come to the conclusion that in spite of the schoolboy pranks and the exciting hours as leader of the Crown Street Clan, my happiest days were spent by the riverside.[36]

He went on to describe the fascination of the Clyde. This was the golden age of shipbuilding, when many a Clyde-built steamer was immediately snapped up by the Confederacy as a blockade-runner during the Civil War. But just as Clyde ships were to be found in every part of the world, so too was the Clyde a Mecca for the world's trade. Young Lipton haunted the Broomielaw, studying the steamships and craft of all kinds, chatting to seamen and stevedores, dockers and engineers. His favourite question was 'Where has *your* ship come from?' In this way he learned more geography that he ever picked up at school. He bought a cheap map of the world and pored over it, taking great delight in tracing the routes of the various ships that came to the Clyde from China, Calcutta, Peru or wherever. But the American boats fascinated him most of all. Often he watched with envy as parties of emigrants bound for New York went up the gangplanks, their faces shining with hope. Even then, in the early 1860s, New York was the magic lodestone that drew countless thousands from Europe each year.

Lipton's passion for ships extended right down to the tiniest craft. By the time he was eleven he could ply a pair of oars or single-scull a coble, and not long afterwards he learned to sail a lugsail boat with the best of the Clydeside watermen. Whenever he had scraped together a few pence he would hire a cat-boat and indulge his hobby to the full.

It was at the age of eleven that he had his earliest experience of yachting. 'As a matter of fact I founded a Yacht Club and was its first commodore!'[37] From the massive lid of an old wooden chest he whittled the hull of a boat with his clasp-knife to which he added a mast and a bowsprit, complete with rigging and paper sails. Across the river not far from Crown Street was the great expanse of Glasgow Green. Fireclay had been quarried on the part then known as the High Green for brickmaking and the 'dubs' or holes had filled with muddy water. On the largest of these ponds Tom launched his yacht, appropriately named *Shamrock*.

> Joy of joys! Not only did she float, and on an even keel, but she sailed across the pond like a thing of life at the first time of asking. Not once in all the crowded years which have come and gone since then have I ever recaptured the thrill of the launch and the first 'race' of the original *Shamrock*.[38]

Where Lipton led, the others dutifully followed and soon they, too, were racing their model craft on the waterholes of the High Green.

As a founder of the new sport and of the club, my word in all
matters affecting the races was accepted as absolute. In all the
important races I acted as referee unless, of coure, the *Shamrock*
was a competitor. I won many races and lost a few. And I think I
can say with all truth that it was on the muddy banks of the clay-
holes in High Green that I learned one of the greatest lessons in life
– how to win with pleasure and lose with a smile.[39]

The chapter dealing with his boyhood ended with a long homily
extending over two-and-a-half pages. As he looked back
nostalgically to 'the one really blissful period in existence' he
reflected that the children of the very poor were often far happier
than those of the rich; though it could be argued that the Lipton
family did not know the meaning of real privation or hunger.
Their diet might be very plain and simple but there was always
sufficient; and the parents who could afford to pay for their son's
education, even if it only cost them threepence a week, ensured
that he would have a grounding in the basics, at least to put his
foot on the bottom rung of the ladder. There were thousands of
others growing up in the teeming slums of the Gorbals at that
time who never had the benefit of the most rudimentary
education, ill-shod and poorly clad, suffering from malnutrition
and starvation and prey to the ills and diseases that came in their
train. A photograph of Lipton taken about the age of twelve
shows a remarkably well-dressed young man, complete with
three-piece suit, stiff white collar and broad bow tie. But the
most remarkable aspect is the smug expression exuding self-
confidence.

Interestingly, Lipton quotes at length from 'My old friend,
Andrew Carnegie, himself a child of the people':

I pity the sons and daughters of rich men who are attended by
governesses and servants. They do not know what they have
missed. They have fathers and mothers – very kind fathers and
mothers too – and they think they enjoy the sweetness of those
blessings to the full, but this they cannot do. For the poor boy who
has in his father his constant companion, tutor and model, and in
his mother – holy name – his nurse, teacher, guardian angel, saint,
all in one, has a richer and more precious fortune than any rich
man's son can possibly know and compared with which all other
fortunes counts as little.[40]

The parallels in the childhood of Carnegie and Lipton are very
close. Both came from the urban proletariat rather than the

peasantry. Indeed, the Carnegies, like the Liptons, were linen weavers, forced to seek some other form of semi-skilled employment when handloom weaving gave way to mechanisation. Both fathers were rather shadowy figures – we know rather more about Will Carnegie than we do about Lipton Senior, which is not saying much – whereas the mothers were very much the dominant figure in each household. Carnegie eventually managed to throw off the shackles of his mother-fixation, but Lipton never did. His thralldom to his beloved mother prevented him developing a fully rounded personality, with the maturity to form a close relationship with another woman, on a different level.

On the other hand, the two self-made men differed in one respect. Whereas Carnegie was a rather solitary figure as a child, Lipton was much more outgoing. His parents gave him 'a more liberal education in the give-and-take, the rough-and-tumble of life' than he could have got at an English public school:

> By mixing freely with other children I early came to a knowledge of human nature and the necessity of keeping my own end up. We are told that the race is 'neither to the swift nor the battle to the strong'. There may be exceptions to the general rule; in my case it was borne in upon me very early that the 'race' is usually won by both the swift *and* the strong![41]

2. EARLY EMPLOYMENT
1863–70

When all the world is young, lad,
And all the trees are green;
And every goose a swan, lad,
And every lass a queen;
Then hey for boot and horse, lad,
And round the world away:
Young blood must have its course, lad,
And every dog his day.
    Charles Kingsley, *Songs from the Water Babies*

In his autobiography Lipton says that 'it was an eventful day in our family history when my father and mother decided to embark upon a new method of gaining a livelihood'. Tantalisingly, he does not tell us precisely when this occurred, though the inference, a few pages later on, is that this momentous decision was taken in 1858 or 1859. He then goes on to describe the 'tiny, wee shop with three steps down from the street level – to let at 13 Crown Street which they decided to lease and start in the retail provision trade'.[1] He makes much of the fact that, at the age of nine, he left school to seek full-time employment 'one dismal November morning in 1860'. He goes on to explain that the reason for taking a job was to help his parents out of the dire straits in which they now found themselves.

> Business had been very bad in the wee shop for some months. Profits were scarcely sufficient to keep the household going in the bare necessities. The few sovereigns my father and mother had been able to save when trade was fair were gradually eaten up and there came a time when it was very doubtful if the shop could continue to pay its way. I was only between nine and ten years of age, but I realised how tight was the corner in which the Lipton family now found themselves.[2]

So here we have an impression of a little business flourishing at first, then going downhill and finally teetering on the brink of insolvency. But the chronology is wrong, and, as it has an important bearing on the Lipton saga, it deserves to be examined in some detail.

In the first place, the Lipton shop was not established till some years later. It first appears in the Glasgow directory for 1865-66, compiled late in 1864, which shows that Thomas Lipton, butter and egg merchant, had his premises at 11 Crown Street and his home next door at number thirteen. That the Lipton family were not living in Crown Street much earlier is borne out by the fact that the 1861 Census, taken on 7 April that year, shows them as still residing at 57 Rutherglen Loan – a stone's throw away, but certainly a different address. Furthermore, at that date, Thomas was still employed as a printfield worker. No occupation was entered for Frances, so it is clear that the little corner shop had not yet come into existence. As previously stated, the move to Crown Street must have taken place a few months later, for Thomas Lipton was shown at that address in the Valuation Roll compiled that year.

The entries in the Glasgow directories were confined to businessmen, tradesmen and professional people. Thus the entry for Thomas Lipton at 11 Crown Street merely referred to the shop occupying the ground floor, and took no note of the swarms of people who occupied the apartments and single-ends on the upper floors. Similarly the listing for 13 Crown Street is confined to the three professional men – James Boyle, Colin Granger and Thomas Nairn – who resided there. Farther up the street, towards the river, we find that J. Lawrie kept a dairy at number three, John McIntyre, wine and spirit merchant, had his shop at number five, and Henry Steven ran a 'cooking department' at number seven. Successive editions of the directory up to 1871 show Thomas Lipton as a butter and egg merchant at 11 Crown Street.

In the 1871 Census we find the Lipton family ensconced in the top-floor, four-room flat at number thirteen – the house Tommy Lipton claimed as his birthplace. The entry is slightly inaccurate, insofar as it gives the age of Thomas's wife Frances as fifty-seven when she was actually at least sixty-one. Margaret's age was given correctly as twenty-five, while Thomas Junior was likewise shown as twenty-two, being then just a month short of his twenty-third birthday. Interestingly, the apartment was shared with Janet Kirkwood, a twenty-year-old general servant from Mauchline, Ayrshire. From being on the verge of bankruptcy a few short years before, the Liptons were now enjoying a measure of affluence, with middle-class aspirations.

To put matters into perspective, it should be noted that the population of 13 Crown Street numbered no fewer than 142, in thirty-five families, up a single close! Of the heads of families, only George Craven (iron-moulder at Dixon's Blazes) and John Wilson (wire-worker) were natives of Glasgow; everyone else was an incomer. Only ten hailed from Ireland, though one suspects that James Boyle (railway advertising agent), Mary Mulrine (fish-dealer) and John Scullion (merchant) were second-generation Irish. The rest came from every part of Scotland, from Ardnamurchan and Sutherland to Dumfries.[3]

Bearing in mind the error regarding his age which he perpetrated in later life, it seems, therefore, that the corner shop was leased when young Tom was well into his teens. His parents had no experience of shopkeeping but, they argued, people had to eat to live so why should they not start a small shop from which they could sell basic foodstuffs? The decision to open this shop was not come to suddenly, and Thomas Senior and his wife endlessly discussed the pros and cons. When Lipton speaks of 'many anxious and prayerful hours' spent by his father and mother 'discussing ways and means, difficulties and prospects' one may read between the lines and picture the scene: old Thomas timid and fearful of squandering his few hard-won sovereigns on a reckless venture, and Frances the resolute one, persuading, cajoling and nagging her husband.

> They had only a few pounds saved up and failure would have meant disaster. But they had faith and energy and determination; all they desired was a bare living and the thought of 'success' – in the ordinary sense of the word – and moneymaking never entered into their calculations.[4]

The shop was a single room, so tiny that half a dozen people could not have squeezed inside. Frances kept her shop like her house, spotlessly clean. From the outset the main stock in trade consisted of ham, butter and eggs which Frances arranged to import direct from an old farmer friend near Clones, James McAviney. Every week McAviney consigned the three basic products by train from Clones to Belfast where they were loaded aboard the Glasgow steamer. Every Monday evening Tommy took a handcart across the river to the Broomielaw and waited for the Irish boat arriving at Lancefield Quay. Having loaded up the week's supply of provisions – six hams, two firkins of butter and two crates of eggs – he then trundled his barrow along the Broomielaw, across Jamaica Bridge and then back to Crown

Street, a round trip of about three miles for which he earned the princely sum of twopence. Here again, we may discount the fanciful tale of the little boy of nine performing this arduous task; it would have been tough enough for a strapping teenager to wheel a heavily laden hand-cart for a mile and a half along the cobbled streets.

Young Tom took a keen interest in the enterprise from the outset. The business was founded on the principle of giving the customers good, wholesome, fresh food at an affordable price. By cutting out the wholesalers and other middlemen, and dealing directly with a small farmer, the Liptons offered value for money. 'What was more important,' adds Lipton, the customers 'were served by transparently honest people whom they had known for years in the district where the shop was situated'. As well as acting as the youthful porter Tom helped in the shop, sweeping the floor, cleaning the counter and polishing the one and only window. Between times he ran errands for his mother and delivered groceries. Even at this early stage he was showing a natural talent for salesmanship, demonstrated by a remark to his father one morning after he had seen him serve a customer with half-a-dozen eggs.

> I asked him: 'Why don't you let mother serve the eggs, dad? You see mother's hands are much smaller than yours and the eggs would look much bigger in her hands than they do in yours.' For many years afterwards I was often chaffed regarding this suggestion, which was held to be a wise and precocious notion for a small boy.[5]

Not long after his fifteenth birthday, in May 1863, the session at St Andrew's Parish School came to an end and boys of that age were faced with the prospect of continuing their education at the grammar school founded by the Hutcheson brothers (who had given their name to Hutchesontown, the district in which the Liptons lived), with a view to going on eventually to the University, or of leaving school and finding full-time employment. By now, eking out a precarious living with the little shop and with an invalid daughter to support, the Liptons would have had no choice but to take the latter course. Tommy Lipton was undoubtedly bright though, on his own admission, an indifferent scholar, but his wages were needed to augment the family's slender income.

The third chapter of his autobiography opens with a colourful account of him playing truant at the age of nine to wander round the city in search of work, and coming home that evening to announce that he had found himself a job. How his mother wanted him to continue his schooling but he would not listen. 'To abandon the post I had been so lucky to secure was unthinkable. Besides, I argued, I would be earning money and helping to keep myself.'[6]

Lipton's first employment was as an errand boy and general dogsbody with the firm of A. and W. Kennedy, lithographers, printers and stationers of 13 Glassford Street. The wage was meagre – half a crown a week (twelve and a half pence in modern money) but Lipton never forgot the reward earned for six days' drudgery:

> I felt that the wide world was mine for the taking. Tightly clenching the half-crown in my right hand and keeping that same hand hidden deep in my trouser pocket, I hurried to the wee shop in Crown Street and proudly placed my wages in my mother's lap. You can imagine for yourself our combined emotions.[7]

And in a newspaper interview many years later he added that the happiest day of his life had been when he handed over that first half-crown and was rewarded with a kiss. Lipton is characteristically vague about this period, so it is not known how long he stuck this job; but presently he was lured away by the prospect of four shillings a week, working for Tillie and Henderson of 39 Miller Street, the largest firm of shirtmakers in Glasgow at that time. Although the wages were greater Lipton lacked the freedom he had enjoyed in his first employment: 'My job here was the singularly dull and uninspiring task of cutting cloth patterns and gumming them into the sample books carried by travellers.'[8] Now and again, however, there were interludes that varied the monotony, as when he had a terrific fight with another boy in the pattern department which was unfortunately witnessed by John Henderson, the head of the firm, 'an elderly Scot of stern countenance, and a martinet to business application on the part of his staff'. Lipton, of course, had got the better of the fight, sending his adversary off with a bloody nose and a black eye. When summoned by the boss to explain his disgraceful conduct, the unrepentant youth replied, 'I hit him, sir, because he cut the toorie aff ma bonnet.'

'That does not justify you making a fellow-worker's nose bleed,' said Henderson.

'Well, I admit I can get a new bonnet and he canna get a new nose!' was the cocky response.

Remarkably Lipton appears to have held on to his job, for we next hear of him, after a month or two with the firm, applying in writing for an extra shilling a week. All day he waited apprehensively for a response from the management, but all he received was a curt note, in pencil, from David A. Sinclair, the firm's cashier: 'You are getting as much as you are worth and you are in a devil of a hurry asking for a rise!' Half a century later, Sir Thomas Lipton received a letter from the same David Sinclair, now the chairman of the company, asking him to look after a young nurse from Glasgow who was going out to Serbia on Sir Thomas's steam yacht *Erin*, then being used as a hospital ship under his personal supervision. On receipt of this letter, Lipton telephoned Tillie and Henderson and asked Sinclair if it was he who had worked there all those years ago. When Sinclair confirmed that it was, Lipton went on to say: 'What a contrast this letter is from the last one I received from your firm!' He then recounted the incident when his application for a rise was rebuffed and added the sting in the tail: 'A bit of a change in the tune of the two letters, eh?'

Poor Sinclair was bemused and embarrassed, but then he heard Lipton chuckling on the other end of the line. 'He realized that I was only pulling his leg,' concluded Lipton with a note of satisfaction, 'He became from then onwards one of my greatest friends.'⁹ A variant of this anecdote, which appeared in many newspapers early in 1915 following the telephone conversation with David Sinclair, maintained that it was Lipton's mother who had written the letter. In this version Sinclair is alleged to have said to the boy: 'Tell your mother that you'll never be worth more than four shillings a week to us!' In view of this widely publicised version, although Sinclair was not identified, it seems hardly probable that he and Lipton would have become great friends.

The curt refusal of his application for a rise in wages discontented Lipton and although he continued to work for Tillie and Henderson for a few months longer he lost all his enthusiasm for the dreary task of cutting out shirt patterns. During this period he attended the Gorbals Youths' School at 16 Greenside Street, a night-school for working boys run by Thomas Neil whom Lipton describes as:

> A crusty, ill-tempered old crank, who wore big-rimmed, blue spectacles and was known to everybody in the district as 'Auld Specky'. That he was sound enough in the fundamentals of his profession I have no doubt and must admit that I made considerable progress under his tuition. But the man did not seem to have the

slightest atom of humanity in his make-up; he was a fish-blooded tyrant of whom Dickens would have made a character. 'Specky' was a whole-hearted adherent of the biblical theory about sparing the rod and spoiling the child. Heavens! How he must have loved us! During school hours we even trembled when he looked at us and few of the pupils escaped condign punishment from time to time.[10]

Eventually Lipton and some of the schoolmaster's other victims decided to get their own back and planned, with a couple of former pupils who still smarted at the memory of Neil's tawse on their backsides, to pay a surprise visit to the school at a late hour when they knew that the master would be there alone. Having secured the doorhandle firmly with a rope so that Neil could not escape, they plugged the keyhole with an evil-smelling substance known in those days as Deil's Fodder, which they had purchased from a pharmacy in Crown Street. This awful compound was then set alight and with the aid of pipe-shanks the boys blew the fumes into the schoolroom. Specky's rage and mortification and utter discomfort were gloatingly beheld from one of the windows, and it was not until the wretched dominie was on the point of suffocation that the boys relented and untied the door.

Some time in 1865 Lipton left Tillie and Henderson. Whether it was because he had lost heart over the failure of the wage increase to materialise or merely because he craved a change he could never recollect later on. In hindsight, however, he supposed that he had a hankering to see a bit more of the world. He was never happier than when he was 'in the atmosphere of ships, sailors, boats and the waterside generally'. By a lucky chance he heard one day that the Burns steamers that plied between the Broomielaw and Belfast needed cabin-boys. Lipton hastened to the offices of the steamship company and applied for a position. By now almost seventeen and a strapping six-footer with a good appearance, he was immediately taken on, at a weekly wage of eight shillings and all found. Feeling six inches taller and twice as broad, he went home and broke the good news to his mother. 'Naturally, she did not like the idea of so small a boy leaving the roof-tree,' he adds improbably.

The work as a cabin-boy on a small cross-channel steamer was onerous and endless, with no set hours of either day or night. The crossing was short but often very stormy.

Day merges into night, and night into day, in a remorseless sort of continuity. It is work, work, all the time, until the eyes become heavy and the feet weary. Yet I can honestly say that I was completely enthralled, both night and day. I took an endless delight in the ship herself; in the engines which drove her, in the sailors on the deck, and in the captain on the bridge. There was fascination for me in the casting-off at Glasgow and in the tie-up at Belfast; in the ships we passed at sea, in the lighthouses which flashed their messages through the darkness; in the stars, and in the moon, and even in the wind and waves. I felt that the world was being opened up to me. That it was good to be alive and better still to be a cabin-boy on a gallant Clyde-built steamship.[11]

These short voyages gave him a taste for sea travel which would never leave him. Often he would stare at the great Atlantic steamships berthed at the Broomielaw and gaze wistfully at the steerage passengers on the quay, clutching their bundles as they waited in line to board ship for a new life in America. He often heard passengers speak of New York and Philadelphia and Boston, as they crossed from Belfast to catch the Atlantic liners. Some members of the crew had made trips to America and never tired of telling of its vastness, its wealth and the boundless opportunities which the great new world across the ocean was offering with open hands to all and sundry. Fortunes were to be picked up for the asking. The boy listened eagerly to all this and determined that sooner or later he would try his luck in America.

The opportunity arose sooner than expected. On arrival at the Broomielaw one morning in the spring of 1866 the shore steward's representative came on board to carry out a snap inspection. On finding that the ceiling in one of the cabins had been discoloured by smoke from a badly trimmed lamp he asked the chief steward to name the culprit whose negligence had caused the damage. Young Lipton was hauled before the official and given a week's notice on the spot. Many years later Lipton often entertained Lord Inverclyde, Chairman of the Burns Line, on the *Erin* during the Clyde yachting fortnights and never tired of telling him how he had once worked on his ships as a cabin-boy. 'At dinner on his yacht, or when he came to dine on mine, we have repeatedly laughed over the old story.'[12]

On the day he was paid off, Lipton went straight to the offices of the Anchor Line to make enquiries about a steerage passage to New York. 'At one time I had the idea to set sail without telling my mother and father, as I apprehended the usual objections from them to a mere lad going abroad. But I could not bring myself to this course. It would not be playing the game.'[13] So he trudged home, with his ticket in his pocket, and told them that his mind was made up. He pleaded eloquently to be allowed to go, and his enthusiasm won the day. 'The parting was sad, but I really think that my mother, at least, had such faith in me that she believed I would soon return a rich man.'

Lipton claims that he sailed to America aboard the Anchor liner *Devonia* but this ship was not launched until 1877 and it is more likely that he sailed on her older sister ship, the *Caledonia*. In the mid 1860s the only ship called *Devonia* was a 160-ton schooner engaged in coastal trade and plying out of Dartmouth. The SS *Caledonia* was a much more commodious vessel with a gross tonnage of 628, although only a fifth of the size of the *Devonia* which was launched a decade later. The *Caledonia*, under her master Thomas Ferguson, took emigrants from the Clyde to New York at a cost of seven guinesa for the one-way steerage ticket. There are so many anomalies and discrepancies in Lipton's various accounts of his time in America that there is considerable confusion regarding the actual time he spent there in his youth. On the assumption, however, that the earlier interviews are likely to have been more accurate than the heavily embroidered accounts he gave out in later years, he probably spent rather more than four years in America, between May 1866 and the autumn of 1870.

The ship took so long to cross the Atlantic that some of the steerage passengers were convinced that the captain had lost his way. Sailing records indicate that the *Caledonia* left the Clyde on 21 April 1866 and arrived at her destination on 4 May. This partially agrees with Lipton's recollection that he landed in America shortly before his birthday, although it was his eighteenth, and not his fifteenth as he claims in his autobiography. It is also significant that, in 1903 when Lipton was interviewed by American reporters about his first visit to their country, he stated that he had been seventeen years of age at the time. He had only thirty shillings in his pocket, but many of the other emigrants had considerably less. As the ship edged slowly towards her berth at Castle Garden on the lower west side of Manhattan Island, the eager youth leaned over the rail and scanned the crowd below. His attention was caught by the gaggle of boarding-house keepers touting for business. Running down the gangway well ahead of the early landers, Lipton hustled around among the canvassers until he came across a decent-looking man with a thick Irish brogue. Taking him aside, he told him that he had many friends on board, and great influence with them.

'What will you charge me if I bring you a dozen lodgers tonight?'

'Not a cent, me bould lad,' came the response. 'I'll board you free for a week!'

Back on board Lipton approached a group of passengers who were in his debt because, being illiterate, they had relied on him to write their letters home. He soon corralled thirteen of them, and brought them off the ship to Mike McCauligan's boarding-house at 27½ Washington Street.[14]

Washington Street was one of the seedier side streets near the docks, the houses of flaking red brick decorated with rusting ironwork. Part of this street survived till the 1930s, and on a number of occasions many years later, Lipton would take a nostalgic stroll along its grimy sidewalk; but the McCauligan boarding-house – 'anything but a Biltmore or a Waldorf-Astoria' – was unrecognisable by the turn of the century. In *Sights and Sensations of the Great City*, published in 1865, the anonymous author quoted at length from a report by the city health inspectors. This unsavoury tenement was the property of one, 'Butcher' Burke and was 'one of the most filthy and horrible places in the city'. It was still standing in 1930, serving its purpose as the 'domicile of transients from foreign shores who only wait a turn in their luck to seek better lodgings'.[15] Waugh visited the area just after the Second World War but found that the entire street was in the process of demolition and redevelopment.

Castle Garden had only recently become the official entry point for immigrants, although there was little formality at the time – no passports, visas or other documents, and no insistence on means of support. It sufficed to give your name to an immigration official, who then entered it in a ledger, and provided you passed the rather perfunctory medical examination you were free to pass through the gate and out into the bustling city. In 1903, during one of his challenges for the America's Cup, Lipton was shown his entry in the ledger and was given a photograph of it as a souvenir.

The port of New York was the great gateway for immigrants coming to the United States; of the 7,892,783 immigrants to the country between 1855 and 1882, 5,169,765 landed at New York. Germans were the principal ethnic group, but the Irish were not far behind.

> The Irish emigrants who settle in New York are to a considerable extent a deposit left by the stream of emigration which enters the country at that port. The more energetic and thoughtful, and those who have any money, push on to the west; the penniless and the

shiftless are apt to stay where they land, and furnish the city with most of its unskilled labour, although, of late years, they have been exposed to considerable competition from Italians, mainly from southern Italy. The resource of a large number of the more pushing is apt to be liquor dealing, which generally brings them influence in ward politics, and secures recognition from the party leaders as a means of communicating with and controlling the rank and file. The great body of the porters and waiters in the hotels and second-class restaurants, of the carters and hackney-coach drivers, a large proportion of the factory workers, and almost the entire body of household servants are Irish also, and for the most part a saving and industrious body.[16]

Lipton was certainly not shiftless, but he was well-nigh penniless, and he was hard-headed enough to realise that any sort of roof over his head was better than none at all.

Often we slept eight in a room o' nights. The boarders were drawn from all nationalities under the sun, and unless when a row sprang up, which was not infrequent, there was very little talking for the good and sufficient reason that hardly anybody understood his neighbour's language.[17]

Many years later, when Lipton was a multi-millionaire hitting the headlines with his attempts to win the America's Cup, the American newspapers frequently ran stories about him, or invented interviews. Although they invariably referred to his time spent in America in the 1860s they were remarkably vague. When they stated what appeared to be a hard fact, it was generally untrue. Thus the newspaper which said that he had been born in County Tyrone in 1856 and that his mother's name was Mary was unlikely to be any more accurate when it remarked that his first job in New York was as a newspaper boy, and that on hearing that labourers were needed in the rice fields of South Carolina he tramped many hundreds of miles there in search of work.[18] Lipton himself is virtually the only source of what he did in America during this period, and while he does provide a certain amount of circumstantial evidence, and even occasional names of people and places, his adventures must be taken with a pinch of salt. There is no reason, however, to doubt his statement that he was advised to put his name down in an employment registry which in due course offered him work on a tobacco plantation in Dinwiddie County, Virginia. From this would arise the canard in many newspapers of the late 1920s, that Lipton had been born there. If he was aware of the connection of that county with his natal city he makes no mention of it. In fact it was named in honour of Robert Dinwiddie, the Glasgow-born governor of Virginia, best-remembered nowadays as the man who gave young George Washington his first military commission. The Dinwiddies of Dumfriesshire and Glasgow were an ancient family; Lawrence Dinwiddie had been one of the great Tobacco Lords and also the founder of a pottery and glassworks at Stobcross, where Lipton was to open his very first shop. But Lipton merely states that, on getting the appointment from the registry, he set off the very same evening for the tobacco fields of the south, full of hope and high spirits:

> To reach my destination, which was Wilson's Depot, I travelled by way of City Point on the St James's River and then on to St Petersburg. I had only a few dimes in my pocket but this did not prevent me from taking a keen interest in the journey, and I remember as if it were yesterday how tremendously impressed I was by the new and wonderful country in which I now found myself. The planter for whom I was due to start work was one Sam Clay. I liked him from the start. He passed me over to his manager and I commenced work in the tobacco fields forthwith.[19]

This was gruelling, back-breaking work which, until quite recently, had been performed by slave labour, but since the emancipation of the slaves, the tobacco planters were hard put to get sufficient black field-hands at the miserable wages offered. Instead, their place was taken by recently arrived migrants, reduced to taking this most menial of jobs by sheer necessity. Since the end of the Civil War in the previous summer, the demobilisation of troops of the Union armies had created a problem of unemployment in the great cities of the east coast. Any illusions Lipton may have had about getting rich quick were soon dispelled by the harsh reality of his new situation. But, looking back on this period from the affluence and comfort of the 1920s, Lipton could afford to write that, hard as this new job was, he liked it and thrived on it, adding 'for everyone was kind and considerate'. There is a naïve, bland description of plantation life:

> I and my fellow-toilers trudged home every night to the little cabin where we lodged, so tired and weary that we were glad, our hunger appeased by a square meal, to sink down and forget our exhaustion

in almost instantaneous sleep. Take my word for it, there was no restless tossing on the beds of that Virginian cabin; its occupants slept like logs until it was time to tumble out for another day's 'hard darg', as we say in Scotland. But by each mail, I used to write home that I was getting on fine and saving money – which was quite true. For, noticing that I was big and strong, the foreman promoted me to still harder work and as this carried increased wages I was only too willing to tackle it. Months elapsed and every week I added a bit more to my store of savings. The more I earned the more I saved.[20]

In newspaper interviews sixty years later, Lipton said he was so hard-up he had to scrounge the stamps to frank his weekly letters. One might have expected that Frances Lipton would have treasured every letter, every scrap, that her dutiful son sent home; but regrettably none of this youthful correspondence appears to have been preserved. This is all the more remarkable in view of the vast amount of documentation covering the later years of his life. Lipton kept no diary, either as a boy or as a grown man, and it can only be assumed that, in giving this rather sketchy account of his adolescence in America he was relying solely on a rather selective memory.

This life of rather meaningless drudgery might have gone on indefinitely had it not been for a serious accident in the spring of 1867. Lipton was cutting wood one morning when the hatchet slipped and severely injured his right foot. When Sam Clay was informed he had the boy removed from his straw palliasse and installed in a spare bedroom in his own house. For weeks Lipton writhed in agony, consoled only by the assurance of the doctor that he would not lose his foot. Clay and his wife nursed the young giant back to health and as soon as he was able to hobble about they insisted on him taking things easy, and even drove him to church with them on Sundays. Many years later, Lipton repaid their kindness by entertaining their granddaughter at Osidge, his London home.

When he was fully recovered Lipton went back to work in the fields, but somehow the job had lost its appeal. After a few weeks he gave notice saying that he had a notion to try his luck in New York once more. Heading north Lipton took time out to do some sight-seeing, though he is maddeningly vague about what he did and where he went. 'I spent a day or two at Virginia' – he could scarcely have been more imprecise – although he adds that he visited the home of Jefferson Davis, lately president of the Confederate States and only recently released from Federal confinement.

Young as I was I remember with what eagerness I visited all the historic spots around Virginia; it seemed to my mind that I was walking on holy ground indelibly associated with the glorious early romance of the vast new land, the new people, and the new spirit amongst which I now found myself a very humble but admiring unit. At nights I lived in the cheapest boarding-houses I could discover. Even then this holiday appeared to me to be wildly extravagant, but revelled in every minute of it.[21]

It was autumn by the time he was back in New York, but the employment situation had not improved. As the days passed and his precious, hard-won little hoard of dollars melted to a handful of quarters and dimes, he became very depressed. But just as things were at their blackest the employment agency told him that there were some vacancies for strong, able-bodied young fellows on a rice plantation in South Carolina.

So once more he headed south, and spent the winter of 1867–68 'at Coosaw Island on the Edisto River, sixty miles from Charleston and forty from Savannah'. Coosaw Island, extending to 6,500 acres, was one of the cluster of sub-tropical, swampy, malaria-infested Sea Islands, west of St Helena Sound near the southern tip of the state. Early in the Civil War, Port Royal fell to Union forces who found themselves with over 10,000 negro slaves – officially termed 'contraband of war' – on their hands. In January 1862 General Sherman put into operation a plan for the maintenance of the slave population. In March as a social experiment, a contingent of doctors, teachers and 'superintendents' was sent down from New York, with the aim of keeping the blacks employed and shipping the crops of Sea Island cotton and rice back north. This scheme rapidly proved unworkable and by 1864 all the government plantations had been farmed out to private contractors. The Sea Islands, in fact, became a model for the methods, later employed generally throughout the southern states, which came to be known euphemistically as 'Reconstruction'. Despite a special field order by General Sherman that the islands and abandoned rice-fields for thirty miles back from the sea were to be specially reserved for the sole and exclusive management of the negroes, the island plantations, abandoned by their original owners, were sold off at rock-bottom prices to speculators, the forerunners of the scalawags and carpetbaggers The net result of this well-meaning, but ultimately unjust, system was that the entire economy of the area was turned upside down. In 1865–66 production of rice and cotton fell to an all-time low and never fully recovered before the dreaded boll-weevil killed off the Sea Island cotton industry in 1918.[23]

The newly emancipated blacks preferred a regime of economic self-sufficiency, raising enough sweet potatoes and corn to supply themselves with hominy and grits. What cotton they raised themselves was sold off in the autumn and yielded just enough cash to pay their taxes and buy some new clothes. The rest of the year they were quite content to get by without money. Speculators like Robert Chisolm therefore had to import poor, white labour, mostly in the form of recent immigrants, and it was in this bizarre situation that young Lipton now found himself, along with a motley crew drawn from every country in Europe. Lipton lodged with a Spaniard and his Irish wife 'who took quite a fancy to me. We were the best of friends all round.'

One day the Spaniard confided in the boy that during the recent war, he had been stationed on Fort Sumter, the rather grim fortress dominating the harbour of Charleston and the scene of the first action in the Civil War. It was during this spell of garrison duty that the Spaniard had fallen in love with a pretty Charleston girl. After he returned to his Irish wife, the Spaniard continued to correspond with his mistress, though the fact that the Spaniard had difficulties in letter-writing is one of the improbables in this anecdote. For this reason he confided in Lipton who naïvely agreed to assist him. One night the two men stole out of the cabin and went into the nearby woods in order to compose the letter. Lipton pocketed the letter, meaning to put it into the mail for Charleston the following day. Later, when the Spaniard asked him if he had posted the letter, Lipton was amazed to find that it had disappeared from his pocket. Both men were apprehensive that the Irishwoman had purloined it and it was with quaking hearts that they returned to the cabin that evening.

> Sure enough, the bombshell fell. Immediately she had cleared away the dishes she turned to her man and upbraided him bitterly for his deception. Quick action followed. The hot-blooded Spaniard, convinced that I had betrayed him, turned on me and before I realized what was happening he had drawn a knife from his belt and slashed me across the face with it. Only my agility and fleetness of foot prevented me from being murdered. Dodging the infuriated man, I rushed to the door and out of the cabin. He pursued me all the way to the overseer's house. Fortunately, Mr Mathews, the overseer, was on the spot and he not only gave me instant shelter, but held off the enraged Spaniard with a loaded revolver. My

wounds were dressed and I remained with Mr Mathews that night. In the morning the Spaniard came up with profuse apologies. His wife, fully believing that her husband had killed me, told him that she had been suspicious of us going off to the woods together, taking the ink-bottle and pen with us, and that after we had gone to sleep she had searched our pockets and found the letter. The whole dramatic incident had a happy ending. Husband and wife agreed to let bygones be bygones; they implored me to return to their cabin, which I did, and the three of us were the best possible friends for the rest of the time I remained on the rice-fields.[24]

The naïve, simplistic tone of this yarn typifies Lipton's narrative of his adventures which belong more in the realms of R.M. Ballantine's juvenile fiction than to real life. According to Lipton, Mathews was so impressed at the manner in which Lipton made up the quarrel with the Spaniard that he promoted the youth to the plantation office as accountant and bookkeeper. Coming after months of hard, physical work in the fields this was a stroke of luck, giving Lipton the opportunity to expand in a new direction.

I had a natural aptitude, I found, for figures and my skill in penmanship was given full scope. I did my level best to keep the plantation books better than they had ever been kept before. All through life I have discovered that the boy or man who can do things even a shade better than the other fellow is the one to whom the plums will fall sooner or later. This is obvious, I can hear some of my readers say. It is, but nevertheless it is astonishing how many people miss the obvious in life and in business.[25]

Lipton adds that he held down the bookkeeper's job for almost twelve months, so it would have been late in 1868 when he got the urge to move on in search of something bigger and better. One day a big schooner put in at one of the island anchorages not far from the plantation. Lipton heard that she was bound for Charleston and immediately broached the subject of a passage to the mainland. The skipper was not averse to helping him but advised him to come aboard after nightfall without telling a soul. Borrowing the Spaniard's canoe, Lipton and another boy paddled out to the schooner just before she weighed anchor. On the passage to Charleston they called at a real desert island. Spread along the shore were many piles of carefully cut timber, evidently cut and stacked by some person or persons who intended to return and ship the lumber to the mainland. The schooner's captain, acting on the principle that findings were keepings, ordered his crew to load the timber on to the schooner's deck and sold the 'salvage' on arrival in Charleston. Lipton dramatises his arrival in the great seaport, discovering:

> The entire population seething with excitement over a disastrous fire which had broken out the previous day and was still raging and threatening the complete destruction of the town. This was bad luck for Charleston and thousands of its citizens, but it was good luck for me because I immediately got a job with one of the fire engine squads at 50 cents an hour! I became an enthusiastic fireman at this remunerative pay and would not have minded very much had the conflagration lasted a month. But it was all out in a day or two, and soon my boy friend and myself were tramping the streets and docks looking for work.[26]

Here, at least, is a verifiable incident which, had it really occurred, would have helped to pinpoint Lipton's movements. But the Great Fire of Charleston had occurred in December 1861. It began on a wharf on Cooper River above the market, where negro slaves heading up-country were cooking their supper. It was a windy night, their fires got away from them, and set a hay barn on the wharf alight. All hope of checking the blaze vanished as the rising wind drove the flames in great beams through the air. There was no fire brigade to tackle the blaze, as all the men had been conscripted into the Confederate forces. The fire swept unchecked through the city, cutting a huge swathe from north-east to south-west. All the great antebellum mansions and public buildings were razed to the ground and the devastation was total as far as the rice mills along Ashley River. There was little loss of life but an immense amount of public and private property was destroyed. As a result Charleston was virtually abandoned by its civilian population; in the latter part of the war the city was besieged by Union forces for 567 days. What the fire did not consume General Sherman's army accomplished, when marching northwards from Savannah. Although rebuilding began in 1866 the city must still have presented a tragic sight when Lipton passed through two years later. Gaunt, burnt-out ruins stood amid a veritable jungle. Everything was overgrown with rank, untrimmed vegetation, the streets a tangle of tall grass and shrubbery amid the broken glass.[27] Lipton's only truthful remark was that although an occasional odd job or two came their way, the fire, instead of causing employment, had the reverse effect.

One day Lipton and his companion were despondently strolling along the quayside when they came abreast of a steamship, the *Moneka*, taking on the last of her cargo for New York. Great bales of cotton were being pushed aboard across a flat gangway. Why not help to push one on board – and stay on board? Lipton suggested this ploy and the other lad agreed. The ruse worked splendidly and in no time they were making themselves scarce in the steerage quarters. They remained concealed until the ship dropped her pilot at Fort Sumter. They then emerged and surrendered to the purser.

> It was my idea to make a clean breast of our presence aboard – carrying the war into the enemy's camp, so to speak. We were speedily taken before the captain, and here again my candour and straightforward admissions seemed to impress him. In any event, he told me off for work on the deck and the other boy was sent below to help the stokers. I think I had the better share of the 'punishment'![28]

Back in New York Lipton was parted from his unnamed companion 'for whom I had developed a real liking – as people will do for those introduced to them by adversity', as the boy went home to his parents. Lipton hoped that it would be a case of third time lucky; but he had no more success in obtaining employment on this than on the two previous occasions. This time he was so short of cash that he could not even afford a roof over his head. One wonders what happened to all the money he must have saved from his twelve-month stint as plantation book-keeper. With the onset of winter in 1868 he headed south to warmer climes. 'For the next few months I wandered over different parts of the States, taking a job at this thing or the next, and passing on when the work was finished or I felt that I could better myself.'[29]

Eventually he landed at Carrollton, seven miles from New Orleans, where he obtained work with the local tramcar company, and lodged with the foreman of the caryard, Harry McBride and his wife. Lipton remembered his landlady with fondness and she, in turn, beamed with pleasure when he told her that her pancakes were just like his mother's. More than forty years later, in the autumn of 1912, Lipton was back in New Orleans but staying at the St Charles Hotel 'at a cost of, figuratively, five dollars a minute, as against the five dollars a week I paid for my lodgings when I first struck town!'. According to his autobiography, the day after his arrival had been well publicised in the local newspapers and he was visited by none other than his old landlady from Carrollton who had followed his career with interest. Lipton entertained her to lunch, during which she leaned over and said: 'Do you remember saying, Sir Thomas, that my pancakes were every bit as good as those your mother used to make?' Lipton chuckled as he recalled not only saying that, but he remembered the pancakes even better. 'This meeting was for me a most refreshing link with the past; and I can truthfully say that in all America there was no one with whom I would rather have renewed my friendship than with this dear old lady.'[30] The truth is rather different. Mrs McBride did not seek him out; but through the good offices of the Southern Yacht Club, the cottage where Lipton had lodged was identified and the elderly widow and her one-time lodger were tearfully reunited. When he left New Orleans Mrs McBride received a massive chest of tea and an envelope, the contents of which she never divulged to a soul. On a later visit to New Orleans (in 1926), Lipton gave an interview to R. Lee Edwards which clarified the position. He had worked there for five months, not as a regular car-driver (as he stated in his autobiography) but as a clerk in the administrative office above the mule barn; although when one of the regular drivers failed to turn up he would sometimes take out the trolley himself, hauled by a pair of mules – a revelation that provoked a spate of features in the American papers with the headline 'Millionaire was a Mule-skinner'.[31] He also reminisced with affection about Poydras Market 'where you could get the largest slice of pecan pie for a nickel'.

One would have expected that, when Lipton was rich and famous and a frequent visitor to the United States, some of the newspapers from the towns where he had lived and worked might have dug up 'local boy' stories; but it is surprising how few factual accounts were preserved in Lipton's voluminous scrapbooks. The *Chicago Sunday Tribune* was the first paper to get an interview with the great tycoon, and publish an outline of his early life in America, later reprinted by many other papers. This account, sketchy though it is, is illuminating as representing the earliest version of the story that would – much embroidered and embellished – eventually find a permanent place in the autobiography. After saying that he began as a messenger boy in a Glasgow stationery shop – 'I was ten years old. My father, Thomas Lipton, was a workman' – he went on to describe his time in the United States:

I ran away. I took an Anchor Line boat out of Glasgow and came to America. I came in the steerage. I landed at Castle Garden and went through the regular form there. Next I got down to South Carolina and worked on a well-known rice plantation. But money was scarce there and wages had to wait till the crops grew and were sold. This was discouraging to me. After many difficulties I made my way to Charleston and became a stowaway on a ship bound for New York. Of course I had to work my passage. In New York I got a situation and stayed there a time, finally going back to Glasgow.[32]

Oddly enough, it was another Chicago newspaper which was to provide the fullest account of Lipton's sojourn in New Orleans, as well as shedding light on subsequent movements which were not dealt with in the autobiography. According to this account, he drove a tramcar for a month, but his employment ended abruptly when the workers came out on strike. Two strikers jumped on to Lipton's car and bellowed; 'Are you with us?'

'Who are you?' he asked.

'We're a committee from the strikers.'

That was enough for Lipton to halt his car and join the strike, but he did not stick around to see the outcome. Instead he got work as a door-to-door salesman for a crayon portrait concern. According to this newspaper, he had brought from Scotland his most cherished possession, a violin which he played in the evenings for relaxation. He became acquainted with a New Orleans merchant who was fond of music and almost every evening he would go over to the merchant's shop and play old Scotch airs for him. When the shop caught fire one day Lipton rushed in and, braving the flames, managed to rescue his violin. As he exited, however, he ran into the arms of a policeman who arrested him as a looter, and it was some hours later before the merchant arrived at the police station and confirmed his story. He had only eighteen dollars when he left New Orleans. He went to New York and obtained employment aboard an Anchor Line steamer scheduled to sail next day. On the trip across the Atlantic he played his violin in his off-duty hours. 'He played so well that he attracted the attention of the passengers, and the big Scotchman was the principal performer one night at a concert in the saloon.'[33]

This account was even accompanied by a line drawing vividly illustrating the arrest of the 'looter'. Lipton himself makes no mention of this incident although, at a later stage in his autobiography when he was back in Glasgow, he refers to a period when he took up the violin, implying that this was an interest developed some years later. This intriguing tale also omits the fact that Lipton spent several months in New York before deciding to return to Glasgow. According to another newspaper account, Lipton also spent five months as a farm-hand at Dunnellen, New Jersey. The widow of his employer, Robert Newhall, recalled many years later that when he left he had saved $150.[34] From the comfortable farmhouse at Dunnellen, Lipton was reduced to living in Casey's bed-house at twenty-five cents a night. In his autobiography, however, he merely tells how he returned to New York and was fortunate in obtaining a post as an assistant in a prosperous grocery-store.

> Here, at last, was a business that appealed to me. I liked it from the outset. I could see possibilities in it. People must eat, I told myself, and the store that tempted people to buy good goods would never be empty of customers. Certainly our store was a busy place; it was run on up-to-date methods. These I studied keenly all the time I was employed there. I thought I could see the subtle differences between shopkeeping in America as compared with the methods of tradespeople in Glasgow.[35]

The wares offered, the food sold, might not be any better, but it seemed that they were displayed to fuller advantage, and the shop assistants took a more personal interest in the customers they served. There was a much more positive, up-beat atmosphere in a New York shop even in the 1860s, which seemed to Lipton to invite trade and hold it. Nowhere does he mention the store where he was employed but from casual references in newspapers many years later it transpires that he was employed by Alexander Turney Stewart, a native of Ulster who had emigrated to New York twenty years earlier and established a fine department store at Broadway and Tenth in downtown Manhattan. In its heyday, Stewart's was *the* New York store, and in the grocery department of this great emporium the eager young Lipton soaked up the techniques of retailing with intense eagerness. After Stewart's death in 1876 the store went into a decline, but in 1896 it was acquired by John Wanamaker and continued until 1952. Long before that time, however, the fashionable stores had moved uptown.[36]

Lipton, now in his twenty-first year and with a wealth of experience under his belt, prospered in Stewart's, and won rapid promotion. 'Probably I would have done very well there had I stuck to it, but about this time a tremendous longing assailed me to see my father and mother again. The feeling became overpowering as the months went on. So I saved all the money I could from my wages and when I had $500 I booked my passage for Glasgow.'[37] Homesickness was the primary reason for Lipton's return to Scotland, although, looking back on this period many years later, he felt that he must have had some 'undefined resolve' to apply his 'American experiences and wit-sharpening adventures' to some project in his native land. 'I did not know it at the time, but, as events proved, I went home to make my fortune, thus reversing the usual order of things, whereby emigrant lads have gone to America from all corners of the earth to improve their lot.'[38]

It was in the autumn of 1870 that Lipton, now aged twenty-one, left the United States after a sojourn lasting rather more than four years.[39] What must, at the time, have seemed like rather aimless drifting probably gave Lipton his shrewd insights into America and the Americans. Robert Smallwood, President of Thomas J. Lipton Inc., neatly summed it up when he said that Lipton saw America as a true immigrant – 'an experience more valuable than a college degree'.[40]

3. ON HIS OWN ACCOUNT
1870–78

To found a great empire for the sole purpose of raising up a people of customers, may at first sight appear a project fit only for a nation of shopkeepers.

Adam Smith, *Wealth of Nations*

Before leaving New York, Lipton purchased presents to take home. Characteristically, no mention was made of the gifts for his father or sister, Maggie, but the choice of suitable presents for his mother cost him 'many hours of anxious consideration'. The choice, after long deliberation, was a curious one: a barrel of flour and a rocking-chair. The unnamed ship which bore him back across the Atlantic docked at the Broomielaw early on a Saturday morning. Most returning migrants would have rushed off home as fast as possible; instead, Lipton hung about the ship as long as he dared and dallied on the quay till midday when he calculated that his old mates would be heading home after the week's work. Then he hired a cab and, loading the precious flour barrel and rocking-chair on the roof, told the driver to proceed to Crown Street – not the direct road straight to the low numbers on the south bank of the river, but by a circuitous route which led him to the far end of the street. Then the cabbie was instructed to drive *slowly* through that busy thoroughfare, thronging with midday pedestrians.

A horse-cab in Crown Street was an uncommon sight, and all heads would have turned to behold the spectacle anyway; but a cab with a flour barrel *and* a rocking-chair lashed uncertainly to the top – now that was a rare sight indeed. And who was this tall stranger, gesticulating to the crowds as if he were the Prince of Wales himself? Tommy Lipton, barely recognisable as a grown man, moustache and all, hung out of the window, waving and shouting to all the passers-by he fancied he had once known. 'Thus my return caused quite a sensation among my friends,' he congratulated himself on his showmanship, naïvely assuming that the denizens of Crown Street would immediately recognise this local boy made good. No matter, this strange apparition was doubtless the talk of the neighbourhood for weeks, and the word would spread like wildfire that young Tommy Lipton was back from America. Many people went from the Gorbals to America, but no one could ever recall any of them coming back. The sight of the tall, bronzed young man with the huge moustache, laden with parcels, alighting from the cab outside number thirteen was just the thing to attract a crowd in no time at all. Lipton savoured his brief moment in the limelight before stooping to go down the three steps into the family corner shop. How tiny it seemed. How tawdry the street was, even by the standards of New York.

Frances and Thomas Senior apparently had no inkling of their son's return, but they were overjoyed to have him back.

> Far into that night and again on the Sunday we sat round the fire while I told them the stories of my adventures. And when my mother said that her rocking-chair was the most comfortable thing she had ever sat in, I felt that all my hardships and hard work had been well worth while.[1]

The following morning, however, he came down to earth with a bump as he started as an assistant in the wee butter-and-ham shop. 'The old shop seemed very small indeed,' he confessed. But it was small in more ways than the purely physical. After many months in the palatial grocery department at Stewart's, young Tom found the family shop claustrophobic. Very soon it became abundantly clear to him that his parents were barely making ends meet; the small scale of their business and the slimness of their profit margins could scarcely have made things different. 'On my return, trade began to improve and soon my mother had quite a tidy bank balance on the right side,' he wrote, without revealing how this change was wrought. Clearly, from the outset, he effected subtle changes, making the most of the small window to present an attractive display of goods, so that the housewife, tempted inside, might purchase more than she had intended. Young Tom had a brisk but genial manner, chatting up the customers. Gradually he took over most of the serving and most of the buying. A genuine interest in people never interfered with the serious business of giving them what they wanted – at a price they could afford.

Above all, he had an instinct about Glasgow. The city itself had changed out of all recognition in the four years he had been away. The Gorbals might be more congested than ever but across the river the city was entering its golden age of architecture.

Many splendid public buildings were going up, reflecting the commercial and industrial progress. Previously Glasgow's fortunes had been made with the southern states of America, by trading in tobacco, sugar and cotton. The Civil War had grievously set back this trade, but now the city was flourishing as never before. Iron and coal, procured locally, had replaced American imports and the Clyde was rapidly becoming the ship-building centre of the universe. Locomotive manufacture and heavy engineering of all kinds had dramatically transformed Glasgow, now second city of the Empire and its industrial nerve-centre. Glass, ceramics, textiles and paper joined iron and steel as the great primary products and, increasingly, Glasgow was becoming the home of a thousand-and-one manufacturing industries that took raw materials from every corner of the globe and spewed them back again as finished goods. Even before he had set foot on dry land, Lipton had been impressed by the sight of the great new Kingston docks, on the opposite bank from the Broomielaw. The Clyde, deepened and widened, was a forest of masts all the way to Jamaica Bridge in the very heart of the city. There was a brashness and raw vibrancy about the place that set his pulse racing as he took that memorable cab-ride home.

Only Crown Street itself was something of a let-down. Glasgow clearly had potential for an energetic young man like himself, but the way ahead was not in the semi-basement of 11 Crown Street. Lipton still had the better part of the nest-egg he had brought back from America; translated into sterling it worked out at around a hundred pounds, no mean sum in an age when it represented two years' wages for the average working man. 'This knowledge caused me to begin dreaming the dreams which I was so soon to translate into realities.' For a long time, however, he hesitated about broaching the subject of expansion and diversification with his parents, but as the business prospered and profits rose steadily his restlessness increased. When the family's (as opposed to his own) bank balance passed through the magic three-figure barrier, he felt that the moment had come to take the bull by the horns.

That evening he dropped his bombshell. What was the use of money lying in the bank? It was doing no good there. 'Money makes money,' he told them. 'But it only makes money rapidly if it is used properly. We are doing as well in the Crown Street shop as we can ever hope to do. If I open another shop, I can double the profits!'[2]

The reaction of his parents was predictable. His father thought he had lost his wits, and his mother castigated him at the very idea of squandering their hard-earned savings, painfully gathered over many years, on such a wildcat scheme with all the worry and anxiety that that would entail. No, it was quite out of the question. All Tom's hopes and ambitions were stifled in a matter of seconds, though not for long. He was not the man to let such adamantine opposition deflect him from his cherished dream. He said nothing for the moment but resolved to raise the matter again, whenever an opportune moment arose.

This came sooner than he had anticipated. A Philadelphia steamer arrived in Glasgow after a very stormy passage which had severely delayed her. As a result parts of the cargo had to be sold off on the quayside for whatever they would fetch. Tom saw an advertisement for the sale and hurried over to the Broomielaw. As luck would have it, a consignment of hams was one of the first portions of the cargo to come under the hammer. For a few pounds, which Tom had drawn from his bank account, a large quantity of hams and sides of bacon were his. The rest of the morning was spent going round all the little corner shops in Glasgow's side streets unloading this stock. By the end of the day he had made a profit of eighteen pounds. This was his first business gamble and its total success exhilarated him. Repeatedly he told himself that if he could make eighteen pounds by selling a few hams, he could make hundreds of pounds by selling a thousand of them. He had grasped the principle of buying as cheaply as possible and making a modest profit on a rapid turnover. The quantities did not matter; it was the system that counted. 'Success and fortune seldom came stalking up one's home street, uninvited.' Only by going out and hustling for business would he ever get on.

He was rather crestfallen when his parents failed to share his enthusiasm. From time to time he continued to preach to them but they remained obdurate. In one of the very few passages that mention his father, Lipton paints a picture of the old man's total lack of vision.

> 'We are only humble folks, Tom,' he would say, 'and we should be thankful that we have done so well. If we followed your plan, people would say that we were riding for a fall, that the peas were shooting above the sticks. Come back to earth, my boy, and stop building castles in the air.'[3]

Significantly, Lipton paints his mother in a more positive light, but far from being the guiding star and the instigator as he often liked to make out, we have the young man pleading, cajoling and persuading, and Frances gradually coming round to his way of thinking. When he got her on her own, Tom felt that he could reason with her. One day he took her into his confidence: his big idea was to launch not just one shop but to have shops all over Glasgow. Who could say, but perhaps the day would come when there would be a Lipton shop in every town in Scotland. He impressed on Frances the urgency of putting this plan into operation before anyone else got the same brilliant idea. At that time the little shop in Crown Street was making about three pounds profit every week; but Tom argued that he could make six pounds with two shops and thirty pounds with ten. The scope of his plan was quite breathtaking.

Already, he had his eye on an empty shop at 101 Stobcross Street, on the north side of the river, not far from Lancefield Quay where the Irish steamers berthed. It had been a grocery, run by James Alison, but it had in fact been empty for the previous five years and was in a very poor, run-down condition.[4] He made discreet enquiries and discovered that the lease was available for no more than a nominal sum. Every time he went across to the Broomielaw to load up his hand-cart with produce from Ulster he would take a short detour, and reassure himself that this shop still had the vacant sign above the door. The opportunity was too good to miss. Frances was half-convinced but Old Tom was more dubious.

Young Tom decided on a daring course of action, to show the old man what he meant by modern business methods. Drawing heavily on his own savings, he ordered a smart, freshly painted grocer's van with the word LIPTON on each side. Between the shafts was a smart pony in a shining set of brand-new harness.

> My father was standing at the door when the equipage drew up. I kept in the background and watched him with anxious eyes and a beating heart.
>
> 'What on earth does this mean?' I heard him ask the man in charge as the latter jumped down from the van and saluted him.
>
> 'It's your new horse and van ordered by your son, sir!' replied the man. 'And I must say that it's a fine smart turn-out and does your son credit.'
>
> 'Well, I don't want anything to do with it,' promptly said my father, 'and you can take it back to where it came from!'[5]

Without another word the old man turned back into the shop. Young Tom had to hurry after the retreating van and explain the situation to Messrs Leckie and Company, the saddlers at 60

Stockwell Street from whom he had ordered the outfit. Eventually he persuaded John Leckie to take back the horse and van, promising that he would return shortly. 'I shall soon want the horse and van myself, as I am opening up on my own account in Stobcross Street very shortly.' His chagrin and humiliation knew no bounds, and we may suppose that his father's negative attitude provoked a bitter altercation later that day, though all Lipton says about this incident of the horse and van is that it 'broke down my father's last scruples about letting me have my business head'.

By the time Tom had got back to Crown Street his mind was made up. The wee shop in Crown Street was not big enough for the three of them; he would have to move out. Lipton claims that his mother now openly sided with him, pointing out to her husband that it was better to have a son 'who was pushful, self-reliant, and ambitious than one who would simply be content to accept things as they were'.

When the census was taken in April 1871 Tom was still living under the parental roof at 13 Crown Street and listed, like his father, as a butter and egg merchant, but a few weeks later, on 10 May, he opened his own shop. 'So it came about that on my twenty-first birthday I started business on my own account,'[6] he writes. He was, of course, actually twenty-three, but the myth of being two years younger may have started at this time. In the census, his age was given as twenty-two – which was strictly correct.

Lipton commenced his business career with a capital of one hundred pounds, but cannily he expended only half that sum on furnishings and stock-in-trade, keeping the balance for contingencies and extensions. Over the days prior to the grand opening, he worked round the clock in order to have his little shop ready for business. It was actually twice the size of the Crown Street shop, with a large window on either side of the doorway. Yet it was no bigger than any of the other shops in that crowded street. What marked it out from the others was the bold inscription across the fascia board: LIPTON'S MARKET. Such a grandiose title was bound to attract attention. The premises were painted and decorated inside and out and he introduced many innovations in the fittings and general equipment, but it was to the stock that he paid the closest attention. 'Most of it came direct from Ireland, and it was purchased at such keen rates that on my opening day I was announcing prices which quickly caused a sensation amongst my competitors all over the district.' The word that the new young grocer was offering good ham at fivepence or sixpence a pound, with an extra special brand at sevenpence, spread like wildfire through the Anderston district. Even other grocers, whom Lipton significantly describes as 'opponents', hurried along to see who was undercutting them so drastically. Before he had been open many hours there were clusters of housewives round his window – 'and they didn't all stay outside, either!'. Lipton records that his first day's takings were two pounds six shillings, 'considerably more than we had ever drawn in a single day at the wee shop in Crown Street'.

Today Stobcross Street, like Crown Street, is virtually non-existent. Most of the Anderston district through which it ran was swept away during the massive redevelopment of the city in the 1960s; where Lipton's first shop stood there now runs the Clydeside Expressway, and no memorial, or plaque, marks the location of the modest beginning of one of the world's greatest grocery chains. To the south, and running at right angles down to the quays, was a series of streets with the imposing titles of Cheapside, Piccadilly, Hydepark and Whitehall, but they were as unlike their London namesakes as they could possibly be. This was another of Glasgow's congested districts where factories and manufacturing businesses, large and small, sat cheek by jowl with overcrowded tenements. The lower reaches of these streets were occupied by ships' chandlers and model lodging-houses for seamen and dock labourers. It was a ghetto inhabited by West Indians, Chinese and Lascars – Glasgow's first coloured community. Stobcross Street itself represented the respectable end of this industrial dockland, its tenements inhabited by decent working men and their families. It was essentially a working-class district, with small lock-up shops fronting the pavement and a public house on every corner. What made Lipton's Market stand out from countless other little shops along this bustling thoroughfare was its brightly painted exterior and eye-catching window displays which were far ahead of anything else in Glasgow at the time.

Lipton kept open at all hours and, as darkness fell, he would turn up the gaslight, so that the windows flashed like a beacon to passers-by, the bright, cheery glow tempting them inside. Lipton himself worked from early morning until late at night. 'I was manager, shopman, buyer, cashier, and message-boy all in one.'[7] If he had provisions to collect off the Irish steamers he would go down to Lancefield Quay himself with his hand-cart before dawn; if his customers required groceries to be sent to their homes, he would shut the shop temporarily and make the delivery in person. He kept his shop scrupulously clean, and wore fresh white overalls and an apron every day. When business was slack and there were no customers to serve, he would go outside and polish the windows, giving him the opportunity to exchange a cheery greeting with any housewives who happened to pass up or down the street. Then he would draw their attention to some special offer or some titbit or other which he strongly recommended. Lipton had a nifty line in patter and took delight in chatting-up customers, or even anyone passing who looked as if she might be tempted into the shop. Once inside, there would be few housewives who could resist the quality of his wares that positively cried 'value for money' at them.

More importantly, he was not long in Stobcross Street before he got a contract to supply the kitchens at the new University which had sprung up in the late 1860s on Gilmorehill, overlooking the River Kelvin. This lucrative contract lasted three years and, more than anything else, put the energetic go-getter on his feet. For Lipton, his grocery store was the be-all and end-all of his existence. He poured his heart and soul into that first little shop.

> I got it into my head that a man could attain almost anything he liked, if only he had the mind. So I stuck to my work all day long and far into the night. Often I was on duty from six in the morning until midnight. Frequently, indeed, I slept in the little back shop so that I could be up bright and early next morning to take advantage of some bargain in butter, or eggs, or bacon which I knew would be on offer. But the work was a thrill and a joy to me. I lived for my little business.[8]

He adds that, to the credit of his parents, from the first day of his going to Stobcross Street, they never interfered with him in any way, not even with suggestions. 'You're doin' fine, Tom,' was all his mother would say, 'but dinna kill yersel workin' ower hard!' So much for Frances Lipton being the guiding star he proclaimed in later years. The impression is also given that he continued to reside under his parents' roof, when he was not sleeping in 'the back shop'; but the earliest Glasgow directory, published early in 1872, that mentions 'Thomas J. Lipton, butter and egg merchant', indicates that he had his home at 3 Radnor Street.

This is intriguing on two counts. It shows that Lipton, at the age of twenty-three, had moved away from his parents and sister. Secondly, it marked a decided improvement for this upwardly mobile young man, for Radnor Street was in the heart of Glasgow's West End, about a mile north-west of the shop in

Stobcross Street and very close to Kelvingrove Park which was
then in course of being laid out. Back in 1871 this was arguably
the most desirable district then being developed.

Clearly business was booming in Lipton's Market, but that in
itself would not explain the sudden and dramatic move from the
Gorbals to the most salubrious part of the city. Perhaps the
answer lies in the momentous step which Lipton took on 12 May
1871, only two days after opening his shop. The records show
that Thomas Lipton, who gave his age as twenty-one, was
married on that date in St Francis Chapel in Cumberland Street,
Gorbals, after banns of the Roman Catholic Church. The bride
was nineteen-year-old Margaret McAuslan, cotton-carder of 31
Thistle Street (one block distant from Crown Street). The
witnesses were the bride's brother Patrick (her father was dead)
and Mary Conly, and the ceremony was performed by Father
Brendan Butt.[9] Interestingly, the groom gave his address as 8
Mathieson Street, Gorbals, a cheap lodging-house.

The immediate reason for this marriage was the birth of a son,
Thomas, on Christmas Day 1871. The birth was registered by
the father on 10 January 1872, at which time Lipton and his
young bride were living at 12 South Wellington Lane. This was
obviously a temporary lodging, but it was only about 200 yards
from Stobcross Street. It is probable that the move to Radnor
Street took place early in the new year.

There is, of course, no mention of the marriage in Lipton's
autobiography. In later years when he had suddenly sprung from
nowhere into the glare of publicity, there was endless speculation
about the world's most eligible bachelor. Waugh makes the point
that a very important factor in his social success in the 1890s was
that he had arrived unencumbered:

> Nine times in ten the self-made man is handicapped by an early
> marriage, by a wife who does not fit into the new world to which
> success and wealth have introduced him, a wife who does not 'go
> down' with his new friends. In the case of nearly all self-made men
> there is a 'little woman' in the background; or else there is a divorce,
> which in England, even in Edwardian days, would have involved
> the closing of certain circles.[10]

Later, however, Waugh makes a cryptic comment, 'Once it was
rumoured that he was married all the time', but fails to give details
of how such rumours originated or what precise form they took.

Unless baby Thomas was two months premature it seems
likely that the marriage was forced on Lipton because Margaret

McAuslan found herself in the all too common predicament of pregnancy. In those circumstances and in those times the usual course was to do the decent thing by the girl and marry her, even if the match was palpably unsuitable. Margaret was a Catholic whereas the Liptons were staunch 'black-moothed' Presbyterians. The boy's parents, growing up in the increasingly sectarian atmosphere of Ulster in the 1820s and 1830s, would have been horrified by the news that their only son had got himself tangled with a 'taig', but apart from the religious factor, Margaret was far beneath Tom in the social scale – even by the standard of the Gorbals – for she was illiterate and employed in one of the most menial jobs then available to women. It is open to speculation that Tom may never have told his parents about the trouble he had got himself into; though equally, the news of this unfortunate liaison must inevitably have reached the Liptons.

Baby Thomas was not long for this world. At the age of ten months he contracted a bilious fever and died on 6 November 1872. Significantly, his death was registered by Margaret, who made her mark in the appropriate register. On this occasion she was accompanied by her widowed mother for moral support.[11] For a while Tom and his child bride seem to have jogged along, for she fell pregnant again and gave birth to William on 15 September 1873.[12] On this occasion Margaret made her mark unaccompanied. As her address was now given as 36 Bolton Street, Tradeston, a district on the south side of the Clyde, to the west of the Gorbals, it may be inferred that the couple had already parted company. Thereafter Margaret and her surviving son vanish without trace. In the Scottish records down to 1950 there is no mention of a remarriage or death for Margaret, nor mention of marriage or death for William. It seems highly probable (for reasons that will become clearer later) that they sought a new life in Canada; if this were the case, it is logical to assume that they were paid off by the reluctant husband and father. Herein would lie the basis for those rumours and this episode, unresolved by divorce as it would be nowadays, explains Lipton's avoidance of matrimony later in life.

In his autobiography, Lipton studiously avoided any details of his private life. The chapter dealing with his early days in the grocery trade concentrates on the meteoric growth of his business. After only six weeks this had expanded to such an extent that he was obliged to hire an errand-boy. Jim was very shabbily dressed and though apparently a good worker his ragged appearance was at variance with the smart image that Lipton was so keen to project.

One day he drew a shiny gold sovereign from the till and told the lad to go off and purchase a decent suit during the lunch-break. The boy duly returned that afternoon clad in his new suit, and Lipton beamed with satisfaction. Jim was now a credit to the establishment. Next morning, however, Jim failed to turn up for work as usual. After three days, Lipton called on the boy's mother to enquire whether he was ill – only to be informed that Jim was looking so respectable in his new suit that he had obtained a better job as a result.

A second assistant did not last long either. One day he was sent to the post office to buy five shillings worth of halfpenny stamps to put on some circulars which Lipton had had printed – his first essay in advertising. When he returned and was asked for the five shillings change out of the half-sovereign he had been given, he replied, 'There's no' ony change, Mr Lipton. The price of stamps has riz!'[13]

Eventually Lipton found more reliable staff, some of whom were destined to be associated with him for many years and to rise to important positions in his organisation. The first of these young men was a youth of about eighteen whom he encountered one day trying to push a heavily laden wheelbarrow up the incline of the Victoria Bridge. The lad was making heavy weather of the task, for there must have been half a ton of ironmongery tools in the barrow, yet the boy was putting his shoulder to the wheel with right good will. Let us imagine the scene. Slowing his pace, for a minute or two Lipton stalks the boy, noting the rippling muscles through his thin shirt, the growing patch of sweat running down his back, the trim buttocks and the straining calves. He is unaccountably stirred by the spectacle; his heart goes out to this sturdy boy struggling so manfully with the ungainly load. He quickens his step and draws alongside. 'Here, let me help you!' The boy returns his ready smile. In an instant, a bond is forged that will last for forty years.

Together they trundled the barrow across the bridge. In the course of conversation Lipton learned that the boy worked for a firm in Crown Street, and that the work was hard but that he enjoyed it. On impulse Lipton asked him what he earned.

'Seven shillings a week.' Lipton looked him up and down.

'Come and work for me and I'll give you fourteen shillings a week,' he said.

'Right you are!' agreed the youth. And Lipton concludes, 'That young man became, in after years, one of my principal directors!'[14]

Except in a single, unrelated anecdote, nowhere in his autobiography does Lipton mention this boy by name, far less admit that he was his inseparable companion and closest confidant for many years. The boy was William Love, born in Wigtownshire in June 1854 and thus six years Tom's junior. In the early days of the Stobcross Street shop, William worked as long and as hard as his boss whom he hero-worshipped. He was energetic, highly intelligent and utterly dedicated to Lipton. Most of his life would be given up to the service of his brilliant master. By 1874, perhaps even earlier, William had likewise left his parents' home and had moved in with Tom. The exact nature of their relationship, business or otherwise, can only be guessed. In later life Lipton often referred to him as his partner, though there was never any formal agreement of partnership and in press reports, for example, Love is usually referred to as General Manager. Lipton trusted him implicitly; in later years, when he was often abroad for weeks or months on end, he was secure in the knowledge that William, his alter ego whom he had trained to perfection, whom he had moulded in his own likeness, would act and think exactly as he would himself.

Discussing Lipton's hasty and unsuitable marriage with an eminent psychiatrist, I was given a profile of Lipton's sexual behaviour. It appears that he was a classic and extreme case of mother-fixation. Such a man would never be able to form a normal sexual relationship with a woman, unless she was far beneath him in morals and manners, for the very idea of sexual intercourse with a woman approximating the dearly beloved mother would be unthinkable. Margaret McAuslan, the illiterate mill-hand, probably fitted this pattern. Worldly wise and sexually aggressive, she must have made all the running, seeing the young grocer as a good catch. Soon disgusted and revolted with her and himself, Lipton turned away from her and then discovered his true love, the aptly named Love. It is significant that, although there was no one of the name in either the Lipton or McAuslan families, the second child of this brief union should have been named William – after Lipton's lover.[15] Later in life Lipton enjoyed a considerable reputation as a ladies' man but, in line with his policy of inventing himself, it was a carefully cultivated persona and calculated to the precise degree, so that although his name was frequently linked in the gossip columns with some society belle or other, there was never any substance to the stories, and rumours of an engagement were usually followed swiftly by denials by one or other of the parties concerned. It is indubitable that William Love, the inseparable partner of the years before Lipton came into the limelight, was more than Lipton's right-hand man. Even when they parted company in 1893 they remained on the most intimate of terms. Later, of course, there would be others, such as Joe Slade and John Westwood, though it can only be a matter for speculation to what extent their relationship had a sexual element.

The rough and ready manner in which Lipton recruited William Love became standard practice, if not on the same intimate level, in the hiring of employees thereafter. He would look out for a likely lad, and the streets of Glasgow thronged with them, ask him how much he was currently earning, and then offer to double his wages. This ploy never failed and Lipton never had any cause to be disappointed with his choice. Without the formality of references or a job interview, Lipton would secure the services of many young men who would give their lives for him. As an employer, especially in the 1870s and 1880s, Lipton had a charismatic quality that inspired fierce loyalty in his staff. A flair for advertising and a keen business sense were certainly ingredients in the Lipton recipe for success, but the *esprit de corps* which he engendered among his employees was something unheard of at that time. At the core lay the fact that Tommy Lipton never lost the common touch, an astonishing ability to relate to people, and they to him in return.

This was essential to his strategy of opening further shops. Lipton's Market in Stobcross Street was a great success from the outset but within months it had been expanded to its utter limits. During this period Lipton had taken his first tentative steps in advertising, not only by circulars but in eye-catching drawings which adorned the upper parts of the windows. At the same time, however, his restless mind was forever scheming over ways and means of expanding the business. Soon he was branching out into contract work as an adjunct to the Stobcross Street enterprise. He was beginning to realise that 'the first aim in business is to secure more business, and also that the more business you can do the less profit you can work on'.

His first important deal came when he secured the contract to supply provisions for the staff of one of the largest drapery firms in Glasgow. When he told Love that he intended tendering for this contract, the youth shook his head. 'They'll never give it to a wee shop like ours, Mr Lipton. You'll just get a disappointment. Don't try to run before you can walk.'

'Just see how fast I am going to run on this contract,' was the riposte. 'The other firms won't see my feet for dust!'

Lipton carefully worked out quotations for top-quality merchandise at prices which left him only the barest margin of profit. Not content with undercutting potential rivals, he sent in his bid with samples of ham, butter and eggs, all daintily packaged. 'Confronted by such enterprise the directors of the drapery establishment at once gave me the contract.' Characteristically, Lipton used this contract to good advantage when advertising his business, making as much capital as possible out of the fact that Lipton's were supplying such a prestigious firm with their household provisions. In this manner similar contracts with other businesses – including the University – were negotiated. In the early days all the goods connected with these contracts passed through the Stobcross Street shop and Lipton and his assistant were often hard-pressed to cope with the volume.

In hustling after such lucrative contracts Lipton was fairly exceptional (especially at the lower end of the grocery trade) but not unique. What gave him the edge over much larger competitors, however, was his grasp of advertising techniques. Advertising as a tool of retail selling was still very much in its infancy. The principal medium was the press. This was the era in which the whole of the front page of a newspaper would be taken up with advertisements, but aside from stock woodcut ornaments used to head each section, there was virtually no attempt at pictorialism. Advertising relied entirely on the written word. This applied also to the small posters and placards that appeared at the sides of shop windows. Doubtless Lipton had seen a more pictorial approach developing in New York, but he was certainly one of the first retailers in Britain to employ this technique.

Never a man to hide his light under a bushel, Lipton boasted of his role in revolutionising advertisements in Britain: 'I was one of the first Britishers to see the immense possibilities and advantages to be reaped from novel and judicious advertising.'[16]

He began in a modest way with a very simple handbill urging housewives who wanted superb value for money at the lowest possible prices to patronise Lipton's Market in Stobcross Street. This leaflet was distributed by hand to passers-by, but it was soon followed by a circular detailing Lipton's prices and inviting a comparison with those of other grocers. Taking advantage of the recently introduced halfpenny postage rate for printed matter, he mailed this price-list to a few hundred specially selected addresses in the vicinity. Then he tried a small advertisement in a Glasgow evening newspaper, drawing attention to a line of extra-fine bacon to be had at the shop at a price that defied

competition. This advertisement cost seven shillings and sixpence
a far cry from the many hundreds of thousands of pounds
expended annually on advertising by the Lipton organisation in
the 1920s. Lipton would forever be on the lookout for new
advertising media; his firm would be one of the first, for
example, to advertise on the sides of tramcars and omnibuses,
and in the early 1900s he would be among the first to advertise
in stamp booklets following their introduction.

Very early in his career Lipton tumbled to the fact that people
were more likely to spend money if they were in a good humour.
It occurred to him that the most successful advertisements were
those which raised a chuckle; people were more likely to
remember an advert which made them laugh. Appreciating this
point was one thing, but making it work was something else.
Then one morning he hit upon the idea of having a large wooden
ham, painted as realistically as possible, hung from a pole outside
the shop door. In no time at all, the ham sign was swinging
merrily in the breeze and immediately attracted a lot of attention.
It made its début on a very hot day, the new paint melted and
blistered and the sign began to resemble a large, luscious ham
straight from the boiling. This caused endless amusement among
the passers-by and soon people were coming from all over
Anderston and Finnieston to see Lipton's dripping ham.

The next ploy was to commission Willie Lockhart, a local
cartoonist, to draw a series of comic sketches which Lipton used
to adorn his windows. Lockhart's first cartoon showed a solitary
pig, eyes streaming with tears, perched on the back of an Irish
drover. Nearby stood an old lady, concerned for the poor
porker's grief. Below the picture was the sort of wordy caption
beloved of cartoonists at the time:

> OLD LADY: 'Why, my good man, what ails your pig?'
> THE IRISHMAN: 'Sure ma'am, he's an orphan; the rest of the
> family have gone to Lipton's.'

This simple cartoon drew thousands of people to Lipton's
window and, thereafter, a fresh cartoon was pasted up every
Monday morning. People came from all over the city to see the
cartoons and they always went away with a smile and a chuckle.
Sometimes Lockhart gave his cartoons a topical twist, as when
Gladstone's ministry fell in January 1874. One half of the picture
showed a procession of dejected ex-Cabinet ministers, while the
other half showed the same men emerging happy and triumphant
from Lipton's brandishing sturdy hams. So long as Lipton's

Market was to the fore, there was no excuse for despondency anywhere, not even in a defeated Cabinet.

Soon Lockhart was extending his repertoire to include pictorial price tags and mini-placards which forced passers-by to spend more time in front of the window. The longer they stood there laughing at the cartoons, the more likely they were to see something they fancied and come into the shop. Lipton's competitors scoffed at his 'comic-cuts', failing to grasp the basic psychology behind them. Lockhart, 'under my guidance and encouragement' diversified into sculpture, producing 'statuary in butter' which was added to the attractions drawing people from near and far. Lockhart's masterpiece in this line was a tableau representing a stout policeman making love to a dairymaid. Lockhart also produced sculpture from sausages and cheese, his figures invariably stout and jovial, which is how Lipton liked to see his customers as well.

To cope with the steadily increasing demand, Lipton went beyond his old habit of buying produce straight off the steamer. In the early 1870s he began travelling across to Ireland to buy direct from the farmers. Oddly enough he recorded no impressions of those business trips when he must often have slept in the very cabins he had cleaned a few short years before. By this time he had acquired a well-trained staff and could therefore go off to Belfast with an easy mind. From there he travelled to the market towns and villages of the north and west, paying cash on the nail for his purchases. In this way he acquired a reputation for fair dealing and, as the size of these cash transactions increased, so he ensured that he got the best quality goods for the lowest cash price.

On one occasion he travelled to Lisnaskea in County Fermanagh, not far from the ancestral home at Shannock Green though he made no mention of this.[17] On the steamer he had met a businessman who was also heading for Lisnaskea, though in a different line. This man gave him some useful advice on how to get the better of his rival butter-buyers. Acting on this tip, when he got to the market in the village square he hired a stall and a set of scales from Noble, the market manager. Then he looked around for a smart young man and paid him five shillings to go out on the highway and intercept the farmers on their way to market. Lipton wrote the prices he was offering for best-quality eggs and butter on slips of paper, and these the youth handed out to the farmers with the information that Thomas Lipton of Glasgow would pay spot cash for all the produce they could offer him.

Within half an hour the farmers began to roll up at Lipton's booth, 'much to the mortification of all the other would-be buyers'. Lipton was kept hard at work weighing butter and counting eggs. True to his word he paid cash on the spot, and as the word spread more and more farmers clamoured for his attention. After two hours of hectic trading he was disconcerted to discover that he was running out of cash. His competitors were quick to realise his predicament and began jeering at the young upstart from Scotland and accusing him of breaking his promise. In fact, Lipton was only short of about thirty shillings to complete deals with the last two or three farmers, but he refused to be beaten. Quickly he ran to the pawnshop on the other side of the square and popped his silver watch for the required amount. Then he called at the post office and telegraphed home for additional funds, in order to settle his hotel bill and redeem his precious watch. This was his first and last experience of the inside of a pawnshop.

It was during this early period, when his only shop was in Stobcross Street, that Lipton imported a thousand turkeys and geese from Canada, through Messrs R.G. Tennant of Montreal. An undated cutting, one of the earliest preserved in the Lipton scrapbooks, describes this venture:

> The poultry before leaving Canada were naturally frozen and have arrived here in fine condition, quite ready for the manipulation of the cook. This is probably the beginning of a very important branch of business with the Colony, as, not only do the poultry arrive in prime condition but Mr Lipton can sell it in retail at from 7d to 8d per pound. Mr Lipton expects a further consignment of 2,000 turkeys this week in Glasgow.

The birds were packed in ice, a technique which, if not entirely new, was still sufficiently novel for a newspaper to comment on the enterprise of Mr Thomas J. Lipton of 101 Stobcross Street. Incidentally, this was the first reference to Lipton's middle initial, which also made its début in the Glasgow directory that year. It seems that, perhaps emulating the American custom of a middle initial, he merely adopted Johnston by taking his mother's maiden surname. In later years he even tacked the letter 'e' to the end, though for what reason is inexplicable. In this he was also inconsistent, spelling his middle name with or without the final letter almost at whim. In standard works of reference, however, beginning with *Who's Who* (whose details he furnished himself), the name was invariably spelled Johnstone, but on his tombstone it was correctly spelled.

The narration of the Lisnaskea incident was followed, in the autobiography, by one of the very few glimpses into Lipton's home life:

> As may well be imagined, I had very little leisure time on my hands. It was a case of work, work, work from sunrise – and frequently before it – until late at night. But what glorious fun it was! I never felt that I wanted more amusement or excitement than my business afforded me. After the first few months I stopped sleeping in the back-shop and went home to the old roof-tree in Crown Street. No matter how late I arrived home, my father and mother were anxious to know what had happened 'down at Stobcross Street', what new scheme or idea I had hatched, and generally how things had prospered or gone awry.[18]

Here again, however, the bare facts do not match up to this cosy domestic picture. In 1873 he moved his residence from 3 Radnor Street, but only round the corner and across Dumbarton Road to an elegant apartment at 12 Franklin Terrace (which was also numbered 297 Dumbarton Road). This would be his home, shared with William Love, until 1877.[19]

In the aftermath of his unsuitable marriage and its subsequent breakdown, it is more likely that a rift, or at least a coolness, would have developed between the Liptons and their headstrong son. As he became more and more absorbed in his own grocery business he would have had less and less time for the wee corner shop in a district which, by the mid 1870s, had degenerated into a festering sore.

There are endearing touches, which Lipton added to show that he still had a little time for leisure pursuits. 'After supper I would get out an old fiddle and scrape away for the better part of an hour.' He does not mention what kind of music he played; indeed music of any sort gets scant attention in the rest of his memoirs, which tends to reinforce Blackwood's opinion that Sir Thomas Lipton had no interests outside his work, until the yachting mania overtook him at the turn of the century.

Apparently he went through a phase for self-improvement, but the boy who made little progress under the great James Lochhead, and who seems to have spent more time and energy at the evening classes to playing practical tricks on Thomas Neil, was hardly likely to have had the self-discipline or the motivation for educating himself. 'If I didn't practise the violin,' he says airily, 'I would give myself a French lesson,' but there is no evidence that he ever attained any written or spoken fluency in that or any other language. 'I was so full of this zest for self-improvement that I would willingly have spent several hours a day to that end had I been able to spare the time which, of course I was not.' Nothing must interfere with the grocery business.

In his autobiography Lipton states with customary vagueness that 'three years after opening the Stobcross Street shop' he had sufficient funds in the bank to open another, and much larger, establishment in Glasgow's High Street, about a mile to the east of his first shop. In fact it was not until late in 1875 that the shop at 21–27 High Street was opened. As its numbering implies, it was actually a very much larger store than its predecessor, although in many respects it was a replica of it, with the same layout of produce and the same use of butter sculpture and window cartoons. Where one man and a boy had sufficed in the early days of the Stobcross Street shop, the High Street store had a staff of six at the outset, and this number rapidly expanded as the business mushroomed. By now Lipton was a name to be reckoned with, in Glasgow at any rate, and the High Street shop was 'an instantaneous and tremendous success'. A few months later he opened a branch in Govan, at 199–201 Paisley Road. In 1877 Lipton divested himself of the shop in Stobcross Street to a grocer named Cochrane who would, in turn, operate quite a chain of stores around the city. Stobcross Street was too down-market for the scale of the Lipton enterprise and it was now replaced by much more commodious premises at 137 Main Street, Anderston, a stone's throw away so that the original clientele were not inconvenienced by the move.

Lipton also states that only a few months after opening his shop in the High Street, he acquired 'a magnificent shop in Jamaica Street, one of the best shopping thoroughfares in the city, and here again it was a case of scoring an immediate and sensational success'. Lipton's memory was at fault, for the Jamaica Street shop, which eventually became his flagship store, opened in 1879.

Early in 1877 Lipton took another major decision, by diversifying from retailing into manufacturing when he established his own factory for dressing and curing hams. This was located at 8–12 Robertson Lane in the city centre. Hitherto Lipton had purchased his hams cured in Ireland, but by now he was buying 'on the hoof' and arranging for the slaughtering and curing in Glasgow. The decision appears to have arisen on two counts: a desire not only to cut out middlemen but to gain some control over the processes between livestock and the dinner table.

The idea of curing his own hams seems to have occurred to him on one of his jaunts to Ireland where he was increasingly concerned at the uneven quality of the produce being offered. He had quickly established a reputation for paying best prices in spot cash, but sometimes he was disappointed on finding that produce was not always as fresh as it should have been, or had been damaged by careless handling.

From the outset, the Robertson Lane factory attracted considerable attention. The factory premises were gutted and entirely refitted specifically for the business of ham-curing. The largest of the three drying houses processed 9,000 hams while two smaller buildings handled 3,000 each. One curing tank held 1,200 hams and there were several smaller ones. The factory processed 6,000 hams and sixteen tons of bacon every week. The same account, entitled 'Enterprise in the Provision Trade',[20] stated that Thomas Lipton was selling 16,000 dozen eggs a week, as well as 200 Stiltons, Cheddars, Dunlops and American cheeses. Butter, however, was the mainstay of the business, Lipton importing a colossal ten tons each week from Ireland 'in lumps, crocks and firkins'. Lipton was now exporting huge quantities of dairy produce 'to the West Indies and elsewhere', besides supplying the leading hotels, restaurants and institutions of Glasgow. He now had 100 employees and his 'splendidly horsed' vans delivered daily to all parts of the city and suburbs. The report concluded extravagantly, 'We think these particulars of the extent of Mr Lipton's trade fully entitle him to claim to be the largest retailer in the world.'

Certainly, by 1877, Lipton was a force to be reckoned with in the Glasgow provision business. It was early in that year that he hit upon the idea of making unsolicited gifts of a nicely packaged ham to people of some consequence in the hope of getting an effusive letter of thanks which might be utilised in future advertisements. Typical of the response was the letter from Lieutenant-General MacPherson on 28 August, thanking him for the parcel of hams – 'the finest I have ever tasted'. The General mentioned that he had given one of the hams to 'a friend of mine, the Countess Montidjio [sic] who declared they were better than anything she had tasted on the Continent'. The Countess Montijo was the daughter of William Kirkpatrick of Closeburn and mother of the Empress Eugénie whose late husband, Napoleon III, had lost his throne six years previously. Eugénie herself was destined to become one of Lipton's closest friends, after he became rich and famous.

Fired by the success of this venture, Lipton now embarked on a series of stunts. The first of these was to have small handbills printed in imitation of the pound notes of the National Bank. They were lithographed rather than engraved, but were a perfect colour match, in the exact dimensions, and printed on one side only just like the real thing. Superficially the design of the imitation was very similar, but for the bold heading LIPTON'S below the royal coat of arms. Whereas the genuine note had an inscription across the top UNDER ACT 16 & 17 VICT. CAP. 68 alluding to the legislation under which it was incorporated, the imitation had the clever slogan TRY LIPTON'S CAP. HAMS. The side panels bore the addresses of the shops in Paisley Road and the High Street. The small print, which in the genuine note carried the promise to pay the bearer on demand one pound sterling, stated that the 'Great Irish Ham, Butter & Egg Markets' would give a pound's worth of provisions 'as given anywhere' for only fifteen shillings. The notes did not offer a discount and merely served to advertise the fact that Lipton was undercutting his competitors. The notes were dated at Glasgow, 11 March 1877, in the same way as the real notes were dated at Edinburgh, and in the panel bottom right each note was hand-signed by T. Lipton as Proprietor and William Love as Cashier. The 'notes' were handed out in the streets to passers-by in exactly the same manner as any other handbills.

According to his autobiography 'the broadcast issue' of the Lipton Notes caused a sensation and led to many unexpected and comical happenings.

> Many of the notes found their way into circulation as genuine representations of 'real money'. Rival shopkeepers found them in their tills at night and even the cashiers at one or two Glasgow banks were deceived. I myself was hoist with my own petard for no fewer than five of my own spurious notes were discovered among the takings at my High Street shop one Saturday night![21]

Several pages were devoted to humorous anecdotes concerning church elders getting Lipton notes in the collection plate, or the naïve housewife whose purse was snatched and complained to the police that it contained four Lipton notes and twopence in coppers, or the out-of-work comedian whose fellow thespians had a whip-round of thirty-five pounds – all in Lipton notes – as a practical joke at the poor man's expense. Lipton, of course, 'was moved to console him with a few real notes' when apprised of his hard-luck tale. Lipton brings himself into one of these anecdotes:

One afternoon, I was driving through Dumbarton with some friends when, in a traffic hold-up, a tramp came up, begging. Jocularly, I offered him one of my 'own' pound notes. This he greedily seized and disappeared before I could throw him a copper or two. Next day I read in the papers that a vagrant had been up before the local magistrate and sentenced for trying to pass a Lipton pound in exchange for a glass of beer at a public house.[22]

The true story was much grimmer. Archibald McCallum, a labourer of Old Kilpatrick, found one of Lipton's notes in the roadway and, being illiterate, assumed he had chanced upon a genuine pound note. Scarcely believing his good fortune, he made straight for Ferguson's pub in Dalmuir where he tendered it to the publican for a glass of whisky and a glass of ale, receiving nineteen shillings and sixpence change. The good-hearted McCallum thereupon stood drinks all round and a right merry party ensued. Archibald was quite drunk before Ferguson realised his mistake and summoned a constable. McCallum was arrested and brought before Sheriff Steele at Dumbarton court the following morning where he pleaded guilty to passing a counterfeit note and was sentenced to thirty days in prison.[23] Solomon McCall got twenty days from stipendiary magistrate Samuel Gemmell for trying, albeit unsuccessfully, to pass a Lipton note, but James Castel was sentenced on 13 September to sixty days imprisonment. In the case of Helen Stewart, who proffered a Lipton note for two meat pies, the verdict was 'not proven' because it was unclear whether she realised the note to be false.

Inevitably the law caught up with the perpetrator himself. On 3 April Francis McConnal, a collector for the Glasgow and Govan Building Society, had received cash from six investors, but on checking the takings in his cash-box that evening he had discovered a Lipton note. Unable to figure out which of the investors had lodged the note, McConnal made no attempt to question any of them. Instead, he applied to the Small Debt Court for a writ against Lipton in the sum of one pound. The case came before Sheriff Lees on 17 April but was adjourned for a week so that fuller evidence could be obtained. The main hearing took place on 24 April, when John B. Wann, cashier of the National Bank's city branch, said that the Lipton note was a passable imitation of his bank's pound note. Wann had personally remonstrated with Lipton, after one of his tellers had mistakenly accepted one, and warned the young grocer not to issue any more, but hinted that Lipton had ignored this advice.

Samuel Irvine, tea merchant, said under oath that he, too, had been duped by these false notes.

Lipton himself did not appear in court. Instead he passed this buck to William Love who gave evidence as to how the notes were handed out to passers-by in the street and that no one could have been in any doubt as to their true nature. Sheriff Lees likened this action to a previous case in which someone, who had unwittingly accepted a gilt button hammered flat to resemble a gold sovereign, had sued the tailor for redress. Lees took the commonsense view that Francis McConnal should have exercised more care in taking cash from his investors, and by failing to question them after the event he undermined his own case. The case was dismissed as incompetent, but the Sheriff awarded no costs to the defendant, and characterised Lipton's stunt as 'a most impudent and reprehensible act'.[24] This is hardly the same as giving judgment in Lipton's favour, as claimed in his autobiography.

Nor did the worthy sheriff state that 'a mere moment's examination would have proved to any intelligent person that the note was only an advertisement'. From that viewpoint, however, the note could scarcely have been more effective. The story, in various forms, not only appeared in many of the Scottish newspapers but attained prominence in the *Irish Times* which reported on 3 May, the involvement of 'Mr T.J. Lipton, a well-known dealer in Irish butter and ham' in the escapade, and added its own reproof:

> The fact that actions have been brought against him by the police, the bank authorities and several persons who had been innocently imposed upon will probably impress upon the mind of this unfortunate butterman the danger of copying too slavishly Yankee modes of advertising.

And it is clear that the case was even reported in the English press, prompting at least one notaphilist, E. Barker, to write to Lipton, 'I would take it as a favour if you could oblige me with one of your notes, on the understanding that it would be kept in my private collection.' Lipton himself was quite unrepentant over the matter, even when the number of cases of poor, illiterate people going to prison as a result began to proliferate. In one of his earliest letters to the press (26 April 1877) he defended his action by saying that people should keep their eyes open when accepting notes. This was in response to an editorial in the *Glasgow Evening Citizen* which had previously warned the public against mistakenly accepting these notes.

While Thomas and Frances Lipton gave up their little corner shop in 1873 but continued to reside at 13 Crown Street for a further four years, by 1877 Young Tom had purchased a surprisingly modest mansion in Cambuslang, a village some miles to the south-east of Glasgow. By that time the low-lying parts of the village, around the railway line, had become home to a wide range of industrial concerns, and tenements to house their workers had been thrown up close by. But on the slopes of the hills to the south of this development the wealthy merchants and industrialists of Glasgow were erecting their sandstone houses. Many of these were semi-detached, but large and spacious for all that. The house which Lipton purchased on North Avenue was one of those and he named it Johnston Villa in honour of his beloved mother. Whatever rancour may have remained from the unfortunate marriage had long since been forgotten and forgiven. In due course Thomas and Frances took up their new abode, and their son moved back under the same roof.

Along with Tommy came William, his bosom pal, partner in crime and inseparable companion.

4. CAMBUSLANG

1879–86

Because the thrifty housewives of Newport
To Dundee will often resort,
Which will be to them profit and sport
By buying up cheap tea, bread and jam,
And also some of Lipton's ham.
    William McGonnagall, 'On the Newport Railway' (1894)

One of the tallest stories in Lipton's autobiography concerns the manner in which he claims to have opened his first store outside Glasgow. As no date was given, it did not matter that the facts as set out in the tale bore no relation to reality.

One day, so the story goes, he decided to learn German, and made arrangements with 'a certain Herr Schultz to come to the back-shop in Stobcross Street' and give him private lessons. It is more probable that the lessons were to have taken place at the flat in Franklin Terrace. For someone as canny as Lipton was, he made the stupid mistake of paying Schultz in advance for the lessons. On the appointed evening the German did not turn up. Evening after evening passed without any sign of him, and finally Lipton's patience ran out. One night he went off in search of the professor and tracked him down to his lodgings near St Vincent Street. Schultz got the shock of his life when he answered the doorbell and found an exceedingly irate six-footer on his doorstep.

'I have been waiting for you to teach me German,' said Lipton without any preamble, 'and now I'm going to teach you!' *His* lesson lasted five minutes, but it was a good one.

The following morning, Frances Lipton happened to be in the shop when Sergeant Swanson of the Western Police Division came in and alarmed her with a report that a German professor of languages had filed a complaint against her son for grievous bodily harm.

> The sergeant, who was a great friend of mine, urged my mother to prevail upon me to make myself scarce for a few days until the affair blew over. This she did with all the pleading at her command. The

mere idea of her Tom being 'in trouble with the police' badly upset the poor soul. For my part, I was very unwilling to 'flee from justice' because I knew I had done no wrong in chastising a swindler; but in the end I decided to clear out temporarily, and I took the train the same day for Dundee.[1]

As in all his stories, Lipton cast himself in a heroic light, regardless of the fact that he had taken the law into his own hands. A couple of pages later his assault on the teacher was justified when it turned out that he had swindled many other people in the same manner.

Far from being censured for taking the law into my own hands and administering a sound 'leathering' to the rascally Schultz, I was highly commended for my action; a well-known Glasgow magistrate even went the length of saying that I had performed a useful public service![2]

Needless to say, the Glasgow directories reveal no one of the name of Schultz living in the vicinity of St Vincent Street, or indeed any other street in the city at this period. To be sure, there *was* a Michael Schuller, a designer with Dalglish, Falconer and Company, who lived at 29 St Vincent Place and may have given German lessons to supplement his income. But then again, he may not have done. The canny grocer who was a past master at the art of driving a hard bargain with Ulster farmers was not the man to be hoodwinked by a con man, German or otherwise. Nor was the prosperous young businessman likely to have gone to so much trouble, and risked prosecution, for the sake of a few shillings. The eighty-four volumes in which Lipton carefully preserved the press-cuttings that documented every aspect of his later career contain not a single scrap that pre-dates April 1877. Even supposing that Lipton had changed the professor's name to Schultz, and that the story was fundamentally true, the case of the German swindler is not to be found in any of the Glasgow newspapers, far less any report of a 'well-known Glasgow magistrate' commending young Lipton for his public spiritedness. One is left with the inescapable conclusion that this colourful yarn was a figment of the Lipton imagination, got up to explain how he came to be in Dundee. According to Lipton, his four days' self-imposed exile as a fugitive from the long arm of the Glasgow police provided the chance discovery of an empty shop in the Murraygate, a prime site which he snapped up on the spot, for his first shop outside Glasgow.

> Had I not gone to Dundee, and had I not taken a determined fancy
> for that shop in the Murraygate, it is no certainty that I would ever
> have extended my activities outside the radius of Glasgow. Up till
> this stage I had more than once pondered over starting another shop
> as soon as I had saved enough money for the purpose, but it was
> not until I had visited Dundee that the vision of a nation-wide
> enterprise – Lipton Stores in every large town in the Kingdom –
> gradually began to take possession of me.[3]

The truth was far more prosaic. Lipton never did anything
without long and careful deliberation and meticulous, almost
military, precision in the planning. The likelihood is that he had
been contemplating expansion, to realise his dream of having a
chain of shops all over Scotland, and eventually targeted Dundee
as a good working-class location. Furthermore, the opening of
new Lipton shops was taking place in Glasgow itself, long before
Lipton contemplated expanding to other parts of the country.
But the way Lipton tells it, the Dundee shop came before any of
the Glasgow branches, which is patently absurd.

The Dundee shop opened in July 1878 at 8–10 Murraygate, in
a handsome block which had recently been erected by the
developer Laing on one of the city's slum-clearance sites. The
shop, modelled on that in the High Street, was very light, airy
and spacious. In the evenings it was brightly lit by no fewer than
sixty gas lamps with opal globes, while above the doorway itself
was the largest and brightest lamp Dundee had ever seen. Interestingly, credit for designing the decor and layout of the store and
installing the horseshoe counter and other fittings was given by
the newspapers to William Love who took personal charge as
manager of the new store until a successor had been fully trained
for the position. From the outset this store had a staff of fifteen
male shop assistants and three cash-boys. Reporting on the
opening of this shop, the *Glasgow Herald* added: 'We understand
that Mr Lipton intends shortly to open similar branches in
Aberdeen, Edinburgh, Greenock, Paisley and other towns.'

This shop was an unqualified success from the beginning. Nine
months later, the local press was reporting the forthcoming
mammoth Easter sale of a quarter of a million eggs, 25,000
hams, 100,800 pounds of bacon and 22,400 pounds of butter.
Prices were slashed for the two-day sale that commenced on
Good Friday, something quite unheard of at that time. 'With a
cheap sale in full swing the method of doing business alone will
be worth going to see.'[4] Other reports in the Scottish newspapers
went so far as to credit Lipton with altering the celebration of

Easter in Scotland. The legacy of John Knox's Reformation was that even Christmas was hardly observed, being regarded as something Popish; but by the 1870s the more secular aspects, such as the Christmas tree imported from Germany by Prince Albert, had caught on. Easter was not a matter of any importance to Scotland's predominantly Presbyterian populace, but the consumption of hot cross buns was spreading from England. To Tommy Lipton alone, it seems, was due the revival of the medieval custom of painting and rolling hard-boiled eggs.[5]

In the same year Lipton moved his factory from Robertson Lane to Lancefield Street. The wheel had almost come full circle, for this short thoroughfare ran from Stobcross Street to Lancefield Quay, cobbled streets so familiar to Lipton. As he inaugurated his vast new premises, he must have pondered just how far he had progressed in an astonishingly short space of time. Even if the thought had never crossed his mind, the media were always at his elbow to remind him. One report, in June 1879, stated that he was handling 10,000 hams a week. At that time the great bulk of his dairy produce was coming from Westport, County Mayo, but soon afterwards he erected a vast depot at Ballina in the north-east of the same county, from where supplies could be shipped across to Lancefield Quay by coastal freighter.

On Saturday, 28 June 1879, Lipton himself opened his latest branch, at 21 High Street in Paisley. There was a stupendous display of 2,000 hams, 'flitch, smoked and rolled', with a free ham to the first customer through the door (a pauper woman, as it happens). The large open area was dominated by a horseshoe counter with a dozen shopmen and three cash-boys. It was, in fact, an exact replica of the Dundee store and, inevitably, it was presided over by the indefatigable William Love who noted with satisfaction that by the close of business at eight o'clock that evening over 50,000 eggs, 500 cheeses and three tons of butter had been sold. Paisley had never seen anything like it before, and soon the catch-phrase 'Have you been to Lipton's?' was on everyone's lips. The local paper commented on the counter 'of a novel design' with its wire-mesh guard rail running the entire length to protect the stock from too eager customers.[6] Even Tim Driscoll, the local bard, composed a ballad entitled 'Lipton's Big Store' which the newspaper duly published.

Lipton's autobiography states that the store at the corner of Jamaica and Howard Street was opened 'a few months' after the shop in the High Street. In fact it was not until Saturday, 8 November 1879, that this store – which would for many years be regarded as the flagship of the enterprise – was inaugurated. This magnificent emporium with its palatial decor of gleaming marble slabs, burnished brass fittings and tasteful majolica tiles, attracted a better class of shopper from the outset, although Lipton never lost sight of the fact that his business was firmly designed for the working classes. Commenting on Lipton's enterprise one humorous weekly magazine hailed him as 'a veritable Herod among piggy-wiggies' and likened the Lancefield Street depot to 'those gigantic Chicago factories, where, as we read, endless streams of lively grunters enter at one end, to emerge at the other, in an equally endless stream, scalded, dressed, pallid, passive – pork'.[7]

It is very difficult to appreciate what a boon the Lipton markets were to working men and their families. Wages were stable but improved public health had lowered infant mortality without providing any basis for the limit on the number of children being born. Many a workman, earning less than a pound a week, had to house, clothe and feed a family of seven or eight. All too often, a basic diet of potatoes and herring was supplemented only by dry coarse bread. Luxuries such as sugar and tea were unheard of, while dairy products were barely affordable before Lipton came on the scene. By slashing prices he stimulated a working-class demand that had barely existed before.

Some idea of the importance of this switch to a higher protein diet may be gained from the poem entitled 'The Master and Man: Lipton to the Rescue'. It was composed in 1877, when long-running disputes between the shipbuilders and their workers culminated in a series of strikes and lockouts:

> Says Mr Shipbuilder to Johnny McPhee,
> 'Come here, you scoundrel and listen to me.
> For twenty long years I've kept you, I'm sure,
> On one pound a week – how dare you want more.
> There's you and the wife and the children five,
> On herrings and tatoes I've kept you alive.
> So go back to your work and don't dare to mutter,
> Or I'll lock you all out to stand in the gutter.'

> Then Johnny McPhee to the master did say:
> 'I don't care a fig, for what you can dae.
> You have held the reins tight, for a long time now,
> But yet I defy you, and I'll tell you how.

There's Lipton that worthy you've heard of him I'm sure.
The Hero of High Street, the friend of the poor.
5,000 fat pigs he has bought and will kill.
He's determined the lockouts shall still have their fill.
He has prime Hams, and Butter, Eggs, Tongues and Cheese,
So I don't think that we'll starve on such dainties as these.'

It is probable that Lipton wrote those verses himself, for the poem, in beautiful copperplate handwriting, was lithographed and distributed as a handbill, with the addresses of his Glasgow stores at the bottom. He was doing good for others – and well for himself – but was never slow to blow his own trumpet.

At that time working men were generally paid every two weeks, at midday on a Saturday. The opening of new Lipton stores was invariably geared to a pay Saturday. Of course, the biggest pay-out of the year came at the festive season, which explains why the next shop to be launched, at 15 Cathcart Street, Greenock, opened on Saturday, 20 December 1879. Ignoring the truth, Lipton, now in his thirty-second year, states that he celebrated his twenty-sixth birthday 'by working fourteen hours on the opening day of a new shop in Greenock'.[8] For several weeks prior to the launch, Lipton had plastered the hoardings of that town with posters stating laconically 'Lipton is Coming'. Similar bald statements appeared in advertisements in the local newspaper. On the inaugural day, however, the *Greenock Advertiser* not only carried a large display advertisement from Lipton, but smaller advertisements by other merchants and tradespeople in the town, urging the public to buy pots and pans to cook Lipton's hams, good geese and turkeys to flavour Lipton's hams – even coals to cook Lipton's hams. Such a co-ordinated campaign leads one to suspect a deal between the enterprising grocer and these firms. Perhaps he even paid for their advertisements, or supplied them with hams as an inducement to support him.

In all of these new stores Lipton's now tried-and-tested methods of salesmanship and window display were slavishly followed. In Paisley and Greenock, as in Dundee, Lipton was applying techniques which had never been seen there before, and the response from the public was overwhelming. What effect this had on existing grocers is difficult to quantify. Some, at least, must have been driven out of business as a result of a Lipton's market opening in their vicinity. On the other hand, he studiously avoided competing with them in the basic foodstuffs, such as bread, milk, potatoes and salt herring. He had no effect on the high-class Italian warehousemen or the stores, such as Cooper's, which aimed at a better clientele. These establishments regarded Lipton's Yankee methods with disdain or ridicule, dismissing his window cartoons and butter sculptures as vulgarities.

In his autobiography Lipton describes some of his other publicity stunts, conveying the impression that they were, like the pound notes, employed from his earliest days in business, and that it was but a short step from the two-dimensional Lipton's Orphans of Lockhart's cartoons to the spectacle of real-live Orphans in the streets of Glasgow. In fact, although he graphically describes the antics of two of the largest, fattest porkers he could obtain from the livestock market as they made their way to Stobcross Street, the first of these porcine parades took place on 9 July 1878, following which the Glasgow papers reported the considerable amusement in the neighbourhood of Glasgow Cross at the appearance of three pigs dressed in gaily coloured cloth with the slogan 'The Orphans, Home-fed, Bound for Lipton's' on their flanks. The Orphans were driven by a man dressed up as the stereotypical Irishman, in knee-breeches, green cutaway coat and billycock hat, brandishing a shillelagh. Whether by accident or design, when the trio got to Glasgow Cross they decided to take their siesta in the middle of the street, effectively bringing the horse-trams to a halt. Although cautioned by the police for creating a public nuisance Lipton, as usual, remained unabashed. The parade of Orphans bound for Lipton's was repeated, with variations in dress and slogan, on a number of occasions. As many as six pigs were eventually employed, and as word of the latest procession spread like wildfire the crowds, larger and noisier than ever, were kept in stitches at the antics of the terrified animals as they tried to elude their driver and dodge among the traffic. Lipton repeated this ploy over and over again, using different routes and, it is to be hoped, only subjecting the wretched pigs to the terrifying ordeal once before sending them to the slaughterhouse.

There must have been many in Glasgow who regarded Tommy Lipton as a clown and a buffoon, but such criticism was easily brushed aside. The main thing was to get himself talked and written about, and in this he was certainly succeeding. From April 1877 onwards he kept a series of folio-sized scrapbooks in which his cuttings were meticulously preserved, even those which were critical or uncomplimentary. But there was also a serious side to him, as revealed in a number of letters which he wrote to *Freeman's Journal*, one of Ireland's most influential newspapers. These reveal a man who was both articulate and visionary. The

TOP: Thomas Lipton at the age of twelve
BOTTOM LEFT: Frances Lipton (*née* Johnston), Lipton's mother,
from an oil painting, *c*.1885
BOTTOM RIGHT: Thomas Lipton senior, Lipton's father, from an oil painting, *c*.1885

TOP: The alleged birthplace of Thomas Lipton, at the corner of Crown Street and Rutherglen Road, Gorbals, from a sketch drawn in the 1920s
BOTTOM: Lipton's first shop, at 101 Stobcross Street, Anderston, 1871

Opposite Page TOP: Thomas Lipton in 1877, at the age of twenty-nine
CENTRE LEFT: *(top)* 'Lipton's Leading Article', the first of the shop window cartoons by Willie Lockhart; *(below)* One of the earliest cartoons displayed in Lipton's shop – 'What's the matter with the pig, Pat?' 'Sure, Sirr, he's an orphan so, out of pity, I'm taking him to Lipton's!'
CENTRE RIGHT: A famous Phil May cartoon – Lady: 'No wonder Lipton is a bachelor if that's him!'
BOTTOM: One of the earliest window advertisements

LIPTON'S
LEADING
ARTICLE

THE FIRST PICTORIAL ADVERTISEMENT UTILIZED BY LIPTON

LIPTON

COMING FROM LIPTON   GOING TO LIPTON

LEFT: Johnston Villa, Cambuslang, in 1890
CENTRE: Osidge in the present day as a home for retired nurses
BOTTOM: Osidge, Lipton's home (1896–1931), from the painting by W.S. Tomkin, *c.*1910

At Mr T. J. Lipton's Festival, 24 February 1891, from
The Bailie cartoon supplement, 4 March 1891
INSET: Lipton (in straw boater) and William Love (in
Highland dress) receiving guests at the staff garden
party, Osidge, 1895

TOP LEFT: London horse-drawn omnibus with advertisement for Lipton's Tea,
*c.*1895
TOP RIGHT: Lipton's Pound Note and a genuine note of the National Bank of
Scotland for comparison
BOTTOM: Bullock cars laden with chests of Lipton's tea, Ceylon
(courtesy of Unilever Archives)

TOP: Exterior of a typical Lipton store, *c.*1920
BOTTOM: Interior of a typical Lipton store, *c.*1920

TOP: Sir Thomas Lipton, the theatrical impresario Sir George Alexander, Andrew Carnegie and J. Pierpont Morgan piling up the money bags (detail from a cartoon by Charles Sykes in *The Throne*, 11 May 1907)

CENTRE: The Princess's Dinner to the Destitute Poor: an artist's impression of the dinner at the Great Assembly Hall, Mile End Road, June 1897

BOTTOM: West Auckland Football Club, winner of the Lipton World Cup, 1909–10

first letter drew attention to the serious inroads on the British market by butter imported from America, and a deterioration in the quality of Irish butter.

> We must start at the fountainhead – the cows. It is important that they be well fed, but even more so that they have access to a plentiful supply of fine fresh water, all stagnant pools being carefully avoided. The byre must also be improved and cleanliness and order more studied in the dairy. It is most important that the butter be kept clean and cool after churning, and before being taken to the market.[9]

Because of the manner in which butter was stockpiled by the farmers, waiting for an improvement in price, butter was often six months old before it reached the shop. Lipton strongly urged them to consign their butter to the markets every week, as it was in their best interests to do so. He also wrote at length on all aspects of the handling, salting, packaging and branding of the product in a bid to improve quality control. Significantly, this letter was reprinted verbatim in the *American Dairyman and Butter, Cheese and Egg Reporter* at New York on 28 August. His second letter, written from 99 Lancefield Street on 31 July, was published in *Freeman's Journal* four days later. In this he advocated sending milk to large central dairies for churning, and the proceeds divided among the various farmers in proportion. 'Should this idea be taken up by men of standing, I shall be glad to take shares in the concern to the amount of fifty pounds.' He was also willing to subscribe five pounds a year for five years to help provide the best possible instruction to be given in these butter factories, and he also added trenchant views on the generally poor quality of packaging then used. In due course Lipton's ideas were acted upon, and central creameries eventually became the standard, revolutionising the Irish dairy industry. A third letter from Lipton appeared in this journal on 16 December 1879, this time offering constructive but blunt criticism on the quality of Irish eggs.

As a new year dawned Lipton revelled in the fact that a music-hall song entitled 'Lipton's Butter and Ham' was on everyone's lips. It had been composed by James Willison, then one of Glasgow's leading comics, and sung to wide acclaim at the Argyle Theatre of Varieties by Willison on his benefit night. Halfway down the programme, however, one notes that one of the major attractions was a raffle with a live Lipton's Orphan as the prize. That kind of support did a power of good, for Willison went on to repeat his success with the song at music-halls all over Scotland. Within months there was a rash of comic songs and ballads, such as 'The Boss of Lipton's Store' by George Landale and popularised by such singers as Joe Anderson and Dan Cavannah, which even found its way into the *City Songbook*. Willison composed a comic monologue entitled 'Soosie Spare-Ribs'[10] while Robert Vokes apparently brought the house down at McFarlan's Varieties Music Hall in Aberdeen with his spirited rendition of 'Can Anyone Tell Me Where Lipton's Is?'. A sizeable anthology could be compiled of the odes and elegies, music-hall songs and street ballads which helped to spread the gospel to parts of the country which had not, as yet, received the benefit of a Lipton's market.

That year would be dominated by a bitter controversy over butterine, a vegetable substitute that looked like butter but certainly did not taste like it. Feature articles and editorials as well as endless tirades in the correspondence columns of all the newspapers fulminated against 'the large quantities of that unpleasant compound oleomargarine' which were flooding the Glasgow market and masquerading as butter. This dispute dragged on for several years, occasionally dying down, only to re-emerge more rancorous than ever before. Dishonest grocers made huge profits by foisting this cheap substitute on an unsuspecting public. Lipton leaped into this fray, vigorously denouncing those who were lining their pockets at the expense mainly of the poorer classes. He was at pains to add that he had nothing against margarine as such, and conceded that it was a healthy and wholesome product; but it should be sold in packets clearly marked MARGARINE and he decried the use of the term butterine as intended deliberately to confuse the public. He also pointed out that in the United States, where oleomargarine (a French invention) was first produced on a large commercial scale, the Federal government had passed stringent laws to prevent misrepresentation. Only Denmark, among the countries of Europe, had enacted similar legislation to protect its indigenous butter industry, though later it was discovered that exporters, operating out of Kiel and Hamburg, were adulterating Danish butter with large quantities of margarine in order to bring down the basic price of the commodity.

A letter signed 'True Colours', but clearly from Lipton's hand, averred that over 200,000 packets of butterine were sold in Glasgow every year, but only a fraction was retailed under its real name. He began very reasonably by stating that 'It is a palatable and wholesome article and the fact that its intrinsic merits are so inestimable is all the more reason why it should be sold under its own name'. But he strongly objected to it being passed off as butter:

> The other day I went into a first-class restaurant in the city and ordered tea. While partaking of what was set before me I observed that butterine had been put upon the bread instead of butter. I directed the attention of the proprietor of the establishment to the fact, and the astonishment which he expressed was by no means assumed, and I have every reason to believe that he had bought and paid for what he assumed to be genuine butter. The responsibility for the fraud rests entirely with the retail dealer.[11]

He went on to criticise the present system of inspection by the Sanitary Department whose inspectors were well dressed and had 'City Chambers official' written all over them. Lipton thought it would be much more effective to use females 'in the garb of working men's wives' to buy sample packets for analysis. Subsequently Lipton was instrumental in getting an Act through Parliament making the proper marking of margarine obligatory.

In July 1880 Lipton opened a branch in Dumbarton Road, Partick, and concluded a busy year by opening a branch at Bridgeton Cross on Christmas Eve. This completed the circle of branches that now more or less covered the working-class districts of Glasgow. Oddly enough the Gorbals, where his family had begun operations fifteen years earlier, was not included. In the same year he completed his plans for the central depot and creamery at Ballina, County Mayo, the first of its kind anywhere in Ireland, and the prototype for many similar establishments as the century drew to a close.

Towards the end of July he crossed the Atlantic for the first time since that epic voyage at the age of seventeen. In his autobiography he stated that his first trip, in the spring of 1866, had been aboard the Anchor liner *Devonia*, though Waugh noted that this was impossible as the ship was not launched till 1877. In fact, this was the vessel in which he crossed the Atlantic in 1880. The ship's purser made a speech welcoming the king of provision merchants, which was duly printed in the ship's newspaper, the *Atlantic Daily*, and in due course the cutting was pasted into the scrapbook. Alongside is a cutting which reveals that he was staying at Hunt's Hotel in Cincinnati on 6 August.

The reason for this trip can be summed up in one word – cheese. As the number of Lipton markets grew, and the volume of business soared beyond his wildest dreams, Lipton began to run into problems of supplying this demand. Having systematically tied up the Irish suppliers, he had turned to the Continent and employed agents from Helsinki and Copenhagen to Brittany in the quest for good quality merchandise. These sources sufficed, for the moment, but it was in the matter of good quality cheeses that he first experienced a major problem. In the summer of 1879 he despatched 'a bright Irish youth of an enterprising nature' to New York and installed him there as his North American agent. 'By having a representative on the spot, I found I was able to buy butter and cheese at such prices that I could pass on the advantage to my customers.'[12]

Typically, he tells us that his own decision to visit the United States was taken at seven o'clock one evening as the family were sitting down to supper. 'Mother,' he announced, 'I'm off to America tomorrow. You must help me pack tonight!' This second trip to America was vastly different from the first. He was no longer the penniless immigrant but a wealthy young businessman. From New York he went to Philadelphia and Cincinnati and eventually arrived at Chicago. This was a city in which he could have seen many parallels with Glasgow, but he was not concerned with the sights or the people. Instead he allegedly headed for the stockyards, intent on learning as much as he could about the meat-packing industry as possible. At first he prowled around on his own, making discreet observations and enquiries. He took every opportunity to tour the great stockyards and abattoirs, even then regarded as a tourist attraction. Certainly no tourist paid more rapt attention to everything the guides had to impart.

Eventually he found what he had been looking for, a building with the capacity to kill and dress up to 400 pigs a day. According to his own account, he had this factory up and running within two weeks of his arrival in Chicago. This was one of the more outrageous untruths in the entire autobiography for it was not until 1 November 1885 that the Johnstone Packing Company commenced operations.[13] By this time Lipton was affecting a final 'e' in his middle name. The actual building in which the company conducted its business was known as the Cork Packing House which may have been its original name, and not a reference to the Irish city or county with which he had, of course, no personal connection. In his autobiography Lipton paid a warm tribute to his competitors, 'Men of such weight and position as P.D. Armour, Louis Swift, Nelson Morris, John Hately, and T.C. Boyd', who showed him immense kindness. Their help and advice, he says, 'kept me from making many blunders in a branch of business absolutely new to me and, as may well be imagined, studded with pitfalls for the unwary new-comer'.[14] And he concluded this nonsense with a reminiscence from the daughter of one of those pork barons, to show what a tremendous impact he had made on them at the time. Her father used to refer to Lipton's arrival among them:

> Do I remember Tommy Lipton sitting in at the pork-packing game
> in Chicago? I'll say I do. Until I met him I always thought that your
> Britisher was slow to get a move on at anything, but this Lipton guy
> quickly knocked *that* notion for nix. Why, he just shooted around
> like an express train so that none of us ever saw him for more'n ten
> seconds at one time![15]

Lipton's descent on the meat-packing business, when it finally came five years later, could hardly be described in such breathless fashion. The company commenced operations in November 1885, but by the end of March 1886 had produced only forty-eight barrels of pork and a 108 sweet pickled tierces. In the same period Armour, Swift and the other giants of the industry were counting their barrels by the hundred thousand. If they thought of Tommy Lipton at all, it was probably as some dilettante, and the Cork Packing House as nothing more than a rich man's toy.

Lest there be any doubt that Lipton had merely confused the date, it should be noted that, having allegedly got his meat-packing plant in running order, he then took himself off on a holiday – 'the first luxury of the kind I had ever allowed myself in my life thus far'. He made for the nation's capital and had hardly been there many hours when he was shaking hands with President Rutherford B. Hayes. He had been told that the President held frequent receptions which were open to all and sundry, and assuming that this particular day was a reception day, he took a cab to Pennsylvania Avenue and bowled straight up to the front door of the White House where he rang the bell. Eventually a manservant appeared and Lipton asked him quietly if the President were at home.

'He is, sir!' replied the servant: 'Will you please follow me?'

Feeling a bit apprehensive at the total absence of the crowd he had expected to be joining, Lipton followed the man into a spacious chamber occupied by a solitary individual, very amiable in aspect, whom he took to be a secretary or clerk. He came forward and shook Lipton warmly by the hand. Lipton, now at his ease, chatted with the fellow in the friendliest manner. They conversed for some twenty minutes and Lipton, thoroughly enjoying the company, invited him to join him for lunch at his hotel after he had had the honour of meeting the President. 'Can you tell me when the reception is likely to begin today?'

His new-found friend regarded him quizzically. 'But I am President Hayes!' he quietly observed.

Lipton was aghast at his gaffe and apologised profusely, but the genial President only laughed heartily, and it was only later on that Hayes confessed that he had mistaken Lipton for an important visitor who had an official appointment. Hayes would be the first President of the United States that Lipton met, but by no means the last. The point of this story, however, is to fix the date of the visit, as Rutherford B. Hayes demitted office to James Garfield early in 1881.

It is much more likely that the trip to the United States in the summer of 1880 was in connection with the import of American cheese into Britain, for this was a matter which now loomed large, not only in the mundane matter of supplying his shops but as the subject of a series of stunts less troublesome to the traffic than the Lipton's Orphans but calculated to generate even greater publicity in the national press. Here again, Lipton could not present this as a straightforward business venture, well planned in advance (as it undoubtedly was), but had to dress it up in one of his yarns. Five pages of the autobiography[16] are devoted to a long, rambling tale of how he got the better of a trio of conmen in Washington leading, of course, to their arrest and conviction. He claimed to have the satisfaction of reading all about himself and the tricksters in a graphic story which occupied three columns of the daily press bearing the streamer headline: 'The Three-Card Monte Men. How the Plan and the Plotters were Neatly Foiled by a Young Britisher on Holiday'. Strangely enough, no such press-cutting has been preserved in the relevant scrapbook, nor has a perusal of the Washington newspapers for August and September 1880 yielded any such stirring tale.

Back in New York, and intent on catching the next steamer back to Liverpool, he allegedly ran into a friend who was a cheese merchant in Montreal who persuaded him to go north on the overnight train, the pretext for another tall story about being stranded at Rouse's Point when the train went off without them, and having to hire a special to take him and his companion all the way to Montreal. This should have cost him $150 but on arrival at Montreal he merely handed over his ticket and refused to pay for the special. As the train had departed from Rouse's Point after only ten minutes, when it was scheduled to remain there for a breakfast stop of twenty minutes, it was obviously the fault of the railroad company. Lipton stood his ground, and as he had only three dollars in his pocket there was not much the railroad manager could do about it. He went to his friend's store, examined his cheese, and caught the train back to New York that afternoon. One of the passengers on this trip south was a Yankee salesman who, impressed that Lipton had got the better of the Canadian railroad, offered him a meal and refreshments at his expense. Every time Lipton and his new friend went to the refreshment rooms at the various halts they found the conductor and brakeman at the adjoining table. Eventually Lipton asked them how it was that their appetites kept pace with his, and they replied, 'We have been given strict orders never to let that long fellow out of our sight, as if we did we would find him arriving at New York on a special train.'[17]

Having opened his latest shop at Bridgeton Cross at Christmas that year, Lipton wasted no time on planning further expansion. So far he had established stores in various parts of Glasgow, as well as in the leading towns and cities of Scotland. Now the time had come to take the plunge and sally forth into England. Early in January 1881 the *Leeds Express* began carrying mysterious advertisements, occupying a substantial space but merely stating cryptically 'Lipton Is Coming'. It was a repetition of the ploy used at Greenock and Paisley but it worked just as well in Yorkshire. For several weeks readers of the newspaper puzzled over the meaning of these three words, coming to the conclusion that it was some theatrical spectacle. Then he headed south in person and on Saturday, 22 January 1881, opened his first English store at 18 Kirkgate.

One of the few dates quoted in his autobiography is 1881 – 'I give the exact year because there have been scores and scores of arguments about it ever since' – when Lipton pulled off what he admitted was 'the cleverest piece of advertising which had been successfully attempted by any British trader'.[18] What he had in mind was a Christmas attraction which would make people really sit up and take notice. In his autobiography he makes the curious claim that, by that time, he had only three shops and he racked his brains for weeks on end trying to think of something special for their Christmas window display.

> Then all at once, when serving a customer one afternoon with a two-pound slice of cheese, the idea came to me that I would import, display and sell the largest cheese ever made in the world. There was only one man who I knew could make it – Dr L.L. Wright of Whiteborough, New York. The cables were set humming at once.

> Within a few hours of the idea being conceived every detail was
> fixed and I knew that six weeks before Christmas my monster
> cheese would arrive at Glasgow from New York.[19]

The stupendous nature of this undertaking may be imagined
when it is realised that, prior to this time, the largest cheese ever
made was under a hundred pounds in weight. The idea was
perhaps not so sudden as Lipton makes out, for earlier that same
year he had startled the grocery world by importing several 500-
pound cheeses. Actually the name of the maker of monster
cheeses was Dr L.L. Wight of Whitesboro, the proprietor of the
largest dairy in the United States.

Two giant cheeses, each weighing 3,472 pounds, were ordered.
To produce them required six days' milk from 800 cows. Lipton,
who was passionate about statistics, in due course informed the
British press that each cheese required 32,000 pounds of milk
(sixteen tons or 4,000 gallons), and that they were eleven feet in
circumference and two feet thick. They were shipped aboard the
SS *Surania* and landed at Glasgow on 12 December 1881. One
was immediately sent south by rail for display at the
International Cookery and Food Exhibition at the Royal
Aquarium, Westminster, while the other, immediately nicknamed
Jumbo, was paraded on a steam-traction-engine through the
streets of Glasgow from the Broomielaw bound for a window of
the store in the High Street. To his horror, however, Lipton found
that he had miscalculated; Jumbo could not be got through the
shop doorway, far less mounted in the window. With remarkable
aplomb he had it hoisted back on to the steam engine and
paraded back through the city to Jamaica Street where,
mercifully, the doorway was much wider. Even so, it took a gang
of strong men some time before the monster could be rolled
safely into position in the centre of the largest window. For the
next twelve days Jumbo would be the talk of the town as
thousands flocked in from the neighbouring countryside to gape
at the giant cheese. When he returned to Cambuslang that
evening, feeling that he had accomplished something out of the
ordinary, and bragged about his latest exploit which would
generate the greatest publicity so far, his mother remarked
quietly, 'It will be a better advertisement still, Tom, if the cheese
is good cheese!'

By 20 December its companion, fresh from its London début,
had been installed in the window of Lipton's brand new store at
the foot of the North Bridge in Edinburgh. After his mother's
dour put-down, Lipton had scurried the following morning to

Jamaica Street to test a discreet sliver of Jumbo. To his relief he found that it was every bit as good and flavourful as any normal cheese. Then the idea came to him of converting his Giant Cheese into a Golden Cheese by hiding a large quantity of sovereigns and half-sovereigns in its vast interior. Forty gold coins were secreted in various parts of the cheese, and advertisements were published to the effect that it would be cut up and offered for sale on Christmas Eve. As a precaution, Lipton had arranged with the police to have a dozen constables on hand to control the anticipated crowd. He considered that this would be more of an advertising dodge than anything else, but as it happened, a hundred policemen could not have coped with the vast hordes who converged on Jamaica Street from every part of the city. Lipton himself, clad in an immaculate white suit and matching slippers, mounted the monster at the appropriate moment and began cutting chunks. He claimed that Jumbo melted 'like snaw aff a dyke' in less than two hours. In fact, according to press reports, it kept his staff busy the better part of the day. Sheer pandemonium broke out as the first purchasers tore the wrappers off their portions and began breaking up the cheese in search of the gold coins before they had left the counter. Others, anxious to get served, pushed, jostled and elbowed their way through. Groans of disappointment mingled with whoops of delight as successful and unsuccessful purchasers milled about. Lipton himself provides a richly embroidered account, vividly describing the 'laughing, perfectly good-natured pandemonium and the merriment all round'. Even the policemen, detailed to maintain order, joined in the fun, and one constable, having discovered a sovereign in his portion, danced a fandango in the doorway and lost his helmet. Had Jumbo been five times as large Lipton reckoned he could have sold the lot. And, he concluded, 'the newspaper reporters came along in force and next morning I had columns of free publicity'.

In succeeding years Lipton and Jumbo cheeses became synonymous in the public consciousness. The following December Dr Wight shipped across three cheeses, each of more modest dimensions than the original Jumbo, at 2,400 pounds. These were brought to the Clyde by the Anchor Line steamer *Bolivia* and in due course installed in the main windows at Jamaica Street, and the Edinburgh and Leeds stores.

The giant cheeses were only seasonal diversions from the main business of opening up new stores. Lipton's Market came to Aberdeen in January 1883, established in Union Street, the Granite City's most prestigious shopping centre. By the end of the year a second English store, at Old Haymarket, Liverpool, was opened. Stores in Sunderland, Newcastle, Nottingham, Manchester and Birmingham followed, and by the time the Lipton market at Wine Street, Bristol was opened in May 1886 Lipton could boast of some thirty stores with an annual turnover in excess of £350,000. With the butterine controversy continuing to fester, and the problem of ensuring quality control an ever-present headache, Lipton was at pains to maintain public confidence. With the opening of the Bristol store he introduced a novelty to the British retail trade, a buy-back guarantee if any of his goods were found not to be of the very highest quality. Such a promise had never been made by any retailer before.

This rapidly burgeoning empire was firmly controlled from Lipton's palatial office at the top of the building in Lancefield Street. 'The organization of this great headquarters depot kept me engrossed for many months.' Lipton habitually worked a fourteen-hour day, catching an early morning train from Cambuslang and often getting the last train home, at eleven o'clock. Virtually the only time he ever deserted his post was when still another branch was being opened in some distant part of the country.

> This was a rule I set myself in the early days and did not break for many years – the rule that Thomas Lipton in person should be behind the counter on the opening day of every new store. More than that, I made it a practice to serve the first customer myself. By this time my reputation was pretty firmly established, thanks to the Press publicity, which my 'modern' methods of shopkeeping had won for me, and thanks also to the unique 'advance booms' I organized in each new town marked down for attack; the result was that there was generally a rush of custom the moment the doors were opened. With white jacket and apron, I watched the entrance of the first housewife.[20]

Nothing succeeds like success, and eventually property-owners all over the United Kingdom wrote to Lipton whenever they had a shop to let. If the town was of any size Lipton would pay a discreet visit. 'It did not take me long to decide one way or the other, and as often as not I arrived by one train and left for home by the first available one thereafter, having in the meantime fixed up all necessary details for opening still another Lipton Market or – as occasionally happened – turned the proposition down altogether.' During one of these forays he was asked by a prominent Member of Parliament what his political convictions were.

'My politics are to open a new shop every week!'

That was a pardonable exaggeration, though towards the end of the century, new stores were opening thick and fast. As to his politics, there is ample evidence to suggest that Lipton never forgot his roots. He could be described as a radical populist with an attachment to Irish nationalism that was not merely sentimental. As a frequent traveller in Ireland, Lipton was acutely aware of the tensions as the Land League, having won important agrarian reforms, now agitated for Home Rule. It was at this time that Lipton made the acquaintance of Joseph Biggar, the firebrand Nationalist MP for Cavan, and this developed into close friendship.

After the collapse of his government in 1874 Gladstone had relinquished the leadership of the Liberals to the Marquess of Hartington. The Balkan crisis of 1875-78 brought him back to prominence and in 1880 the Grand Old Man returned to power. Gladstone's second administration was dominated by distress and unemployment, industrial unrest and the rise of socialism, all of which the Liberals hoped would be alleviated by an extension of the suffrage to include all men over the age of twenty-one – regardless of property qualifications. This measure was hotly contested by the Conservatives and matters reached fever pitch in the summer and autumn of 1884 when the Reform Bill was introduced in Parliament. Mammoth demonstrations were organised to mobilise public opinion. A great reform demonstration took place in Glasgow in Saturday, 6 September; the parade through the streets to George Square was headed by five Lipton lorries disguised as political tableaux. The first of these had a man cleverly got up to resemble the Prime Minister, seated on a mound of Irish bacon and hams and festooned with dairy produce; but the float that drew the greatest cheers and hoots of derision was a cartload of black pigs labelled 'The House of Lords – we'll cure them!' The biggest and fattest porker in this group had the word MARKISS painted on his flanks, a dig at the unpopular Marquess of Hartington who had briefly supplanted Gladstone as leader of the party. Similar Reform parades were staged in Dundee and other Scottish towns and in each case Lipton lorries were well to the fore.

Less contentious but still very effective as headline-grabbers were the later generations of monster cheeses. On a visit to the United States in September 1884 Lipton visited the Cloverfield Combination Factories operated by Richardson, Beebe and Company of East Aurora, New York, and subsequently ordered twelve cheeses totalling 27,000 pounds at a cost of $4,000. Seven of them arrived at Liverpool aboard the *Aurania* and five landed at Glasgow from the *State of Pennsylvania*. The largest cheese, weighing 3,473 pounds was sent off to London where it was displayed on stand 45A at the Food Exhibition and earned for its proud proprietor a bronze medal and a diploma of merit. The two runners-up, weighing in at 3,472 pounds each, were displayed in the windows of the stores at Jamaica Street, Glasgow and North Bridge, Edinburgh, while a third cheese of only slightly smaller dimensions was sent to Sunderland to launch the latest Lipton store in fine style.

In the course of the autumn Lipton, following his return to Britain, had arranged for a large quantity of gold sovereigns to be shipped over to East Aurora, to be dropped into the curds at the churning stage. In that way it was hoped that a more even distribution of the gold coins could be achieved. Given the weight of the gold, however, it is probable that they all ended up at the bottom. To counter this, therefore, Lipton decided that, on the day he inaugurated the Sunderland store, he would personally, and in full view of the assembled crowds, insert a further quantity of sovereigns into the giant cheese. As this ploy was well advertised in the local press beforehand it is not surprising that a magistrate took a dim view of the proceedings and issued a warrant restraining Lipton from selling the cheese, on the grounds that such a transaction constituted an illegal lottery. When the police swooped on the opening ceremony, Lipton, with considerable presence of mind and tongue firmly in cheek, announced that, in order to keep within the law, the finders of any coins must immediately return them to the shop manager. Every ounce of cheese was sold in double-quick time and – surprise, surprise – not a single coin was ever returned.

When the Lipton store at Clayton Street, Newcastle, was inaugurated in Christmas 1886, Lipton launched it with a two-ton cheese but as he was in the act of inserting sovereigns and half-sovereigns before the assembled multitudes the police again descended on him with full magisterial force and put a stop to the proceedings.[21] For the first time, the Phineas T. Barnum of the grocery trade was stopped dead in his tracks. In his autobiography, of course, he paints a rather different picture. This time he says that the police objected solely because the lives of the populace might be endangered through swallowing sovereigns unawares.

So I warned the Newcastle public by prominent advertisements in
the local papers, that any man or woman buying a portion of the

Giant Cheese at Lipton's Christmas Market, stood in very grave danger of being choked by the large number of sovereigns with which the cheese was liberally sprinkled throughout. I headed this announcement *Police Warning* and people rolled up in their thousands, eager to be choked. And I never heard that anybody was![22]

A good story, no doubt, but unfortunately not backed by any actual announcement to that effect. It would have been an excellent ploy, had Lipton anticipated trouble from the Newcastle police. Still, he was never the man to let such a minor irritation as the truth to stand between him and a good yarn.

After that incident Lipton began to take a back seat. Opening stores and serving clamouring crowds began to pall, and thereafter he tended to rely on some prominent personality as a crowd-puller. Actually this idea had come to him in December 1884, when the celebrated Tichborne Case was at its height. Lipton contacted 'Sir Roger', the notorious Tichborne Claimant, and offered him £100 if he would come north and make personal appearances behind the counters of his shops in Aberdeen, Dundee, Edinburgh and Glasgow. Lipton even had a crazy idea of parading Tichborne through the streets behind a herd of Orphans, but even a blackguard as black-dyed as 'Sir Roger' apparently had his vestigial scruples, and he declined the contract. Lipton, naturally, ensured that the offer was well publicised in the Scottish newspapers.[23] At Christmas 1885 Lipton tried the same tactic with Viscount Hinton, a rather louche aristocrat who had recently hit the headlines on account of some unsavoury business transactions. The viscount was offered £100 if he would come to Glasgow and cut up the latest Jumbo, but the deal fell through when Hinton was arrested and charged with obtaining a pair of Purdey shotguns by false pretences. By the time he should have been hacking away at the monster cheese he was being sent to prison for twelve months, so Lipton was obliged to do the honours himself.

Though his greatest cheese stunts were still some way off in the future, Lipton now cast around for other means of hitting the headlines. In March 1886 he secured the services of Carl Herrmann, the celebrated mesmerist whose demonstrations of hypnotism had been the sensation of the music halls. Lipton was fascinated by this, but succeeded in giving it a fresh twist, harnessing Herrmann's powers to the latest technology of the age. One Saturday afternoon at the end of March a demonstration was arranged in Lipton's office at Lancefield

Street for the benefit of the local press. Present with Lipton were Dr J. Kerr Love of Strathbungo and his brother William, along with Dr Grainger of Hillhead and the firm's chief accountant, James Ross. About a mile away, Herrmann was ensconced with witnesses and other reporters in the office of Messrs Currie, Thomson in Union Street. At the appointed hour the telephone rang in Lipton's office and Herrmann proceeded to hypnotise the two medical men, one after another, down the line. It was apparently the first time that hypnotism had been attempted telephonically. As a publicity stunt it was a dead loss, but at least it got good press coverage.[24]

5. A NEW STORE
EVERY WEEK
1886–89

'Oh, where are you going to, all you Big Steamers,
With England's own coal, up and down the salt seas?'
'We are going to fetch you your bread and your butter,
Your beef, pork, and mutton, eggs, apples and cheese.'

Rudyard Kipling, 'Big Steamers'

If not yet a name on everyone's lips, Lipton was becoming a household word in Scotland and the north of England by the time he was thirty-eight. By 1886 the first profiles, in word and line drawing, were beginning to appear in the press on both sides of the Atlantic. Significantly perhaps, the first attempt to put a face to the name occurred in the trade journals of the United States, a country which, since 1880, was getting an annual visit. The articles about Lipton, however, gave absolutely nothing away. He was variously described as an English merchant, an American or an Irishman but, strangely enough, never as a Scot. Any trace of a broad Glasgow accent had long since been eradicated and in its place came a soft, well-modulated voice which could affect a New England twang or an Irish brogue with effortless ease. Lipton took a pride in his ability to mimic the different regional accents of the Emerald Isle. At an early stage, probably during his four years in America as a boy, he had learned that it was better to claim to be Irish rather than British. Some papers, especially in Ireland, claimed that he was born in County Tyrone, one actually naming Cookstown as his birthplace. Others gave Fermanagh as his home county, stating that he had first seen the light of day on a small farm near Enniskillen, which was, in fact, a pretty accurate description of Thomas Senior. The earliest newspaper portraits of him were rather crude, but with his piercing eyes, hair parted down the centre and enormous moustache even these caricatures were readily recognisable. Later these characteristics would be endlessly exploited by cartoonists on both sides of the Atlantic.

Even more important were the epithets which the press

bestowed on him. Expressions such as 'king of the provision trade' or 'the world's largest food retailer' were bandied about. Extravagant reports in the American grocery press stated that the ramifications of his business empire stretched from Denmark to Australia and from India to the Rocky Mountains, a preposterous claim which was parroted unquestioningly even in some British journals by early 1886.[1] True to the conventions of the period, there was absolutely no reference to his private life.

Mention has already been made of the visit to America in 1885 which led to the opening of the Johnstone Packing Company on 1 November that year, and of its farcical performance in its first five months in operation. Lipton returned to the United States the following May, and one of the New York trade journals mentioned him dropping in just after his arrival by steamer. It stated that they were 'glad to see his handsome and genial face once more',[2] though they were disconcerted to hear him say that Danish butter was now superseding the American product in the British market, as it took only two days from the churn to the British shops, compared with ten or twelve days from the United States – and transportation costs were very much lower.

What had brought Lipton hot-foot to America on this occasion was the industrial unrest in Chicago, fomented by the Knights of Labor who were fighting a losing battle on behalf of the workers in the meat-packing industry. At the heart of the problem was the stark reality that as the sub-continent was opened up and developed, the corn belt had inexorably moved farther and farther west. Hogs in the Mid-West were bigger, fatter and cheaper to raise than those in Illinois and Indiana. Faced with competition from Nebraska, or higher transportation costs in bringing the pigs to Chicago, the giant meat-packing companies looked for ways of cutting costs. Men were laid off, or faced the bleak prospect of substantial cuts in wages. Inevitably their response was to go on strike. The trouble began in the stockyards operated by John P. Squire who took the drastic action of dismissing his entire workforce of 750 men. The strike spread to the Armour, Libby and Nelson Morris plants and all that summer strikes and lockouts raged throughout the industry. Matters came to a head when Philip D. Armour sent a force of armed Pinkerton agents into his plant on 12 September. There was an ugly confrontation but Armour personally intervened and withdrew the Pinkertons. Work in the plant resumed, but the men sullenly went about the building, merely putting away tools and equipment and leaving everything tidy. At the end of the shift, they walked off, and the mighty Armour plant came to a standstill. The Knights of Labor maintained iron discipline throughout the dispute, even prevailing upon the local pubs not to sell hard liquor which might have inflamed the situation. But the atmosphere remained tense.

On reaching Chicago, Lipton quickly came to a decision. Realising that the fundamental problem was that the stockyards and abattoirs were in the wrong place, he took a train to Omaha in southern Nebraska and began prospecting for a likely location for his meat-packing works. In no time at all he had found a disused factory near the railroad depot. Within five months the Johnstone Packing Company had moved, lock, stock and pork-barrel, from Chicago and was in production. Starting from scratch, Lipton personally designed and supervised the installation of an assembly line. Live pigs were slaughtered, skinned, stripped of lard, gutted and dressed, the refuse being converted into fertiliser. Then the dressed carcases were chilled, cut, salted and packed in barrels. When fully operational, the plant could handle 2,500 hogs a day. Lipton started with a workforce of fifty men, but this rapidly expanded to 250, and within a year rose to over 400. It is not surprising that the arrival of this plant was warmly welcomed. When operations began in November 1886 the local newspaper ran the banner headline 'Lipton Begins Packing: Omaha Gets Another Jewel'.[3] Many of the workers bought or rented houses in Lipton Place, a development near the plant which was inaugurated in January 1887. The works grew so fast that they had to be closed temporarily a month later for extensive refurbishment and expansion. Within a year the Johnstone Packing Company, which had begun in Chicago so inauspiciously, was a force to be reckoned within the industry. Phil Armour shrewdly recognised this at an early stage and, acting on the basis if you cannot beat him then join him, he negotiated an agreement with Lipton, enabling the latter to use the Armour refrigerated cars for transportation, in exchange for preferential treatment in the supply of carcases from the Mid-West. The bulk of the output from the Omaha plant, however, was destined for the ever-expanding chain of stores in the British Isles, enabling Lipton to sell ham at threepence a pound, a price to which none of his competitors could come anywhere close. In 1887 the first Lipton markets in Ireland were opened, in Dublin, Belfast, Derry and Newry, and later the same year Lipton attacked the food retail market in Wales, hitherto regarded as an impregnable bastion of the Co-operative movement. It was this quasi-political institution which had deterred Lipton from opening up in Aberdeen for many years, having been told that people were so firmly wedded to their dividends that they would not patronise his shop. But the Aberdeen store was a tremendous success from the outset and, thus encouraged, Lipton opened· a branch at St Mary Street, Cardiff in April. Significantly the arrival of Lipton was regarded as 'proof of the growing importance of Cardiff as an industrial and commercial centre'.[4] The store was twice the size of the Dundee shop, with a staff of twenty shop assistants, ten boys and two girls, under the management of Mr Gray, one of Lipton's bright young Glaswegians.

Lipton's reluctance to tread on Co-operative toes stemmed from his unvoiced political convictions. Although he might proclaim that he was quite apolitical, his actions often betrayed his true sympathies. His political philosophy might be summed up as giving the public a fair share and value for money. As an employer he demanded, and usually got, unswerving loyalty. He paid better rates than his competitors and saw to it that working hours and conditions were the envy of the industry. But he was a benevolent dictator and behind the genial visage was a flinty ruthlessness tempered by bitter experience. Early in his career he had the humiliation of being dragged before the Small Debt Court by a disgruntled ex-employee, Robert Shaw, who claimed fifty-two pounds for unpaid wages (reduced to twelve pounds when the case actually came to court). The main bone of contention was that Lipton had sacked Shaw for dishonesty, but instead of prosecuting him Lipton had put the word around the grocery trade that Shaw was a thief. Shaw claimed that this was an unwarranted slur on his character and tried to sue his former employer for slander, but the case was dismissed and Lipton was awarded seven shillings and sixpence in costs.[5]

Eight years later, when his three shops had increased tenfold and turnover was estimated at £600,000 per annum, Lipton remained in close touch with his workforce. He visited his stores whenever he could and liked nothing better than to don a white apron and overalls and serve bemused housewives, to show that he had not lost that skill and flair which had led him to fame and fortune. In Glasgow, still the nerve centre of his empire, he was a familiar, everyday sight to the headquarters staff, now over a hundred strong. In March 1886 the first annual *conversazione* of the headquarters staff took place at the Assembly Rooms in Bath Street, over 150 staff 'and their lady friends' taking part. Lipton himself was absent on the Continent, and the chair was taken by James Ross, the chief cashier. When the second *conversazione* came round, on 26 January 1887, Lipton himself presided over the evening's entertainment and led the singing in his fine baritone voice.

Shortly after the turn of the year the nation began making plans to celebrate the Golden Jubilee of Queen Victoria, on 20 June. Not since 1810, when George III had been fifty years on the throne, had a British monarch reigned so long. Coming at the end of a period of industrial and agricultural depression accompanied by widespread unemployment, the Jubilee was a shot in the arm. Lipton was quick off the mark in perceiving commercial advantages to be gained from the forthcoming celebrations. On 7 March he wrote a personal letter to Her Majesty offering her the largest cheese ever made. The milk from 8,500 cows would be required to produce a cheese weighing fully five tons. He was at pains to point out that this monster would be manufactured in Canada, rather than the United States, and that it would be ready for presentation in six months' time.

A week later Lipton received a frosty reply from Sir Henry Ponsonby to the effect that the Queen could not accept any presents from private individuals to whom she was not personally known. Lipton probably knew that all along, but he promptly sent both sides of the correspondence to all the leading daily papers, many of which published it in full on 16 March. Lipton inevitably gained considerable publicity from this ploy. In fact, judging by the vast number of press cuttings arising from this, and the even greater volume of editorials and letters to the editor, it seemed that Lipton was now a household name, as well known as Victoria herself. Predictably, some of this coverage was less than sympathetic, on the grounds that he should not have revealed his letter to the Queen or her indirect response to it, though press comment was seldom as hostile as the pompous poem published in *The Pioneer* which concluded with the stinging rebuke:

> Snubbed by a Queen!
> Go, think of it in silence and shame
> And weigh against a piece of cheese
> The glories of a throne.

An unexpected outcome of this incident was the number of appeals sent to Lipton's office from Newcastle, Sunderland and Birmingham as well as Glasgow, urging that, if the Queen turned down the gift, Lipton should distribute it among the poor and needy. More specifically, he received a letter from George Holmes, chairman of the Birmingham relief committee trying to raise funds on behalf of the families of the chainmakers of Cradley Heath, made destitute by a strike which had lasted for thirty-four weeks. Holmes's account of the plight of the families, on the verge of starvation and many suffering from the illnesses brought on by malnutrition, struck a deep chord in Lipton, perhaps echoing the harrowing tales he had heard of the Great Hunger that had driven his parents out of Ireland forty years earlier. His immediate response was to reply saying that the cheese would not have been ready till September, but in the meantime he would make arrangements to supply the families with much-needed provisions. James Deuchar, a master-baker, wrote to Lipton saying that if he would supply the cheese, he would provide the bread to go with it. In the thirty-sixth week of the strike Lipton despatched five hundredweight of bacon and 2,400 eggs so that the strikers could have 'an Easter treat'. Each man with a wife and five or more children got three pounds of bacon, seven eggs, six four-pound loaves and two shillings in cash, smaller families and single men receiving proportionately smaller amounts.[6] When the Lanarkshire miners went on strike the same month, Lipton promptly sent 560 pounds of bacon and 2,400 eggs to Samuel Colville of the strike committee, together with a cheque for ten guineas and a warm letter of support:

> I consider it a disgrace to a civilised country that men should be found doing a hard day's work and risking their lives all for the miserable pittance presently earned. I am of the opinion that the miners are the worst-paid and most ill-treated class of men in Europe.

When the Liberal Party put up fifteen working-men candidates at the 1885 General Election, Lipton contributed funds which ensured that two at least were elected to the House of Commons. In later years the great Labour leader Keir Hardie paid warm tribute to the generous support, both moral and financial, which had come from Thomas Lipton over the years.

In the spring of 1887 Lipton opened a vast complex of warehouses in Seel Street, Liverpool, to supply the ever-growing number of shops in the north of England. On this occasion William Love (who masterminded the project) granted an interview to a local newspaper and showed the reporter over the premises which were the last word in food-handling technology.[7] This was William's first encounter with the media and he told the reporter that he had been with Lipton from the very beginning. 'We started together in one little shop in Glasgow and did everything ourselves.'

'You had pretty hard work, I suppose, at first?'

'If I told you how hard you might think I was exaggerating. We simply thought of nothing but work and took very little notice of the hours or of the difference between day and night.'

The reporter added that William Love, Lipton's Chief Manager, bore an uncanny resemblance to the great man himself. Indeed, in general build and appearance they were very similar, and William even parted his hair and sported a moustache in imitation of his master.

In his late thirties, Lipton was more of a driven man than ever. When he was not touring the country inspecting stores and opening new branches, he was in Ireland, Europe or America negotiating fresh deals for the supply of provisions. At an age when most businessmen would have settled down to raise a family, become a kirk elder or a member of the golf club, perhaps even a patron of the arts or take an interest in municipal politics, Lipton had time for none of these things. His pious parents might be regular attenders at the Cambuslang parish church, but their busy son never put in an appearance. But a portent of things to come was the Glasgow Daily and Letter Press Printers United Regatta on 27 August 1887; in the list of the thirty-two patrons the name of Thomas Lipton appeared last.

For Lipton, the annual staff *conversazione* was all the social life he needed. At the third such gathering, early in 1887, he proposed a novel idea for the Glasgow International Exhibition which was scheduled to take place in the summer of 1888. He would mount a demonstration of pig-slaughtering, together with all the processes that followed. He would enthrall the paying public with a spectacular display from the live porker to the rashers on the table. He would process 200 pigs a day, and it would be a *sensation*. By the time the exhibition opened, the following May, his original rather gory idea had been considerably toned down, though he did provide a Model Dairy, with more acceptable displays of cow-milking and butter-churning, and could console himself with the thought that he had been awarded the lucrative contracts to supply the provisions for the Exhibition restaurants as well as the Bishop's Palace Temperance Café.

What the public would chiefly remember him by were the two mirrors mounted on the wall outside the Exhibitors' Club close to Lipton's Model Dairy. The mirrors, one convex and the other concave, were designed and manufactured specially for the occasion by H.J. Humphreys and Company of 156 Sauchiehall Street. According to his autobiography, Lipton implies that these mirrors were among the earliest of his advertising stunts. To be sure, the concept of pictures of skinny people 'Going to Lipton's' and fat, jolly people 'Coming from Lipton's' was one of the first to be put into cartoon form by Willie Lockhart back in the days of the Stobcross Street shop, but it remained in that medium for several years, although a subsequent variant was the procession of skinny or fat people with sandwich boards bearing the appropriate slogan which often formed part of the antics surrounding the launch of a new store. Nevertheless, the mirror marked 'Going to Lipton's', which showed the faces of all who gazed at it elongated and miserable, and its companion which puffed out everyone to an enormous girth and made the faces round, jolly and carefree, were first displayed at the Exhibition.

> These mirrors were a sensation for months. Millions of people must have looked into them, children came from near and far to enjoy the free novelty and there was more spontaneous laughter outside and inside my shops than in any music-hall or theatre in town. Once more originality and enterprise reflected themselves immediately and conspicuously in my turnover.[8]

Lipton was certainly right about the millions, for over five million people flocked to the Exhibition between May and November and most, if not all, must have looked at their distorted reflection in the mirrors whose novelty was rapturously greeted by the press.[9] Almost as big an attraction was the biggest Jumbo of the lot, the long-promised, much-trumpeted five-ton cheese. On the inaugural day, Lipton, clad in a white silk suit and white slippers and wielding a pick-axe, mounted the monster and began digging into it. After a few token strokes he handed over to a team of diggers clad in the same gleaming white raiment. That summer the song 'Lipton's Stores', sung to the tune of 'Tara's Halls' was on everyone's lips. There was also a rollicking ballad to the tune of 'The Laird of Cockpen' entitled 'The Digging o' Lipton's Big Cheese':

> Great Jumbo the Monster does a' folk surprise
> Wi' his fine yellow coat and prodigious size.
> Ower a' fairy Grottoes or fancy Bazaars
> He stauns oot as clear as the moon 'mang the stars.
> There's some nervous folk have got a sair shock,
> Mistaking the Monster for Dumbarton Rock,
> But o' trifles like that, tak nae note if you please,
> But rin to the digging o' Lipton's Big Cheese.

And five more stanzas in similar vein.

Lipton himself was off to Russia that summer, attending the vast Nizhni Novgorod Trade Fair. The main purpose of his visit was to tender for arguably the largest single contract of all time, to supply provisions for the Russian Army of over a million men, and the Navy of 25,000.[10] As there is no mention of this in the autobiography, it can only be assumed that he was unsuccessful in the bid.

Until now, Lipton had concentrated on establishing stores in the provincial towns but in April 1888 he opened a branch in Westbourne Grove, London, right opposite the impressive Bayswater emporium of William Whiteley, 'the Universal Provider'. This was an act of barefaced cheek on Lipton's part, but the housewives who came along out of curiosity to see the new shop were staggered to discover that butter of a quality offered by Whiteley for one shilling and eightpence a pound could be obtained across the road at Lipton's for a shilling. Lipton's ham was fourpence a pound cheaper, and better quality into the bargain, In general, goods sold at Lipton's were twopence in the shilling cheaper than at Whiteley's. Whiteley's fortune had been amassed by attracting a better class of customer, the sort of person, it was believed, who would not mind paying a bit more, rather than have to push and shove through the crowds to get to the counter, but soon angry letters began appearing in the west London newspapers complaining that housewives had been duped by Whiteley's, whose profits were far too large.

On 30 January 1889 a branch of Lipton's was opened in Islington, north London, right opposite the Home and Colonial store. The opening ceremony was performed by Joseph Biggar, the prominent Irish Nationalist MP who had himself been a grocer before entering Parliament. When Biggar also opened the store at the New Arcade in Swansea a month later, the press somehow formed the impression that Joe Biggar was the true proprietor of the Lipton chain-stores. From this, it was but a short step to circulating rumours that Joe Biggar and Tommy Lipton were one and the same person, provoking at least one newspaper to quip that they preferred his bacon to his politics. Though both Biggar and Lipton denied the canard, the rumour that they were one and the same person persisted well into the 1890s. In connection with the plans for this store Lipton tells an amusing anecdote:

> In these days I had a manager in my employment of the name of Love. He had been in London at the taking-over of the Islington

119

shop and, desiring to get in touch with the contractor who was going to make the necessary structural alterations, he wired him to his home as follows: 'Meet me at the Angel at eight tonight, Love'.

Mr Love waited fully an hour for the contractor but he did not show face and my manager had to return the same night to Glasgow. A few days later he was again in London, and this time he called upon the contractor at his place of business and upbraided him for his carelessness in not keeping the appointment made by telegram.

'What telegram? I never got a telegram from you, Mr Love!' exclaimed the man. Then suddenly a light seemed to dawn upon him. 'By heavens!' he ejaculated. 'I see it all now. My wife has been impossible to live with for three days. She must have opened your telegram signed Love for she certainly left the house that night and was away for two hours and came back in a devil of a temper. I must run home and explain!' And off the contractor went.

The poor man's surmise proved correct. His wife had opened the telegram. Even yet she would not accept his explanations.

'I don't believe this story about a Mr Love – as if anybody could believe a cock-and-bull tale like that!' raved the still angry woman. 'Why, I went down to the Angel and saw the woman standing there with my own eyes. There were several other females standing round the doors but I knew her at a glance and I had hard work to keep my hands off the huzzy. You and your Mr Love!'

Not until Mr Love had been prevailed upon by the distracted contractor to go along with him and explain matters to his wife was peace restored in that troubled household.[11]

By this time new branches were opening more or less every week, but in a single day he opened two large shops in London, at 128 Lambeth Walk and Strutton Ground, Westminster. Branches at Clapham Junction, Deptford and Greenwich followed in short order. By the end of 1889 Lipton had 150 stores and an annual turnover in excess of a million pounds. Now, the London media were bestowing on him the title of the Universal Provider which they had once applied to William Whiteley.

'I believe I was the first advertiser to use the air,' says Lipton in his autobiography.[12] This was long before the advent of the Wright Brothers, but ballooning was a fashionable craze of the 1880s.

Hearing that a famous aeronaut was coming to Glasgow to give an exhibition ascent at a local gala, I promptly got in touch with him and arranged for one of my representatives to 'go up' in the balloon and distribute 100,000 telegrams from the clouds extolling the merits of Lipton's bacon, and the purity of his butter. Prizes ranging from twenty pounds in cash down to a flitch of bacon and ten pounds of tea were offered to the first twenty people presenting the 'sky telegrams' at the nearest Lipton branch shop.

It was on 22 June 1889 that Professor George Higgins made his memorable flight over Glasgow in a balloon launched from the Shawfield sportsgrounds. Higgins was actually giving a demonstration of a dangerous new sport – parachuting – and the balloon was piloted by an Italian named Bellini. The honour of going aloft with the intrepid parachutist fell to the long-suffering William Love, who released the shower of telegrams on the vast crowds below. Higgins was blown off course and landed in a ploughed field near Paisley Half-Way House, Ibrox, while the thousands of advertising flimsies were scattered far and wide by the strong winds. Here again, Lipton's memory played him false for the first person to hand in one of the telegrams at the Jamaica Street store got a prize of two guineas, while the nineteen runners-up got various rewards, from thirty shillings in cash to a two-pound packet of tea.[13]

By 1889 Lipton was opening new shops, if not every week, certainly at an astonishing rate. Everywhere, he applied the same principle: select the best site and the best shop he could lease, fit it up regardless of expense so that it stood out like a jewel among its drab neighbours and use the local newspapers to an extent 'which made me distinctly popular with their advertisement managers'. Considerable thought and effort went into planning a stunt appropriate to the opening of each shop. 'Everywhere a different notion was exploited according to the character of the town, its trade, and the proclivities of the people'.[14] At the opening of Edinburgh's second store on the South Bridge, he secured the boisterous assistance of some medical students who dissected hams and cheeses to the accompaniment of much wit and banter from the customers. At Liverpool a stupendous model of the latest crack Atlantic liner was carved in butter and, in Dublin, a newly married couple were persuaded to sit for a couple of days in the window, brewing tea for the customers. Lipton certainly never overestimated the taste of the general public. But, harking back to the parades of Lipton's Orphans, his favourite ploy undoubtedly was the procession, and this stunt he raised to spectacular perfection towards the end of the decade.

All the profits of the business went straight back into it. Lipton had no shareholders to whom he must answer. Although his headquarters staff of accountants and book-keepers included an architect and a solicitor, all major decisions pertaining to the business were his and his alone. Though probably now a millionaire, on paper at any rate, his lifestyle continued to be very modest:

> It is true that as I prospered it was my pride and joy to see that my mother and father had a bit more comfort, even luxury, but for myself my wants continued to be few. If I got enough to eat and a nice bed to rest in for six out of the twenty-four hours I was well content. The 'game of business' was always much more to me than the financial results of the game, but it would be stupid on my part to deny that the knowledge of my firm's rapid and successful expansion was at once delightful and exhilarating. Here was all the excitement, all the romance, all the encouragement, and – if you insist – all the literal 'rewards' which I required to make my strenuous life happy.[15]

This is one of the few brief references to his parents, with whom he and William were living in Cambuslang. For glimpses of Thomas and Frances one has to look elsewhere. In a brief account of Cambuslang there was a passing reference to the Lipton parents:

> Even when far advanced in years, it was not an uncommon thing to see old Mr Lipton at the Western infirmary on a Sunday morning inquiring as to the condition of some patient of his acquaintance. An old shop-boy once described him as the most kindly-hearted and genuine man he had ever met. Sir Thomas's mother was also very kindly, thrifty and economical. She was also a woman of rare talent and tact. She had the knack of stretching a shilling its full length, and a great deal further than many can extend it now.[16]

At Cambuslang, Lipton had the reputation of keeping the finest pair of horses in the county, and if he took any recreation outside his business it was driving a coach and pair. His team was not often seen in the city, Lipton preferring to take the commuter train to the Central Station, whence it was a five-minute walk to Lancefield Street, but it was a well-known sight in the country roads and lanes between Cambuslang and Lanark in the Clyde Valley. One of Lipton's boyhood dreams had been that some day he would provide his parents with their own carriage and horses – an ambition which he shared with Andrew Carnegie. This was no idle fancy, for only the very wealthiest people could afford to maintain such an equipage, the modern equivalent of which would be to run a Rolls-Royce limousine. Walter Freer, a boyhood chum who later became editor of the *Sunday Post*, recalled an occasion when he was with Lipton in Glasgow's Central Station waiting for the train bringing his parents into the city from Cambuslang. It was a memorable moment:

> As we stood, the four of us, in the station there drove up a carriage drawn by two beautiful grey horses and with all the regal equipment associated with such a turn-out. Lipton led his father and mother to the carriage, handed them in, gave the signal to the driver to drive off and stood hat in hand as the horses stepped out.
>
> I was touched as I remembered my chum's ambition of earlier years and would have reminded him of it, but what I saw stopped me and I knew this was no time for reminiscing on the past. Tears streamed down the cheeks of my friend as he stood on the kerb looking on the fulfilment of his greatest ambition.[17]

Lipton himself briefly mentioned that his parents 'had everything they wanted, even down to the carriage-and-pair for my mother, which, as a wee boy, I had confidently promised she would ride in some day'. Then he adds that although she enjoyed the sensation of driving behind two spanking horses, 'I think she enjoyed even more the little pleasantry which always obtained between us when, as sometimes happened, I wanted to please her by humbly asking if I could have the use of the carriage for an hour or two.' Then Frances would regard the apple of her eye archly and say, 'Only on one condition, Tom. That is that you keep the carriage to drive you all day long and bring you home in the evening!' This triggered off the memory of 'a little tiff' which he had had with his mother one morning as he set off to work and they did not part on the usual affectionate terms. During his six miles' drive to the office he became increasingly wretched and on reaching Lancefield Street, could not concentrate on business. At first he thought of telegraphing to make his peace, but then decided to go straight home and put matters right between them. When he got back, he pretended to be in as much of a tantrum as ever. But it was no use. Frances was not to be deceived and said quietly, 'I know well enough what you've come back for, Tom', and there was no more to be said. They embraced emotionally and 'I went back to my work at peace with myself and everybody else because I had left my mother happy'.[18]

Freer also recalled that throughout his career Lipton's life had been ruled by two great passions, his business and his love of his parents. In her late seventies, however, Frances contracted chronic bronchitis which meant that she was seldom able to go out of doors. Just after the New Year of 1889 her condition worsened and she took to her bed where she died at 4.55 p. m. on 2 February.[19] At the end she was attended by her physician, Dr A.L. Kelly, but the duty of registering her death was performed by the ever-faithful William Love who was, in many ways, more of a son to her than her own flesh and blood. Significantly one of the very few dates quoted in full in Lipton's autobiography states that his mother died on 1 February 1889 – a day earlier than that recorded on her death certificate. Inexplicably (and inexcusably) Waugh and Crampsey say that Lipton's mother died in October 1889, both indulging in fanciful descriptions of the funeral: 'on a warm October afternoon' (Waugh), which gets embellished by Crampsey as 'the very warm out-of-season October day with which Glasgow sometimes climatically teases its inhabitants'.[20] When Frances died, Lipton lost:

> my best friend and trustiest counsellor. Without her unfaltering love, her constant encouragements, her amazing shrewdness and foresight, I could never have fought the business battles I did or achieved one tithe of the success that came my way. A few months later my father slipped away to join the wife he loved, leaving me a sad and very lonely man. I am lonely today, for I have not one living relative in the world.[21]

When these words were penned in 1930, Lipton himself had not long to live. That last sentence is probably the saddest in the entire book. Did he, one wonders, ever speculate about the fate of Margaret McAuslan? In the New World, or perhaps the Antipodes, had she made a new life for herself, perhaps bigamously married? If so, it would explain her reluctance, or inability, to come forward when her estranged husband was so rich and famous. Perhaps she died young, but he never knew. Though unencumbered long before he first emerged into the spotlight, he would always have harboured that lingering doubt that somewhere, at some time, Margaret would come out of the shadows to haunt or embarrass him. And even if she were dead, and he was free to marry again, his natural predelictions lay in other directions. At Johnston Villa he had the perfect set-up; living with loyal but ever-so discreet William under the same roof as his parents, who could suspect Lipton of unnatural desires?

Not only his parents, but the world at large, seem to have been singularly naïve, despite the scandal of Oscar Wilde and the suicide of General Sir Hector Macdonald, who would take his own life in Paris while on his way home in disgrace after having been caught *in flagrante delicto* with his Sinhalese houseboy. As Governor and Commander-in-Chief of Ceylon, he must have been a very familiar figure to Sir Thomas Lipton.

Without his beloved Frances, old Thomas deteriorated rapidly. He had been 'losing the place' for some time, but now the onset of senile decay was rapid. He passed away quietly on 4 March 1890. His death was registered by James McKnight, one of the servants.[22] Both parents were laid to rest in the family plot in the Southern Necropolis where son John and daughter Margaret were already buried.

Many years later, Lipton still cherished his mother's memory. Freer recalled an occasion when he was visiting his old friend in London and Lipton enquired casually whether he ever went to the Southern Necropolis. Freer admitted that he had never been there, whereupon Lipton begged him to pay a visit and let him know how the ground looked, where his parents were buried.

'What is the number of the lair?' enquired Freer.

'Oh, never mind the number. Just look for the best-dressed grave, and you will find it.'

Some weeks later Freer kept his promise. The graveyard superintendent, knowing him, was intrigued regarding the object of his visit and asked him for the number of the lair. Freer told him he had come to see the place of interment of a friend and would just wander around until he found the place. Freer and his wife strolled among the headstones, when she suddenly drew his attention to a grave surrounded by a granite kerb. The place was a mass of violets, truly the most beautiful of all the place. Freer picked a violet and sent it off to London, with an appropriately worded note to Lipton. A day or two later Freer received a letter:

> I received your letter enclosing the violet which you plucked from my mother's grave. You know that my house is loaded with valuable presents, which came from every part of the world, and which I prize very much, but nothing has ever touched me more than your kind act. Immediately on receiving it I went up to my bedroom and placed it between the leaves of my dear mother's Bible, where it will lie as a most sacred possession.[23]

Years later, on a visit to Osidge, Lipton's north London home, Freer raised the subject of their families, now long gone. Lipton got up, left the room, and returned a minute later carrying an old Bible, a relic of the past. 'With true reverence he opened the book to show me the violet which, years before, I had plucked at the grave and sent to him.' It was a soft, sentimental side of the great tycoon which the world at large never knew. By that time Sir Thomas Lipton was rich and famous, the world's best sportsman and the friend of the high and the mighty, the great and the good. But he was still, at heart, a simple man who never ceased to be the friend of the folk he had known in other times.

Perhaps there was a twinge of conscience, a hint of remorse, in this touching tale. One cannot help wondering why Lipton, a frequent visitor to Glasgow for years after he moved his business to London, never took the time to visit the cemetery himself.

Neither Frances nor Thomas Senior made wills and, to all intents and purposes, left no property. Everything they had, they owed to their son. Soon after the death of his parents Lipton decided to move to London. At or about this time he and William Love came to the parting of the ways. Frank Reihill was appointed General Manager in his stead and thereafter there is no mention of the hitherto ubiquitous Mr Love in the company's affairs. The parting, in both the business and emotional sense, seems to have been quite amicable, for Lipton allowed William to go on living at Johnston Villa rent-free. In addition, he transferred the ownership of several of his shops in Glasgow to William Love. A study of the Glasgow directories over the ensuing forty years reveals that William gradually lost them, one by one. The 1903 *Glasgow and Lanarkshire Illustrated* concluded an account of Johnston Villa by stating that 'Mr William Love, who at present resides there, was at that time manager for Sir Thomas, and lived with the Lipton family. A lengthened period of association binds Sir Thomas and Mr Love together in the closest friendship.'

That was surely an understatement.

6. TEA TOM

1889–97

Tea, although an Oriental,
Is a gentleman at least;
Cocoa is a cad and coward,
Cocoa is a vulgar beast.
   G.K. Chesterton, 'The Song of Right and Wrong'

According to Chinese legend, the virtues of *cha* (or *te* in the Amoy dialect) were discovered by the Emperor Chin-nung in 2,737 BC. It was certainly the subject of poems by 550 BC and a thousand years later a tax on its consumption was one of the principal revenues of the Chinese government. The use of tea spread to Japan in the mid-ninth century, and actual cultivation there began four centuries later. Until well into the nineteenth century China and Japan were virtually the only tea-producing countries which meant the product reached western markets only through the narrowest channels and most oppressive restrictions. This Far Eastern monopoly was only gradually broken. In 1826 the Dutch established the first tea plantation in Java. Britain might have got their first, but for a stupid mistake on the part of Dr Wallich, the government botanist at Calcutta, who in 1820 identified certain leaves sent to him from Assam as belonging to the genus Camellia. Fourteen years later Captain Francis Jenkins vigorously rebutted this identification, proving that what Wallich had examined were the leaves of a tea plant which grew wild in Assam. Later still, scientists would prove that this tree, which grows to a height of twenty feet, was in fact the ancestor of the small shrubs cultivated in China and Japan. In 1836 the first one-pound parcel of Assam tea reached London. By 1839 almost one hundred boxes of Assam tea were exported and the following year the Assam Tea Company began commercial production.

Indian tea might be quite different in taste from China tea, but it had the same stimulating effect at a fraction of the price. When the first *chaw* was imported by the East India Company in the middle of the seventeenth century, prices ranged from six pounds to ten pounds a pound. In 1660 Thomas Garraway, proprietor of a well-known London coffee-house, began importing tea on a large scale, and as a result the price fell drastically to between fifteen and fifty shillings a pound, depending on the quality. Samuel Pepys sampled his first cuppa on 25 September that year, proving the novelty of the drink even at that date. By 1689 it was becoming fashionable enough for the government to tax it, at the rate of five shillings per pound. Thereafter it became, like French brandy, a staple commodity of the smuggling trade. In John Galt's *Annals of the Parish*, the Revd Micah Balwhidder castigates his flock for the sin of tea-drinking on two grounds: that it was smuggled and thereby evaded the duty on it, and that it was a luxury item to which ordinary folk should not be aspiring.

There was also a hint of depravity about tea-drinking. Henry Savile echoed popular sentiment when he wrote to his uncle in sharp reproof of certain friends of his who 'call for tea, instead of pipes and bottles after dinner, a base unworthy Indian practice . . . The truth is all nations are growing so wicked as to have some of these filthy customs!' Medical men and others pontificated on *thea*, 'a drug not less destructive than opium or some other drugs which we have at present learned to avoid'.[1] The celebrated Dr Lettsom railed against tea-drinking which caused such a weakness and debility of the system among its addicts as to lead them eventually into the worst excesses of alcohol.[2] Samuel Johnson was a self-confessed addict, 'a hardened and shameless tea-drinker . . . whose kettle had scarcely time to cool'.[3]

Nowadays tea is such a cheap, popular beverage that it is hard to imagine a time when it was not universally drunk. The retail price in Britain remained relatively high until 1834 when the monopoly of the East India Company was abolished. Within two years the price had fallen to two shillings and sixpence for Congou and four shillings and sixpence for Hyson and domestic consumption had risen to almost three million pounds. Following the reduction in the tea duty to sixpence in 1862, the average price fell to around two shillings and consumption rose sharply. By 1885 it had reached the astronomical level of £182 million per annum, an average of five pounds per man, woman and child. The British were, by that time, second only to the Australian colonists as the world's most heavily addicted tea-drinkers.

The sharp rise in tea consumption coincided with the expansion of the Lipton shops and the tea wholesalers were not slow to perceive this grocery chain as the ideal outlet for their wares. 'Here was an organization all cut and dried, with many thousands of customers, ready-made and only requiring the simplest of exploitations! That was what the wholesalers told me, not once but many times.'[4] Lipton toyed with the idea; the addition of tea to the list of comestibles for sale entailed no great alteration or revision of his business arrangements. But as he examined the structure of the tea trade, and in particular the substantial profit margins of the wholesalers and the tea estates, it became clear to him that the only way ahead would be for him to apply to tea exactly the same principles on which he had operated so successfully in the dairy trade.

There is no record to show at what precise point Lipton began to take a serious interest in tea. He began in a small way, buying relatively modest amounts of tea direct from the merchants in Mincing Lane, London. Making allowances for operating expenses, he found that he could sell a first-class tea to his customers for one shilling and sevenpence per pound, as against half a crown which the ordinary retailers charged for practically the same quality. The wholesalers tried to deter Lipton from beating them at their own game, pointing out that the key to success lay in the proper blending of tea, and that this was a rare and arcane skill which simply could not be bought, let alone dispensed with. Lipton's answer to that was to search out skilled blenders, find out what they earned, and then offer them double if they would come and join him. It was a red letter day in Lancefield Street when Lipton and his departmental chiefs sat down in the executive dining-room to sample the first brew. 'We sipped it, we drank it, we smelt it, we rolled it on our palates and on our lips, looking at each other the while.' They compared it with brews of much more expensive teas, and concluded that theirs was the equal of the best. 'So the new tea department of Lipton's was in lively being in the course of a week or two,' he concluded airily. 'I believe I am merely stating a fact when I say that my entry into the British tea market created a sensation of the first magnitude.' The public flocked to buy his one shilling and sevenpence tea, and liked it so well that before many weeks had elapsed Lipton added two cheaper blends retailing at a shilling and fifteen pence respectively, prices unheard of in the tea trade up to that time.

Even Lipton must have been astonished at the success of his latest venture. He had not appreciated what a hold the tea habit had on the great British public. People who had never set foot inside a Lipton store previously now came to buy cheap tea, and of course tarried long enough to purchase other groceries as well.

Within months turnover had risen substantially across the entire chain. Tea was the quantum leap that took Lipton into the really big league, and it is significant that the frequency with which new stores opened accelerated sharply after this time. This, in turn, stimulated further sales of tea, to the point at which any shop which did not achieve sales of at least a ton of tea each week was deemed to be doing badly.

On 1 May 1889 Lipton sent a cheque for £2,584 to the Commissioners of Excise, representing the duty on 103,000 pounds of tea. According to the press, this was the largest sum paid in a single amount in recent years. As identically worded reports were published in many newspapers, one suspects that Lipton himself was the source of the story. That same month, he considerably expanded his tea business by opening a separate warehouse at 76 Howard Street, Glasgow. No less than eighty tons of tea, in chests, were loaded at the Broomielaw on to forty horse-drawn lorries festooned with bunting and garish slogans. The cavalcade then proceeded slowly along the street, led by De Banzie's pipers and brass band, followed by fifty men dressed in a colourful costume (variously described in the press as Arab, or 'the airy garb of the mild Hindoo') and carrying gaily decorated umbrellas. Thereafter, parades of Lipton's Life Guards, in their splendid white silk tunics, baggy trousers and scarlet waistcoats embroidered with gold, became a familiar sight, especially at the opening of new stores. On one occasion, however, this had most unfortunate results. On 21 May 1892, a brougham containing Herbert Gladstone, son of the Prime Minister and himself a prominent Liberal MP, crashed and overturned when the horse, startled by the bizarre sight of a Lipton procession in Brunswick Street marking the opening of the store in Oldham, broke from its traces and bolted. The brougham was badly damaged and both driver and passenger were bruised and severely shocked.

Characteristically, Lipton's account of the début of his Howard Street tea warehouse was rather different from the press reports and, written with the benefit of hindsight, described 'the little army of about two hundred men' as being clad in 'Cingalese costumes'. Congratulating himself on his latest brain-wave, he added 'Actually, many of the citizens thought that I had imported the natives from my tea estates in Ceylon', although no such estates existed until well over a year later. Based on this falsehood was another long anecdote, the nub of which was that one poor woman, whose husband had been employed by Lipton as a sandwich-man, assaulted one of the 'black fellows' who were doing honest Scotsmen out of their jobs. A policeman restrains her with the words, 'Wheesht woman, wheesht! Them chaps only arrived frae the Indies this mornin' an canna understaun a word ye're sayin. So save yer breath, woman, save yer breath!' The punchline comes when the lady returns home that evening, to discover that the very man she has assaulted is her own husband, 'occupying the proud position of the leader of the Cingalese and chosen for the honour by reason of his ability to play the part!'.[5] And Lipton concludes this fantasy by saying untruthfully: 'I took good care that the story found its way into the evening papers!'

In truth, the consumption of tea in the Lipton stores at this time may have been a fleabite compared with the retail sales of this product nationwide, but apart from the showmanship and the hype, Lipton made a valuable contribution to the distribution of tea. Hitherto it had been sold loose in paper bags, or even displayed in open chests and barrels where it inevitably suffered from contamination and atmospheric pollution. From the outset Lipton understood that the secret lay in excellent packaging. The man who had taught the Irish farmers their business years earlier, now proceeded to revolutionise the handling of tea. His Howard Street factory employed 400 girls as tea-packers. The tea was carefully weighed out and packed in brightly coloured packets decorated with pictures of the Orient and bearing the slogan 'Direct from the Tea Gardens to the Tea Pot'. In this connection he established his own printing works and package-making plant in a building adjoining his administrative headquarters in Lancefield Street. At its zenith, this plant employed 200 people and was the largest private printing works in Scotland.

At a time when the cheapest tea sold on traditional lines cost two shillings per pounds, Lipton was able to offer the discriminating housewife a reasonable product at fivepence less. It is hardly surprising, therefore, that within six months he was selling over thirty tons of tea every week. Significantly, he was also rapidly emerging as a major exporter, selling packaged tea through his outlets in New York, Chicago, Omaha, Philadelphia and Boston. The last named occasioned him some merriment, with quips about the last time there had been a tea party in that city. Beside tea, his latest line – hermetically sealed jars of Wigtownshire cream – paled into insignificance.

Hitherto Lipton's assault on well-entrenched ham and butter markets had gone unchallenged, probably because these markets were in no sense organised when he entered the fray. When it came to tea, however, this was a different matter. The wholesalers and retailers responded with an immediate reduction, so that the cheapest tea became available at two shillings per pound. Just along Jamaica Street from Lipton's flagship store, John Charteris was well established at number sixty-one as Glasgow's leading tea and coffee merchant. He immediately reacted to Lipton's poaching on his preserve in very vociferous fashion, his chosen medium being the tried and tested method of the handbill distributed to passers-by in the street. This was a foolscap broadside headed pithily 'The Sin O' A Lie Is The Scrimping O't'. This was followed by a four-line quotation from Robert Burns, 'Some books are lies frae end to end . . . An nail't wi Scripture'. It seems that Charteris had previously thrown down the gauntlet, offering the sum of £100 to the Glasgow infirmaries if his tea was judged to be of inferior quality. Lipton had ignored this challenge and now Charteris was resuming the attack.

> Why has my challenge not been taken up by those Pinchbeck tea dealers? Because they dare not. They know I am up to all their tricks and their capers; they know I would expose their huge exaggerations, egregious miscalculations and gross mis-statements, and I would expose their claptrap bounce and bunkum.
>
> LOOK OUT FOR AND BEWARE OF Pig Dealers, Cheap Bacon Vendors, Sausage and Pottedhead Makers, who, when they have destroyed their own business by selling rubbish not fit for pigs to eat, take to the tea trade and by unscrupulous advertising try to dupe a fresh crop of fools and idiots.[6]

And much more in the same scurrilous vein. Lower down, Charteris changed tack and began making extravagant claims of his own. For example, Emin Pasha was drinking a cup of Charteris Tea when he was discovered, in the heart of the Dark Continent, by H.M. Stanley. 'Stanley joined him in a cup . . . and declared, with a supply of Charteris Tea, he was ready to start on his return journey. He got it, hence his safe return.' Lipton probably permitted himself a quiet chuckle over this farrago of nonsense and continued to ignore it.

Farther afield, John Findlay of Alyth, Perthshire, placed a more soberly worded advertisement in his local newspaper pointing out errors and discrepancies in Lipton's claim that his tea came direct from the tea gardens to the teapot, and he warned the public of the dangers of tannin poisoning from drinking cheap and inferior tea.[7] Another disgruntled competitor resorted to verse and published a song in twelve verses plus chorus entitled 'The Phenomenal TWO SHILLING Indian Tea':

> Though we can't boast great foreign plantations
> Or Tea Gardens far o'er the sea,
> Still, we call from the best of all nations
> Our wonderful **Two Shilling Tea**.

At first Lipton merely ignored the rantings and ravings of the opposition, but he was forced to sit up and take notice when Valentine and Company, tea merchants of Belfast, offered £100 to the Belfast hospital charities if a panel of three impartial experts deemed Valentine's tea (at one shilling and fourpence per pound) to be inferior to the Lipton blend which retailed for one shilling and sevenpence. Valentine's overstepped the mark when they plastered posters all over Newry (where one of Lipton's stores was located) repeating the challenge. The posters were almost immediately torn down or mutilated, leading Valentine's to offer a reward of five pounds for information leading to the apprehension of the culprits. When Valentine's placed similarly worded advertisements in a number of Irish newspapers, Lipton's response was to write to the editors and advertising managers stating bluntly that if there was any recurrence of such advertisements mentioning his firm in this light he would immediately cancel all further advertising. Needless to say, Valentine's found themselves squeezed out.

Robert Kennedy, a tea dealer of 347 Dumbarton Road, Partick, published a broadside stating emphatically, 'I know something about TEA, and feel called upon in the interests of those whose means are limited, and whose sources of information are apt to be unreliable, to try and deliver them from the spell of unscrupulous wind-bags'. In October 1889 Lipton's methods in general and tea advertisements in particular were attacked in the *City of Perth Co-operative Examiner*, while a leader in the *Hull Express* of 10 January 1891 was downright libellous in its vitriolic attack – no doubt acting at the behest of old-established firms facing ruin from this upstart.

Numerous jibes about the slogan 'Direct from the Tea Gardens to the Tea Pot' may have influenced Lipton's decision, early in 1890, to make his first journey to the Orient. In late spring he booked a passage to Australia, letting it be known that he needed a vacation. The grocery trade suspected that he had an ulterior motive, and there was speculation that the trip to the Antipodes would swiftly result in a rash of Lipton markets in Sydney, Melbourne and Adelaide. In May he set sail, but two weeks later, at the beginning of June, he jumped ship at Colombo in Ceylon (now Sri Lanka).

Up to 1878 Ceylon was principally renowned for the quality and quantity of its coffee, and the amount of tea grown was minimal, but in that year the island's staple industry was virtually wiped out by coffee-leaf blight. This compelled the plantations to consider an alternative crop and serious attempts were made to introduce tea as a substitute. Within a decade tea-growing had extended from a few hundred acres to over 170,000 acres yielding an export crop of fourteen million pounds. By 1890, when Lipton came on the scene, acreage under tea cultivation had reached 250,000, with a yield in excess of seventy-one million pounds. The industry would continue to grow at this spectacular rate. Lipton could see the figures for tea sales through his stores rocketing and decided that, like butter and pork, this was a commodity whose production he should be controlling. According to his own account, he was approached in the first instance by certain London bankers, representing a group of tea estates.

At Colombo he was met by Frank Duplock, one of his employees whom he had sent on ahead to spy out the land. On Duplock's confirmation that the prospects looked pretty good, Lipton abandoned his voyage to Australia and checked in at the Grand Oriental Hotel and after a few days' rest and acclimatisation went up-country to inspect the estates which Duplock had prospected. Confessing that he knew 'as much about tea-planting as Euclid knew about motoring', Lipton liked the look of the estates he visited in the Kandy and Matele districts and immediately cabled a very low offer to the Chartered Mercantile Bank of India, China and London. When the bank wired back, 'Can't you do better?' he knew that the plantations were his. His shrewdness was amply confirmed, so he says, the following morning when another would-be buyer came to his hotel and offered him £10,000 profit on the deal. In his autobiography Lipton described his initial purchases:

> The first estates I acquired in Ceylon were known as the Downall group in Haputale and they included the plantations known as Dambatenne [sic], Laymostotte and Monerakande . . . Having embarked now as a real tea-planter I rather enjoyed the sensation, so much so that a few days later I bought another estate, this one the Pooprassie plantation at Pussellawa. Before leaving the island I made arrangements for the taking over of other properties as and when they could be secured. Between the estates I had bought and the big sum of money I left with my agent for immediate future use I think I must have invested well over £100,000 [in] Ceylon within

a week or two of my arrival in that lovely and delectable island of spicy breezes.[8]

According to the Ceylon newspapers at the time, he paid over £130,000 for Haputale and a further £80,000 for Dambetenne, totalling 5,000 acres and employing 3,200 hands. The *Ceylon Independent* reported an unprecedented boom in land values as a result of Lipton's purchases. Lavish entertainment of the local reporters probably blinded them to the true facts, which were later revealed anonymously in the *Aberdeen Journal* of all places. An article, obviously written by a fellow Scot in the Ceylon tea trade, revealed that Lipton paid no more than a sixth of the £130,000 which had allegedly been refused previously for the Haputale estate. What he actually paid out was between £20,000 and £30,000.[9]

The *Ceylon Times*, the island's leading newspaper, published a report on 7 June 1890 giving a sober, factual account of Lipton's purchases, though it, too, swallowed the tale of the large sums paid. Several months later, having received excerpts of this report as relayed to the British press, the *Ceylon Times* was provoked into setting the record straight. On 18 August it published a feature showing that Lipton had doctored its June report for dissemination by the British newspapers. It thereupon reprinted the Lipton version with his alterations in brackets:

> The Ceylon Times, June 7, says: Mr Lipton has secured some of the finest tea land in [Ceylon] Uva. [His estates, viz.] Dambetenne, [Laymastotte, Morakande, Mahadembetenne, Mousakellie, Pooprassie and Gigranella] has [have] already made a name for its [their] fine and delicately flavoured teas.

It then went on to concede that in modern advertising the line between exaggeration and falsehood was difficult to draw, but this blatant tampering was unpardonable: 'And this is what commands success now-a-days – we will say nothing about deserving it!' The *Ceylon Times* felt that it was wholly unnecessary. Furthermore, it hinted at legal action if Lipton did not apologise and publish a retraction, adding that it now bitterly regretted having given him the publicity in the first instance. Needless to say, no retraction was ever forthcoming. In due course, however, the *Ceylon Times* amended report was reprinted in several British grocery trade papers which doubtless felt that Mr Lipton was getting above himself.

Lipton caused a ripple of disapproval in Colombo when he

entertained the notorious Arabi Pasha to tea on the verandah of the Grand Oriental Hotel. Ahmad Arabi was about ten years Lipton's senior, born in Lower Egypt of a *fellah* (peasant) family. As a youth, he was conscripted into the Egyptian army but rose through the ranks and received a battlefield commission in 1862. He served under Ismail Pasha with distinction in the Abyssinian campaign of 1875, but a charge of embezzling regimental funds (unproven) led to his retirement on half-pay. Disgruntled at his treatment, he joined a secret society formed by Ali Rubi with the aim of getting rid of Turkish officers in the Egyptian army. Egypt, nominally under Turkish suzerainty since 1517, had enjoyed considerable autonomy since 1805 under a hereditary dynasty of governors and khedives (viceroys) founded by an Albanian tobacco dealer, Mohammed (Mehmet) Ali. As Turkish power waned, however, the British, French and Italians moved in, gradually obtaining control of much of the country's commerce and industry, as well as the Suez Canal and the railway system.

In 1878 Ahmad Arabi was employed by Ismail Pasha to foment a disturbance against the government of Nubar, Rivers Wilson and de Bligniéres, and was rewarded with a wife from Ismail's harem and the command of a regiment. In the agitation against the corrupt government of Khedive Tewfik (1879–92), Arabi was thrust into the limelight as the leader of the discontented Egyptians, but in reality he was little more than the mouthpiece for Ali Rubi and Mahmud Sami. On 1 February 1881 Arabi and two other Egyptian colonels, arrested and brought before a court-martial for acts of disobedience, were rescued by their soldiers. The Khedive was forced to dismiss his then minister of war in favour of Sami. A military demonstration led by Arabi in September forced the Khedive to raise army pay.

In 1882 Sami became prime minister, and Arabi was appointed minister of war with the rank of pasha (general). After a brief fall from office, Arabi returned with virtually dictatorial powers, much to the alarm of the British and French governments. An Anglo-French naval expedition was despatched to Alexandria; severe rioting on 11 June led to the murder of many foreigners. When Arabi armed the forts at Alexandria, this was treated by Britain as a hostile act. Though the French warships declined to get involved, the Royal Navy proceeded to bombard Alexandria on 11 July. A British force under General Sir Garnet Wolseley landed soon afterwards with the aim of securing the Suez Canal. Arabi was defeated on 11 September at Tel-el-Kebir, and as a consequence British troops remained in Egypt till 1954. Arabi fled to Cairo where he was arrested and tried in December for rebellion. Some plea bargaining was brokered by the British minister Lord Dufferin, as a result of which Arabi pleaded guilty but the death sentence was commuted to banishment for life to Ceylon. The same sentence was meted out to Sami and others.

Lipton was in Alexandria in the summer of 1882, shortly before and after the British bombardment, though he was actually in Constantinople when the Egyptian port was attacked. It was during this trip, incidentally, that he paid one of the *fellahin* at the Pyramids to incise the word LIPTON into the stone above the entrance to the Great Pyramid – a source of considerable merriment (or irritation, depending on one's outlook) among British tourists to Egypt for many years thereafter.

Nowhere in his autobiography does he mention this trip (other than *en passant* the stone-carving incident), nor his subsequent connection with Arabi, but newspaper reports of the 1890s reveal Lipton's warm sympathies for the cause of Egyptian independence. Doubtless the conditions he found in Egypt reminded him of the troubled situation in Ireland around the same time. The man who secretly supported Parnell and the Land League was not the man to turn a blind eye to the corruption and exploitation of the *fellahin*, though his feelings must have been very mixed when he visited Tel-el-Kebir shortly after the battle, shed a tear over the graves of the mainly Scottish soldiers who had been killed in action, and had the honour of planting the first tree in the war cemetery.[10]

In Ceylon Arabi, along with his family and entourage, lived in somewhat reduced circumstances in Elsternwick, a village some miles from Colombo. Unabashed by the hostile comments of the expatriate community, Lipton sought out the erstwhile revolutionary and subsequently entertained Arabi Pasha at his Dambetenne estate. He was quoted in the British press as saying that he had a very high opinion of him. Arabi Pasha repaid his hospitality by publicly endorsing Lipton's coffee and chicory essence, saying that it was 'superior in quality and flavour to any Mocha or other coffee I have ever tasted in Egypt or elsewhere'. Clearly Lipton was not the only man capable of extravagant statements that were palpably untrue. When this interview with the former Egyptian rebel was published in the daily press, *The Grocer* was moved to speculate drily whether it was Lipton's tenpenny brand which Arabi Pasha had sampled.[11]

Thereafter, Lipton paid frequent visits each year to Ceylon and his friendship with the Arabi family deepened. On his return to Colombo in 1891, Lipton was distressed to find his friend in poor health, recovering slowly from a bout of influenza. Obviously the heat and humidity of the coast had a severely debilitating effect. There is no doubting the sincerity and generosity of Lipton's intentions when he appointed the Egyptian as general manager of his estates, with a fine residence at Haputale in the much more salubrious hill country, and a salary of £1,000 per annum. What Arabi knew about tea could be read in a teacup, and the British and Ceylon press were not slow in criticising this sinecure, which even led to questions in Parliament.[12] There was even a jibe about the question being 'the medium for a vulgar advertisement, Mr Lipton being the well-known advertising tradesman'. Lipton was quite unabashed by all this commotion and not only remained steadfastly loyal to his friend but tirelessly campaigned for his return as a free man to Egypt. It was not until May 1901 that Khedive Abbas II exercised his prerogative of mercy and allowed Arabi and his family to return to Cairo where he died ten years later. No less a figure than Sir Evelyn Baring (later Lord Cromer), appointed British resident and consul-general in the aftermath of the 1882 disturbances, conceded that the rebellion of Arabi Pasha was a genuine revolt against misgovernment. It was Lipton's friendship with the Prince of Wales (later King Edward VII) which eventually led to the string-pulling with Cromer (effectively administrator of Egypt till his retirement in 1907) which secured Arabi's return from exile after almost twenty years.[13]

Over the ensuing years Lipton did, in fact, add considerably to his estates in Ceylon, but even when he had become the largest tea-planter on the island he was still prone to exaggerate the size of his holdings. By the end of the decade he was importing, from one source or other, more than half the United Kingdom's tea requirements. One of the odder statistics he revealed to the press in 1895 was that the sale of the scrap lead lining the chests in which the tea was imported netted him more than a hundred pounds every week.

Interestingly, at the turn of the century, he was one of the very few planters who was persevering with coffee production; needless to say, Lipton's coffee was the best-ever grown in Ceylon. By the end of 1892 he had established a huge tea-processing plant at Laymestotte, from where wires from the various tea gardens high in the neighbouring hills brought the baskets of leaves hurtling down every evening. He had even created Lip-town, his own company village for up to 5,000 hands and their families. Unfair jibes in the tea-trade journals about the inferior quality of the tea grown on the Lipton estates were well and truly squashed when a small quantity of golden-tipped tea from Dambetenne was auctioned in Mincing Lane and sold for the record price of thirty-five guineas (thirty-six pounds and seventy-five pence) per pound. According to press reports, it was said to be the finest sample of tea ever sold. In time, this would join all of the other superlatives in a seemingly endless array of press features about Lipton and his unique business organisation. Oddly enough, the actual purchaser of this valuable tea was never named, though, of course, there was never any hint that it might have been Tommy Lipton himself.

In the spring of 1890 Thomas Lipton Senior was hardly cold in his grave when his hyperactive offspring began planning the major upheaval of his life. Glasgow was now too small, too provincial, too remote from the greater commercial bustle for his liking. Typically he explains his problem:

> I found myself spending half my life in railway trains between Glasgow and the metropolis and vice-versa, while my principal colleagues were doing the same thing. For the money which the firm was spending in railway fares it could have hired a series of Lipton Special Trains, with constant steam up on the engines![14]

Having established a number of branches in the metropolis, the time had come for Lipton to set up his headquarters there. This was achieved by stages, but in view of his penetration of the tea market, the first phase was to acquire offices in Mincing Lane, the Mecca of the tea world. When the *Daily Graphic* of 2 April 1890 reported the theft of a quantity of tea from the premises of Mr T.J. Lupton of Mincing Lane, the *Sporting Review* was quick to quip: 'There has always been a mighty difference between I and U – Lupton is in the Bankruptcy Court. Lipton is on the high road to fortune.'[15]

At the headquarters staff *conversazione* on 21 March 1890 in the Grand National Halls, Glasgow, Lipton announced triumphantly to the assembled gathering that business was now eight times greater than it had been four short years before. He got a rousing cheer when he announced a shorter working day, a weekly half-holiday and better wage and overtime rates. A further concession, soon extended to all his shops, was early closing on Thursdays, at five o' clock instead of the customary eight o'clock. In advocating such measures, he set an example which he hoped other retailers would follow, but he went further and stated that such measures should be made compulsory, and that he would do his utmost to ensure the passage of the necessary legislation. Then he dropped his bombshell; he proposed to remove the staff of Lancefield Street, numbering several hundred people, to new premises in Bath Street off the City Road in London. The announcement was greeted with stunned silence.

Lipton says that the transfer was delayed for several months due to sentimental reasons. Glasgow was his birthplace and he had started his mercantile career there. 'To uproot my office and factory organization would be a task of great magnitude. Hundreds of people would have to be transplanted to a new soil and, to a great extent, new conditions.' That is, perhaps, a mellow view of the matter, written so many years after the event, but the staff in Lancefield Street were given no alternative but to accept the move or face dismissal. This was no idle threat for Lipton, despite his undoubted concern for the welfare of his workforce, had insisted that every person, on entering his employment, should sign a document waiving their rights to notice at the termination of their employment, for whatever reason the management chose. The move to London took far longer than the six weeks stated in Lipton's autobiography, and it was not until 5 February 1892 that the last batch of twenty men and women (including half a dozen of the new 'lady typewriters') boarded the night train at the Central Station. Reporting on this exodus the *Evening Citizen* added that the departure of Lipton's headquarters meant a loss of revenue in excess of £1,000 a week to the Glasgow General Post Office.

Of course, there must have been many employees who, for family or other reasons, were unable to face this enormous upheaval, and therefore chose to seek work elsewhere. John Barclay, a twenty-four-year-old from Belgrave Street, however, was not content with the automatic dismissal he received when he refused to make the move, and took his employer to the Small Debt Court in the sum of two pounds, being a week's wages. This sum, actually well above the average for a junior clerk, was merely the pretext to bring Lipton before the court on a matter of wrongful dismissal, Barclay arguing that he was entitled to a week's notice. It was in the course of this hearing that the peculiar nature of the agreement between Lipton and his workforce came to light. The document specified that employment could be terminated 'at close of business on the first or any subsequent Saturday, without notice or warning on either side'. Although Sheriff Guthrie raised his eyebrows sharply at this revelation there was nothing he could do about it. The signed agreement was a valid contract, and he had no option but to dismiss the case and award costs to the defendant.[16]

To be sure, there were some setbacks that year. When fire broke out in the cellar of his grocery warehouse and tea depot in Dame Street, Dublin, the fire brigade were quickly on the spot and doused the flames within fifteen minutes. Not so fortunate was the Lipton Market in Newry, County Down, which went up in flames on 30 January 1891, with the loss of £15,000 worth of provisions. On that occasion fire engines from as far afield as Belfast and Dublin had to be summoned to cope with the conflagration. Edward Williams, Lipton's Outside Manager (with a roving commission as troubleshooter), was on the spot immediately, obtained a disused warehouse and with a team of workmen slaving all through the night, had an alternative market open for business the following day while the firemen were still playing their hoses on the smouldering ruins nearby.

The cause of the Newry blaze was never ascertained, though arson was not ruled out. It will be remembered that this was the town where Lipton had clashed with Valentine over his tea claims. While it would be going too far to suggest a connection between the poster campaign and the destruction of the Newry shop, these ugly incidents were followed by concerted efforts by an organisation calling itself the Belfast and North of Ireland Grocery Protection Association to get to grips with the great tea tycoon. The man who had played a signal part in securing the passage of the Marks Merchandise Act of 1887 (largely over the butterine dispute) now found himself hoist with his own petard.

On 2 April 1892, in the course of the prosecution of a Bristol shopkeeper under this Act, the defendant claimed that he had purchased butter adulterated with margarine from Lipton's store in Bristol. On this occasion Lipton took swift legal action and secured an immediate retraction which was then circulated, along with a covering letter from himself, to all the major newspapers in Britain. Ironically, only two weeks later, Lipton found himself on the receiving end of a writ to appear in the Belfast Summons Court on 16 April, charged with selling bacon under false descriptions, contrary to section three of the Act. He was found guilty of passing off inferior American bacon as 'prime Wiltshire' or 'best cured Cumberland'. The resident magistrate who summarily tried the case obviously did not think much of the offences, for Lipton was fined a shilling on each of the two counts. When he came before the same court the following June, however, the bench was not so lenient, and he was fined ten pounds on each of three counts of selling American hams wrongly labelled as best Irish or English products.

These cases received extensive coverage in the papers on both sides of the Irish Sea and one may detect a note of sanctimonious reproof in the accounts published in the grocery trade journals, though these paled into insignificance compared with the poem entitled 'Lipton in Excelsis' signed H.H.B. The eight stanzas attacked the King of the Provision Trade on various counts, ranging from his friendship with Arabi Pasha to his chicanery in the tea trade. A sample of this will suffice:

> With brawn and broken pekoe, and with print and paper thus
> I ridicule the world with trash and tea of sorts and sus.
> It's Lipton here and Lipton there, and Lipton takes the lard.
> Still a trade mark, in the future, it were wisdom to regard.[17]

During the latter part of 1890 and the whole of 1891 the transfer of operations from Glasgow to London went on apace. Having already established so many branches in the various London districts, Lipton had opened a suite of offices and a small warehouse virtually in the city centre at the corner of Bath Street and the City Road. Attached to these premises was a considerable strip of waste ground. The way Lipton tells it, he merely got on the telephone to his London manager and asked him how long it would take to erect the necessary buildings to accommodate the Glasgow staff and fit them out ready for operation. When the manager replied 'six weeks', Lipton remarked, 'Very good. We all start in London at nine o'clock in the morning six weeks from today.' He adds smugly, 'And we did – almost to the minute arranged.' In fact the move took more than eighteen months. The headquarters staff were still in Glasgow when the next *conversazione* came round, on 24 February 1891. Now grandly renamed Mr T.J. Lipton's Festival, it was of sufficient social importance to merit a full-page illustration in *The Bailie* cartoon supplement of 4 March. As well as the great man himself, Frank Reihill (General Manager), James Ross (Chief Accountant), W.S. Carmichael and Edward Williams were singled out for individual illustration; but William Love was conspicuous by his absence.

Lipton paints a vivid but entirely fanciful picture of the coming of the Lipton army, a thousand strong, to London. The movement of personnel and their families was carried out piecemeal and excited absolutely no comment in the London press, but the story enabled him to indulge in a little bit of chauvinism:

They all settled down very quickly and happily in London, proving once again the astonishing adaptability of their race. Give a Scot plenty of work, good wages and a glance at an occasional Glasgow newspaper and he'll be happy and contented in Hankow or Timbuctoo or Spitzbergen! And happiest of all in London! They'll tell you that the 'competition' there isn't so keen as in their own land.[18]

Meanwhile the douce citizens of Glasgow heaved a sigh of relief at the departure of the Lipton clan. Early in January 1892 those living within a couple of miles' radius of the Lancefield Street complex were startled out of their slumbers by a piercing whistle that rent the still-night air at the ungodly hour of 5.30 a. m., only to be repeated half an hour later. For several weeks the Glasgow newspapers were full of letters from irate burghers complaining about 'That Dreadful Whistle'. No one knew where it came from, for the sound ceased before it could be pinpointed. One correspondent described the sound as 'an abominable whistle coming from about the locality of Finnieston, beginning with a most pitiable lament and carrying on howling (dog fashion). By mid-January the noise was being repeated at hourly intervals, on the hour, right through the day from six in the morning till six at night. As the mystery deepened the letters of complaint to the newspapers increased in number. Just who was the perpetrator of this racket, and what purpose it served, were never revealed, for the whistle stopped mysteriously in the first week of February. Lipton never owned up to being the culprit, and no one in Lancefield Street betrayed him to the authorities. But the fact that a vast number of press cuttings pertaining to these letters were lovingly pasted into the Lipton scrapbooks leads one to suppose that he had a hand in the matter. Whether anyone subsequently connected the departure of the last contingent of Lipton staff for London with the cessation of the noise, no such speculation ever appeared in the papers. It was not a factory hooter, signalling the beginning or end of the day's work, that much is clear from the eldritch sound and the fact that it was repeated every sixty minutes. Perhaps it was part of some stunt – keep everybody guessing till the last moment – that never quite reached its logical conclusion.

Even in the midst of the move to London, Lipton was continually thinking up some new wheeze. The latest ploy was a variant of the Lipton Life Guards, in which marshals, mounted on magnificent chargers and clad in sumptuous costume, kept the Oriental sandwichmen in step with the precision of the

Household Cavalry. Apart from the carving of his name on what is nowadays a World Heritage Site, there seemed no lengths to which Lipton would not go in promoting himself. On a trip to Ceylon in 1897 he sailed through the Red Sea on the SS *Orotava* which ran aground on a sandbank near Ras-el-Tin. Although several dhows came close out of curiosity, none made any attempt to help the stricken vessel. In an attempt to float the ship off the reef, much of the cargo was jettisoned, and ever the opportunist, Lipton paid the now idle engine-room crew to cut a stencil and provide him with a paint-pot and brush. Armed with these, he went on deck and, to the vast amusement of the passengers and crew, painted the words DRINK LIPTON'S TEA on as many bales, cases and crates as he could before they were consigned to the shallows around the ship. Months later he heard of the jetsam from the *Orotava* being recovered 'by Arabs and other tribes' on the Red Sea coast. 'Whether they had the good sense to follow the advice to drink my tea, I cannot say.'[19]

On another occasion he had the bright idea of utilising all the buoys marking the channel in the Firth of Clyde from Greenock to Glasgow with his advertisements but this proposal was rejected peremptorily by the Clyde Navigation Trust. Similarly his proposal to the municipal authorities to solve the problem of the giant chimney-stack in St Enoch Square in the heart of Glasgow fell on deaf ears. This relic of the city's earliest industrial phase was in disuse by January 1892 and palpably unsafe. Lipton proposed having it repaired and repointed at no cost to the ratepayers, so long as he was permitted to adorn it with his tasteful advertisements. The matter was thoroughly ventilated in the Glasgow press, both editorials and letters highlighting quite fiercely opposed viewpoints. The consensus of opinion was that Mr Lipton was a tiresome fellow whose advertisements would only make an eyesore considerably worse. The city fathers, bowing to the wishes of the people, cut the Gordian knot by ordering the demolition of the stack. In his autobiography Lipton expresses pained surprise at the palpable philistinism of the city council. He would have made it 'a thing of beauty, telling its tale to the world of the excellence of my products, but these dolts in the City Chambers could not see this'.

One of Lipton's most familiar advertisements, ranging in size from a small handbill to a giant hoarding, showed a dusky Sinhalese maiden wistfully savouring a cup of Lipton's tea. This provoked an ode of eleven verses addressed to the tea maiden:

There are depths of unsearchable meaning
'Neath thy seemingly meaningless smile.
And the fringe which thy forehead is screening
Is remotely suggestive of guile.

* * * * * * * * * * *

Wilt thou go and take with thee thy hoarding?
Then, though poor as proverbial rat,
Thy reluctant departure rewarding,
We will certainly send round the hat.

This provoked a response the following week, allegedly found scrawled on one of the posters. Supposedly the maiden's reply defending her position, this poem ended with the punchline:

I don't see why I should be rated,
Although this monstrosity should.[20]

During 1892, the provisions depot and the factory where Lipton's notorious coffee and chicory essence was manufactured were moved to an adjoining site at Old Street. Over the ensuing year the Bath Street complex of buildings was expanded and added to as the exigencies of the burgeoning empire demanded. The fundamental problem was that the warehouses erected in 1892 had a floor space of only 200,000 square feet, whereas the Lancefield Street site was twice that size. Then, at eight o'clock on the evening of Thursday, 19 October 1893, a fire in the model lodging house at the rear of the Old Street premises spread to Lipton's warehouses. Although virtually every manual pump and steamer in the London fire brigade was eventually on the site, and over a hundred fireman fought the blaze all night long, by morning the complex of factories and warehouses was reduced to ashes. Even the headquarters building suffered severe damage from smoke penetration and water. It was a severe blow which might have driven a lesser enterprise into liquidation, but Lipton was organising the rebuilding operation before the ashes were cold. The eminent architect Mark King was commissioned to design a new headquarters worthy of the world's largest grocery empire. Work began in 1894 and took over two years to complete, but the phoenix which rose from the ashes was much bigger and infinitely grander than ever, and at the turn of the century was regarded as the commercial showpiece of London.

Over a four-year period Lipton gradually extended his land-holding to take in all the ground bounded by Bath and Cayton Streets and between Peerless and Old Streets. In a city which boasted many splendid buildings, the Lipton complex emerged as one of the more spectacular pieces of late nineteenth-century architecture, contrasting sharply with its older, more staid neighbours. The façade, of red brick interspersed with white stone, was dominated by the main doorway standing forty feet high and flanked by polished marble pillars. Above the doorway was carved the single word LIPTON in colossal lettering, and above it, carved on the metope, was the royal arms, signifying the grant of the Royal Warrant by Queen Victoria. Continuing upwards were central boardrooms on two floors, with huge bay windows. At the top, under a mansard roof, the windows of the top floor were dominated by a central tower adorned by the word LIPTON in even more gigantic lettering, with a clock at the very summit.

Entering by the main doorway at ground level, one came to the chief despatch department, occupying 6,000 square feet. Here a staff of 300 processed orders from stores all over the country, leaving them little time to admire the noble proportions of the lofty hall. On the upper floors were the administrative offices, the personnel and accounts departments, the typing pool, the secretaries, administrators and senior executives of the organisation. At the apex of this pyramid was the surprisingly small *sanctum sanctorum* of Thomas Lipton himself, decorated sumptuously and expensively to his own taste which was eclectic to put it mildly. One reporter commented that it reminded her of a ship's cabin, with its heavy panelling in ten different timbers. The walls were covered with photographs of the tea estates, and in a prominent position was a frame containing a cheque drawn on the National Bank of Scotland for £35,365 9s 2d, dated 30 April 1894 for the previous *week's* clearance of tea from bond. This was far and away the largest single sum paid to Her Majesty's Customs in respect of tea duty, even though it had recently been reduced to fourpence per pound. In fact, by that date Lipton was accounting for half the total tea duty paid weekly in the United Kingdom. At this rate, Lipton reckoned he was paying for the government's proposed naval building programme! When the Chancellor of the Exchequer raised income tax by a penny, the national press was unanimous in suggesting that he ought to have consulted Mr Lipton first.

Ever since his first trip to Ceylon in 1890, Lipton had been hooked on Oriental art, and his office and the corridor leading to it were cluttered with figures of richly caparisoned elephants, bas-reliefs and frescoes derived from the Ajanta caves and the guardstones of Anuradhapura. In keeping with the exotic flavour of this upper floor the attendants were clad in what Lipton fondly imagined was Sinhalese uniform, dazzling white trousers and tunic, with rich brocade waistcoats trimmed with gold. Four handsome youths served as the great man's personal messengers and impressed important visitors no end.

From the outset, the building was illumined by that wonder of the age, Mr Edison's incandescent electric light. Telephones were installed in every part of the building for both internal and external calls. The Lipton headquarters even boasted its own post and telegraph office, and the bill for telegrams alone ran to many thousands of pounds a year. Direct lines connected the nerve centre of the empire with the regional offices in Glasgow, Liverpool and Dublin. Towards the rear of the building were separate departments such as the printing works (moved from Glasgow in 1895), producing promotional material as well as packaging in up to twenty languages, reflecting the global nature of the enterprise. In the basement was a suite of strongrooms housing the company's records, and an enormous safe supplied by Messrs Milner, in which the cash was kept secure. Nearby were the forty-horsepower steam engines which powered the Holmes generators providing the electricity for the lighting as well as the operation of machinery.

Separate factories employing more than 800 operatives were erected at the rear of the main building. These structures, of six or seven storeys, included separate establishments for the manufacture of cocoa, chocolate, candy and coffee essence. Visitors gaped at the giant Lehmann presses that reduced cacao beans to dust. Dominating the scene was the huge tea factory whose two giant zinc blending machines were ranked among the industrial wonders of the age. Needless to say, they were bigger, better, faster and more efficient than any mechanical blenders previously employed in the tea trade. Here sufficient tea was blended each week to supply over a million one-pound packets which kept 500 girls working an eight-hour shift, six days a week. Their speed and deftness was a wonder to behold. It was claimed that every ounce of tea processed had emanated from Lipton's own estates in Ceylon. Although this statement was widely disseminated in the world's press, only those in the trade knew how false that claim was. By the mid 1890s Lipton's agents were buying up the greater part of the production of all the other estates in Ceylon, and were prominent bidders at the tea auctions in India as well.

Nor was Lipton's original business overlooked, for a separate factory converted the product of the Omaha plant into pork pies and sausages, ten tons of the latter being spewed out of the giant machines every day. Some 30,000 hams passed through the curing works every day, while a separate depot handled the vast quantities of cheeses from all parts of Europe and north America. Separate departments manufactured boxes, crates and barrels.

Journalists, from every part of the British Isles and even much farther afield, were positively encouraged to visit this temple of industry and marvel at its size, scope and advanced technology. The sheer scale of operations left visitors gasping. In 1894 Lipton was one of the first manufacturers to purchase petrol-driven vehicles, and within three years he had a fleet of Crossley lorries that was the envy of the distributive trades. One of the greatest marvels of all, however, seldom got reported, and that was the high wages earned by Lipton's workers. Even the girls who worked in Lipton's jam factory in Bermondsey were taking home at least twenty shillings every week, at a time when many a working man, raising a family, would have been content with that wage.

The Lancefield Street premises were not given up. Instead they were swiftly converted into bakeries where a staff of 200 men and women produced cakes, shortbread, biscuits and pastries, not just for the notoriously sweet-toothed Scots but for universal consumption because, by 1893, Lipton's stores and agencies had spread throughout the colonies, from Newfoundland to New Zealand. When the printing department moved south in 1895 the bakeries were doubled in size to occupy the space vacated.

Probably Lipton's greatest achievement of the early 1890s was to persuade Americans to switch from coffee to tea. Having got over his astonishment at the extent of the tea addiction in Britain, he was no less surprised to discover, on one of his frequent visits to the United States, that tea as a beverage was virtually unknown. He started by asking for a cup of tea at his hotel in New York, not long after disembarking, and was greeted with a look of blank amazement from the waiter. Eventually he returned with a pot of coffee saying that 'the stuff you asked for was not stocked in this hotel'. Lipton found the same sorry state of affairs in other hotels and restaurants. Tea of a kind was obtainable in some of the New York and Chicago stores but when he brewed it the result was unpalatable. What tea was available tended to be Oolongs and Japans, common types of green tea, and a most inferior China Congou. He was horrified to discover that storekeepers kept tea in open sacks or chests, and in one store on

State Street, Chicago, it was actually exposed to all weathers outside the shop door. Tea was weighed loose into indifferent paper bags, and for this anything up to a dollar a pound was charged.

He approached the problem with the skill of a seasoned military strategist. Instead of going in quite as baldly as his autobiography implies, he encouraged the Indian government, through its trade commissioner, Mr Blechynden, to take a prominent stand at the Columbian World's Fair in Chicago. Staged in 1893, the largest exhibition the world had ever seen belatedly celebrated the quatercentenary of the discovery of America by Columbus. Lipton himself had one of the more prominent stands, an ultra-modern plate-glass affair where the full range of retail products was proudly displayed. When the prizes were announced, Lipton surpassed Fry's cocoa, Crosse & Blackwell's pickles, Keen's mustard and Parkinson's baking powder; they only scooped one gold medal apiece, whereas he took three large gold medals, for his tea, coffee and coffee essence. In the food section of the exhibition, however, it was the Canadians who stole the show with their twelve-ton cheese, widely hailed as 'The Wonder of the World's Fair'. This monster put Lipton's previous Jumbos in the shade, for this leviathan, produced at the Dominion Experimental Dairy Station at Perth on Tay, Lanark county, Ontario, required the milk from 20,150 cows, milked by 2,177 dairymaids. Nearly 30,000 gallons of milk yielded a cheese weighing 250,885 pounds. It was twenty-nine feet in girth and stood over six feet tall, requiring a special staircase to enable visitors to examine it properly. With impressive statistics like these, it is hardly surprising that Lipton was drawn to it. It might have come from Canada but it was a Scottish product, supervised by Professor James Robertson and actually made by James A. Ruddick. Soon it was revealed that the monster cheese had been purchased by Mr Thomas J. Lipton who intended shipping it over to Liverpool when the Fair ended. The cheese was almost two years old when it reached Chicago; after exposure in a broiling summer, with temperatures soaring into the nineties, the monster had shrunk by six per cent, shedding almost 5,000 pounds in weight in the process. Nevertheless, when tested at Chicago prior to loading on a Lipton boxcar for the train ride to New York, the cheese was pronounced in good condition, if a trifle sharp to the palate. Stowed in the forward hold of the SS *Laurentian* of the Allan Line, however, the cheese deteriorated rapidly. When it was disembarked at Liverpool on 29 November the pong could be detected miles away; on the quayside it must have watered the eyes and gagged the throat. When apprised of this disaster Lipton, who had expended $10,000 on transportation and an undisclosed sum on the cheese itself, merely shrugged his shoulders. Besides, the attendant publicity even of this disaster was well worth the expense. This episode, however, put a damper on his extravagant plans to launch a chain of grocery stores all over the United States, and in the end he confined his American tea operations to wholesaling.

He obtained premises in Franklin Street, New York City, from which an army of salesmen and agents was recruited to hustle hotels and restaurants into trying parcels of Lipton's tea. The chief buyers of the retail chains were also approached and, backed with a coast-to-coast advertising campaign, a new and cheap beverage was launched on an unsuspecting American public. Within eighteen months Americans were consuming over sixty million pounds of tea per annum, virtually all of it supplied by Lipton. He dated his spectacular entry into the American tea market to 1892 and, indeed, this is verified by the glowing press reports arising from his first world tour, undertaken that year.

In March he set off on an extended trip to Ceylon, the Far East and Australasia, purchasing further tea estates, inspecting the tea trade in Japan and opening stores in Australia and New Zealand. In Ceylon his friend Arabi Pasha repaid his kindness by throwing a lavish banquet for him at the Grand Oriental Hotel on 27 April. Among the guests on this auspicious occasion were Arabi's son Mahomed Bey, Ali Fehmy and Lord Percy Douglas as well as Lipton's local agents Joseph Frazer, Frank Duplock and F.J. de Saram. During the course of dinner Lipton regaled the others with a display of envelopes which had come to him from all over the world, often addressed simply to 'Lipton, Glasgow', 'Lipton, Ireland' or even 'Lipton, Europe' (the last named being found on envelopes bearing postmarks from as far afield as Chicago and Colombo). In each case the General Post Office had correctly routed the letter to its destination.[21]

On the following day Lipton, accompanied by his new personal secretary Joe Slade, boarded the P & O steamship *Thames* for the Far East. In Hong Kong he ran into a European police officer who fell upon him like a long-lost brother. The police inspector turned out to be Samuel McLennan, formerly constable 100 of Glasgow's Western Division, one of the men who had had such trouble rounding up Lipton's Orphans when they ran amok in the High Street. The story of the meeting of the grocery king and the ertswhile bobby at a Chinese theatre in the crown colony was soon winging its way to all the newspapers in Britain and, remarkably, they all printed it word for word. From Hong Kong Lipton and his companion sailed to Yokohama and then crossed the Pacific aboard the *Empress of Japan*, arriving at Vancouver, British Columbia, on 27 June. Interviewed by the local newspaper Lipton boasted that he now had over 300 stores the length and breadth of the British Isles, 'in every town from Land's End to John o' Groats'. Some of the statistics bandied about on this occasion were that he sold 300,000 pounds of tea every week, and that his advertising bill last year had amounted to over £40,000.

He had no time for sight-seeing in Vancouver but immediately took a train east. By 29 June he was in Minneapolis where he granted an interview in his suite at the West Hotel to a reporter from the *Journal*: 'Mr Lipton talks with a broad Scottish accent, addresses his secretary Mr Slade as Joe, and is a thoroughbred son of the heather country, *sans* frills or any other superfluous decorations'. The interviewer was most impressed by the continuous quick-fire dictation of telegrams to Joe Slade ('at sixty cents a word!') by which means Lipton kept close contact with his business empire.

The following day he was in Chicago for a very important meeting with P.D. Armour and his partner, Michael Cudahy. From time to time Phil Armour had made overtures to Lipton, with a view to buying him out of the Omaha operation which Armour desperately wanted in order to expand his pork distribution to the Pacific coast. Up to now, Lipton had always managed to turn him down, courteously but firmly, but now he was of a mind to think again. He had discovered by this time that Nebraska hogs were rather too fat for the British taste, but were what the American market liked best. Negotiations were spread over several days, but in the end the men shook hands on the deal, auspiciously on 4 July, the American national holiday. But Lipton drove a particularly hard bargain. Part of the deal appears to have been a letter from P.D. endorsing the product now dearest to Tom's heart:

> I consider both my own house and the homes of my relatives are incomplete unless they are well supplied with Lipton's Teas. We cannot get tea anywhere in our country to give us anything like the same satisfaction.[22]

The sale of the Johnstone Packing Company in South Omaha, however, brought Lipton back into the Chicago market, eventually acquiring the Meyer Packing House. After making the most discreet enquiries concerning this property, Lipton used the offices of John Craig Hateley to finalise the deal and negotiate a fair price. By this clandestine method he obtained the premises at a 'rock-bottom price'. The Meyer House turned out to be a real bargain. It occupied a four-acre site and was soon processing 2,000 to 4,000 hogs a day. A fleet of express refrigerator cars was purchased a few months later. These wagons, with the single word LIPTON painted in very large lettering on their sides, were soon speeding to every part of North America 'carrying my products and advertising them wherever they went'.[23]

From Chicago Lipton went on to New York to conclude the deal for warehouse premises on the waterfront and then, well satisfied with his whirlwind world tour, he boarded the steamer taking him to Liverpool and his new home. In London that autumn he rented Wellfield, 'a nice but unpretentious villa' set in twenty acres of lawns in Muswell Hill. Some years later the house was demolished and its grounds developed by speculative builders. Where Lipton lived there now stands Muswell Hill post office. It was a pleasant enough district but it was not long before Lipton moved farther out into the surrounding countryside. He leased a large, sprawling two-storey mansion set in fifty acres of gardens and paddocks at Southgate in Hertfordshire and acquired a team of Kentucky trotting horses behind which, reins in his own hands, he generally drove to and from his office in the City Road. Someone told him that his house had been mentioned in a charter of the monastery of St Alban's in the reign of King John under the name of Huyeseg. Over the centuries this had become transformed and refined into Osidge. He was not the least put out when one of his friends opined that it was more probably a corruption of the Anglo-Saxon word for sausage.

Lipton implied that he had purchased this estate, though without giving details. In fact he merely leased the place, though a few years before his death he eventually bought it. At least sixteen different spellings of the name now known as Osidge are to be found in documents from medieval to modern times, but scholars agree that the name signifies the boundary of a place where trees were felled for timber. It was in fact on the edge of Enfield Chase and in the Middle Ages was the property of the church, but at the dissolution of the monasteries in 1539 it was sold by the crown to various landowners. Osidge passed into the hands of the Conyers family and had tragic associations with Lady Arabella Stuart, cousin of King James VI and I. Over the centuries it passed through various hands until 1834 when Daniel Lambert sold it to Augustus Henry Bosanquet, scion of a well-known Huguenot family whose descendants would include celebrated cricketers (including the inventor of the googly) and the late lamented Reggie Bosanquet, the television personality. Augustus died in 1877 and his widow Louise in 1883. Mrs Bosanquet's trustees let the estate to tenants, and in 1893 Lipton signed a twenty-one-year tenancy agreement. He extended this agreement in 1914 for a further twenty-one years, with an option to purchase, which he took up in June 1926.[24]

Here he began to cultivate a few of those interests for which he had never the time nor the inclination while his mother was alive. Osidge boasted a fine hothouse and here Lipton began breeding exotic orchids. From then onward every manager and departmental head received a fresh orchid for his buttonhole every morning. In addition to the winter *conversazioni* in Glasgow, Lipton had encouraged a summer outing, or 'pic-nic' to such picturesque sites round about Glasgow as Strathblane and East Kilbride. Out of this grew the Lipton sports club and even a soccer team rejoicing in the name of Lipton's Reserves. The final match in Glasgow was played at Woodvale Park in mid-January 1892, shortly before the departure of the staff to London. On that inauspicious occasion Lipton's team beat Louden 3–0, the game being abandoned before half-time on account of the icy state of the pitch.[25] In London Lipton lost no time in purchasing land at White Hart Lane, next to the Tottenham Hotspur grounds, and laid out a sports ground for the Lipton Cricket and Athletic Club. His star player was R.S. McGregor, a brilliant athlete, batsman and soccer player whose prowess on the pitch ensured accelerated promotion within the organisation. Lipton organised two cricket teams, of Scots and Englishmen respectively; usually they played against each other but joined forces when playing outside clubs.

At the Columbian Exposition in Chicago in 1893 Lipton had been cock-a-hoop at winning three gold medals, but later he would become rather blasé: 'I won so many prizes at functions like this all over the world that I got tired of entering!' On 28 February 1895, however, his greatest prize to date came to him at long last – the Royal Warrant as purveyor of tea to Her Majesty Queen Victoria. The timing of this award could not have been better, for he was then smarting over the decision of the Grocers' Association, only a month previously, to continue to exclude him from membership. This matter had been raised at an executive meeting on 11 January, but dropped after heated and acrimonious discussion. As a news item, the grant of the Royal Warrant rated no more than two lines in any newspaper, but as almost nine hundred papers carried that titbit, the resulting cuttings, meticulously annotated with the date and publication from the cuttings service of Messrs Romeike & Curtis, were lovingly pasted into the appropriate scrapbook and filled fifteen large folio pages. Admittedly, Lipton may have come perilously close to losing the coveted warrant when, shortly afterwards, he let the national press know that 200 pounds of best quality Lipton's Tea had just been despatched to Balmoral in time for Her Majesty's summer holiday there.

The annual *conversaziones* and picnics for the Glasgow staff were modest affairs compared with the two social events which Lipton masterminded each summer in London from 1894 onwards. The Glasgow gatherings were relatively democratic and involved all grades, but in London the organisation had grown to such an extent that it was deemed advisable to split the summer social into two events, a week apart. On Saturday, 7 July 1894, the administrative and clerical staff boarded a train at Moorgate at 9.15 a. m., arriving at Palmers Green at 9.47 a. m. precisely. There, a fleet of ten large brakes was assembled to take them through winding country lanes to the village of Old Southgate. At the gates of the lodge, the Guv'nor, resplendent in a polka-dot bow-tie and straw boater, was waiting to greet them with his bosom pal, William Love, down from Cambuslang especially for the occasion and appropriately clad in a Glengarry bonnet, doublet, hose and kilt. Races and other sporting events began promptly at 11 a. m. and continued until 6 p. m., punctuated by a delightful *al fresco* luncheon under the trees at 1 p. m. and a strawberry and cream tea at 4.30 p. m. After the sports came a proper high tea, Scottish fashion, followed by dancing on the lawn till 9.30 p. m. Tired, but happy, the revellers reboarded their brakes in time to catch the 10.05 from Palmer's Green back to London. By contrast, the afternoon outing a week later for the manual employees was much larger but shorter in duration; and significantly was held at a park in Theydon Bois, Essex, and not Osidge. Nevertheless, the Director of Sports on both occasions was the irrepressible Lipton himself who ran the programme with split-second timing but otherwise ensured that everyone had a good time. Inevitably selected members of the press were invited to attend one or both functions. In ensuing years these twin events generated an astonishing press coverage, replete with sketches and cartoons and latterly photographs. The programmes reflect the pecking order in the organisation, with such prominent figures as Frank Reihill, Edward Williams, James Ross, Frank Beckham and Duncan MacDiarmid as judges and umpires. William Love, by the way, was listed at the foot of the programme as the starter.[26]

Remarkably, these well-publicised outings seem invariably to have had beautiful weather. By June 1896 the manual staff annual outing to Theydon Bois was a monster of an event, requiring all the logistical back-up for which Lipton was famous. No fewer than sixty-four horse-brakes were required to take 2,000 people in a cavalcade that stretched for over a mile along the road. The relatively slow movement of this procession brought the main east-west traffic to a standstill. While the factory hands had the brass band of the Midland Railway providing their music, the staff garden party at Osidge that year had the pipe band of the Scots Guards, who also gave spectacular displays of Highland dancing. Inevitably even something as mundane as a staff picnic grabbed the headlines – if your picnic required the quantities of comestibles which Lipton gladly reeled off for the benefit of the obligatory reporters who now seemed to be covering his every move.

A notable feature of both social events was the evening entertainment; with such a large workforce, Lipton had no shortage of talent from which to draw. Whereas the factory hands made their own entertainment, a feature of the 1896 staff concert was the appearance of the Marchioness of Breadalbane who sang 'Cam Ye by Athole' and then tactfully added an English ballad by way of an encore. In addition to the administrative and clerical grades, the staff garden party was noteworthy for the impressive list of guests who included the Hon. Charles Russell, H.C. Richards, MP, Alderman Shanks (ex-Lord Mayor of Dublin) and James Thomson (Chairman of the Caledonian Railway) as well as the Marquess of Breadalbane and his charming young wife. This Scottish aristocrat, once the laird of broad acres in Argyll but now living in somewhat straitened circumstances in London, had met Lipton at a dinner party hosted by Lord and Lady Brassey in March 1895, arguably Lipton's début in London society.[27] The following year Lord and Lady Breadalbane accompanied Lipton on his voyage to Ceylon and were his house guests at Dambetenne.

In October 1896 work on the City Road complex was finally completed and Lipton formally inaugurated it, pulling a drape down to reveal the royal arms above the doorway. On the plinth below the arms was carved WORK CONQUERS ALL. The architect had wanted the Latin version *Labor Vincit Omnia* but Lipton, whose knowledge of Latin was nil, bluntly dismissed that as too pretentious. At the age of forty-eight he was already one of the richest men in Britain. As he surveyed the vast complex of factories and food processing plants from the rear windows of his administrative building, did he ever wonder what was the point of it all? An essentially simple man, Lipton probably never gave it a thought. He lived for nothing else but his work. 'It was my joy to be continually immersed in the big developments of the business and to take a fatherly interest in the great human machine which had grown up around me.'[28]

When in London his daily routine was unvaried: up at the crack of dawn to drive into the city, at his desk early – often before his employees – and late home to bed. Lunch in the executive dining-room was exactly the same as dinner at home in the evening: a soup, fish, meat or chicken and a rice pudding – always a rice pudding. Lipton consumed large quantities of rice twice a day and swore by it. It was prepared in a special way by John, the senior of his two Sinhalese houseboys, and whenever he stayed at a friend's house he would insist that John's recipe be supplied to the cook.[29] He eventually developed an interest in music and in his early years at Osidge he would listen in to concerts from London down the wire of a special telephone called a theatrephone. This essentially solitary pursuit was his only evening recreation, apart from pasting cuttings into his scrapbooks which filled a large glass-fronted bookcase, especially constructed for the purpose.

Life never seems to have been quite the same for him after the death of his beloved mother: 'Still feeling very much the deaths of my mother and father and a sense of utter loneliness taking possession of me, I threw myself more strenuously than ever into the maelstrom of business.' That was an understatement. On several occasions in the early 1890s he opened three new stores in a single day. No wonder one of his building contractors complained to him that the trouble with his firm was that it was like a boy who grew so fast that he needed a new suit of clothes every week. When he decided to sell jam, he personally inspected the six fruit farms in Kent and Essex which had to be purchased for that express purpose. In turn, diversification into jam brought him inevitably into the sugar business, and soon he was offering granulated sugar to his customers at three and a half pence per pound, cutting out the middlemen and eventually making inroads into the manufacturing business as well.

He was the wonder of the age, and hardly a day passed without a reference to him in the national press. Significantly after the move to London, he was much more accessible to reporters and never refused an interview, though the formula was much the same in each case: born of poor Irish parents in Glasgow, running away from school at nine (or ten) to help the family business, going to America at fourteen and opening his first shop at twenty-one, often sleeping in the back-shop at night. Thus was the myth of Tommy Lipton created in the 1890s. The pump was primed by a series of identical articles from an unknown hand, which found their way into various magazines from 1892 onwards. It is probable that they were all the work of William Blackwood, the young Scottish journalist working in London, whom Lipton befriended about that time. The feature articles often waxed rhapsodic about the Lipton manufacturing processes and distributive system, but contained remarkably little of a more personal nature. Not until May 1896 did a reporter (a lady scribe from *Woman's Life*) venture to ask him if he was married, to which Lipton smiled quizzically and replied sharply: 'No. For twenty-four years I have been wedded to my business, and it is a partner which has brought me a good return and is always at peace – so I have no desire to make a change.'[30]

Significantly it was a Glasgow paper which came closest to stumbling on the truth when it dutifully reported a rare visit of Lipton to Glasgow and Cambuslang in June 1895. The article concluded with the titbit that though he now lived in London, Mr Lipton still had his villa in Cambuslang:

> It is sacred to him; he will not lease or sell it. It is occupied at present by a friend of the old days – one who helped in the early struggles, and who now prospers in Glasgow himself. He is not a tenant; he is simply 'a friend', and as 'a friend' he preserves the sacred character of the chimney corner in Cambuslang.[31]

By the middle of the decade press reports and interviews were describing Lipton as 'just over forty, strongly built, six feet high, his erect carriage, which would do credit to a guardsman, makes this commercial genius look taller'. He was described as having a heavy dark moustache and a full head of dark brown hair now tinged with grey. Reporters invariably commented on his 'keen, blue eyes' which gazed in a penetrating way beneath his arched eyebrows. Argus noted that 'his face, which expresses firmness, tempered with a certain hearty kindness, betrays evidence of great mental powers'.[32] There were comments on his organisational genius, his ready wit, anecdotal prowess and fascinating conversation. To the cautious canniness of the Scot and the impetuosity of the Ulsterman he had now added the 'go-ahead smartness' of the Yankee. He was a phenomenon, an enigma. His name was a household word, but his private life was a closed book. In the years from 1890 to 1897 Lipton worked with a new, manic intensity which must have exhausted many of his colleagues or driven them to the verge of mental and physical breakdown. By May 1896 he was campaigning tirelessly on behalf of Sir John Lubbock who introduced a Bill before Parliament to limit shop hours; ironically Lipton's oft-quoted argument was that shopkeepers and their staff deserved a social life the same as everybody else.

From time to time there were rumours that he was about to go public, but he was always quick to refute them. Still there was no holding him back. He must be forever striving onwards and upwards, building and expanding his one-man business.

7. SIR THOMAS
1897–98

A man he was to all the country dear
And passing rich with forty pounds a year.
   Oliver Goldsmith, 'The Deserted Village'

Undeniably the highlight of the Grand Opening of the Lipton headquarters in October 1896 was the unveiling of the large oil painting in the main hall. The three-quarter-length portrait of Thomas J. Lipton seated at his office desk was the work of Professor (later Sir) Hubert Herkomer, RA. The 3,000 employees of the Lipton organisation in the United Kingdom subscribed their shillings and sixpences to present the Great Man with his portrait. It shows the Napoleon of the Provision Trade at the age of forty-eight, the wavy brown hair beginning to recede at the temples, the jowls and jawline filling out nicely as befitted such a captain of industry. The following year the portrait was lent for the Royal Academy's summer exhibition and excited considerable comment for here was proof at last that there *really* was someone called Lipton. Rumours that there was no such person had been rife for years, despite Lipton's valiant attempts always to get behind the counter of each new store to serve the first customer in person. But in an era before the cinema, radio and television when newspapers, at best, were illustrated with crude woodcuts if at all, it was impossible for most people to envisage the entrepreneur who had revolutionised their eating habits.

It was even alleged that he was unknown to the vast majority of his employees in the provincial stores, and by way of illustrating this point the *Sheffield Telegraph* wrote up an amusing anecdote. On a visit to Glasgow, Lipton had paid a lightning visit to his store in Jamaica Street and was examining the poultry counter when an alert young shop assistant came up to him and began praising the fowls and extolling their merits. The customer smiled and was about to move on, but the persistent salesman became more and more pressing. Eventually he achieved a sale, but was nonplussed, on asking where the bird was to be delivered, to be told to send it to Thomas Lipton at 99 Lancefield Street. The following week the young man was even more agreeably surprised to find an extra florin in his wage packet, and to be informed by the manager that Mr Lipton himself had made enquiries about him and had authorised a raise of two shillings a week. If Lipton were taken aback at the salesman's failure to recognise him, he was mollified when the manager informed him that the young man had only started work in the store a week or two previously.[1]

The paradox of being simultaneously the best-known and least-known man in the country was neatly encapsulated in an anecdote which Colonel Menzies of the Glasgow Highlanders loved to recount. In May 1895 he had dined with the Marquess of Breadalbane at Holyroodhouse, Edinburgh. Among the guests was Thomas Lipton and as they were waiting for their cab to be drawn up, the policeman engaged on speeding up the parting guests called out, 'What name, Sir?'

'Lipton,' answered the owner of that name.

'None of your jokes!' said the policeman. 'Give me your right name.'

Mr Lipton with a chuckle patiently explained to the exasperated constable that he was really '*The* Lipton'.[2]

A correspondent of the *Edinburgh Evening Dispatch* who merely signed himself 'D.H.' but was described as 'a gentleman whose own business career is not much less remarkable than the subject of the present sketch', contributed an article entitled 'The Provision King':

> Amongst all the interesting people I have met, I certainly rarely met one who has more interested me than a fellow traveller in the express on my way to London recently. Was he perhaps an American colonel or the President of a South American Republic? We conversed and I gave him my card. The other gentleman very simply said, 'My name is Lipton.'
>
> 'Not *the* Lipton?'
>
> With a merry twinkle in his eye, he replied, 'Certainly.'
>
> 'No. The son of the great originator surely – not the man himself? I'd been told that he was an elderly man living in a quiet way near Glasgow, from where he regulated all his vast undertakings.'
>
> The opening being thus made, Mr Lipton in the most frank and kindly way gave me in the course of our two hours' railway ride so much information about himself as to greatly interest me, and I am sure that others will be equally interested.[3]

Bronze medal struck in 1903 to mark the America's Cup challenge
(*top*) 'Good Speed to *Shamrock III*' (*bottom*) Sir Thomas Lipton
(courtesy of Ronald Breingan)

Shamrock IV and *Resolute*, 1920 (Topical Press)
INSET: The village of Southgate cheering Lipton as he sets off on the
America's Cup challenge, 1901

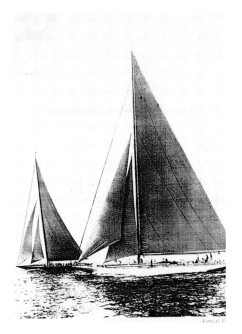

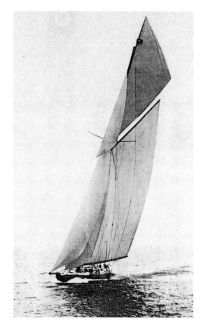

TOP LEFT: *Shamrock V* and *Enterprise*, 1930 (Topical Press)
TOP RIGHT: *Shamrock IV*, best of all the challengers
BOTTOM LEFT: Lipton in yachting cap
BOTTOM RIGHT: Sir Thomas Lipton in the uniform of His Majesty's Lieutenant of
the City of London, 1903

TOP: The gold loving cup
BOTTOM: Lipton at the City Hall, New York, November 1930, receiving the gold
loving cup; (*left to right*) John 'Honey Fitz' Fitzgerald of Boston, Mayor James J.
Walker of New York, Sir Thomas and Barron Collier

TOP: Lipton photographed on board the *Erin* on his
eighthieth birthday
BOTTOM: Lipton among his trophies

TOP LEFT: Western film star Tom Mix, world boxing champion Jack Dempsey and Lipton (astride a wooden horse labelled HAM) at the Breakfast Club, Los Angeles, 1928
TOP RIGHT: Lipton at the wheel of one of his many cars
BOTTOM: Lipton laying a wreath at the tomb of David Kennison, the last survivor of the Boston Tea Party, 4 July 1927

Lipton and Sir Harry Lauder in New York
(Topical Press)
INSET: Colonel Walter Scott (*left*) and Lipton
(*right*) with Sir Harry Lauder on stage at a
theatre in Philadelphia

CLOCKWISE FROM TOP LEFT: Stamp booklet showing a Norwich tram advertising Lipton's Tea; Lipton's tombstone, Southern Necropolis, Glasgow; *Columbia*, *Shamrock I* and the America's Cup, 1899, on a souvenir sheet from the Grenadines, 1987; Sir Thomas Lipton and *Shamrock V*, on a stamp from Dominica, 1988

Clearly D.H. had confused the dairy impresario and tea tycoon with his late father. Yet within five years Lipton was the most talked-about man in the country, and within ten years would be the most talked-about man in the world. The *Westminster Budget* Christmas supplement of December 1894 had included a full-page reproduction of a painting showing two elegant young ladies 'Enjoying a Cup of Lipton's Tea', but within months people were commonly speaking of 'a cup of Lipton's'. It seems strange that Lipton did not put his own portrait on the tea packets, but as an alternative to the Sinhalese version of the Mona Lisa he introduced in 1896 his Tam o' Shanter brand which shamelessly cashed in on the mania for anything Burnsian in the centenary year of the poet's death.

With 300 stores in the British Isles and new ones opening up virtually every week, speculation about Lipton's net worth was a constant topic in City circles. It was generally conceded that Lipton, still a relatively young man, must now be a multi-millionaire. Everything he touched seemed to turn to gold. Amid renewed speculation about such a mammoth enterprise which was unlimited, Lipton stated flatly that his business was still in its infancy. If and when he went public he would confine the offer of shares to his customers; as his books revealed that he now averaged 300,000 customers a day, this was no mean boast. When he went to Johannesburg in 1896 it was immediately rumoured that a chain of Lipton stores would shortly be opening in South Africa, but plans were aborted by the Jameson Raid; Scotsmen were no longer flavour of the month in the Transvaal, and the outbreak of the Boer War in 1899 delayed expansion in South Africa by several years.

At home, Lipton studiously avoided any questions about his politics, saying that he was 'thoroughly satisfied to feed his enemies and friends too, of both parties, if they will allow him'. From time to time, however, his political leanings were revealed in his practical support of strikers. When the textile workers at the Manningham Mills in Bradford were locked out Lipton sent them a generous gift of tea. Similarly he was a generous supporter of the Lord Mayor's appeal for the poor and crippled children of London, not so much in cash as in kind. In June 1897 Queen Victoria was due to celebrate her Diamond Jubilee, but mindful of the snub delivered to him ten years earlier Lipton kept a low profile this time round. When the Prince of Wales (later King Edward VII) launched his Hospital Fund on 9 February and urged everyone to donate a shilling if they could manage it, Lipton dashed off a cheque for a thousand times as much before leaving for Ceylon on the ill-fated *Orotava* the following day. By the time he returned, early in May, he discovered that Princess Alexandra, the Princess of Wales, had got herself into an embarrassing predicament. Not to be outdone by her portly husband, she had launched her own charity which aimed at providing 400,000 poor people with a celebratory meal. To achieve this it was estimated that £30,000 would be required but the British public, suffering charity fatigue after the Indian Famine Fund and the Prince of Wales's Hospital Fund and sundry other Diamond Jubilee appeals which had already netted £672,161 that year, had been extremely slow in responding to Alexandra's appeal.

On 9 May the national press carried an announcement that 'Mr Lipton has kindly offered to provide the whole of the tea that may be necessary to give away in connection with the meals for the poor people'. A week later, when it was revealed that only £5,000 had been subscribed to the fund, and that as a result it was in danger of being aborted, on impulse Lipton wrote out a cheque for £25,000 and sent it to Sir George Faudel Phillips, the Lord Mayor of London, accompanied by a letter:

> I was exceedingly sorry to learn that the subscriptions were coming in so slowly for this laudable project. Feeling that it should not be allowed to fall through for lack of support I have very great pleasure in enclosing a cheque for £25,000. This, with the amount already subscribed, will enable the Princess's kindly and considerate scheme to be successfully carried out.

The Lord Mayor circulated the letter to the press but, bowing to the wishes of the donor, he refused to divulge his identity. Phillips, who knew of Lipton as the Phineas T. Barnum of the grocery trade, was fully aware that this was merely a ploy to get additional publicity, but he was in no position to refuse the gift. Cynically wondering just how swiftly this cat would be out of the bag, he gave the bare details to the press. Reaction varied from the inevitable speculation as to the donor, to the high-minded leader in the *Birmingham Argus*:

> There is great virtue in the anonymous shilling. How much more when it comes to 500,000 shillings, still preserving the pure pleasure of giving, letting no alloy of wide advertisement to come in and destroy the perfect purity of the spirit of benevolence. This is a very pretty set-off to the vulgar ostentation which we began to fear was to be the dominant note of the Diamond Jubilee Com-

memoration. It is sincerely hoped that the identity will never be divulged.[4]

But the ink had hardly dried on that editorial when the Press Association released a brief statement to the effect that the anonymous donor was Mr Thomas J. Lipton, adding that a bank official who had handled the cheque had made an unauthorised disclosure. That may or may not have been the case; it does seem like an unwarranted slur on the integrity of the banking fraternity, and it is more probable that Lipton leaked the details himself, perhaps piqued at the appearance that day of a humorous poem in the style of 'Who Killed Cock Robin?' whose stanzas pointed a finger at William Waldorf Astor, the South African diamond millionaire Barney Barnato; the Nottingham bicycle magnate Ernest Terrah Hooley; the swashbuckling journalist and conman Horatio Bottomley and the financier Lowenfeld, but not Lipton himself.

Reaction to the revelation was mixed. At one end of the scale was the American newspaper which acerbically congratulated Lipton on keeping the secret for a whole afternoon. At the other, many of the British papers ran identical stories headed boldly BRAVO LIPTON. One wonders who orchestrated this positive puff. The socialist newspaper *Reynolds News* printed the text of the story, but predictably provided its own headline – THE TOADIES' JUBILEE. Among the few truly independent comments was that which appeared in the *Islington Gazette*. Under the headline 'The Poor and the Jubilee' it spoke warmly of 'our bounteous parishioner Mr Lipton'. The tabloid *Sun* went over the top in clamouring that Mr Lipton should be made a peer of the realm. The hideously mawkish column was contributed by T.P. O'Connor, a prominent Irish Nationalist MP no less, who attributed Mr Lipton's philanthropy to the wretched misery of his boyhood and the sufferings of his poor Irish parents. Probably less toe-curling and more gratifying to the donor, however, was the cartoon of a mysterious knight in armour proffering his lance to the Prince and Princess of Wales. The scarf tied to the point of the lance was clearly inscribed £25,000.

Whatever publicity Lipton had previously had was nothing in comparison to the deluge of articles which came in the aftermath of the revelation. He was the hero of the hour, and unprecedented crowds flocked to the Royal Academy summer show to view his portrait. Sir George Phillips, who had been saddled not only with raising the funds but organising the dinner, was not slow in turning to his new-found saviour for advice on putting the Princess's well-meaning gesture into effect. Businesslike as ever, Lipton responded that £30,000 would feed 400,000 people on a one-pound meat pie, a two-pound loaf, a quarter-pound plum pudding, a quarter pound of cheese and half a pound of cake. This would require 700 tons of provisions. He also pointed out that, assuming that a man could pack a parcel in two minutes, it would take 16,000 men a full day to pack the food parcels and 4,000 to distribute them. He suggested that the poor should be fed locally, with an even distribution throughout the British Isles.[5] This was going much further than Princess Alexandra had envisaged. When she had written to the Lord Mayor at the beginning of May she had concluded vaguely, 'I leave it to your very kind and able organisation to arrange that the very poor in all parts of London should be equally cared for,' and with a personal donation of £100 she doubtless felt that she had done her bit.

Ever the populist, Lipton now expressed forthright views on the criteria to be applied to those on the receiving end of this bounty. To be sure, there had been a certain amount of criticism of the Fund because of its rather condescending and patronising references to the deserving poor. As always, Lipton came straight to the point. 'We should not be concerned with extending an invitation to the respectable poor or the deserving poor, but to the hungry. We must feed a man whether he is deserving or not.' This struck the right chord, and the press were quick to latch on to it. 'By so doing he deserves, alas for how short a moment, to be the life-giver of that memorable day; and we wish him joy and blessing in his calling.'[6]

In the end, however, the dinner for the poor was scaled down to more manageable proportions. On 22 June tens of thousands of poor men, women and children flocked to the largest public halls in nine different locations in the greater London area, where they sat in closely packed benches and received their parcels while a battalion of lady helpers poured mugs of tea. The teetotal Lipton had strongly advocated that strong drink should not be included; Lipton's tea was stimulating enough. Though far short of Lipton's grand plan – and given time and a free hand there is no doubt that he would have achieved his aims – the dinner was hailed as an unqualified success. As the *generalissimo* in charge of the catering arrangements, he was in his element. For Lipton personally, Jubilee Day was both a humbling and strangely uplifting experience. Not since the miracle of the loaves and fishes had anything been attempted on such a scale. He made a point of visiting the Great Assembly Hall in the Mile End Road and all the other mass venues and was touched at the sight of those countless thousands of wan, pinched faces whose eyes lit up as the parcels were doled out.

The national and local papers were as one in singing his praises and highlighting his public spirit. To O'Connor's plea for a peerage – 'if sterling character, if the instincts and boundless charity establish claims to such an honour, he certainly would stand a good chance' – other papers responded with a more measured appreciation. Of course, it must not be presumed that any such thought occurred to Lipton when he whipped out his cheque-book and wrote out that five-figure sum. According to O'Connor, however, Lipton had had lunch with the Lord Mayor only two or three days before the donation was made public. O'Connor knew Lipton well enough to realise that for the Great Man to be prised out of his sanctum to have lunch with anyone, let alone the Lord Mayor, the occasion must have been very serious indeed. So arose the notion that Sir George had appealed to Lipton direct and he, without giving the matter a second thought, wrote out the cheque. The ploy of concealing the donor's identity, in retrospect was seen as merely a ruse to whet the public's appetite, thereby creating a far greater impact when the identity was made known. Significantly, the *Birmingham Argus* made no comment when Lipton was identified. Assuming that the Lord Mayor had importuned Lipton in the manner suggested, it is not improbable that a hint of some sort of honour was made. Of course, Lipton had a long and honourable track record for helping the needy, but hitherto the object of his charity had been striking miners and locked-out textile workers, and the scale of his generosity had been infinitely smaller. To get a better idea of the immensity of his Jubilee gesture, its present-day equivalent would be in the region of two and a half million pounds. It was a powerful sum of money by any account, but if that were the price of saving the beautiful face of the Princess of Wales then it would not have been unreasonable for Lipton to hope that some reward might come his way.

In the meantime there was a rapidly growing empire to mastermind and a host of new society acquaintances to cultivate. That Lipton got a tremendous buzz from his association with the aristocracy was revealed during his annual trip to America that summer. Interviewed on 1 August by the *New York Journal* he sang the praises of his friends, the Marquess and Marchioness of Breadalbane. The Marchioness, he informed the reporter, was the Lady Alma Imogen Leonora Charlotte Graham, sister of the Duke of Montrose, adding: 'They are the most illustrious of the peerage, you know.' Back home, he was being widely tipped as the Liberal candidate for the Enfield constituency (which included Osidge) in the next general election. Characteristically, within months of the introduction of motion pictures, Lipton had organised a short commercial for his tea which was screened in bioscopes and picture palaces all over the British Isles from August onwards. Four frames of 35mm film have been preserved in the Lipton scrapbooks indicating that they were 'exhibited by the cinematographic process at Douglas, Isle of Man'. The film strip was hand-tinted, so that the commercial appeared in full colour.

In October the newspapers carried the story that Lipton had just sent a cheque for £50,513 11s 3d to the Inland Revenue in respect of tea duty, and claimed this as an all-time record, but this was immediately shot down by the *Saturday Review* of 9 October which stated that a leading tobacco company had once paid as much as £150,000, adding, 'And thus Lipton has again been convicted of blowing his own trumpet more loudly than the occasion warranted.' Lipton was swift to respond, demanding proof of this assertion. When none was immediately forthcoming he put out a press statement reaffirming his claim to the record. In fact, on 16 April 1894, Gallagher's had paid £56,067 12s 9d tobacco duty in one go but remarkably the Lipton claim was not refuted by this hard fact. A few months later the rival Mazawattee Tea Company paid out £63,147 2s 10d, but as Mazawattee was not a name on everyone's lips, their record went unnoticed.

During the typhoid epidemic in the summer of 1897 Lipton helped Sir George Phillips by donating a thousand jars of beef extract to the Lord Mayor's appeal. Worst hit was Maidstone, with 1,590 cases and seventy-five deaths, and Lipton went so far as to pay a personal visit to the overworked hospitals in that town. Sir George Faudel Phillips, who had every reason to be grateful to Lipton, was the grocer's key to the highest echelons of London society. No doubt appreciating this opportunity himself, soon after his return from his latest world trip, Lipton presented the Lady Mayoress with 'a large ornament made from the lower portion of the foot of the largest elephant in Ceylon, richly ornamented with silver'. On 21 October Lipton was one of the guests at the Lord Mayor's Ball singled out for mention in the press, and on 6 November *The Times* reported that Thomas Johnston Lipton had been nominated by the Lord Mayor to a lieutenancy of the City of London. This story nicely coincided with the widespread report that Lipton had just purchased the entire Irish output of honey. Most of this emanated from the poor counties in the west of Ireland, and the deal gave a much-needed boost to the local economy. In the very same edition that reported the lieutenancy *The Times* commented on Lipton's latest coup that, once more, he had shown an uncanny knack in 'combining a good commercial stroke with a proceeding of the most practical patriotism'.

Six months after the Jubilee dinner, Lipton finally met the Prince and Princess of Wales, when he was formally presented to them by the Lord Mayor at Marlborough House on 23 December. The man who was equally at home with Irish pig-dealers, Chicago pork-barons and Egyptian revolutionaries instinctively had the measure of the portly Prince of Wales; he was affable without being familiar, deferential without being sycophantic. He was himself, charm and geniality personified. He was an excellent raconteur, and Edward enjoyed a good story. He was immensely wealthy, yet at heart a simple man. He was what people used to call 'one of nature's gentleman' and Edward, who possessed the common touch as well, readily took to him. Princess Alexandra, on the other hand, was quite dazzled by him. Tall, good-looking, with a soldierly bearing, he had an easy way with women of all classes. Alexandra, who was inclined to be headstrong and passionate, chatted animatedly with Lipton for several minutes. Sir George Phillips had organised this meeting to present to the Princess an illuminated address from the sixty local committees involved in organising the Jubilee dinner. The address was inscribed with the names of the sixty chairmen, but the Lord and Lady Mayoress *and* Thomas Lipton actually signed their names. On Christmas Day a small package arrived at Osidge by special messenger. It contained a beautiful diamond scarf pin from a grateful Princess Alexandra.

In the days that followed there were enigmatic puffs in the press suggesting that a certain provision merchant might get his just recognition in the New Year Honours List. Sure enough, came the day, it was announced that Thomas Johnstone Lipton was to be created a Knight Bachelor. When he entered his office the following morning, the usual businesslike quiet of the place was routed completely. The staff yelled and cheered ecstatically and sang 'For He's a Jolly Good Fellow'. When the commotion had subsided Lipton said quietly, 'Now, I think that'll do. You'd better all take a holiday to recover,' and waved cheerily as the 300 office staff rushed for the door before he changed his mind. Press reaction to the knighthood was generous, if not always accurate.

The *Greenock Herald* of 8 January, basking in his reflected glory, boasted: 'Thomas Lipton may be a Glasgow man but

Gourock was his favourite coast town, and he might have been seen any morning, not so long ago, hurrying along to catch the train for Glasgow.' The reference to Gourock on the Clyde estuary is intriguing, for Waugh in his biography of Lipton came up with the preposterous story of the one great love of Lipton's life, a girl called Catherine McLeod who was in 1885 living 'in a small village between Gorrock [*sic*] and Ashton on the north-east coast of Scotland'.[7] Inevitably the lady in question denied that they had ever been more than just good friends and at no time had she been engaged to him, or jilted him as had been implied.

With his usual impeccable timing, Lipton released an announcement, duly reported in all the papers on 3 January 1898, that the success of the Jubilee dinner had inspired him to open a nationwide chain of twenty-five restaurants for the poor. There they would get cheap but nourishing meals at cost price, as well as the free use of recreation and reading rooms. He had earmarked £100,000 for the pilot scheme, but although the press was generally enthusiastic about the project, the restaurateurs and café proprietors of Britain, fearful that he would do to the catering industry what he had already done to the grocery trade, ganged up on him and forced him to abandon the idea. It was a bold and imaginative idea, and that it would have been quite practicable was demonstrated during the Second World War when the government established the chain of British Restaurants where cheap meals could be obtained without the need to produce a ration book. In the end, however, the concept was revived a year later under the umbrella of the Alexandra Trust. The trustees consisted of the Princess of Wales, the Duke of Norfolk, Sir Francis Knollys (a member of the Royal Household), Sir Francis Jeune (a divorce court judge) and James Knowles (editor of *Nineteenth Century*). Lipton himself was not a trustee, although he served alongside Lady Faudel Phillips on the executive committee. The Trust's main activity, continuing up to the Second World War, was to provide free or very cheap meals to thousands of children, mostly in the East End of London. By 1914 the Trust was serving 45,000 meals a day to poor children at 200 feeding centres in London, as well as 5,000 meals to ordinary (adult) customers who paid a penny for a bowl of soup and a hunk of bread. A wash and brush-up and even shoe-cleaning were thrown in for good measure as a small step towards giving the destitute back their self-respect. While this was most laudable, it was but a shadow of what it might have been had Lipton directed all his energy and organisational talent into the original Restaurant Scheme.

Infinitely more successful was Lipton's launch, in January 1898, of his own beef extract. Hitherto he had been content to retail Bovril through his grocery chain but it was inevitable that he should wish to gain a slice of this market for himself. Under the unprepossessing brand name of Lipton's Meat Extract and Fluid Essence, the new product was in the shops by the end of February, and within a year was making a severe dent in Bovril's profits. Abroad, Lipton stole a march on his Chicago competitor Phil Armour when he secured the extremely lucrative contract to supply meat to the Klondike gold rush. On 8 January he announced that he had concluded a deal with the Alaska Commercial Company of San Francisco to supply 500 tons of smoked ham, packed in 100-pound crates with rope handles so that the prospectors could manhandle them as they toiled up the Chilcoot Trail. More than 35,000 pigs were slaughtered in Lipton's Chicago plant to fulfil this order, and soon the ham was heading west in Lipton's own refrigerated freight-cars.

On 18 January, along with the Queen's solicitor, two of her doctors and three senior colonial officials, Mr Lipton took the ferry across the Solent for an audience with the Queen herself, in the India Room at Osborne House, with Colonel Lord Edward Pelham-Clinton making the introductions. The tall, rather gawky grocer knelt awkwardly on the tasselled cushion for the accolade, and took the next boat back to Portsmouth as Sir Thomas. We can only imagine his feelings. Perhaps, his chest bursting with pride, he had only one regret: his mother was not alive to witness his greatest triumph. Unfortunately, Lipton's autobiography is completely silent on the matter. Nowhere does he mention his knighthood, nor the circumstances which led to it. Perhaps he felt, many years after the event, that he had bought his honour, but if there had been any justice in the world he should have had it years previously, for the solid achievement of creating a business empire that gave employment to thousands and high-quality sustenance to millions at an affordable price. Single-handedly he had revolutionised the provisions industry. Many men got higher honours for doing very much less.

Three days later Lipton stepped off the overnight train from London at Glasgow Central, inspected his factories in Lancefield Street and several stores in the Glasgow area, and that evening presided over the annual *soirée* of the Caledonian Railway staff. One of the two comedians providing light entertainment after dinner was an up-and-coming young man named Harry Lauder – out of this chance encounter would develop one of the closest and most enduring friendships Lipton ever formed. The following day he was among the guests of honour at the grand opening of the People's Palace by the Earl of Rosebery, before catching the train back to London.

Sir George Phillips demitted office at the end of 1897 and was rewarded with a baronetcy in the New Year Honours List. On 24 January the Jewish community of London's East End staged a banquet at Bonn's Hotel, Whitechapel in honour of Sir George. At the top table Sir George and Lady Phillips were flanked by the Chief Rabbi, Dr Herman Adler, and Professor Marks, head of the Reformed Jewish movement, along with Emanuel Barnet, Woolf Joel and other prominent figures in London Jewry. In their midst, and probably the only *goy* present, was Sir Thomas Lipton, to whom fell the honour of making the principal speech and presenting Sir George with his portrait in oils, painted by Solomon Solomon.

He was brought sharply down to earth again on 27 January when he was summoned to appear before magistrates at Bermondsey, where he was fined ten shillings for a black smoke nuisance from his jam factory. The magistrate commented, 'He is the new knight, is he not?' to which the factory inspector quipped, 'Yes, your worship, and rather a black knight in this instance.'[8]

The knighthood thrust him into the limelight and for the first time in his life Lipton, the consummate publicity-seeker and self-publicist, experienced the embarrassment of publicity of a kind which he did not seek. In truth, Lipton was a dual personality. On the one hand there was the affable, occasionally garrulous extrovert, the life and soul of the company garden party, the self-made millionaire who would grant an interview to the local cub reporter or T.P. O'Connor himself at the drop of a hat. On the other hand there was an intensely private man who had, perhaps, more reasons than most for keeping cupboards firmly locked, in case their skeletons should come tumbling out. Since those first interviews a decade previously he had become increasingly adept at brushing aside any probing questions; and it has to be said that the press, by and large, respected the privacy of the individual and did not pry in the manner so common nowadays. In a village like Cambuslang there must have been some tongue-wagging about those two good-looking fellows – 'confirmed bachelors' was the common expression – living together, albeit with the parents of one of them; yet no hint of impropriety ever leaked to the press.[9] Reporters who beat a path all the way out to Osidge often remarked on the fact that Lipton employed an all-male staff, but beyond describing the smart turn-out of the Sinhalese servants they never got beyond such comments as 'Rodrigo, Mr Lipton's Cingalese servant, is an accomplished musician' or that John cooked rice divinely.

Predictably it was the less-inhibited American press which caused Lipton the greatest embarrassment where his matrimonial intentions were concerned. In July 1898 he was in Chicago visiting his pork-packing enterprise and sorting out some problems which had unexpectedly arisen. A reporter from the *Chicago Tribune* had requested an interview, to which he had readily assented; but because of the exigencies of business he telephoned the paper to postpone the meeting until late that evening. The reporter was upset, despite the fact that Sir Thomas had been unfailingly courteous and suitably apologetic. Instead of keeping the delayed appointment, the hack had merely tapped out on his Remington an imaginary interview– after all, he had ample material in the cuttings file to concoct a plausible account. Most of what he wrote followed the usual bland formula, but not satisfied with this he decided to spice it up with something more personal. He had Sir Thomas confess that he was tired of the solitary life. 'The time has come for me to take unto myself a wife, and I have a long-standing preference for American ladies.' Within an hour of the paper hitting the news-stands Lipton's hotel was besieged by throngs of determinedly nubile women of all ages, shapes and sizes. Like pop idols of the present, Lipton was a prisoner in his suite, not daring to show his face in the public corridor, far less venture down to the lobby or the restaurant. He immediately contacted the newspaper and gave out a statement in which he tried to shrug off the offending article, quipping that 'it was a mean advantage to take of an unprotected fellow'. Privately he was seething at the indignity of it, and bitterly complained to President McKinley himself about the outrageous manner in which he, a visitor to the United States, had been treated.

Back in Britain at the beginning of 1898, rumours concerning the new knight abounded: he was about to become a director of the Caledonian Railway; he had just purchased Kier House, a mansion near Stirling; he was proposing to diversify into newspaper and magazine publishing; he was about to become Junior Sheriff of London; he had been selected as Liberal candidate – at least half-a-dozen constituencies were mentioned in this context. Inevitably his name was linked romantically with a young lady, a matter that caused intense embarrassment to Lipton, while the feelings of the girl may be imagined. It was *The*

Sun which broke the news that: 'We understand that Sir Thomas Lipton is engaged to a daughter of Sir George Faudel Phillips.'[10] The *Evening Times* followed this by speculating that Lipton might soon be following his prospective father-in-law as Lord Mayor of London. Three days later, however, every newspaper in the land carried a two-line denial of the engagement. Indeed, the denial was much more widely reported than the announcement that had triggered it off. As Sir George Faudel Phillips had two daughters, and neither was mentioned by name, both got fed up denying the rumours and turning down well-meant felicitations. An unpleasant aspect of this embarrassing episode was the element of anti-semitism evident in certain sections of the 'yellow press', which found hilarious the prospect of a marriage between a man who had made his money out of pigs marrying 'a daughter of Judah'. The *Ladies' Home Journal* of 6 August, however, put the matter in perspective:

> Sir Thomas Lipton is proof against being lionised; he is far too sensible a man, and too good a sort for that. A man who by sheer hard work and capacity has built up a huge fortune is very unlikely to care much for the very artifical conditions of fashionable life.

The most persistent rumour of all, which the press had aired continuously for at least two years, was that Lipton was about to go public. This had got as far as 'confirmed reports' in 1897 that Ernest Hooley, the bicycle millionaire, had offered Lipton two and a half million pounds for his business. Ironically, Hooley went bust in June 1898 claiming at that time that he blamed irresponsible financial journalists for blackmailing him, though the precise nature of these allegations was never made clear. It seems probable that Hooley had engaged in very sharp business practices, if not actual fraud. After months of mounting speculation, however, Lipton announced on 3 March 1898 that he was about to launch an issue of shares in his company.

While the lay press were generally enthusiastic about the prospective launch, the stockmarket paper, *The Statist*, echoed the sentiment of the City in its comment two days later:

> If all the paragraphs about the probable conversion of Lipton which have appeared in the newspapers since May 1897 were paid for as advertisements the outlay would be nearly as much as would provide another free meal for the outcasts of London. The alternate assertions and denials of imminent conversion have been used over and over again, according to transatlantic methods, but the thing

has been overdone; and, moreover, it is doubtful if the public generally in this country are yet educated up to approval of the 'authorised' statement by almost every newspaper of statements which have more than once been contradicted and reasserted also by express authority. It may be said that this is merely a way of drawing attention to a new company, and that, as it is pretty generally understood, no great harm is done. We do not like it, and we are inclined to think that, in the case of Lipton's, it will not have tended to attract the better class of investors. Of course, after the continuous proclamation about the shares being at a premium (before the prospectus has appeared), there may be a rush to make applications, as there was for the Burma Ruby Mines' issue, and it is well to bear in mind that boomed issues have often shown a speedy reaction from an undue market hoist.

Soon afterwards a prospectus was published which, for the first time, gave the true facts concerning the Lipton empire. He had been openly boasting that he now had 450 stores nationwide and 5,000 agents, but the prospectus revealed that there were only 242 stores and 3,300 agents. It was proposed to raise capital of one million pounds in Cumulative Preference Shares, one million pounds in Ordinary Shares of one pound for which a premium of five shillings would be required on each share published, and half a million pounds of Debenture Stock to be redeemed after September 1920 at 115 per cent. The trustees for the Debenture Stock were named as the Marquess of Breadalbane, Sir George Faudel Phillips and Henry House (Lipton's bank manager). Inevitably the proposed launch was hyped in the popular press which took the opportunity, yet again, to go over the spectacular rise of the grocery millionaire. The City press were much more reserved, judging the Lipton business to be stable but no longer capable of the dramatic expansion witnessed in recent years. The shares would probably be a safe bet, although *The Statist* of 12 March cautioned:

The sensational response to the elaborately worked-up boom in Lipton's conversion seems to us to imply that a vast number of people are ready to take part in a scramble with a chance of picking up premiums. No such rush for shares has been witnessed for many years. As the vendor and his friends together take nearly half of the capital, the Debentures and shares will very likely be kept pretty steadily for a time at a premium, and the vendor in any case will get in cash more than what a business man would consider to be the full value of all the assets of the business, including the goodwill, and he will have his shares and Debentures besides. It is noteworthy that no indication is given in the prospectus of the amount at which the Ceylon tea estates are valued, and a still more important omission is that there is no statement of the expenditure on advertising during each of the eight years. But probably most of the people who have applied for shares did not take the trouble to read the prospectus, and would have applied just the same if there had been nothing but the application forms.

No matter that the reality was less spectacular than the myth, just as *The Statist* predicted, the public responded to the offer of two million one pound shares with unparalleled enthusiasm, subscribing fifty million pounds in all, or more than a pound for every man, woman and child in the country. The allocation of shares was handled by the National Bank of Scotland's branch in Nicholas Lane, London, an unpretentious little thoroughfare which, on the day of the launch, was hopelessly choked with would-be subscribers determined to make their bids in person. Four policemen were rushed to the scene to control the crowds, described by one newspaper as 'the Klondike at Home' and another as resembling the railway booking office at Waterloo Station on Boat Race Day. Some of the claimants importuned Lipton personally. One man claimed priority on the grounds that he had once sat opposite Lipton at dinner aboard a P & O ship nine years earlier and passed him the mustard. A lady claimed inaccurately that she had been drinking Lipton's tea for more than forty years. Immediately after the launch of the prospectus, the first post on 9 March had brought 18,000 applications, the largest delivery the Post Office had ever made to a single address in its history. Over the ensuing days registered letters containing cash poured in by the thousand, and just as many ordinary letters contained cheques. More than 160 clerks were drafted in merely to open the mail, sort the cash and cheques, and enter the details in the ledgers. Characteristically, Lipton arranged that the notices of refusal should be sent out before the actual share allocation was announced, thereby increasing the tension and ensuring that the shares, once on the open market, would get off to a flying start. He himself went off to the Riviera for a well-earned break while the share frenzy reached its climax. So much cash was temporarily tied up in the scramble for Lipton shares that the launch of the prestigious Chinese Loan had to be postponed.

Needless to say, this stockmarket fever, the most intense since the ill-fated South Sea Bubble of 1720 – caused by intense speculation following the South Sea Company taking responsibility for the debts of the southern islands in return for a trade monopoly – provoked articles and commentaries galore. Perhaps the most bizarre was the sonnet which appeared in, of all places, the *Vegetarian*:

> Lipton! Albeit with affrighted breath
> In sonnet I'd perpetuate your name.
> Who in these days of villainy and shame
> Days of decrepit creeds and falling faith
> Called for two millions and with gnashing teeth
> Men fought that they should'st fifty million claim
> So great their faith in one whose sounding name
> To million hogs's synonymous with Death.
>
> Lo, on thy statue men shall read, 'I am
> The man who turned his heav'n-enlightened wit
> On hurling pigs to cold Destruction's pit,
> Who, spite of competition quack and sham
> Raised millions from mankind, whose name is writ
> In miles of sausage, continents of ham!'

When the dust had settled and the uproar subsided, the City's grudging verdict was that Lipton had done well out of the process, effectively putting two million pounds in his pocket while retaining a majority shareholding that gave him continued control of the business which he had created. The idea of charging a five shilling premium on every one pound share came from Lipton's financial adviser, the flamboyant Panmure Gordon, a former cavalry officer and a dandy of remarkable extravagance from an impeccable aristocratic background. After leaving the Tenth Hussars he had gained his financial training with Jardine Matheson in China and had subsequently earned quite a reputation in the City as a swashbuckling buccaneer – just the sort of man that Lipton would have warmed to. Doubtless Panmure Gordon did well out of the deal; Lipton himself claimed that the bonus arising from the share issue (amounting to well over £300,000) paid for the construction of *Shamrock II* and the costs of his second challenge to the America's Cup.

The first statutory meeting of the Lipton shareholders took place in the Cannon Street Hotel on Friday, 2 June 1898. Although Lipton enjoyed quite a reputation as an after-dinner speaker, his performance on this occasion was rather disappointing. He spoke hesitantly at times, and was not in total command of the situation. He had memorised his speech but made a number of mistakes and required the prompting of a fellow director. It seems that he was unnerved at having to deal with a room full of shareholders. A man who had built up his huge business single-handedly, or at least had always believed that he, and he alone, had been responsible for his runaway success, was perhaps not the person to take too kindly to the accountability forced on him by shareholders. To be sure, the company now had a board of directors, but as they were recruited from the upper executive levels of the company then they were all Lipton's very own chosen men, and proved to be more tractable than the shareholders. When Lipton announced that he intended to diversify into beer, wines and spirits, one of the shareholders, G.P. Ivey, leaped to his feet and claimed that he would not have taken 8,000 shares if he had known that Sir Thomas was getting into the liquor trade. Normally Lipton would have come up with a suitably witty rejoinder but for once he was nonplussed and it was left to some of the other shareholders to shout the protestor down, clamouring to buy his shares.

Under the headline 'Lipton Limited: The Truth Coming Out', the *Scottish Critic* of 1 July commented that it was remarkable that, within three months of the flotation, Lipton Limited should be adding wines and spirits. For a total abstainer this smacked of desperation. The Lipton 'markets' were not doing so well, as a visit to the Jamaica Street emporium would show. The grocery business was played out – and the deluded public had paid Sir Thomas £1,489,881 for the goodwill. The new venture was perceived as a desperate effort to save the company. 'A reasonable dividend on £2,500,000, with merely £1,176,785 representing assets, can be made possible only by going into the wine and spirit trade, and it is very doubtful if the Company will succeed even with that addition.' The article went on to question Lipton's estimate of the worth of his tea estates in Ceylon. The perception in the United Kingdom was that he owned most of the island, but in Ceylon itself he and his estates did not have the same reputation. He was only 'a very small grower and a moderate dealer'.

The system of 'presumptuous advertising to which we are accustomed here' was also to be seen in Ceylon:

> Colombo is covered with ox-wagons bearing LIPTON in enormous letters on either side, apparently doing Lipton's business. A visit to Lipton's factory at Colombo revealed a busted boiler, a disused engine, an old coffee machine – for which there was no use on the

island – two tea-cutters and a lot of empty space. No work was being done, partly because of London prices, partly because orders were awaited from the new Company.

London prices had, in fact, fallen by fifteen per cent since the beginning of the year, while labour costs in Ceylon had risen sharply in the same period, resulting in 'a reversal of trade sufficient to turn a handsome profit into a serious loss'. Mercifully, the article omitted to mention the serious problems which Lipton had been facing since April when his trusty lieutenant of long standing, Frank Duplock, committed suicide at his home in Bambalapitaya. An immediate audit of the books revealed very serious embezzlement.

The source of the story in the *Scottish Critic* is not known, but many of the managers of rival tea estates were Scotsmen and there was no shortage of tittle-tattle on the island which, sooner or later, would find its way back to Britain. Certainly the Ceylon newspapers were often critical of Lipton. There were numerous complaints about his obtrusive signs everywhere. Lipton's store at Slave Island had the name LIPTON in letters standing ten feet high. There were also 'gigantic but inartistic' advertisements at Cinnamon Gardens, a noted beauty spot. The *Times of Ceylon*, which was invariably hostile to Lipton, likened this to plastering Loch Lomond or the Lakes of Killarney with monstrous advertising hoardings.[11] Similar criticism also appeared in the Indian press. Lipton's signboard over his premises in Hare Street was 'about the biggest thing Calcutta has seen in this line yet'. A huge centrepiece showed the great grocer's name in letters ten feet high announcing 'the largest tea, coffee and provision dealer in the world'. The *Planters' Gazette* poked fun at Lipton's crassness:

> It is fortunate that the average hack and *tikha gari* horse is not given to looking upwards, otherwise the entrance to our Hare Street daily contemporary could be blocked up with corpses of horses and fragments of conveyances shying off.[12]

Most of the criticism aimed at Lipton was niggling, with little real substance behind it, and despite his faltering performance (and a noticeable tetchiness) with the shareholders at the June meeting, Lipton seemed unstoppable. His shares continued to rise steadily – contrary to the gloomy predictions of City analysts – and in mid-July it was revealed that he had secured the contract to cater for the great army manoeuvres about to take place on

Salisbury Plain. It was many years since military exercises on such a grand scale had taken place, but with the United States at war with Spain and tension mounting in South Africa, a realistic test of the army's abilities seemed desirable. Over a hundred thousand men, drawn from militia, volunteer and yeomanry units as well as the relatively small regular army, were organised into two opposing forces. A quarter of a century had elapsed since the last large-scale exercise, and that had involved a fraction of the numbers now under arms. Victualling such large formations called for a highly skilled professional, and thus the responsibilty fell on Lipton's willing shoulders.

The idea of putting the job out to a private contractor was not entirely novel; after all Thomas Cook had recently secured the contract to transport the Kaiser and his large retinue from Germany to the Holy Land, while a private contractor in America had been given a free hand to repatriate the Spanish troops from Cuba, after it had fallen to the Americans. But it was the sheer scale of operations that boggled the mind, and provided the press with limitless copy as usual. The project started off well, and Lipton even built a mineral water fountain at Dog Dene Farm to produce 48,000 bottles a day, but soft drinks were not quite what the troops had in mind. Disgruntled at being cheated out of their beer, and outraged at the prices Lipton was charging for his cakes and buns, the last straw came when the Lipton canteens ran out of matches and tobacco. Troops of the Northern Army went on the rampage, looting and pillaging canteen number six at Honington Camp.

This generated considerable embarrassing publicity. Interviewed by the *Daily Mail* on 30 August, Lipton said that he was very surprised at this outburst as he had never received any official complaints, and he was quick to add the usual statistics: he had seconded 1,500 staff to man the 300 canteens, and even supplied 400 horses and six traction engines to transport supplies. Army manoeuvres, however, did not touch the general public, who probably discounted the soldiers' grievances anyway. Within six days of this revelation, Lipton shares were on the move again, allegedly as the result of some people buying huge blocks of them. Four days later, on 10 September, news broke that Lipton was about to establish the world's largest coffee plantation – in Mexico. This was to be the more profitable of the two new ventures on which he embarked as a result of his most recent visit to the United States.

8. THE AMERICA'S CUP
1898–1914

Men prize the thing ungain'd more than it is.
Shakespeare, *Troilus and Cressida*, ii, 310

Shortly after that inauspicious first meeting of the shareholders, Lipton boarded ship for his twenty-fourth crossing of the Atlantic. On the voyage he had the chance to mull over the events of the past few weeks. Being Thomas J. Lipton was one thing; being the head of Thomas J. Lipton Limited was quite another matter. Somehow, for the first time in almost thirty years, the zest had gone out of the business – perhaps he was getting stale. Nowadays one would speak glibly of a mid-life crisis. What he needed was a change of direction, a new challenge. The Restaurant Scheme had gone sour; in the Alexandra Trust he was reduced to one of the bit-players. He needed something else, something that would really make his name. Lipton kept no diary and wrote no personal letters, so we have no way of knowing what led up to his decision to challenge for the greatest prize in the yachting world. The earliest reference to this new-found interest appeared in a periodical called *Man of the World* whose issue of 28 June 1898 mentioned that 'Americans are taking a great deal of interest in Sir Thomas Lipton, who has been across to New York, for they look on him as a possible challenger for the Queen's Cup [*sic*]. This would be a new departure as Sir Thomas does not yet own a yacht.'

The chief reason for the trip was business, of course, and most of the three weeks were spent in Chicago and New York, dealing with myriad matters from pork to tea and coffee. Not surprisingly, the American press latched on to 'Jubilee' Lipton once more as the world's most eligible bachelor and the *New York World* went so far as to publish a feature about four young ladies which it had selected for the millionaire's choice. Under the headline 'Bachelor Millionaire Lipton: Great New York Matrimonial Chances for an American Bride: the Man, the Money, and the Tea', was a cartoon of Lipton framed in the outline of a teapot. On the left were pictures of four young belles captioned 'We four New York beauties love you for your success. We love you for your title'. On the right four old maids were captioned 'We love you for your tea'. This exercise in tastelessness went so far as to give the name and address of each candidate, together with her comments on Sir Thomas, his good looks, wealth and title. Typical was Miss Rose McNul of 183 Avenue C, New York, described as 'a blonde of the Langtry type, and as beautiful as was the Jersey Lily in her girlhood days, with hair of a rich bronze-gold hue, eyes of deepest blue, and a mouth that is irresistible'. She stated that she firmly believed in romance and from looking at Sir Thomas's picture she was convinced that she could love him. If that were not the case, his title and money would not 'win a single smile from her'. She was too young to be mercenary and being a true American girl she would not sell herself for a title. If Sir Thomas wooed her he must lay his heart first at her feet.

The descriptions and comments of the other girls were in the same vein. By this time, however, Lipton was ready for the reporters when they brought up their favourite subject. 'I am not looking for a wife,' he would say quite bluntly, adding, to soften the blow, 'American girls are bright and charming, but so for that matter are English girls and French girls, so are German and Italian girls – all girls, in fact, except Spanish girls.' Doubtless the throwaway line was said with tongue in cheek, but the Spanish–American War was then at its height, and Lipton could always be relied upon to make an appropriately witty remark. He sailed home on the *Lucania* which, hell-bent on winning the Blue Riband for the fastest trans-Atlantic crossing, cracked a piston in the process, thereby delaying its arrival at Liverpool. The day before he embarked, Sir Thomas was fêted by the Empire State Society of the Sons of the American Revolution who presented him with an illuminated testimonial and a huge silk Stars and Stripes. By the end of July rumours that he was about to challenge for the America's Cup proliferated, and the humorous magazine *Moonshine* was inspired to comment in verse:

> If you, Sir Tom, who furnish cups
> To all, from ploughboys up to peers,
> Can only win *this* cup for us
> 'Twill be, indeed, the cup that cheers![1]

As far back as 1887 Lipton had written to William Lynn of Cork, suggesting that it would be a good thing for Ireland if he were to mount a challenge for the America's Cup, using a boat built in Ireland and crewed by Irishmen, but this was no more than a pipe dream and nothing was done to implement it until 1898; but it indicates what was an otherwise unvoiced ambition until the momentous year of the knighthood and the public flotation. The one gave Lipton a new-found status, while the other reduced his previous obsessiveness where his business was concerned. To yachtsmen the America's Cup was what the Holy Grail was to medieval chivalry. It took its name from the *America*, a yacht built in the winter of 1850–51 to the specifications of a syndicate of six American yachtsmen for the express purpose of taking on the almighty Royal Yacht Club which had its headquarters at Cowes in the Isle of Wight. In the summer of the Great Exhibition, the *America* crossed the Atlantic. Commodore John C. Stevens and his crew received gracious hospitality but the members of the Royal Yacht Club felt that it was beneath their dignity to respond to the challenge from the Yankees, and in the end Stevens issued a general challenge to match his schooner against any British vessel for any stake, from one to 1,000 guineas. Again, there was no rush to respond, but Stevens bided his time. In the end the *America* was invited to take part in a race round the Isle of Wight for a 100-guinea cup, sponsored by the Royal Yacht Club.

The race, involving fifteen vessels, took place on 22 August 1851. It was conducted on imprecise, unscientific lines, with no time allowances or limits on tonnage or other specifications. The largest yacht was the 392-ton *Brilliant* and the smallest was the forty-seven-ton cutter, *Aurora*. At 170 tons, the *America* was in the middle rank, but after a slow start she soon took the lead and gradually increased this to eight miles. On rounding the Needles she saluted Queen Victoria's yacht. When the Queen asked who was second her officers had to admit helplessly that they could see no second. The wind dropped towards evening, enabling the tiny *Aurora* to close the gap. Nevertheless, the *America* crossed the finishing line a good twenty-four minutes ahead, and the third vessel did not finish the course until more than an hour later. Most of the other contestants never finished the course at all. The 100-guinea cup was presented to Stevens, and in 1857 he lodged it with the New York Yacht Club as a permanent challenge trophy, to be known henceforward as the America's Cup.

Thus began the great battle between the United States and Britain. It was now up to the British to challenge for the cup, but they had to emulate the feat of the *America* and sail the Atlantic in order to beat the defender in her home waters. From 1870 onwards the British, and later the Canadians, tried to wrest back the cup, beginning with Ashbury's *Cambria* in August 1870 and *Livonia* the following year. Next came Major Gifford's *Countess of Dufferin* (1876) and the Bay of Quinte Yacht Club's *Atalanta* (1881). Sir Richard Sutton made an attempt with the *Genesta* (1885), Lieutenant Henn with the *Galatea* (1886) and the Royal Clyde Yacht Club with the *Thistle* (1887). In October 1893 Lord Dunraven challenged with the *Valkyrie*, and tried again two years later with *Valkyrie III*.

The races between the American yacht *Defender* and *Valkyrie* were sailed at Sandy Hook, but countless vessels of all sizes, packed with spectators and sightseers, obscured the course and interfered with the wind. In these intolerable conditions the much lighter *Defender* had the edge, and easily won the first race. The much heavier *Valkyrie*, built to withstand the rigours of an Atlantic crossing, could not compete on equal terms and, when the problem with the excursionists was even worse in the second race, exasperation gave way to risk-taking. The yachts collided and in extricating herself *Valkyrie* tore away *Defender's* topmast shrouds. The yachts continued on the course and *Valkyrie* won, but was disqualified when the race committee ruled that she had been responsible for the accident. Lord Dunraven appealed against this decision, on the grounds that the excursion steamers had obscured his view of the course and that he himself had been fouled by pleasure craft; whether accidentally or deliberately was unclear.

In an atmosphere which was exceedingly acrimonious, the third race began on 12 September, but *Valkyrie* did no more than cross the start-line before sailing away and leaving *Defender* as the undisputed winner. Dunraven's behaviour was condemned as unsportsmanlike, and the American press had a field day, dragging out every anti-British stereotype that had accumulated since colonial times in howling down the challenger. On his return to England, Dunraven published an article in *The Field* based on the report he had submitted to the Royal Yacht Squadron. He reiterated his complaints about the excursion boats but added:

> In the first race the *Defender*, after being measured, was surreptitiously loaded so as to sink her four inches deeper in the water, that she sailed in that condition on the first day's race, and that immediately after that race the ballast so loaded was secretly removed so that when measured the next day no discrepancy was found to exist between the two measurements.[2]

This was a very grave allegation, and the New York Yacht Club responded with alacrity, convening an enquiry which Dunraven was invited to attend. In due course he did so, accompanied by G.K. (later Lord) Askwith as his counsel. The commission deliberated for several days, weighing up all the evidence as impartially as possible, but it came to the conclusion that *Defender* had not been improperly ballasted, and that this allegation was based upon an imperfect observation of *Defender*'s water-line by the *Valkyrie* crew. It concluded, therefore, that Lord Dunraven's serious charge was totally unjustified. The course of the enquiry and its outcome had been closely followed by the American press and moral indignation ran high in countless editorials which denounced Dunraven in particular and the British in general. In hindsight, of course, it can be seen that Dunraven acted most injudiciously in airing his suspicions in the manner he did – especially as he had already behaved badly at the start of the third race. His pique and frustration were understandable, no doubt, but his pompous behaviour then and afterwards left much to be desired. On the American side it is obvious that the New York Yacht Club bent over backwards to be fair and impartial in their examination of the facts, and, indeed, common sense suggests that yachtsmen of the calibre of *Defender*'s crew would never have stooped to such a ridiculous ploy as tampering with the ballast to gain an advantage which it is unlikely they needed in any case.

Many years later, Lord Dunraven tried to set the record straight in his memoirs:

> I am not sure that I like international contests. In such matters as yacht racing, polo, golf, and so on, I think they tend to demoralise sport by turning it into a serious business in which national prestige is at stake; and to convert amateurs, playing a game for the game's sake, into professional specialists struggling for their country's sake. Moreover, there are critics in sport, as in everything else, and though rules are in all cases identical, and are equally observed, different people view a game from different angles, and misunderstandings may occur.
>
> In those days the course was very badly kept. Excursion steamers thronged it and hampered the yachts badly. Not purposefully, I dare say, for steamer captains did not understand the effect of their lofty vessels upon the wind and were anxious to give spectators their money's worth. Their unwelcome attentions were probably impartially bestowed, but it would be only human nature if a skipper was meticulously careful not to interfere with his own side.

That has all been altered, I believe, and latterly courses have been admirably kept.

The protest that it was my duty to make against the *Defender* in 1895 created an amount of excitement that could not have been exceeded if someone had deliberately hurled an insult at the American nation. The tide of feeling ran very high. It was a curious, serio-comic experience. The London Stock Exchange cabled New York that they hoped that, when war was declared, excursion steamers would not get in the way of our fleet; and the New York Stock Exchange replied that in the interests of a fair fight they hoped our warships would be better than our yachts. All very funny, but not funny to me, for though I found many very good friends I did not have a pleasant time; and the matter was more serious than comic, for indeed it really looked as though a protest about a yacht race was going to cause serious estrangement between two nations.

When I went over to attend a very belated enquiry, I was smuggled out of the liner at Sandy Hook. My good friend Maitland Kersey took lodgings for me close to the New York Yacht Club, where the enquiry was held, and I was under close police protection. A protest has nothing to do with motives or responsibilities. It is a mere question of facts – whether so-and-so happened or did not happen, whether this or that was or was not done, whether the protest was frivolous or justified; but when the facts become submerged in a great wave of emotion, they are lost sight of and a protest becomes absurd. I don't say whether evidence was or was not withheld, but I am very sure that not one of the American crew of the tender in which we lived would have dared to give evidence against the *Defender* had they wished to do so. Well, I am not going to reopen that question even to myself. But I thought at the time, and I think still, that to raise a game or a race to such a pitch is not conducive to real sport.[3]

Three years had elapsed since this unfortunate incident but it continued to rankle in the collective folk memory on both sides of the Atlantic. In the circumstances, it would be an incredibly foolhardy person who would dare to mount a fresh challenge so soon after the event. Lipton's challenge took everyone by complete surprise, and there was speculation that it had been a rash act, done on the spur of the moment, much as he had allegedly written out that cheque for the Princess of Wales the previous summer. But while Lipton liked to convey the impression of acting on impulse he probably never did. In business he planned each move like a master strategist, and there is nothing to suggest that he did not approach this latest venture in exactly the same spirit. It would have occurred to him that more heat had been generated in the press of America and Britain over the contest between the *Defender* and the *Valkyrie* than even the approach of the Spanish Armada commanded by Admiral Cervera, or the ongoing saga of Admiral Sampson scouring the Atlantic in search of the enemy battle-fleet. Lipton, with virtually no knowledge of yachting and certainly no practical experience of seamanship, could never have seriously entertained the notion that he might win back the cup; but he calculated that the challenge would generate far more publicity, on a world-wide scale, than any of his previous exploits. If Lipton was now a name inextricably linked to the drinking of tea, then the challenge for the America's Cup was bound to be good for business.

In 1887 George L. Schuyler, the sole surviving member of the 1851 syndicate which technically owned the cup, attached to the trophy a deed of gift which set forth the conditions under which all races for the cup had to take place. This laid down the parameters of dimensions and stipulated that the races must be between one yacht built in the country of the challenging club and one yacht built in the country of the club holding the cup. The challenging club had to give at least ten months' notice of the race, and accompany the challenge with the name, rig and dimensions of the challenger. 'The challenging vessel must proceed under sail on her own bottom to the place where the contest is to take place.' The challenger had to show his hand in sufficient time to enable the defender to design and build a superior vessel which was not hampered by the need to cross the ocean first. To be sure, this is precisely what the *America* had done in 1851, but yacht-building had become an exact science by the 1890s. It would have been pointed out to Lipton how slim his chances were of wresting the cup away from the Americans. Tantalisingly, however, he gives no indication in his autobiography regarding what led up to his first challenge, far less any explanation of his motives.

Lipton is also maddeningly vague, as usual, regarding dates. Quite casually, at the end of a passage discussing the Alexandra Trust, he slips in a paragraph about, 'The second of the interests which began to link me more closely with the outer world in the late nineties.' Describing the exhilaration from 'the whiff of the briny' during his many Atlantic crossings on business, he goes on:

> But it was not until the year 1898 that I found my thoughts
> definitely and longingly turning again to my boyhood's passion – to

the wind and the waves and the salt spray lashing and a mast bending under a well-filled sail. At all events to the actual possession of some craft which would gratify my zest for the sea and give me more frequent respites from the cares of business. The appeal was almost irresistible. And thus it was that I became owner of the *Erin*, the beautiful steam yacht which, in after, happy years, was to be so well-known all over the world.[4]

The whole of the ensuing chapter was devoted to *Erin* – consisting entirely of a string of anecdotes concerning the great and the good whom Lipton entertained on board. 'Indeed, the *Erin*'s guest-books contain the names of practically every Royal personage in Europe and of illustrious men and women in every walk of life on both sides of the Atlantic.' Inevitably most of the chapter was devoted to King Edward, but Queen Alexandra, Princess Beatrice and her daughter Ena (later Queen of Spain) were also mentioned at length, as was the aged Empress Eugénie who sailed with Lipton to Ceylon in January 1908. Among the commoners the one that stands out was John F. Fitzgerald, Mayor of Boston. 'Honey Fitz' once hijacked the royal barge in order to come out from Cowes to Lipton's yacht. On that occasion he was accompanied by two of his daughters, including the spirited Rose. For several months papers on both sides of the Atlantic rumoured that Lipton and Rose were engaged. What began as a joke seems to have been deliberately allowed to take its course; at any rate there was not the customary instant denial on either side. It appears to have been nothing more than a ruse to get rid of tiresome reporters and the importuning of other would-be suitors. Eventually the 'engagement' story ran out of steam and in due course Rose met and married Joseph P. Kennedy and in 1917 gave birth to the future President of the United States.

    Erin was not Lipton's first steam yacht, although nowhere in his autobiography does he mention the fact that he originally purchased the Clyde-built *Nahma* from the American millionaire Robert Goelet for £80,000. This appears to have been unsuitable, for it was soon discarded in favour of the *Aegusa* which Lipton purchased in the autumn of 1898 from Count Ignacio Florio of Palermo for £60,000. Built the previous year by Scott of Greenock, the 1,500-ton vessel was the largest and most palatial yacht of her time. She was powered by twin screws delivering 2,500 horsepower and had a top speed of almost seventeen knots. She had rakish lines and was painted white all over. Lipton wished to give her an Irish name, and at first toyed with *Killarney* or *Erin's Isle* before settling on the simpler *Erin*.

Having acquired his floating palace, Lipton now set about his challenge to the Americans. The rules called for a challenge to be made by a yacht club and although the Royal Yacht Club at Cowes was not actually specified, it was always understood that any challenge from the United Kingdom would come from it. But Lipton was not a member, and had no hope of becoming one. He might be a Knight Bachelor and a close friend of the Prince of Wales, but he was 'in trade' and that automatically debarred him. Fortunately the Royal Ulster Yacht Club had no such reservations and in due course its latest recruit published his challenge in their name. Reaction at the Royal Yacht Club was predictable: this johnny-come-lately who had so blatantly bought his knighthood was now outrageously flouting hallowed convention. Well might Lord Dunraven and his cronies howl with rage at this ghastly parvenu; was there nothing sacred that the arch-exhibitionist would leave alone? The sneers and snide comments of the English yachting establishment were echoed in the Isle of Wight's local newspaper which ran a story beginning: 'Yacht racing is one of the more memorable ways of losing a fortune. Here at Cowes there is a mingled surprise and mirth that a person should challenge for the America's Cup who hardly knows the stern of a boat from the bow.'[5]

Lipton ignored all this and concentrated his efforts on the design and construction of a suitable challenger. His original intention was to use an Irish-built boat 'out of compliment to my Irish descent and my friends of the Royal Ulster Yacht Club'. He might have added that an Irish challenge was likely to go down well in Boston and New York, with their large Irish populations, and would also have gone a long way towards taking the bitter Anglo–American partisanship out of the contest. Lipton liked America and the Americans and always got on well with them, but it is significant that, from his earliest days in that country, he had always emphasised his Irishness, shrewdly appreciating what an important asset this was. Now he consciously disassociated himself from Britain by his choice of name. Even if, for practical reasons, the new yacht could not be built in Ireland, it would be christened *Shamrock* after the Irish national floral emblem.

The hull of the vessel was to be of metal, mainly bronze, and it seemed to Lipton that nobody was better qualified for the job than the craftsmen of Queen's Island, Belfast, who were then producing some of the world's best steamships and fastest liners. W.J. (later Lord) Pirrie of Harland and Wolff dissuaded him, pointing out that yacht-building was a specialised art which it would be folly to allow sentiment to rule. Pirrie explained that the hull of a racing boat could be much better constructed by a firm with a long experience of producing speedy light craft. Lipton took his advice and in due course placed the order with Thornycroft's of Millwall on the Thames. The first of the five racing yachts to bear the name of *Shamrock* was designed by William Fife, Junior, of the well-known Clyde yacht-builders, Fife's of Fairlie near Largs. The obvious choice should have been George L. Watson, the most celebrated yacht-builder in Scotland and the man who had revolutionised yacht design almost two decades earlier with the *Madge* owned by James Coats of Paisley who had swept the board in all the American races of 1881. This powerful little yacht exercised tremendous influence over the future of yacht design in America. But Watson had designed the *Valkyries* for Lord Dunraven and that automatically disqualified him in Lipton's eyes. Whether this was a manifestation of Lipton's business ruthlessness is arguable, but one of his more chilling maxims was 'Never do business with an unsuccessful man'. When the time came to construct the second *Shamrock*, however, Lipton had no hesitation about giving the job to Watson. On balance, therefore, the decision in 1898 seems rather to have been dictated for diplomatic reasons. Ireland had the consolation of furnishing the masts and rigging which were fitted at Harland and Wolff. Thus the *Shamrock* was very much a joint Anglo-Scottish-Irish venture. By the time she took to the water she had cost her owner £140,000, about £40,000 over budget.

In America, reaction to the news of Lipton's challenge was warm and friendly. Jubilee Lipton had already endeared himself, and his challenge was swiftly perceived as cocking a snook at the stuffed shirts of the Royal Yacht Club. In the early summer of 1899 Lipton and *Erin* were on the French Riviera. A party of wealthy Americans threw a banquet for him and decorated the table with a model of *Shamrock* made of flowers. Each menu card, hand-painted with seascapes, had a four-leafed shamrock brooch affixed to green and yellow ribbons on which was inscribed in gold lettering 'The Shamrock'.

Back in England Lipton began playing his new role in society to the full. At the Prince of Wales Horse Show he purchased the Marshall Belle and the Fille du Regiment for £550. Though he had previously shown little or no interest in music, far less opera, he took a box at Covent Garden for the season. The American press announced that he had three ambitions for 1899: to get the Alexandra Trust under way, to win the America's Cup and to become a peer of the realm. His gifts to charity were many and varied; significantly, he wired $10,000 to the fund for American servicemen wounded in the Spanish–American War. In America the Irish challenge for the Cup was viewed with friendly interest; in Britain, however, the memory of the Dunraven affair still rankled. One London magazine voiced the feelings of the British succinctly:

> If the Americans will kindly take up their submarine contact mines and not arrange a torpedo display on the day of the race there is no reason why an English yacht should not get fair play. The New York Yacht Club must realise that acceptance of the challenge involves responsibility for keeping the course absolutely clear.[6]

In the summer of 1899 *Shamrock*, with the finest crew that money could buy, passed her sea trials with flying colours and then beat all-comers at Cowes, even showing a clean pair of heels to *Britannia*, which the Prince of Wales had recently refitted. Yachting was a rich man's sport which did not normally get much coverage in the popular press, but that summer stories about *Shamrock* and her charismatic owner began to bulk out the Lipton scrapbooks. By September, when she set sail for America, she carried the good wishes of the Prince and Princess of Wales and most of the country, although the Royal Yacht Club remained aloof. *Shamrock* was accompanied by *Erin*, but during a storm they were separated although *Shamrock*'s crew managed to carry on under shortened sail and eventually she was taken in tow by *Erin*. Both yachts fetched up safely on the American side after a passage of sixteen days.

Lipton's arrival was warmly greeted by the American press. The first of numerous official receptions in Lipton's honour was organised by forty prominent New York businessmen and headed by Colonel George Treadwell, representing Teddy Roosevelt, the then Governor of New York State. Later the usual gang of reporters came aboard *Erin* and subjected the challenger to a barrage of questions 'in their customary pointed and cheery fashion'. Lipton added:

> The questions an American Pressman won't ask, I always say, would not fill half a page of the smallest notebook on earth! But I enjoy myself in their company immensely. Their ingenuity and inventiveness and good humour and assurance are things to marvel at. They have always been very kind to me.[7]

He might have added that they never asked really awkward questions or probed too deeply.

Soon afterwards, Lipton had an incredible stroke of luck. The yachts were lying inside the Horseshoe at Sandy Hook when, very early one morning, an armoured cruiser steamed slowly into the bay. At first Lipton and his crew could not identify the stranger; they knew that Admiral George Dewey was on his way back from the Philippines at the successful conclusion of the Spanish–American War, but the Pacific Squadron was not expected for several days. As the warship drew closer, however, the sailors recognised her as the *Olympia*, the Admiral's flagship. The atmosphere was electric: here was the great naval hero who, with his flotilla of four cruisers and two gunboats, had sailed into Manila Bay at dawn on 1 May 1898 and in the space of two hours had destroyed Admiral Montojo's fleet of seven cruisers and five gunboats. Congress ordered a special medal to be struck and awarded to every officer and man of the squadron. Commodore Dewey was given a sword of honour and promoted to rear-admiral on 10 May. Mopping-up operations in the Philippines led to Dewey being placed in control of the new American administration and, in March 1899, he was promoted to the rank of admiral – the only officer since the time of Farragut and Porter in the Civil War to win this title. The previously obscure naval officer hit the world headlines, and the return of his squadron to the United States, via the Indian Ocean, was closely monitored by the world's press; but on the Atlantic crossing, in an era before radio had been perfected, the exact time of arrival was uncertain.

It was just after daybreak that Lipton boarded his launch, armed with all the New York newspapers he could find, and made for the flagship. A gangway was lowered and soon Lipton was on the deck of the *Olympia* enquiring after Dewey's health. He was immediately escorted to the admiral's cabin where he was invited to take breakfast. Dewey expressed tremendous interest in the forthcoming yacht races and the two men chatted animatedly for some time. An hour later, as the launch pushed off, Lipton was astonished to see the crew of the *Olympia* lining the rails and brandishing packets which seemed oddly familiar. Then the penny dropped. Lipton remembered that some weeks earlier, on hearing of the *Olympia*'s impending arrival at Colombo, he had cabled his manager in Ceylon to present every man of the crew with a packet of tea. These packets were now on their way home to the sailors' wives and sweethearts. That evening Lipton returned the compliment by entertaining Dewey and his senior officers to a lavish dinner aboard *Erin*.

A few days later New York accorded the returning hero a

magnificent naval reception. Ships and craft of every size and sort were lined up in two columns at the entrance to New York Harbor to escort the victorious admiral. Although there had been some grumbling in the New York press about Dewey having granted an interview to a foreigner before reporting to his Commander-in-Chief, President McKinley, the consensus was that the millionaire yachtsman had style, and his love for America was genuine. Besides, Mayor Van Wyck was a close personal friend of long standing. To Lipton in *Erin*, therefore, fell the honour of leading the port column in the parade of ships, while J. Pierpont Morgan's *Corsair* led the starboard line. The long parade of steamers and sailing craft was gaily dressed with flags and bunting. *Erin* had a rainbow arrangement of bunting, the American flag on each truck and the ensign of the Royal Ulster Yacht Club at the taffrail. This was undoubtedly a very proud moment for Lipton, provoking the press at home to comment: 'It is difficult to tell whether the festivities at New York are meant for Admiral Dewey or for Sir Thomas Lipton.'[8] To the cheers of countless thousands of onlookers crowding the shores the vessels sailed slowly and majestically up the Hudson from the Battery to Grant's Tomb. Here Dewey disembarked and, accompanied by city and state officials, visiting dignitaries and other important persons (including Lipton), took his place in the land parade which went by Riverside Drive and Fifth Avenue to Madison Square Garden and the great Dewey Arch of Welcome and Triumph, a bizarre concoction based on the Arch of Titus in Rome and the Arc de Triomphe. Lipton, as the city's guest, rode to take his place beside the saluting base with Captain Croker of the *Nixon* and the Hon. Charles Russell.

The land parade was a brilliant spectacle, with Governor Teddy Roosevelt in his silk hat and frock coat (rather than the colonel's uniform in which he had led the Rough Riders up San Juan Hill) leading the New York Troop, followed by the West Point cadets in their shakos, white trousers and gleaming cross-belts. There was a rousing cheer for the colour company proudly bearing its tattered battle flag, followed by the Tenth Pennsylvania Regiment, newly arrived from Manila and still wearing soiled combat uniforms. By contrast, the saluting dais glittered with the dress uniforms and medals of the admirals and generals. On that day the old reservoir on Fifth Avenue and 41st Street performed its last civic function, as the base for a grandstand.

This eventful occasion came to a curious conclusion when Lipton entertained Rear-Admirals Sampson and Schley to a late lunch in his suite at the Fifth Avenue Hotel. How these two men, who hated each other with unparalleled intensity, came to be together in the same room, let alone dining at the same table, is a complete mystery.

At the outset of the war both men held the rank of captain, though Winfield Scott Schley, a year older, had been commissioned in 1860 and was the senior of the two. William Thomas Sampson was commissioned lieutenant in 1862 but both men attained the rank of commander in the same year (1874) and thereafter their careers were on parallel lines. Whereas Schley spent more time afloat, Sampson held a succession of important staff appointments, including head of the Naval Academy (1886–90), delegate to the International Maritime Conference (1899) and chief of the Bureau of Ordnance (1893–97). It was he who had got to grips with Andrew Carnegie over the armour-plate scandal,[9] and almost all the guns employed during the Spanish–American War were made under his superintendence. In February 1898 he presided over the board of enquiry as to the cause of the destruction of the battleship *Maine* in Havana Harbour, the chief pretext for the war. In the same month Schley was promoted to commodore and put in command of the Flying Squadron ordered to attack Cuba. When war broke out in April, however, Sampson was made acting rear-admiral and placed in command of the North Atlantic Squadron. He was thus now technically Schley's superior, but only on a temporary basis. Sampson drew up the plans for the battle of Santiago which led to the total destruction of the Spanish fleet on 3 July 1898, but he was actually at Siboney on that historic day, conferring with General Shafter, the commander of the land forces, so the conduct of the naval battle fell to Schley. On 10 August Schley was advanced six numbers in the Navy List and promoted to rear-admiral for 'eminent and conspicuous conduct in battle', but when the Navy Department recommended that Sampson be advanced eight numbers over the head of Schley who had ranked him for forty-two years, there was a bitter controversy going all the way to the Senate which refused to confirm the promotion. Sampson's substantive promotion to flag rank came on 3 March 1899, and Schley's on 14 April.

The personal animosity between America's two rear-admirals was exacerbated by conflicting opinions concerning the battle of Santiago. In particular, criticism was mounting in the summer of 1899 that Schley had been guilty of delay and inefficiency in cornering Cervera's battle-fleet. More seriously, he was accused of carelessness during the battle in endangering the *Texas* by a peculiar loop movement of his flagship *Brooklyn* which blanketed the gunfire of other American warships at a crucial point in the engagement, and of disobedience to a departmental order of 25 May 1898. Eventually this rancorous dispute would lead to Schley demanding a court of enquiry, which rebounded on him by finding him guilty on all counts, and precipitated his early retirement in 1901. Against this background, therefore, must be read Lipton's description of the meal in his suite:

> Not until afterwards did I learn that these distinguished officers were then actually engaged in a very heated controversy, the causes of which I do not even know to this day. But we all had a jolly good meal. Perhaps they settled their differences over 'a dram' at my luncheon table.[10]

Thus what may well have been a moment of high drama was reduced, in Lipton's autobiography, to a sunny, rather banal get-together. On the last Saturday of September there was a smoking concert at the Waldorf for the crew of the *Olympia*. Lipton was the guest of honour and was enthusiastically greeted with cheers and cries of 'Good luck, Shamrock!'. Lipton marvelled that in a truly democratic country such a dinner could be held at one of the most prestigious hotels for even the lowliest naval ratings. He could not imagine the jacktars of Her Majesty's Navy being similarly entertained at the Ritz in London. Lipton responded promptly when asked to make a speech. Off the cuff he said:

> I am delighted to get this opportunity to meet you all. The country is proud of you and has welcomed you royally . . . I mean to try to get a little American property here myself and I hope that when that little engagement comes off you won't squash it up like you did the Spanish fleet at Manila.[11]

The 'little American property', of course, was the America's Cup, and 'that little engagement' was a sly reference to the forthcoming races.

With the first race scheduled for the following Tuesday, the carnival atmosphere of the Dewey celebration continued over the long weekend. Now Lipton moved into the limelight – from being seen as the plucky underdog he was rapidly becoming transformed into almost as great a naval hero as Dewey. In contrast to the snootiness of the Royal Yacht Club, it appeared as if the cream of British society had crossed the Atlantic to give

Lipton moral support. The Governor-General of Canada and Lady Minto; Admiral Lord Charles Beresford and his wife; Sir Henry Burdett; Lady Cunard; the governors or agents-general of New Zealand and the Australian colonies and sundry European minor royalty were among those who had sailed in from every part of the globe to watch the fun.

Against this festive atmosphere, in which a sizeable proportion of the New York public had a sneaking regard for the Irish challenger, the international situation was grave, and Anglo-American relations were increasingly strained. There was a crisis in the Transvaal and the American press was decidedly sympathetic to Oom Paul Kruger and correspondingly hostile towards 'the high-handed and unscrupulous Chamberlain' who was likened to Lord North whose actions had precipitated the American War of Independence. Parallels between 1775–76 and 1899 were only too easily drawn. Paradoxically, while Britain's behaviour towards the Boers was being condemned as 'sad and shameful' the American press was extraordinarily generous towards Lipton, urging that *Shamrock* should be given every chance and that there should be no repetition of the Dunraven affair, and that the course must be kept clear.

The progress of the sea trials was extensively reported, and tension mounted as *Shamrock* proved to be a far better boat than had been anticipated. There were even sections of the American press which criticised the one-sided nature of the contest, between 'a bluff British ketch' and *Columbia* – 'a glorified skimming dish'. Across the Atlantic, interest in the race was growing. At the beginning, interest had been lukewarm, the *New York Times*'s London correspondent noting a certain apathy owing to the suspicion that Lipton's challenge had been motivated by self-advertisement. But Lipton had not been the mainstay of the newspaper advertising industry all those years for nothing, and soon the British press, notably the Harmsworth publications, were rooting enthusiastically on his behalf. The *Evening News* went so far as to erect a huge hoarding on a site facing the Embankment, with the Sandy Hook course outlined. Two miniature yachts were mounted on tracks in the canvas so that passers-by could watch the progress of the race.

The first race took place on 3 October. Huge crowds gathered on the Thames Embankment to watch the contest on the Cineyachtograph. In conditions of only the faintest of breezes *Shamrock* took the lead, but only half a mile from the finish the race had to be abandoned as both vessels were becalmed and drifting. There was actually much more action at the

Cineyachtograph as the staff of the newspaper applied artistic licence to inject tension and high drama into the non-event, although, in the end, they could not fiddle the result. If *Shamrock* had not won, at least she had not lost either, and understandably the jubilation aboard *Erin* that evening was immense. For the second race on 7 October, the crowds that gathered on the Embankment threatened to bring all traffic to a standstill, so the police ordered that the Cineyachtograph be closed down. Across the Atlantic, fog closed in and the race was postponed. On that very day the Anglo–Boer War broke out, adding to the general gloom in the Lipton camp.

On 9 October the fog lifted and the wind got up. In a smooth sea with an eight-knot breeze blowing, *Columbia* passed the finishing line a mile ahead of *Shamrock*. In the next race, postponed till 17 October because of foul weather, an accident to *Shamrock*'s topmast ended in a walk-over victory for the defender. The last race was conducted three days later in a biting northerly wind of fifteen to twenty knots. This should have given *Shamrock* the advantage but *Columbia* proved to be the superior vessel in heavy winds as in light, and Lipton's first challenge for 'that mug' ended in defeat. Lipton accepted defeat gracefully and philosophically. 'I had enjoyed myself so much in America, and had met with such goodwill and kindness, that almost before the gun in that final race I had resolved to have another cut for the Cup.'[12]

Lipton also records that during the 1899 races, despatches from the course were accelerated by a young Italian named Guglielmo Marconi who had a transmitter aboard the steamship *Grand Duchess* and personally tapped out the messages from a reporter to the offices of the *New York Herald* and the *Evening Telegram*. In fact, Marconi had given Lipton a practical demonstration of wireless telegraphy the previous summer, sending and receiving messages on the lawn at Osidge, over a distance of 200 yards. In view of the enormous developments in radio over the ensuing years, this enterprise was all the more noteworthy.

The Boer War was going badly for the British and the American press did not disguise its jubilation at the mighty British Empire being humbled by a bunch of colonials. It was like a re-run of 1776 and anti-British sentiment was at its height. Lipton needed all his skills and experience in public relations to counter this generally unfavourable attitude. He entertained lavishly aboard *Erin*, and was received hospitably everywhere in return. The memory of the Dunraven episode was finally laid to rest when Lipton was elected to honorary membership of the New York Yacht Club – 'a very exceptional compliment, which I highly appreciated'. Over the ensuing years countless other honorary memberships and awards would come his way. It is no exaggeration to say that, from the dark days of October 1899 onwards, Lipton did more for Anglo–American relations than anyone else, before or since. He may not have retrieved the cup for Britain, but before he left America that autumn he had secured an exchange of cordial telegrams between President McKinley and the Prince of Wales. Henceforth, Sir Thomas Lipton, sportsman extraordinary, would stand very high in the regard of both men.

The Times summed up the general feeling in the aftermath of the races:

> The contest has presented one marked feature on which both nations may be equally congratulated, and that has been the complete absence of any of those elements of disagreement by which a former one was unfortunately characterised. The victory will leave no sting behind and will place no difficulty in the way of a renewal of the challenge.[13]

The American press hailed him as the best sportsman Britain had ever sent across. Having promised to challenge again as soon as the requisite time had passed, Lipton was given a grand send-off, being escorted to the quay by a procession headed by a brass band. A loving cup costing over $5,000 was subscribed for 'as a token of goodwill from the American people'. The cup was presented to him at a banquet in London the following spring, by Joseph Hodges Choate, the American ambassador. In his acceptance speech, Lipton said, 'I know that to lift the other cup I have got to take to Sandy Hook the best and fastest yacht the world has ever seen. But I am not discouraged, I hope I am not expected to be content with *this* cup.'

In the eyes of the general public, Lipton had assumed the status of a national hero, and, in all honesty, in view of the early reverses in the Boer War, heroes of any kind were in short supply. If the country could not find heroes on the field of battle, then the latest exploits of the self-made millionaire were just the thing to boost morale. His achievement was recognised by the Royal Ulster Yacht Club which made him their rear-commodore, and as such, he presided over the Bangor Regatta in July 1900. But while the press and the country at large were generally adulatory, in one narrow section of the community Lipton was still anathema. On 5 August 1900 a rumour surfaced in the *Daily Chronicle* which reported:

> I hear that Sir Thomas Lipton is a candidate for admission to the Royal Yacht Squadron on the personal nomination of the Prince of Wales. Balloting takes place tomorrow and it is not doubted that Sir Thomas will be unanimously elected.

The leading Dublin paper, *Freeman's Journal*, of the same date, however, was doubtful of the outcome:

> It is often found that despite such backing these candidates fare badly at the hands of old fogies who regard every new candidate as an intruder. The fact that the Prince of Wales will be absent from the meeting may also adversely affect the issue in what is one of the most narrowly exclusive clubs in the world.

What actually took place is not known for certain, but an inkling of the proceedings was given in the *Morning Leader* of 7 August which reported baldly that the Earl of Cawdor had withdrawn his own nomination because his boat was too small to qualify, while 'another candidate failed to be elected'. Just who this candidate was the paper did not feel at liberty to reveal, but a week later the *Birmingham Argus* had no such reticence, reporting 'Sir Thomas Lipton has been blackballed and the Prince of Wales is so wrathful that he has boycotted all social intercourse with the Royal Yacht Squadron'. Probably nearer the truth, however, was the report in the *Commercial Advertiser* which stated:

> Sir Thomas Lipton was never a formal candidate for admission to the Royal Yacht Squadron. He was given to understand that his nomination would be opposed and he withdrew. We gather that what stood against him was that he was a yacht owner but not a practical yachtsman.

This is a much more probable scenario. If Lipton were apprised of the fact that his admission was likely to be opposed, and a single black ball would have sufficed, then his uncanny instinct for self-publicity would have immediately induced him to withdraw his nomination. It is a matter to which he never alluded in his autobiography, and the fact that he remained unduly sensitive about the matter is borne out by the fact that he threatened to sue any publication which spread the story that he had actually been blackballed. Not for the first time, the Prince of Wales found himself up against a form of upper-class snobbery that he personally found repugnant, but which he was powerless to combat. And the members of the Royal Yacht Club, still smarting at the way Lipton had turned the tables on Lord Dunraven, resented any attempts by the Prince to influence the membership.

Lipton neatly countered the negative behaviour of the Royal Yacht Club by cementing his ties with the New York Yacht Club, to whom he presented the $1,000 Lipton Cup for competition between seventy-foot yachts at Sandy Hook. The cup was a handsome trophy, and photographs of it appeared in numerous American newspapers and magazines which duly noted that it was by far the most valuable of all the trophies in the NYYC. The first race for the Lipton Cup took place on 13 September 1900 and was won by Cornelius Vanderbilt's *Rainbow*. Ironically, there was an echo of the Dunraven affair when Herman B. Duryea of the runner-up *Yankee* accused Captain Robert 'Ben' Parker, the skipper of the *Rainbow*, of having surreptitiously increased the ballast. The Yacht Club promptly held an enquiry which upheld the charge, although it was at pains to exonerate Vanderbilt himself. Vanderbilt did the decent thing and surrendered the trophy, but Duryea refused the accept it under the circumstances. Subsequently Vanderbilt returned all the trophies which his yacht had won that season, but the scandal seriously tainted the image of this millionaires' sport.[14] Lipton's original *Shamrock* was purchased by Frederick Thompson, the proprietor of Luna Park, where the challenger was a major attraction for many years.

Negotiations between the Royal Ulster Yacht Club and the New York Yacht Club for the 1901 contest went through smoothly and speedily. For his second challenge, Lipton went to 'my old friend' George L. Watson who designed *Shamrock II*, built by Denny Brothers of Dumbarton. Edward VII, who had finally succeeded his mother in January, went down to the Solent with his mistress Mrs Keppel to witness the sea trials, and almost lost his throne before he had hardly begun to enjoy it. The King was on board *Shamrock II* for a race with the yawl *Sybarita* when, without any warning, a fresh breeze came up. The whole canvas filled suddenly, swayed and toppled and, with the mast itself, vanished over the side. King Edward was standing in the companionway, his favourite position when yachting, and missed death by inches when the heavy mast hurtled to the deck. Lipton, standing nearby, witnessed the aplomb of the monarch who kept his nerve and seemed much calmer than anyone else on board. He asked if anyone had been hurt and then, relieved to learn that everybody, including the first mast-hand, had escaped unhurt, he coolly lit a cigar and went on smoking calmly until the entire party could be conveyed back to *Erin*. There, sensing Lipton's distress that such a calamity should have taken place, the King put his mind at rest, saying that mishaps like this were beyond human control. An essentially kindly and considerate man, King Edward insisted on accompanying Lipton in the launch back to the stricken yacht to inspect the damage.

The broken mast had doubled under the vessel and, touching the bottom, was holding the yacht fast. Meanwhile a message had been sent over to Cowes for riveters to come to the yacht and cut away the mast. King Edward watched this delicate operation with the keenest interest. At dinner aboard *Erin* that evening, before boarding his special train back to London, the King was in his usual jovial mood. When someone remarked that it was curious that the boom of the yacht had remained intact, His Majesty wittily remarked, 'Yes, it does seem remarkable for if Sir Thomas's *boom* did not suffer how are we to account for the bringing down of his *sales*.' As puns go, it was a feeble effort, but everyone laughed heartily and the tension was broken. King Edward never stood in higher regard with any of his subjects than he did with Lipton as a result. Shortly afterwards Lipton was able to repay His Majesty by finding suitable employment for George Keppel – at his American headquarters in New York. This neatly removed the one person who might have come between the King and his mistress. The *Philadelphia Times* duly reported this as 'The handsome appointment which Sir Thomas Lipton has given to Mr George Keppel is very agreeable to the Prince [*sic*] who is much interested in the family'.

On the eve of his departure for the United States in August Lipton was given a banquet in his honour. The Misses Morrell presented him with a floral model of *Shamrock II* standing over six feet high.[15] In the contest of 1901, in which the defender was again the *Columbia* – even though newer and faster yachts were now available – *Shamrock II* was highly fancied. Then, a week before the first race, the yacht's mascot, an Irish red setter named Pat, ran away and was never seen again. Although Pat was promptly replaced by Jack, 'an educated rabbit', the loss of the original mascot was regarded as an ill omen. Two days later the first race took place, and in this contest the challenger was only narrowly beaten.

She was just a shade too slow, for over a series of hard-sailed races my boat lost to the American defender by an aggregate of only three minutes, twenty-seven seconds actual time! And this over a total distance of ninety miles – a bit more if the windward work is taken into account! What splendid racing we had that year; I really think that with the slightest shade of luck I might have pulled off a victory. In the last of the series the *Shamrock* crossed the line two seconds ahead of the *Columbia*, but lost because of the time allowance we had to give her. That was a sporting finish, if ever there was one.[16]

The Clyde-built yacht was generally acknowledged to be the best and swiftest challenger so far, but *Columbia* and her redoubtable skipper Charlie Barr were a difficult combination to beat. On the whole, the course was kept clear of excursion boats and the only incident occurred on the day after the first race when the *Erin* collided with the revenue cutter *Gresham*, flagship of the patrol fleet. In the collision Alice Keppel and her friend Mrs Jamieson were slightly injured.[17] The 1901 challenge ended on a more tragic note, however, when Stuart Fitz-James, Duke of Alva and Berwick, one of the most illustrious of Spanish grandees, nephew of the Empress Eugénie and the son of that Countess Montijo who had so enjoyed Lipton's ham many years earlier, caught a chill on the *Erin*. Confined to his bedroom at the Holland House, he developed pneumonia and died on 15 October. He was five times a duke, thirteen times a marquis, fourteen times a count, a Knight of the Golden Fleece and more blue-blooded than many of Europe's crowned heads, but he was about the same age as Lipton and a close friendship had developed between them in the past two years.[18] Shortly before Lipton and his guests returned to Britain, George Keppel contracted typhoid and there were touching scenes as his wife Alice dutifully attended his bedside. George soon recovered and his wife returned to England and her royal lover.

Shortly before leaving America, Lipton presented the Columbia Yacht Club of Chicago with a Lipton Trophy for competition on the Great Lakes. This massive cup, valued at $4,000, was the most costly trophy in America at the time. Interviewed by the press on the eve of his departure from New York, Lipton was in buoyant mood and said that the shamrock, to be perfect, needed three leaves. He would be back with another challenge. The supreme egotism which had brought him to the pinnacle of success in business flaired up when he told reporters: 'The next *Shamrock* will not be the product of a combine or a committee or the mixture of a dozen different ideas. She'll be mine, every spar of her.' He also let slip casually that he was planning to open a series of fruit canneries in Georgia and had an option to purchase 100,000 acres of peach plantations, which the American press generally conceded would be 'good for the South'.[19]

When he returned to Osidge in November Lipton's carriage was halted at Palmer's Green and the horses taken from the shafts. Flags were waving and a band was playing. A torchlight procession was headed with a model of the *Shamrock*. In the middle of the month Lord Tweedsmouth presided over a banquet at the Hotel Cecil in his honour, numbering 400 guests. Lord Rosebery was telling the press that the country needed a business cabinet made up of men like Lipton and Carnegie. When Charles Schwab, Andrew Carnegie's most trusted lieutenant, visited England early in February 1902 it was Lipton who arranged his audience at Marlborough House. In America this historic occasion was greeted by the headline 'Tea King Introduces Steel King to The King'.[20] Two weeks later Lipton was struck down by influenza and for several days he was seriously ill, but eventually his tremendous stamina pulled him through. Needless to say, the press on both sides of the Atlantic issued daily bulletins on the state of his health.

The question of Lipton's election to the Royal Yacht Club flared up again in 1902. Significantly, the British press was silent on the matter, but the American newspapers were not so reticent. The *New York Herald*, which in 1900 had reported the Prince of Wales as saying: 'It is enough for me to put someone up to have him blackballed', now elaborated this theme in an article which viewed Lipton's chances of election as remote as ever:

> Should the King, exercising his royal prerogative, force the matter to an issue, many members of the squadron contemplate withdrawing and forming another organization. Already there is talk of building another clubhouse; but, in view of the deep-rooted opposition of such distinguished subjects, it is not likely the King will push matters further.[21]

There was also a persistent rumour that year that Lipton was to be raised to the peerage in the forthcoming Coronation Honours List. A variant of this, aired in some of the American newspapers, was that Lipton's peerage was conditional on him bringing back the cup. Lipton himself denied these rumours, saying that even if he were offered a peerage he would refuse it. 'I have no desire to get so far away from my friends and am satisfied to remain as I am,' he told the *Philadelphia Inquirier*. The fact that Lord Dunraven, the bogeyman of 1895, was a peer of the realm, had probably not gone down too well in such an egalitarian country as the United States, and Lipton was shrewd enough to realise that a peerage would have created a barrier. His stance neatly covered up the fact that King Edward himself had nominated his friend for a barony, but the Prime Minister, the Marquess of Salisbury, refused to endorse the nomination and was actually quoted in the American press as deploring the fact that 'the hereditary peerage has been sufficiently debauched of late'.[22] True to his principles, Salisbury himself turned down the offer of a dukedom on the grounds that his ancient marquessate was sufficient honour. In the end Salisbury conceded the King's grocer friend a baronetcy – the lowest rank of hereditary title.

Instead, Lipton concentrated on establishing his name in the yachting world. He instituted the Lipton Cup, a trophy for American off-shore yachts who were to be encouraged to race under proper seagoing conditions. In July 1902 the first race for the trophy was run, but was very poorly handled. *La Rita* won the cup but *Arab IV* protested the result. In fact these were the only two yachts which actually crossed the starting line. Of far greater importance was Lipton's third attempt on the coveted America's Cup. Doubtless he was amused when a Broadway musical was launched under the title of *The Defender* in which the challenger was thinly disguised under the name of Sir Thomas Ceylon Teaton. At least that was an improvement on Sir Tea Jam Lipton which had been taken up by the English tabloids. His latest challenge went to the New York Yacht Club with a letter couched in rather high-falutin language:

> In thus desiring an opportunity of making a third attempt to obtain possession of the America's Cup, I hope I may not be deemed importunate or unduly covetous of the precious trophy so long and so securely held in trust by NYYC.[23]

No one had ever challenged a third time, and that was a good news story in its own right. Lipton clearly meant business, and to face this threat the New York Yacht Club mounted an impressive defence. Three of America's leading tycoons – Cornelius Vanderbilt, William Rockefeller and Harry Elkins Widener – formed a syndicate and commissioned Nathaniel Herreshoff (builder of *Defender* and *Columbia*) to design and construct an extremely flat boat with a shallow body and a very deep keel, with over 16,000 square feet of sail, more than 2,000 more than

Shamrock III. The goalposts were moved accordingly, and a new clause was inserted in the regulations about not racing when the weather was rough:

> if in the opinion of the regatta committee the weather shall at the time appointed for any race be or threaten to be of such a character as not to afford a reasonable opportunity of fairly testing the speed of the two vessels . . . unless either contestant insists.

This clause was to lead to prolonged debate later on and delay an effective challenge for many years.

In the spring of 1903 *Shamrock III*, built by Denny Brothers as before, but to a new design by William Fife, underwent her sea trials. With Robert Wringe of Southampton at the helm, one of the most experienced and skilled professional yachtsmen of the period, hopes ran high that, at last, Britain would retrieve the cup. Again tragedy struck, which would afterwards be regarded as an ill omen. On 17 April 1903, as *Shamrock III* was entering Weymouth Harbour, a sudden squall sprang up with terrifying force and dismasted her. Spars and canvas were swept away. Lipton himself was knocked down a hatchway, injuring his hand and smashing his binoculars, but three deck hands were more seriously injured while the steward, William Collier, was swept overboard and drowned.[24]

On 11 June the great yacht-builder George L. Watson married Marie Lovibond at St John's, Putney. It was a society wedding, and among the guests were the Earl of Dunraven and Sir Thomas Lipton. An opportunity to get the two challengers side by side for a photo-call was apparently missed. On the eve of his departure a few days later Lipton received a telegram from 'Edward R.I.' at Windsor: 'As you are just about to leave for America, let me wish you a prosperous journey and all possible good luck for the great race in August.' *Punch* carried a full-page cartoon of Lipton as a medieval sea-wolf riding the waves, with tiny ships bearing shamrock sails attached to his feet. The caption read 'Last of the VI-KINGS and first of the TEA-KINGS'. The same humorous magazine ran a column for several weeks after Lipton got his baronetcy under the title of 'Bart's Progress: Lipton day by day'. The following excerpts parodied the breathless reportage of Lipton's diverse activities during his whirlwind trips to America:

> July 2: Sir Thomas Lipton wins walking race from Wall Street to Washington. Dines and sleeps at the White House, which he paints red.

> July 4: A full day, Sir Thomas Lipton adjudicates as umpire in the walking race of waitresses in the American tea-table company. In the afternoon he kicks-off in a baseball match and in the evening saves a valuable life.
>
> July 19: Sir Thomas Lipton visits Poloniville, Pa., and is kissed at the station by 3,000 ladies, each of whom remarks, 'This is a great day for Poloniville.' *Shamrock III* resumes a yellow tinge of green.
>
> July 20: Sir Thomas Lipton at Harvard. Is made honorary D.C.L. (Disappointed Cup Lifter). Returns thanks in an affecting speech and presents the students with a portrait of himself in Oleomargarine.[25]

Lipton's arrival in America that summer was attended with even greater hype than ever. *Punch* came close to being out-punched by the hectic round of dinners, banquets, speeches and public appearances which punctuated what was still, essentially, a hard-working business trip. In one day alone Lipton judged a beauty contest, attended the Naval Review at Oyster Bay and dined with President Theodore Roosevelt along with William Fife and B.A.C. Smith, vice-commodore of the New York Yacht Club. Charles Schwab and Henry Corbin, Adjutant-General of the Army, staged a banquet in his honour at the Waldorf-Astoria, and then Corbin arranged for Lipton to travel in the presidential railcar to West Point where he inspected the Military Academy and reviewed a parade of the cadets. The following day Lipton was in Washington, dining with Teddy Roosevelt at the White House. Later, he was the President's special guest aboard the yacht *Mayflower* at the grand review of the United States Navy at Oyster Bay. Unfortunately two battleships bumped into each other; no one was hurt, but it was an embarrassing spectacle.

On 28 June he was at Coney Island where he 'looped the loop and shot the chute', and on 4 July, the great national holiday, he witnessed the great firework display put on at Sea Gate by the Atlantic Yacht Club, including a spectacular portrait of himself in firecrackers. He was photographed alongside J. Pierpont Morgan under a banner headline in the *New York World* on 30 June, and quoted as saying in his rich Scottish burr, 'I'm verra fond of Americans!' Everywhere he went, Lipton was fêted, invariably greeted by bevies of beauties who pressed bouquets on him and stole kisses. Lipton took it all in good part, praising the beauty of American womanhood, but usually careful to stick to generalities. The slightest indiscretion, or hint of partiality, was immediately pounced on by the press. The gift of a gold shamrock brooch to Edna Hunter ensured the Chicago actress front-page billing, while the kiss bestowed publicly on Gertrude Quinlan was tantamount to proclaiming the banns of marriage. He was forced to judge whether chorus girls Rose Earle or Miriam Falconer was the more beautiful, or which of the three Broadway 'broilers', Emilie Wellington, Katherine Donohue and Myrtle King, took his fancy. The cartoon in the *Boston Traveller* on 22 July, showing a line-up of beautiful girls waiting their turn to be kissed, was captioned 'Beware Sir Tommy'. On 26 July he was entertained by the burlesque revue *Lifting the Cup* at the Crystal Gardens, the hero being a character named Sir Thomas Liftit. After seeing the musical *The Wizard of Oz* on 15 August he went back-stage where the showgirls lined up to smother him with kisses. More seriously, the gossip-columnist Cholly Knickerbocker, in the *New York Herald* of 26 August, claimed that Lipton was about to announce his engagement to socialite Alice Revell – a claim which was denied by the girl's brother Alexander the following day. Lipton was more determinedly lionised than ever, and society hostesses fought each other for the privilege of having Sir Thomas at their dinner parties. On a fleeting visit to St Louis, his name was romantically linked with two society belles, Mozelle Price and Louise Chappell, more or less simultaneously.

There was also the curious episode of the little old lady, dressed in old-fashioned black bombazine, who was temporarily detained at Ellis Island by the immigration authorities. Catherine Murphy, a widow who kept a haberdashery shop in Anderston, Glasgow, had taken a sudden notion to visit New York and look up the sons she had not seen for over ten years. On impulse she shut up shop, purchased a cabin ticket on the *Columbia* at the Broomielaw and landed in New York a week later. At Ellis Island she said she only intended a brief visit to her sons Peter and Thomas, but all she knew about them was that Thomas worked as a printer on a newspaper. The police were alerted and a couple of days later tracked down Thomas Murphy, a compositor with the *New York World*. After an emotional reunion with her son, and discovering that she was now a grandmother six times over, Mrs Murphy gave the *World* reporter an interview in which she claimed to have known Tommy Lipton 'as a barefoot laddie running about the village [of Anderston]' when she was a girl, and that her father, a Mr Lindsay, had lived next door to the Lipton's shop in Stobcross Street where she vividly remembered Tommy's mother serving behind the counter. 'I don't know if he remembers little Kittie Lindsay,' she added archly, oblivious to the fact that there must have been at least a dozen years between their ages. What Lipton made of this preposterous tale is not known, but he seems to have played along with it, for he arranged for the sixty-eight-year-old widow and her sons to view one of the races.

Then there was the dramatic incident at 5.10 p. m. on 2 July when a sudden squall arose and drove the steam yacht *Giralda* on to the cat-boat *Allita*. The yacht's bowsprit skewered the smaller vessel's mainsail and dismasted her. The *Allita* capsized, pitching its complement of two men and three women into the angry waves. Fortunately, the *Erin* was nearby and Lipton, with immense presence of mind, immediately ordered the lowering of the yacht's two launches. Without a thought for his own safety, he leapt into one and led the rescue. Tales of Lipton's heroism were splashed all over the nation's front pages, with interviews by Mrs Mandelick and Miss McClenahan breathlessly describing how the gallant baronet had saved their lives. The *Illustrated Mail* of 11 July went further and included an artist's reconstruction of the scene. His gallantry was formally recognised when he was made Honorary Deputy Commissioner of the New York Police Department and given his gold badge 'which entitled him to an immediate salute from all 10,000 blue-coats'. He was also appointed Honorary Fire Chief and delighted the pressmen by sliding down the brass fire-pole with great panache. That lucky encounter with the *Allita* ensured that, when the races began, Lipton was already cast in the role of the heroic underdog.

By contrast, the series of races which took place between 22 August and 3 September were virtually no contest. Although designed specifically for sheltered coastal waters, the defender *Reliance* was actually a bigger vessel with a tonnage of 108.41 compared with 104.37 for the challenger. *Reliance* was bigger, much more powerful under full sail and, in the hands of a crack crew, easily led from the start in the first two races. After time allowances, she won by over seven minutes on 22 August, but much more narrowly, by a minute and ten seconds, three days later. Even if *Shamrock* had won the third race, it would not have altered the outcome; but on that fateful day *Shamrock* did not even finish the course. Interviewed by the *New York Herald* after the last race, Lipton tried manfully to conceal his chagrin, but the plain fact was that his yacht was no match for the defender.

> No one has any idea of how I have worried and fretted over this race. No man was more confident of winning anything than I was when I came over. I don't believe in gambling, but I would have

been willing to bet the *Erin* that I would win. It is the greatest disappointment of my life.

What can I do? I have tried my best. I have spent months of sleepless nights worrying over the challenger. They tell me that I have a beautiful boat. I don't want a beautiful boat. What I want is a boat to lift the cup – a *Reliance*. Give me a homely boat, the homeliest boat that was ever designed, if she is like *Reliance*.[26]

This was to be the only chink in his armour, and Lipton's unfailing bonhomie and ready wit endeared him to the American public more than ever. Significantly, the winner of the series hardly rated a mention in the American press, but Lipton was everywhere. When a lady tried to console him over his defeat, earnestly suggesting that his opponents had put something in the water to defeat him, his eyes twinkled and he replied with mock seriousness: 'I knew it all the time, madam! What they put in the water was the cup's defender!'[27] *Shamrock III* was subsequently sold to a mercantile company and ended her days, under the name of *Dorothy W*, cruising out of Brunswick, Georgia, to the West Indies.

Back home, Lipton's popularity soared to an unprecedented height. Articles, interviews, cartoons and photographs of the gallant challenger filled the newspapers and magazines. Editorials gravely suggested that Lipton should be appointed British ambassador to Washington; the Boer War was at an end but magnanimity towards the defeated Boers had not yet softened American attitudes towards England. American tourists, on the other hand, announced that there were only two Londoners they wished to see – King Edward and Sir Thomas. Even *Town Topics* which had attacked Lipton's '*opéra bouffe* style of cup racing' and had dismissed him for thinking that he was either a sportsman and philanthropist or the finest actor that ever lived, was now forced to reappraise him:

You may talk about Lipton as you will; you may deride his penchant for bussing soubrettes square on their mouths – especially you of mature years who have outgrown such luxurious habits – but no matter what you may accuse our cup challenger of, you cannot say that he is anything but the most graceful loser we ever saw. He takes his defeat so pleasantly and gracefully that none can help applauding, and while congratulating him on his successful advertising, we can also compliment him on his manhood and his sportsmanship.[28]

And the writer was generous enough to apologise effusively for 'my flippant envious talk about his girl conquests and take off my hat to him as a true sportsman'.

Lipton did not mind losing, so long as the defeat was of hairbreadth proportions; but the poor showing of *Shamrock III* against *Reliance* forced him to take a long hard look at the rules governing the race. Herreshoff had developed a succession of fast racers noted for their long, flat bodies and deep, thin keels, built for only one purpose – defending the cup. Lipton, to be sure, had bent the rules by having his yachts towed across the Atlantic, but the foul weather clause was now wholly opposed to the spirit of the original challenge. Against a freak machine that was not really seaworthy, the Lipton challengers stood no chance.

The New York Yacht Club did eventually concede the point, and thereafter displacement, as well as length and sail area, were taken into account in assessing the time allowances. Nevertheless ten years would pass before Lipton and the New York Yacht Club could effect a practical compromise that would pave the way to a fourth challenge. In the meantime, in 1907, he built a yacht in the twenty-three-metre class purely for racing in British coastal waters. He named her *Shamrock*. 'Just *Shamrock*,' he emphasised. 'I'm keeping number IV for Sandy Hook.' This vessel was designed by William Fife and built to the highest specifications, using the finest materials and technology then available. In the season of 1908 she swept the board, taking every major trophy in the British Isles. In thirty-five races she won thirty-one flags, and a score of them were first prizes. Lipton's real love of yachting, as opposed to his quest for the cup, dates from that year. Any reservations by the Royal Yacht Club on the specious grounds that Lipton was not a true yachtsman were swept away, but just when (in 1914) that august body was showing signs of relenting, Lipton was engulfed in a scandal which threatened to ruin him. Though he managed to weather that storm it undoubtedly barred his nomination and many more years were to elapse before the Royal Yacht Club admitted him to membership.

As well as the Lipton Cup for ocean-going yachts, instituted in 1902, Lipton instituted a trophy the following year for a race between Mississippi steamboats. Continuing his policy of presenting Lipton Cups for all manner of races, he subsequently established the Lipton Challenge Cup for competition by the rowing clubs of Chile under the auspices of the Valparaiso Regatta Association; the Lipton Cup for American and Canadian yachts on the Pacific coast, under the auspices of the Royal

Vancouver Yacht Club; the Lipton Cup for South African yachts under the Royal Cape Yacht Club; the Lipton Cups in Tasmania and Victoria (with purses of fifty guineas) to encourage yachting in Australia; the Viking Challenge Trophy to encourage Viking-class motor-cruisers under the auspices of the New York Athletic Club; the Lipton Cup for the Grand Lakes Boat Race held in Colorado at an altitude of 9,000 feet and arguably the world's highest yacht race; the Lipton Cup under the auspices of the Winnipeg Rowing Club for annual competition between the rowing clubs of Canada's western provinces, and the Lipton Trophy organised by the Pacific Interclub Yachting Association of San Francisco. This was partly in response to Tom Dewar who gave many cups for all sorts of sports from soccer to billiards, and partly to swamp the boating the world with the Lipton name and outflank the Royal Yacht Club whose trophies were not so large, so prestigious, nor so artistically fashioned as the Lipton prizes.

Undoubtedly, however, Lipton's most ambitious trophy was to have been the $5,000 cup which he offered jointly to the Atlantic Yacht Club, to be held by its commodore, Robert E. Tod, for a race between Sandy Hook and the Needles off the Isle of Wight. The announcement was made on 8 October and widely acclaimed in the American press as 'a cup for *real* yachts'. That evening Lipton was the guest of George Wilson and a party from the Honourable Artillery Company who were then touring America. The following day he boarded the *Cedric* for England. The newspapers on both sides of the Atlantic hinted that the ocean yacht race, to be held in the summer of 1904, was already attracting interest at the highest levels, with both King Edward and the Kaiser planning to take part.

In fact, Kaiser Wilhelm had already come up with the idea of offering a cup for such a race, and had asked his ambassador in Washington to sound out the New York Yacht Club about the feasibility of such a project. Wilhelm was exceedingly chagrined when he learned that his uncle's grocer friend had forestalled him. There was an exchange of correspondence between the Kaiser and Lipton and both letters were reproduced in full in the New York *American* on 30 October. Lipton's letter to the Kaiser was a masterpiece of diplomacy as he graciously backed down. The Kaiser's Cup was to be open to all craft, with no time allowances. On 28 November, however, the Kaiser withdrew his offer 'owing to his health', and begged that the race for his cup be postponed till 1905. The real reason for the Kaiser's *volte face*, however, was the unseemly bickering which had surfaced between the New York and Atlantic Yacht Clubs whom the Kaiser had wished to organise the race jointly. As the NYYC would not share with anyone, there was an awkward impasse which Wilhelm only resolved by withdrawing altogether. An approach was then made to Lipton, but he responded that there was insufficient time now to consider an ocean race in 1904, and the matter was then shelved. Shrewdly, he judged that, had he stepped into the breach, he would have ruffled the Imperial German feathers. As it was, his tactful handling of a ticklish situation only enhanced his standing with the Kaiser who began to regard his uncle's crony with fresh admiration.

The race for the Kaiser's Cup was eventually held in May 1905 and easily won by the American yacht *Atlantic* skippered by the redoubtable Charlie Barr. On his triumphant arrival in London, Barr was entertained to lunch by Lipton and Dewar. Barr might be a formidable opponent, undoubtedly the most brilliant yachtsman of his generation, but the two Toms took some comfort from the knowledge that Barr had been born at Gourock and raised on the Clyde. His brother John had skippered the *Thistle* when the Royal Clyde Yacht Club had challenged for the America's Cup, and Charlie had served as mate on that occasion. Later Charlie had become a naturalised American and skippered the defenders against the first three *Shamrocks*. He was also to die in Britain when on 25 January 1911 he suffered a heart attack at the age of forty-six while in Southampton. Lipton was wintering in the south of France at the time and could not attend the funeral, but he sent the crew of *Erin* and they acted as pall-bearers and guard of honour, making a most impressive turn-out.

The compromise with the New York Yacht Club was not finalised until May 1913 when it agreed to accept the terms for a race using a seventy-five-foot boat under the universal rules. As a result, the next race was scheduled to take place at Sandy Hook in September 1914. *Shamrock IV* would have to sail the Atlantic unaided but on arrival in America she would be entirely dismantled, the hull stripped and the spars and rigging adjusted for inshore racing. Under normal circumstances the construction of the new challenger would have grabbed the headlines. Instead *Shamrock IV* was relegated to the sports pages while the principal news pages exposed the great Army Canteen scandal, discussed in the next chapter. This tragic episode ended in the disgrace and imprisonment of a senior army officer. His sentence to six months' imprisonment came barely 48 hours after the launch of the yacht by Lady Shaftesbury.

The attendant publicity, implicating Lipton, robbed him of the pleasure that should have attended the launch and sea trials of his new yacht. The trial at the Central Criminal Court was nearing its climax when the launch took place. Determined to put a brave face on things, Lipton stage-managed the event with his usual panache. A hundred reporters and photographers travelled in an especially decorated shamrock train from London to Portsmouth while a party of 500 lunched in the boat-shed, which had been transformed for the occasion. The launch had been fixed deliberately to coincide with the Queen's Birthday so the warships in Portsmouth Harbour were dressed overall when *Shamrock IV* slid gracefully into the water as the last shots of the royal salute from the guns of Nelson's flagship *Victory* died away. Lipton tried to be as bright and nonchalant as ever, but he was conscious that, at that very moment, Mr Justice Darling was summing up at the Old Bailey.

The outbreak of the First World War in August effectively erased the taint left by the canteen scandal, but it put an end to Lipton's challenge for the America's Cup as well as his plans to race at San Francisco in 1915 during the Panama–Pacific Exposition. *Shamrock IV* was actually halfway across the ocean when war broke out and was immediately diverted to sanctuary in Bermuda, before being towed to New York in October 'for the duration' and laid up at a South Brooklyn boatyard. A further six years would pass before Lipton again raced for the cup.

9. THE GOLDEN YEARS
1900–14

The optimist proclaims that we live in the best of all possible
worlds, and the pessimist fears this is true.
James Branch Cabell, *The Silver Stallion*

For Lipton, the twentieth century got off to a flying start.
Supplying the Klondike gold rush and then the men on active
service in the Spanish–American War focused his attention once
more on pork, the main source of protein for miners and troops
alike. The outbreak of the Anglo–Boer War in 1899, soon to
draw in contingents from every part of the Empire as well as the
mother country, provided a tremendous challenge to Lipton and
again he rose nobly to the occasion. The war was at its height
when the Boxer Rebellion erupted in China and rapidly sucked
in troops of twelve nations. For the first time since the War of
Independence, British and American troops fought on the same
side. Other men might profit from the sale of arms and
ammunition, but Lipton made a killing in the catering line. In
order to supply the dramatic increase in demand, Lipton, by a
series of clandestine manoeuvres, succeeded in cornering the
pork market, beating Armour and Cudahy at their own game. By
15 October 1900 the price of pork had risen from eleven dollars
to seventeen dollars a barrel, and by the end of the month it
peaked at twenty dollars, although it subsequently dropped back
slightly. Only 35,000 barrels had been produced that year, and
Lipton owned every one of them. Unfortunately, his competitors
had contracted to supply almost twice as many. And among the
customers to whom they were bound by contract, at a price of
eleven dollars a barrel, was none other than Lipton himself. Now
Phil Armour found himself in the ridiculous situation of having
to buy pork from Lipton at eighteen dollars a barrel – in order to
supply Lipton at eleven dollars a barrel. Nowadays such tactics
would be heartily condemned, but back in 1900 the press on
both sides of the Atlantic saw the funny side of the situation.
Inevitably Lipton's cornering of the pork market was described in
nautical terms. After all, this beat yacht-racing any day.

As usual, Lipton at first denied that he had cornered the market, claiming volubly that he detested such business. Then he wavered and conceded that, yes, he had by the merest good fortune acquired a considerable holding in pork, but this was merely to supply his burgeoning chain of stores as well as fulfil his army contracts. Then he divulged to reporters that he planned to release substantial stocks of pork, but only in the southern United States because he did not consider it right that negroes should have to pay eight cents a pound for spare ribs. Finally, when he did come clean, he issued a statement to the press to allay the public's fears:

> I have no intention of raising prices to an exorbitant degree. I am perfectly satisfied to make simply a fair profit out of all my dealings and will do everything possible to avoid causing serious trouble to those who sold short. I let some go the other day to save a few threatened failures.[1]

Oddly enough, the press was silent on the subject of rumoured bankruptcies in the pork business, but the papers were far too polite to question this statement. Lipton literally had his competitors over a barrel, and could have driven the price of pork up to $100 if he had a mind to do so; but that would have hit the consumer in the long run, and Lipton always had the customers' interests at heart. When the story was at its height, Lipton let it be known that he had no wish to squeeze anybody out or force up the price of pork. He made a number of private settlements with his competitors 'so that while bearish speculators received some painful injuries, the wounds were not mortal'. Such headlines as 'Sir Thomas is Not a Hog' (in the *Toledo Times*) and 'Gallantry to his Foes' (in the *Philadelphia Record*) reflect the favourable reaction of the American press when Lipton magnanimously allowed his competitors to purchase pork from him at seventeen dollars a barrel. The *New York World* put it bluntly: 'You don't roar when we beat your sailboat, so we won't chew the rag when you get even in a commercial way.' In fact, Lipton cleared over $350,000 on those 'private settlements', which went a long way towards paying for *Shamrock II* – a connection made humorously by the *Cincinnati Post* of 15 October which showed Lipton in yachting cap at the helm of a pig-shaped boat, with the caption: 'One good corner to pay for another'. The Chicago meat-packers might howl with rage and anguish at the way this interloper had beaten them at their own game, but they got precious little sympathy from the press. In England, the *Pall Mall Gazette* gloated over them:

> Pork butchers in Chicago are cynical creatures. They will scowl and
> smile the smile of contempt, but they will not admire. There must
> be something in the trade that warrants this. Yet those who deal so
> largely in crackling ought to be merry and wise and not lean and
> envious.[2]

One of the secrets of Lipton's success was his infallible sense of
timing. Having got the maximum publicity out of the pork coup
he then judged that the time was right to extricate himself from
the meat-packing industry. After all, the Johnstone Packing
Company had been established in the first instance in
anticipation of developing a nationwide chain of grocery stores
in North America. This ambition was unrealised and now
seemed more remote than ever. It made good sense to rationalise
his operations and get out while he was on top. Soon afterwards
he sold out to Ogden Armour (who had succeeded his late father)
for $300,000 and turned his back on the pork business for good.

Having extricated himself so triumphantly from the pork
business, Lipton engaged in a hectic social round before leaving
the United States. When the Texas port of Galveston was
devastated in September by a hurricane that claimed over 5,000
lives, Lipton had been the first to send $1,000 to the relief fund.
The *New York Sun* of 12 September even managed to reproduce
Lipton's telegram on its front page. Further well-publicised
support for the relief fund no doubt helped to focus attention on
the plight of the hurricane-homeless, but it certainly did no harm
to Lipton's reputation for genial and prompt generosity. On 9
December he was elected an honorary member of the Harvard
Anti-Fussing Association. A fusser was Harvard slang for a
fellow who frequented the company of women, so the
Association was actually an all-male club which openly professed
its disdain of the female sex. Cecil Rhodes was elected an
honorary member at the same time as Lipton.[3] Lipton, of course,
could be perfectly charming to ladies, one of whom was a
reporter from the *Home Journal* who visited him at Osidge
shortly after his return and waxed lyrical about the décor. In
particular, she was charmed by the portraits in oils of Lipton's
parents which flanked the fireplace in the dining-room – exact
replicas of the paintings which adorned the walls of Lipton's City
office.[4] A few months previously another lady reporter had
written effusively of Lipton's famous tree houses. There were two
of them in neighbouring oaks at Osidge, approached by spiral

iron staircases (one for servants, the other for Lipton and his closest friends). The article was accompanied by a photograph of Lipton and his associate John Westwood, with two of the Sinhalese houseboys.[5]

There were numerous stories, or variants of the same story, concerning Sir Thomas's latest protégé. While cruising in the Mediterranean in the spring of 1900 Lipton had picked up a Cretan boy whose parents had been murdered in a recent insurrection. Stellio Arghiri was variously described as eleven or fourteen, although the latter seems more probable from the rather solemn photographs of the lad, in an Eton collar, which appeared in *The Sphere* on 1 September that year. The boy was handsome, with all the attributes of a young Greek god, and was regarded as something of a prodigy. Much was made of the fact that he spoke Russian, French, Italian and a little Armenian as well as his native Greek, although subsequent newspaper reports and readers' letters pointed out that such polyglots were not uncommon in the Levant. Lipton brought him back to England, installed him at Osidge and enrolled him at Enfield Grammar School where his fluency in English was closely monitored by the daily press. He was last mentioned as Lipton's companion on the Mediterranean cruise of August 1900, but thereafter he disappears from the scene.[6]

Soon after Lipton's return to England in December 1900, Queen Victoria died and was succeeded by her portly eldest son Bertie who took the regnal title of Edward VII. The Edwardian era is seen in retrospect as a golden age. The Boxer Rebellion had been crushed and the Boer War was virtually at an end, apart from a few mopping-up operations. King Edward, the most cosmopolitan of Britain's monarchs, was adept at mending diplomatic fences at the highest levels and appropriately he came to be known as Edward the Peacemaker. He played a prominent role in engineering the *Entente Cordiale* with France and Russia as a counter to the Triple Alliance of Germany, Austria and Italy. At the same time he helped improve relations between Britain and Japan and even succeeded in detaching Italy from the Central Powers. And on a personal level he repaired the breach in Anglo–American relations. In this last respect he relied heavily on Sir Thomas Lipton, the one man who moved so easily between Britain and the United States and was so perfectly at home in both, despite the considerable cultural and social differences between these countries. The friendship between the King and the grocery magnate ripened during this decade. They shared an interest in yachting – indeed, there is ample evidence to suggest that the King's interest in this rich man's sport was deepened and took on a new meaning as a result of his friend's exploits at home and abroad. Remarkably, despite the growing estrangement between the King and the Queen, Lipton succeeded on remaining in excellent terms with them both. More and more of his time was devoted to making a success of the Alexandra Trust, even though the original scheme to have a nationwide chain of cheap restaurants was soon abandoned in favour of a much more modest, though eminently practicable, scheme.

In this halcyon age Lipton continued his practice of spending some months each year in America, but he also found the time to travel more extensively and more frequently in Europe. He entertained most of the crowned heads of Europe aboard his steam yacht, *Erin,* and was entertained – and honoured – by them in return. Soon after ascending the throne, King Edward said to him, 'Lipton, I think I shall give you an order shortly.'

'This is exceedingly kind of Your Majesty,' replied the grocer with a twinkle in his eye. 'It will do me a lot of good in business. I shall have a price list sent to Your Majesty at once!'

Of course, both of them knew that it was not an order for tea that was being hinted at. A short time afterwards the King said, 'Here is a surprise package for you, Lipton. Please do not open it until you return home.' When Lipton got back to Osidge that night and opened the box he found the insignia of a Knight Commander of the Victorian Order.

That, at least, is his version of the story, but the truth may have been more prosaic, for he was gazetted KCVO on 8 March 1901 in the new monarch's Accession Honours List.

When the memorial fund for Queen Victoria was launched later that month, Lipton was prompt to subscribe £1,000. His generous donation was only surpassed by the £2,000 given by Lord Rothschild and the 1,000 guineas donated by the King himself. The following month Lipton was reported widely as offering a prize of fifty pounds for the best essay in Irish Gaelic, in a competition organised by the Irish Literary Society of London.

Mention has already been made of the sports facilities at White Hart Lane for the Lipton employees and of the Lipton football team which had existed in Glasgow for many years. Now, however, Lipton began to develop a wider interest in football. If he never went down the road of many later millionaires by acquiring one of the well-known professional teams, he took a keen interest in the game none the less. In April 1901 he could be seen in the stand at Crystal Palace, cheering the Scots on to a 2–2 draw with England. The following year the international was played at Ibrox Park, Glasgow, but part of the terracing collapsed killing twenty-two spectators. Lipton was not present on that tragic occasion but responded swiftly with a large cheque for the relief of the widows and orphans. The following week he attended the Cup Final between Sheffield United and Southampton. A cry went up that Tommy Lipton was in the stand, so the crowds cheered and cried 'Good old *Shamrock*!'. In December 1905 he presented the Lipton Cup to be competed for in matches between Argentina and Uruguay. Soccer had only been introduced to the republics bordering the River Plate a year or two previously. The Lipton Cup, however, stimulated the rivalry between the two and undoubtedly played a part in the emergence of tiny Uruguay as the leading soccer country in the interwar period – the national team taking the gold medal at the 1924 and 1928 Olympic Games, before going on to win the first ever FIFA World Cup in 1930. What is not generally known, however, is that Lipton had instigated his own World Cup twenty years earlier.

Following his investiture as a Knight Commander of the Order of the Crown of Italy in 1904, Lipton decided to repay the honour by instituting a handsome silver trophy for a world football tournament which, after considerable bureaucratic delays, was eventually staged at Turin in 1910. Lipton intended that teams of national status should compete but, as a result of indifference and red-tape in English football circles, the honour of representing Great Britain fell to a local team of coal miners from West Auckland, County Durham, struggling in the Northern Amateur League. Against all the odds, WA (as they were known locally) competed against professionals from Germany, Switzerland and Italy. Undaunted by the paucity of club funds, the players sold their personal belongings to finance the trip and sacrificed their pit wages. At Turin they were greeted by brass bands and banners welcoming the arrival of Woolwich Arsenal; no one had heard of WA! Incredibly, WA triumphed 3–1 against Stuttgart in the first round and in the final defeated Juventus 2–0 to become the first holders of the Lipton World Cup. The following year they journeyed again to Turin where they beat Red Star of Switzerland 2–0 in the first round and again in the final trounced the mighty Juventus 6–0. Under the terms of the championship, the World Cup was now theirs in perpetuity, but, unable to pay their fares home, the team had to pawn the trophy to their landlady who lent them forty pounds to get home. The Cup remained in Turin until 1960 when a village appeal redeemed the pledge and brought the trophy back to its rightful place in West Auckland.[7]

As a baronet, Sir Thomas Lipton attended the Coronation in Westminster Abbey on 26 June 1902. Shortly before that event there was a grand Coronation Review of the Boys' Brigade (then the only youth movement in existence). Its founder, William A. Smith, was a fellow Scot and, like Lipton, destined to become an honorary colonel of Lanarkshire Volunteers. Smith had organised the first boys' brigade in Glasgow in 1883 and within two decades it had become a worldwide movement. Two thousand boys from all over Britain and the Empire were encamped in the grounds of Lambeth Palace for the Coronation. A hundred and eighty of them came from Glasgow itself, with all expenses in connection with their trip to London having been paid by Lipton who also laid on the fleet of charabancs to take them from Euston Station to Lambeth.

In his autobiography Lipton says that he was appointed Honorary Colonel of the Sixth Highland Light Infantry, although in fact it was the Second Volunteer Battalion, popularly known as the Lanark Engineers. This honour was conferred on him on 24 November 1900. The Second Volunteer Battalion had its parade ground and drill hall at Yorkhill, Glasgow, not far from Stobcross Street where Lipton had opened his first market. The appointment was a shrewd one, from the battalion's viewpoint, as Colonel J. Drummond Young was anxious to build a new headquarters. On 2 March 1901 Lipton came north in order to lay the foundation stone of the building. That evening the officers gave a dinner for their honorary colonel at the Grand Hotel, Charing Cross, and expressed their gratitude for the handsome donation he had made to the building fund.

As part of his duties as honorary colonel, Lipton would lead the troops during special regimental occassions. Lipton, who had taken to horse-riding in the 1880s like a duck to water, cut a fine figure on horseback, with his tall, soldierly bearing, his figure still trim though he was now well into his fifties. He recalled the immense joy he felt when he rode on his charger at the head of his regiment as it paraded through the streets of Glasgow, his chest swelling with pride as the column passed the premises of Tillie and Henderson where he had once laboured as a boy. His colonelcy was not without its pains as well, as he ruefully recounted in his autobiography.

> It so happened that at a Royal Review in Edinburgh at which the King was present, I had . . . to appear astride a horse. There was nothing very alarming in this prospect so far as I was concerned for I had horses in London and frequently did a good deal of riding.

However, a friend in Edinburgh wrote to me saying that there was no call for me to bring north one of my own steeds as he had a very fine horse which he could loan to me for the day.

My friend's idea of a 'very good horse' was apparently one that had never been broken in! And on coming to mount the animal just before it was time for my regiment to 'march past' His Majesty, I found that the united efforts of four soldiers were necessary to hold it. Immediately I got my feet in the stirrups the wretched beast dashed off with me far ahead of my battalion and careered onwards until we were opposite the grand stand, on which were seated the King and his nobles and generals and admirals, together with the civic representatives. As if to celebrate my advent under very peculiar circumstances, to say the least of it, fifty massed bands began to blare out at once. This was the last straw. For a few seconds my horse stood stock still, then he turned his head and gave me a most critical stare, examining carefully, it seemed to me, all the decorations on my chest, including the Grand Order bestowed on me by the King of Italy and other shining medals. Then, deciding that he did not like either me or my decorations, he started to 'buck' like an Arizona rodeo-performer. Before I knew it I was fifteen feet up in the air, and when I came down the darned horse wasn't there. Later I woke up in an Edinburgh nursing-home.

A few days later I had an invitation from His Majesty to complete my convalescence as his guest at Balmoral Castle, his beautiful Highland home on Deeside. King Edward was most sympathetic with me over my accident at the review, and, after dinner on the night of my arrival, he singled me out from his other guests with the words:

'And now, Lipton, I am going to bestow upon you a new honour!' Saying this, he tapped me lightly on the shoulder and added: 'I promote you to the Horse Marines!'[8]

The great Volunteer Review took place in Edinburgh on 18 September 1905, and press reports reveal that Lipton was by no means the only rider in difficulties that day. One colonel had the humiliation of riding backwards before the saluting dais. According to the reports, Lipton was thrown from the saddle and kicked in the face by his horse. Professor Annandale examined and dressed the wound, but although in severe shock Lipton was well enough to return to his hotel bedroom where he rested a day before taking the train back to London.

Lipton certainly rode with skill and panache, and enjoyed nothing better than a stiff gallop in the rolling Hertfordshire countryside. He drove with the same panache but his skill as a motorist left much to be desired. When motor cars became fashionable he bought several of the most powerful models then available, a Mercedes, an Oldsmobile, a Panhard, an Argyll and several Daimlers. An article about him in the *Automobile Journal* of 18 October 1902 showed a line-up of no fewer than six cars in front of the garage at Osidge. His first car was a Daimler twelve horsepower, which he purchased for £800 in July 1902, and which he totally wrecked a few days later while driving from Osidge to the City Road. Driving through Wood Green at a speed well in excess of the then speed limit of twelve miles per hour, he swerved to avoid the tramlines and on a wet, greasy surface crashed into iron railings at Green Lanes. John Westwood and a company engineer were passengers in the rear seat. Lipton's accident was front-page news, alongside a story about the Sultan of Morocco, injured in a car crash in the south of France the very same day. In many papers the two stories, with pictures, were printed side by side.

Undeterred by this accident (in which, miraculously, he and his passengers escaped unhurt) Lipton immediately purchased a more powerful model, a Daimler twenty-two horsepower at a cost of £1,200. On 4 September his name appeared thirty-third in the list of candidates for membership of the Royal Automobile Club, proposed by Alfred Harmsworth, the newspaper proprietor, and he was duly elected on 2 October. About the same time he was proposed for membership of the Aero Club on the nomination of his young friend the Hon. Charles S. Rolls, manufacturer of the world's most aristocratic motor cars. Lipton's membership of the Aero Club was justified by a new-found interest in aviation, which included a crossing of the English Channel by balloon soon afterwards. By 1910 he was appearing in a list of celebrities who had flown by heavier-than-air machine, having gone aloft with Samuel F. Cody.

It has to be admitted that Lipton was a road hog, driving at speeds far greater than the country lanes deserved. Before long he was in court, convicted and fined ten pounds for speeding. When arrested by the police he smiled sheepishly and said, 'You have your duty to do; I have always found you to be correct, boys, I am sorry.' The scrapbooks are littered with references to court appearances and convictions all over the country. Eventually Lipton needed two additional sheets pasted into his driving licence to accommodate all the endorsements. In mid-February 1906 he was arrested at Castelsarrasin in France while speeding from Marseilles to Paris, and briefly incarcerated. As luck would have it, the driver of the cart with which he collided, was also the prosecutor, but on this occasion Lipton extricated himself with a large quantity of gold coins.

On one occasion he lent his powerful Daimler to John W. Gates, the celebrated American financier, so that he could drive two American generals (who were also Lipton's house guests) up to town. All three of them were arrested for speeding – twice, on consecutive days – by the same constable on the same stretch of road near Osidge, and subsequently heavily fined.

One of the passengers was Major-General Henry C. Corbin, whose father, David T. Corbin, had been one of the most prominent carpetbag legislators in South Carolina at the time when young Lipton was labouring in the rice-fields of Coosaw Island. Whether General Corbin was aware of the connection of his host with South Carolina is not known; but he was a commissioner for the St Louis World's Fair, planned to celebrate the centenary of the Louisiana Purchase in the summer of 1903 and it was Lipton who persuaded King Edward to give his support to this major international exhibition. In due course, the King would despatch the Prince of Wales (later King George V) as his personal representative. Sir Thomas Lipton was to have been the prince's companion, though, as it turned out, Lipton was unable to attend the Fair himself. Lipton, incidentally, provided the cash for a separate Irish pavilion at the World's Fair.

Potentially the most lethal of Lipton's motoring escapades occurred in March 1907 when his fifty-horsepower Itala got caught on a level crossing near Avignon on his way to Paris. The papers later reported that Lipton had been driving 'at a furious pace' when trying to beat the level-crossing gates and, as the Paris express thundered towards him he spun the wheel and swerved to run along the adjoining tracks as the mighty locomotive missed him by a hair's breadth. This time he made the front cover of *World's News* whose edition of 20 April was entirely taken up with an artist's impression of the dramatic incident.

Much more serious than the occasional spills and speeding incidents, however, was the accident which Lipton had at Alresford, near Winchester, in November 1902. A carter named Bright was leading a horse which bolted when Lipton's car passed perilously close to it at high speed. Lipton drove on, quite unconcerned, but the unfortunate carter was struck by the horse and was later found dead on the road. At the resulting inquest, the county coroner, Henry White, had some trenchant observations to make concerning the behaviour of Sir Thomas Lipton who, now contrite and remorseful, attended the hearing.

In the course of giving evidence, Lipton promised to do what he could for Bright's widow and orphans. White immediately forbade him to touch on this subject and similarly, at the conclusion of the inquest, cut short Lipton's effusive attempts to thank the jury who had, in effect, reached a verdict exonerating him.[9]

During his evidence, Lipton maintained that he had not been driving the vehicle, but had been a passenger in the back seat. The driver was, in fact, his chauffeur, Bernard Humphreys. This was a name that would soon be featuring in magistrates courts all over the country. On 28 March 1903 he was fined five pounds at Winchester Assizes for speeding, having been apprehended at Kingsworthy on the road from Southampton. Police Constable Deacon said that the car was going faster than he had ever seen before. This was Humphreys' second appearance in the same court in a matter of months, and the press were in no doubts as to the real culprit: Humphreys was only obeying the orders of the impatient tycoon in the back seat, and the headlines the following day proclaimed 'Sir Thomas Lipton's Hurry'. Lipton himself was in court that day and paid the fine as well as the thirteen shillings and sixpence in costs. On 15 May 1903 Humphreys appeared before magistrates at Greenock, and was convicted of driving through the douce coastal village of Inverkip at the terrifying speed of thirty miles an hour. This was the first prosecution of its kind in Greenock, and Humphreys was fined two pounds and five shillings.

These well-publicised brushes with the law did not tarnish Lipton's reputation with the King and they were often in each other's company. All his life, Lipton had been a total abstainer and non-smoker. Indeed, in September 1901 he had headed the Anti-Cigarette War in Britain, which aimed at stamping out this habit among boys. Lipton was widely publicised as refusing to give employment to lads who were 'addicted to the little paper cigars'.[10] But within two years many newspapers were commenting on Lipton's penchant for fat Havana cigars, a habit recently acquired from King Edward himself. He even figured prominently in a full-page advertisement in *The Globe* puffing on an Orlando cigar – probably without his foreknowledge.

In the summer of 1903 Lipton was frequently in the company of President Teddy Roosevelt. It subsequently transpired that Lipton served as go-between in a series of extremely delicate diplomatic matters conducted at the highest level, between the President and King Edward, concerning two Irishmen languishing in British prisons. The first was a former MP called P.A. McHugh who had been imprisoned for sedition. The powerful Irish–American lobby clamoured for his release and it was Lipton who passed on Roosevelt's entreaties to King Edward on his return. The King himself interceded with the Home Office and secured McHugh's release.

The case of Colonel Arthur Lynch, however, was much more serious. Lynch, actually born in Australia of Irish parents, had been working as a journalist in Paris when the Boer War broke out in 1899. He was sent to South Africa as a war correspondent but promptly threw in his lot with the Boers and commanded the Second Irish Brigade of volunteers, fighting with considerable distinction at Elandslaagte, Vereeniging and Klip River. Although denigrated by the British as a traitor on that account, he was elected to Parliament as MP for Galway in November 1901, but the government let it be known that he would be arrested if he set foot on British soil. On 11 June 1902 he was taken into custody at Newhaven on arrival from Dieppe and eventually brought to trial for high treason. He was convicted and sentenced to death, but this was commuted to life imprisonment. In 1903 Michael Davitt, the veteran Irish nationalist, was in America and pleaded with Roosevelt to intercede on Lynch's behalf. It is probable that the subject was raised by the President with Lipton; but certainly when Sir Thomas returned to Britain late in 1903 Davitt appealed to him directly to use his influence with the King to free the gallant colonel. In his usual blunt manner Lipton broached the subject with King Edward at Christmas. Shortly afterwards the King informed the Home Office of his views on the matter, and although he would not go so far as to grant a royal pardon, it seems his views carried weight, for Lynch was suddenly released on 24 January 1904. Lipton and Davitt called on Mrs Lynch to tell her the good news. Mrs Lynch was so overcome that she could not speak; instead she seized Lipton's hand and kissed it effusively. Inevitably the American press had a field day with the story, although the British newspapers were relatively muted on the subject. Lynch and his wife settled in Paris, and the magnanimity of a king and the sympathy of a millionaire had a curious sequel. In the aftermath of the abortive Easter Rising in 1916, Lynch published an open letter in the British and Irish newspapers, calling on Irishmen to realise that their real enemy was Germany, and he appealed for volunteers to support Britain in her struggle with the Central Powers.[11]

When he was not hobnobbing with the President in the

summer of 1903, Lipton was enjoying the hospitality of the rich and the powerful. Samuel Felton, President of the Chicago and Alton Railroad, put his personal railcar at Lipton's disposal when commuting between Chicago and New York, and early in September he was the guest of Governor Timothy Woodruff at Kamp Kill Kare in the Adirondacks. It almost became Kamp Kill Lipton after a barbecue on 13 September in which the tycoon dined injudiciously on undercooked corncobs. By the following day, when he was passing through Utica, he was doubled up with a severe attack of indigestion. By the time he reached Chicago on 15 September he was in a state of collapse. The newspapers the following day ran sensational headlines, that he was critically ill with gastritis and had a temperature of 102 degrees. Heavily dosed with morphine, he was confined to a hospital bed in Chicago for several days. Appendicitis was suspected and the best surgeons were immediately summoned. Remarkably, however, his condition improved on 18 September and five days later he was well enough to go for a short car ride with Duncan Neill and Alexander Revell. Although pale and haggard when he left Chicago to return to New York on 3 October, no operation was necessary, but it scuppered his plans to attend the World's Fair at St Louis.

Several years later, the explanation for his miraculous recovery was revealed. His surgeon, on the advice of Sir Andrew Clark, the leading authority on bowel complaints, decided to give Lipton a high-colonic enema, consisting of a pint and a half of molasses mixed well with the same quantity of hot milk before subjecting him to the knife. 'This dislodged a large accumulation of decomposed faeces, high in the colon in the region of the appendix' and gave immediate relief, which obviated the necessity for an operation. Dr Chauvel of Paris also advocated this treatment; in 688 cases of appendicitis which he recorded in 1902, twenty-three out of 188 treated by surgery had died as a result of the operation, whereas all but three of the 480 patients subjected to a milk and molasses enema had made a good recovery.[12] Advised to change his diet as a result, it was at this time that Lipton acquired his obsession with rice.

In the spring of 1904 Lipton was cruising in the Mediterranean, calling at Monte Carlo, Nice and Cannes before heading for Naples where he was a guest of King Victor Emmanuel III at his palace. On the eve of his departure Lipton was invested with the collar and star of a Knight Commander of the Order of the Crown of Italy. A few weeks later he obligingly put his yacht at the disposal of the Empress Eugénie of France, so that she could visit Marseilles, and shortly afterwards he headed north again to attend the yacht races at Kiel, presided over by Kaiser Wilhelm II. The All-Highest was a fearful snob who despised his Uncle Bertie because he went boating with his grocer. If this disdain had ever been communicated to Lipton, he probably shrugged it aside; his hide was thick enough to withstand snubs and insults much closer to home. After the affair of the Kaiser's Cup for the Atlantic yacht race, however, Wilhelm regarded his uncle's grocer in a much more favourable light and when they met at Kiel Week they got on famously. Unlike his friend Andrew Carnegie (who worshipped the Kaiser as if he were God Almighty), Lipton had the measure of Wilhelm and had a happy knack of feeding the German's insatiable vanity without resorting to sycophancy. The Austrian Archduke Leopold recalled an incident when Lipton and J. Pierpont Morgan were guests aboard the Kaiser's steam yacht *Hohenzollern*. The Kaiser was in a thoroughly bad mood that evening and 'coldly polite'. Morgan, in turn, was ill at ease.

> Only Lipton, by his jocularity and high spirits, soon thawed everything and everybody. Wilhelm rocked with laughter at Thomas Lipton's long stream of anecdotes, especially how he tried in vain to get a shilling a week rise . . . The secret of Lipton's success is that he makes everyone around him feel so much at home. He made even the Kaiser feel at home aboard his own imperial yacht.[13]

While Andrew Carnegie was pursuing the chimera of world peace, Lipton was getting on with his business. After the company went public he no longer felt obliged to spend almost all his time at the office in the City Road, but it must often have felt like it, so far as his long-suffering executives were concerned. Lipton might be in New York or Chicago but he spent a fortune on telegrams and succeeded in keeping a very tight rein on company policy and executive decisions, even though he might be thousands of miles away. The company confounded the City analysts and in the period up to the outbreak of the First World War regularly declared dividends of twelve to fifteen per cent.

Mindful of the gloomy predictions of City analysts who claimed that there was no room for further expansion in the provision industry, Lipton began casting around for new ventures. When it was rumoured in August 1900, that he planned to enter the Australian wine trade, a conference of Australian wine-growers in Melbourne unanimously turned down his overtures on the grounds of his inexperience of the trade. In theory, Australia should have been producing good wines – comparable to those of France, Spain and Italy – as the climate, soil and types of grape were all conducive to this, but the plain fact was that, at that time, the growers did not understand the production of fine wine and there were plenty of informed commentators in the press to suggest that Lipton might be just the man to shake up the Australian wine industry, just as he had wrought improvements in the butter, ham and tea industries.[14]

Although he had sold out his pork interests to Ogden Armour, Lipton kept a close watch on other developments in the American meat industry. When the brothers John and Michael Cudahy formed the giant Beef Trust in October 1902, amalgamating the beef industries of Chicago, Omaha and Kansas City, Lipton was quietly working in the background, and doubtless enjoyed his cut from the turnover estimated at £200 million per annum. On 8 January 1904, however, he sold his seat on the Chicago Board of Trade for $3,000 and disposed of his giant packing plant a few months later to the National Packing Company. Having been rebuffed by the Australian wine-growers Lipton next turned his attention to spirits, and in January 1903 news leaked that he was negotiating to buy the Glen Cawdor whisky distillery, but this came to naught. In the same month it was rumoured that he was proposing to purchase Stratfieldsaye from the Duke of Wellington.

In the spring of 1905 he visited his tea estates in Ceylon after a gap of several years. This was no more than a routine inspection but it was sufficient to trigger off wild speculation in the press that Lipton was about to enter the rubber business. Rubber was then enjoying a boom and enormous fortunes (mostly on paper) were being made. Lipton allowed the stories a good airing before denying the rubber rumour. Instead, however, he promised to open a Lipton's market in Paris, in the Place de l'Opéra, one of that city's most fashionable shopping thoroughfares.[15]

On 31 May 1906 Michael Davitt died. When an inventory of his estate was filed for probate it was revealed that he was the possessor of 1,000 Lipton shares. Furthermore, it transpired that these shares had been a gift from Lipton at the time of the flotation. Considering how excessively the share issue was oversubscribed and how many would-be investors were disappointed at the time, the news of Lipton's gift to the Gerry Adams of his day was greeted with outrage in some quarters. It had been nothing more than a typically generous act.

Davitt was a firebrand, anti-English, bitterly Nationalist and often at odds with his fellow home-rulers – small wonder, considering his background. A child of the Hungry Forties, he was forced to leave his native County Mayo when his father was evicted. The family settled in Lancashire where ten-year-old Michael was sent out to work in one of the textile mills at Haslingden. A few months later he fell into the machinery and had an arm ripped off. In some ways this was a blessing in disguise, for he was then sent to school and subsequently found employment as a printer's devil. He drifted into the more extreme forms of Irish politics, eventually joining the Irish Republican Brotherhood. Arrested in 1870 for gunrunning, he was sentenced to fifteen years penal servitude but released on ticket-of-leave after seven years breaking rocks on Dartmoor. His fiery speeches as an organiser of the Land League were regarded as seditious and this landed him a two-year stretch at Portland. During this period he was elected MP for Meath but, being a convict, could not take his seat. In 1892 he was elected for North Meath but unseated on petition. He was then returned for North-East Cork but had to vacate his seat on being declared bankrupt (arising out of the costs in the North Meath petition). Undaunted, he eventually got into Parliament in 1895 when he was elected for West Mayo. His parliamentary career was brief and controversial and came to an end when he resigned his seat as a protest against the Boer War. Members of Parliament did not receive a salary and had to rely on their outside business or landed interests. The one-armed Davitt had no such resources and precious little opportunity to earn money beyond the precarious medium of extreme Nationalist journalism. Moreover, since his resignation, he had alienated many Nationalists by his radical socialism which, in fact, brought him closer to the infant Labour movement. Lipton's gift was a kind gesture which reflected his sentimental attachment to the country of his forefathers, but there were plenty of detractors only too ready to seize upon it and imply a sinister political motive, especially in light of Lipton's connection with Davitt over the Lynch affair.[16]

Lipton, as usual, shrugged off the criticism and continued on his merry way. Disaster on the grand scale struck twice in the spring of 1906. Lipton was cruising the Mediterranean in *Erin* when Vesuvius erupted, only being aware of the catastrophe when the yacht was showered with grey ash. Lipton steamed towards Naples, and later toured the devastated areas on foot and made a very handsome contribution to the relief fund. Lipton's generosity was contrasted in the Italian press with German indifference to the tragedy. Later, however, the Kaiser complained to Lipton that his offer had been rebuffed because the Italians did not want help at a governmental level. A few days later San Francisco was destroyed by an earthquake, followed by a firestorm caused by fractured gas mains. By that time Lipton was in Athens with King Edward for the Olympic Games, but he immediately cabled Mayor Schmitz with a draft for $5,000. In April 1909 the *Erin* was cruising of the Italian coast when Messina was struck by an earthquake. Lipton and Tom Dewar were on the spot soon afterwards and both promptly contributed to the relief fund.

By the beginning of May 1906 Lipton was back in England with young King Alfonso XIII of Spain as his guest, travelling incognito as the Conde de Covadonga. Lipton could claim to have played Cupid for Alfonso and Princess Ena of Battenberg, having introduced them when they were guests on his yacht. Ena, in turn, had a very special affection for Lipton; a queen who owned some of the costliest diamond jewellery in Europe preferred the simple coral necklace which Lipton had bought her in an Alexandria bazaar when she and her mother, Princess Beatrice, had been guests on the *Erin* a few years previously. Now Lipton was driving Alfonso up to London to be reunited with his fiancée. When they got married later that summer Lipton gave them a top-of-the-range player-piano which the Pianola Company later conceded had helped boost their sales immensely.

Lipton had a happy knack of making matches, at commercial and cultural levels as well as matrimonial. In 1905 his guests on *Erin* included the romantic novelist Marie Corelli and the beef baron Edward Nelson Morris. Marie was the daughter of Charles Mackay, the poet and song-writer, while Morris had been a penniless Jewish refugee from the pogroms of Tsarist Russia who started in America as a pork-packer (until his rabbi objected) before turning to beef and eventually became one of the leading figures in the Beef Trust. The Queen of Romance and the Napoleon of Beef, as the press liked to style them, purchased the ancestral home of John Harvard, founder of the American university, at Stratford-upon-Avon, subsequently co-opting Lipton as a joint trustee when Harvard House was established as a heritage site for Americans visiting Britain. [17]

In 1905 Lipton instituted a cup for ocean-yacht races to be staged between New York and Bermuda. The first race, held in May 1906, was a fiasco when only the *Gauntlet* with Thora Robinson at the helm, finished the course. When the race was re-run, however, the American contender *Tamerlane* took the trophy. Lipton was in America to see the start of the race, but his main concern that year was to retrieve something from the wreckage of the scandal that hit the Beef Trust. The result was a packing plant across the border, at Winnipeg in Canada. By the end of the year he was back in England, testing his high-speed motorboat *Britannia I* at the Solent. In February 1907 his stallion Erin go Bragh took all the major prizes at the International Stock Show in Chicago. In April he was in Monte Carlo, taking part in the world powerboat races, and being interviewed by a reporter from the *Neues Wiener Tagblatt*. Under the headline *De beste Politik für England* (England's Best Policy) he advocated naval rearmament in Britain as the best guarantee of continuing world peace. In July he was back in America for the Jamestown Tercentenary Races and instituting yet another trophy, the Lipton Gold Cup for races between deep-sea fishing boats.

By 1908, when he was actually sixty but only admitting to being fifty-eight, his routine was to spend two or three months of really intensive work at his City office, followed by ten or twelve weeks abroad, either cruising in *Erin* or traversing the world by luxury liner. He continued to entertain royalty and be entertained in return. The even tenor of his life was punctuated by the yachting season and the annual staff outings which had now taken on the aura of tribal gatherings. At the Franco–British Exhibition of 1908 he was commissioner for the Ceylon pavilion.

In January that year he took the aged Empress Eugénie with him to Ceylon. As they entered the Suez Canal, the Empress wistfully recalled the day in November 1869 when she and her husband, Napoleon III, had formally opened the canal on board the imperial yacht *Aigle*. Of all the close bonds between Lipton and European royalty, that with the Empress was the strangest, and closest. In many respects she became a mother substitute: their birthdays fell in the same week although she was twenty-two years his senior. Her mother was that Countess de Montijo who had been one of the earliest connoisseurs of Lipton hams. The Countess was, in fact, the daughter of William Kirkpatrick of Closeburn in Dumfriesshire who had settled in Malaga and become American consul there in 1791. Eugénie de Montijo was said to have inherited her blue eyes, fresh complexion and red-gold hair from her Scottish grandfather. Interestingly Kirkpatrick's sister was the grandmother of Ferdinand de Lesseps, so that Eugénie was a cousin of the Frenchman who had constructed the Suez Canal. Lipton was utterly devoted to the imperious old lady and she, in turn, leaned heavily on his support and advice in all matters. He was a frequent guest on her yacht *Thistle* at the Solent, and she was more or less a permanent fixture on *Erin* when it cruised the Mediterranean, and he was often to be seen at her villa in Farnborough or her winter mansion at Cap Martin on the Riviera. It is said that the only time she ignored Lipton's advice was when, in July 1920 at the age of ninety-four, she went off to Madrid to visit her favourite goddaughter, Queen Ena, took ill and died suddenly.

Although never losing his ambition to 'lift that blooming mug', by 1908 Lipton was turning more and more to aviation. At the International Balloon Race in May that year he presented the Lipton Aeronautic Cup as the second prize; the third prize was a more modest trophy contributed by Tom Dewar. When Louis Blériot flew the Channel in July 1909 Lipton hosted a luncheon for the aviator at the Savoy. Lipton hobnobbed with the pioneer fliers, such as Claude Grahame-White, at the Bournemouth Aviation Meeting in the summer of 1910 and it was he who had the unenviable task of breaking to Lord and Lady Langattock the sad news that their son, the Hon. Charles Rolls, had been killed in a crash on 12 July. The following week, he was back on the Solent, following the course of the Bournemouth–Needles Air Race from the deck of the *Erin*.

Scouting was another passion which developed around this time. Previously, Lipton had been a fervent supporter of Sir William Smith and the Boys Brigade, but he was most impressed by Major-General Robert S. Baden-Powell when he came to Glasgow to review the Brigade. A few years later, when Lieutenant-General Sir Robert Baden-Powell founded the Boy Scouts, Lipton was among his earliest supporters and headed the Boy Scout Fund when it was launched in 1910. For this he received one of the first Scout Thanks decorations, a gold swastika which he wore proudly on his watch chain.

In the late spring of 1910 King Edward caught a cold while on holiday at Biarritz. Although he recovered, it left him with bronchitis which was aggravated by the London weather on his return to England at the end of April. During a card game at Mrs Keppel's house he lit a cigar which produced such a paroxysm of coughing that he had to go home. He never left the Palace again, and died a few days later. The last thing of which he was conscious, on 9 May, was that his horse Witch of the Air had won at Kempton Park that afternoon. Later that evening, Queen Alexandra, in a gracious gesture that has immortalised her for generosity of spirit, sent for Alice Keppel and led her by the hand to the King's bedside so that the dying man might have the comfort of his mistress's caress. Edward slipped into a coma and never regained consciousness, dying in the early hours of the following day.

No one mourned the passing of King Edward more than his grocer friend, and for more than purely personal reasons. A paragraph in the journal *Week End* struck a chilling note:

> There was a strong current of commercialism in his late Majesty's choice of companions. It is true that many men of light and learning were honoured with the acquaintance of King Edward, but his closest friends, his 'cronies', were chiefly drawn from commerce and finance. The Rothschilds, Sir Ernest Cassel, Sir Everard Hambro, the Sassoons, Sir Thomas Lipton are all men great in ability and worthy of a king's friendship, yet strongly though they appealed to the late King, it is hardly likely that they will occupy the same position with his son.[18]

Indeed, the Prince of Wales who now ascended the throne as King George V was a man of a very different stamp from his father. A career officer in the Royal Navy, he had the image of a family man, with a fervent belief in Victorian family values. Not until many years later would the truth emerge of how his children were traumatised by his domestic tyranny, but in 1910 he was seen to be embodying the old-fashioned virtues of the family man, faithful to his wife. More of a Victorian than his father, George had a quite different circle of friends, more firmly entrenched in the old aristocracy. In this circle the louche, the raffish and the parvenu found no acceptance. Besides, the new monarch was in his mid-forties. Lipton, now admitting to sixty but actually sixty-two was, frankly, too old to fit in.

Lipton must have noticed the change in climate immediately. The world of business too, was changing and at successive shareholders' general meetings he was increasingly defensive, riled by criticism and quick to take offence if someone made a jibe about the time and money he was expending on his yachting endeavours. How he must have yearned for the good old days when he was truly his own master and had no one to answer to. For the time being, however, the shareholders were kept in line by excellent dividends, and Lipton shares continued to be regarded as a sure thing. But behind the scenes all was not sweetness and light. The old man was becoming increasingly tetchy. Thrusting young executives who overstepped the mark and exceeded their mandate or used their own initiative without achieving the desired results were often dismissed on the spot.

The infamous agreement between employees and management was still in force. To the world at large, Lipton continued to present a genial, affable manner, but his staff and associates were aware of a subtle change in his outlook. The bachelor gay was giving way to that other stereotype, the crusty old bachelor.

He was given to pronouncements on such weighty matters as the state of the economy and Britain's foreign and colonial policies. Much of what he said made sound common sense, but his remarks were often unheeded, or else they provoked a violent reaction. In March 1914 he was on the SS *Maloja*, returning from Ceylon and was sitting one day in the smoking lounge with a group of British Army officers going home on furlough, when he startled them by predicting that within six years every country in Europe would be a republic. The officers, taking great offence at these intemperate remarks, rose as one man and stalked out of the room. Turning to his companion, W.D. Hornaday, Lipton chuckled:

> 'I knew they would take it that way, but what the divvil do I care? I meant ivery word of it. I've told Emperor William [the Kaiser] the same thing; I often said it to King Edward and I've made the prediction to King George. I told King Alfonso of Spain not very long ago, that the day of universal republics was now at hand.'
>   'Do you include Russia with the rest?'
>   'I do.'
>   'How is all this to be brought about?'
>   'My prophecy goes no farther than the results that I have stated; through what process they will be attained I do not know.'[19]

What sort of reaction these predictions made in most cases is not recorded; although King Edward is known to have riposted that if he lost his throne he would ask Lipton for a partnership. When he made the same remark to the Prince of Wales (later King Edward VIII and Duke of Windsor) that young man told Lipton that if he were not king he would become a motor mechanic, and added that his sister (the Princess Royal) would make a capital horse-breaker.

From 1903 onwards a recurring theme was Lipton's criticism of British commercial policy, and he invariably had plenty of ammunition for his attacks. He was prone to making invidious comparisons between Britain and the United States and, with the benefit of hindsight, it can be seen that what he had to say was absolutely correct. He had not got where he was without being able to analyse trends in consumption as well as the fine balance between imports and exports. What he was saying in 1903 still has a ring of truth more than ninety years later. Too much of Britain's prosperity was based on invisible earnings, on money invested in capital projects in foreign countries. This disguised the fact that the value of exports was dropping from the 1890s onwards, while the value of imported goods continued to rise inexorably, thereby creating an imbalance.

Frequent Mediterranean cruises in *Erin* gave him a sharp insight into the soft underbelly of European politics at first hand, and he foresaw the trouble which would fester in the Balkans for years, following Austria's annexation of Bosnia and Herzegovina in 1908. Six years later, Gavrilo Prinzip, a sickly member of the Black Hand terrorist group, would snuff out the lives of an Austrian archduke and his morganatic wife and thereby set in motion the chain of events which would lead to world war. Lipton, however, was more concerned that Britain should take steps to improve its relations with America. He deplored the stuffy, condescending attitude of the British establishment towards the United States, and their failure to realise that out of those thirteen colonies which had thrown off the British yoke 130 years earlier there had grown a great power which, some day soon, would play a leading role in world affairs. More than most, he had good reason to understand American sensitivity towards British patronising, and at the same time he appreciated the fact that friction between the two great English-speaking peoples was so often triggered off by some trifling misunderstanding. After the Dunraven affair he was living proof of the fact that such friction could also be minimised, if not entirely eliminated, by practical diplomacy and plain speaking.

When the press baron, Lord Northcliffe, in 1909 predicted that within a few years Britain would be at war with Germany, Lipton stepped into the breach swiftly to denounce this as 'rot'. Lipton was in America when Northcliffe's prophecies were published and he went out of his way to allay British fears. In due course, Lipton's optimistic views were translated and appeared in a long article in the *Neue Prüssiche Kreuz-Zeitung* of 17 December 1909.

As the twentieth century entered its second decade, therefore, Lipton found himself spending more and more of his time out of the country: winters in Ceylon or the Orient, spring on the Riviera and autumn in America. In his mid-sixties his name was still being romantically linked with this or that society beauty, although, significantly, wealthy widows now vied with débutantes for the title of Lady Lipton. He was now an honorary member of over sixty yacht clubs, though the one which mattered most continued to give him the cold shoulder. One Christmas in Colombo he laid on lavish entertainment for the visiting baseball teams, the Chicago White Sox and the New York Giants. He was as much in the public eye as ever, and this found reflection in light entertainment on both sides of the Atlantic. At the Alhambra in London, Tom Hale impersonated him in the revue *Keep Smiling*, while on Broadway Chauncey Olcott had a hit song:

> Come over, come over, come on over here
> It's a wonderful place, its a wonderful place;
> Sir Thomas Lipton from over the sea
> Is making a fortune in cocoa and tea;
> At the Waldorf you'll meet all the swagger set bunch
> And a dollar will buy you a lovely milk punch;
> I have heard that for ten you can buy a light lunch,
> It's a wonderful, wonderful place.

The chief event of 1911 was the Coronation of King George V, followed by the Festival of Empire in which Lipton was heavily involved in promoting the products of Ceylon, so much so that it was joked that Lipton owned the entire island. For Lipton personally, however, the year would always be remembered on account of the incident which took place at Osidge on 21 January. He took a telephone call from a Detective-Inspector Welldon of Scotland Yard, saying that he had to see him urgently. Lipton agreed, wondering what was afoot, and shortly afterwards the doorbell rang. One of the Sinhalese houseboys admitted the police officer and ushered him into the billiard room. The detective's tone altered rapidly, and when he demanded Lipton's financial help he whipped out a cut-throat razor and threatened him with it. Too late, Lipton realised that he was dealing with a dangerous lunatic but with immense courage he talked to the man and succeeded in pacifying him. Eventually Welldon put down the razor on the billiard-table. Lipton quietly pocketed it and said that he would help him. He slipped out into the hallway and collided with Colonel Duncan Neill who had just arrived on a yachting matter. Swiftly apprising Neill of the situation, Lipton went to phone the Southgate police station while Neill engaged the madman in conversation. Ten minutes later two plain-clothes men arrived, overpowered the maniac and led him away to the lunatic wing of the Edmonton Workhouse, though later he was tried and convicted on a charge of impersonating a police officer. Albert Edward Welldon, an unemployed waiter aged twenty-eight, had a long history of deranged violence.

The year 1912 began inauspiciously when Lipton drove his latest car off the jetty at Folkestone into the harbour. Fortunately the tide was out at the time, so he escaped with cuts and bruises, though the car was a complete write-off. In February he was bouncing back as head of a consortium of financiers who were to build a railway from Salt Lake City to San Francisco, scheduled for completion in 1915 in time for the great Panama–Pacific Exposition marking the opening of the Panama Canal. On 13 May he published a long letter in *The Times*, in the wake of the *Titanic* disaster, advocating the proper training of ships' stewards to cope with such crises, as well as the institution of lifeboat drills for passengers. This letter was widely reprinted and led eventually to the Board of Trade introducing reforms along the lines he suggested. In the same month he was despatching tons of much-needed foodstuffs to the starving islanders of St Kilda, cut off for several months due to severe winter storms.

By December he was in New Orleans, characteristically telling American girls that they were the best dressed in the world and that they should not seek titles abroad as American husbands were the best. A week later he was in Boston, purchasing the biggest doll he could find for the actress Gaby Deslys. When interviewed by Oliver Bainbridge, who was planning a book to mark the centenary of peace between Britain and the United States, Lipton said rather testily that it would be better if Britain talked less and did more to show friendship with America. This tetchy outburst was sparked off by Britain's stiff-necked attitude towards the Panama Canal, then nearing completion. In particular, Britain was angered at the way the Americans, under Theodore Roosevelt, had engineered the secession of Panama from Colombia. The price of Panamanian independence (backed by the United States) had been the concession of the canal. Britain argued that this should be an international waterway, whereas Americans pointedly reminded the British of the way in which they and the French had gained control of the Suez Canal. The United States laid plans several years ahead for a great Panama–Pacific Exposition, and when it was revealed that the British government was boycotting the ceremony Lipton let it be known that he personally would be there and that, by hook or by crook, he intended that his yacht *Erin* should be the first through the locks. And mindful of the way in which he had secured the premier position at the Dewey naval parade, it is quite likely that

Lipton would have been granted his wish – if only to cock a snook at British official attitudes.

Early in 1913 Lipton was in Hollywood, then little more than a village set amid the orange groves, where his new-found friend Mack Sennett even inveigled him into taking part in one of his movies. On returning to London that spring he remarked that he had left behind him in America his best friends in the world. At the Hippodrome he was being parodied in *Hullo Ragtime!*. In March of that year the Miami valley in Ohio, subjected to five days of torrential rain, was inundated and engulfed the city of Dayton. More than 400 people lost their lives and over $100 million worth of damage was sustained. When the floodwaters receded, Dayton was left covered in mud and strewn with debris with pestilence averted only by prompt and energetic action. Martial law was declared, food was distributed and tents erected for the homeless. A relief fund was started by the American Red Cross and, as in the case of Galveston thirteen years previously, Lipton automatically responded with $1,000.

He continued to campaign actively in Britain for a more positive attitude towards the proposed Panama–Pacific Exposition and, putting his money where his mouth was, he sent a handsome donation to the San Diego Burns Club towards the cost of the replica of the poet's birthplace at Alloway which was to be one of the highlights of the exhibition. Characteristically, news of this donation appeared alongside an announcement that Lipton was examining the prospects of growing tea in the valleys of southern California. In April he attended the memorial service for John Pierpont Morgan at Westminster Abbey and was photographed alongside Mrs Asquith, wife of the future prime minister. At Cowes, the Duke and Duchess of Santonia were his guests aboard *Erin*.

Everything seemed to be going well for him. To be sure, he was looking rather older, his hair noticeably receding and his jowls beginning to sag a little but otherwise, to the general public who bought the new tabloid picture papers, Tommy Lipton seemed the same as always, the yachting cap set at a rakish angle in those photographs of him with society beauties and actresses aboard his famous yacht. Just as the Great War burst upon a Europe which had never seemed so peaceful and contented, so too the great scandal that almost destroyed Lipton burst upon him quite suddenly and unexpectedly.

In the years following the Boer War the Hon. Cecil Twistleton-Wykeham-Fiennes, heir of the Baron Saye and Sele, was in the employment of a brewery company called Style and Winch. A former officer of the regular army and at that time a colonel in the militia, he performed duties of a liaison nature, what would nowadays be vaguely termed 'public relations'. Part of his function was to keep in touch with various regiments stationed at home and overseas and pave the way for lucrative canteen contracts. It will be remembered that Lipton was involved in this business on a very large scale when he handled the victualling for the great army manoeuvres of 1898. The system in the early years of this century relied on breweries, grocery firms and other contractors dealing directly with the colonel of each regiment. In practice, the colonel relied heavily on the recommendations of the regimental quartermaster, the regimental sergeant-major, the senior warrant and non-commissioned officers and the cook sergeant in awarding contracts. In a situation like this (which was obviously open to abuse) someone of the social standing of the Hon. Colonel Fiennes was a major asset. In 1903 Fiennes wrote to Colonel Charles Whitaker, the officer commanding the British garrison at Malta which was enjoying a well-earned rest after campaigning in the recently concluded South African war.

'Dear Whitaker,' he wrote:

> I know you are of an enterprising nature. I wonder whether you would care for a free trip to Cyprus and Crete; our agent there is in a very great state of mind about the Dublin Fusiliers. He appears to have got into trouble with Col. Marsh. He is wondering whether you would feel inclined to take ten days leave and do Crete and Cyprus. You could play globe-trotter and at the same time give Marsh a pat on the back and put him right with us. [20]

Cyprus had been under British administration since 1878, although nominally a Turkish province until the outbreak of the First World War. Crete, on the other hand, had only recently declared its independence from Turkey but at the time was prevented from *Enosis* (union with Greece) by a consortium of European powers – including Britain – each of which had its own administrative zone. Colonel Whitaker naïvely accepted the Fiennes offer and apparently conducted his business with Colonel Marsh to the satisfaction of Colonel Fiennes. In connection with this trip to Cyprus he met Style and Winch's Malta agent, a Mr Morris who was also, as it subsequently transpired, the Malta agent for Lipton Limited. His duties in the latter capacity were concerned with the supply through army canteens of a number of articles that were not issued to the men with rations. By what was then known as the Tenants' System, each unit had its own canteen, and the colonel negotiated the contracts individually with the suppliers. An important part of Morris's duties, therefore, was to keep the quartermaster, NCOs and cooks of the Malta garrison satisfied with the Lipton service. Traditionally this goodwill was cemented by a generous gift at Christmas; it was an old-established custom, but it was strictly illegal.

About the time that Colonel Fiennes was arranging the free trip to Cyprus for Colonel Whitaker, Edmund Stratton Sawyer entered the Lipton service in London. One of his functions was to disburse payments to his inspectors to cover the sums which they, in turn, paid over to the army quartermasters in the London District. Sawyer had to make these payments out of his expense account, a system which effectively concealed the nature of the payments but also made it difficult to fix Sawyer's salary. Eventually some disagreement over this matter came to a head and Sawyer resigned in 1911. All would have been well had Sawyer not entered the employment of the Canteen Mess Society, a rival organisation which supplied military units on a co-operative basis. By so doing, however, Sawyer was in breach of his contract with Lipton which, among other things, stipulated that he bound himself not to work for any firm engaged in competitive activities for a year after leaving Lipton Limited. By joining the Canteen Mess Society, Sawyer broke this agreement, and when it came to the attention of Lipton's the aggrieved company brought an action for breach of contract.

The folly of pursuing Sawyer through the courts soon became apparent when the vexed matter of his salary and expenses was dragged out into the public gaze. In a frenzied bid to limit the damage, Lipton's settled the matter out of court and issued a statement to the press disassociating the company from any payment by its inspectors to military personnel, adding that any such payments had been made unofficially and without the knowledge of the company. That ought to have been an end of the matter, but unfortunately for all concerned, the Canteen Mess Society did not operate along traditional lines, and Christmas presents to quartermasters and cooks did not figure anywhere in its budget. The Society was acutely aware that it lost a great deal of business by not indulging in bribery, and was therefore anxious to see this matter thoroughly exposed in order to bring an end to a pernicious system. Consequently Sawyer was informed that he must clear his name or be dismissed.

Sawyer thereupon approached an organisation entitled the Secret Commissions and Bribery Prevention League and handed over a bulky dossier containing all the correspondence he had had on the subject over an eight-year period, together with copies of all the letters which he had written in this connection. The League duly handed over these highly incriminating papers to the Public Prosecutor and on Saturday, 17 January 1914, the case was opened at Bow Street before the chief metropolitan magistrate. Sixteen men stood in the dock: Colonel Whitaker, eight non-commissioned officers of the army and seven members of Lipton's staff. Over the ensuing eighteen weeks the case was to keep the daily press busy, and generate far more publicity for Lipton's than all the ballyhoo surrounding the birth of *Shamrock IV*. Evans was the star witness for the prosecution and gave a total of fifty hours evidence which left no one in any doubt as to the scale and severity of the canteen bribery system.

Eight of the nine military defendants were non-commissioned officers who had risen from the rank of private. There was an element of snobbery in the attitude that their conduct was perhaps no better than might be expected. But on the second day of the case the public was astounded by the appearance in the list of a Colonel Whitaker who, while stationed at Malta, had been in receipt of an annual allowance from Lipton's of £300, disbursed by Mr Morris. Hitherto it had been implied that bribery, if such existed, had amounted to nothing more than a case of Scotch or some similar trifle on Boxing Day; but the size and nature of this stipend indicated that bribery of a much more serious nature was involved. Doubtless many a commanding officer was vaguely aware that his quartermaster was getting some kind of sweetener at Christmas from the local contractors, but he would turn a blind eye to this so long as the canteen was operating efficiently and without complaints from the men. But here was the spectacle of the commanding officer himself engaging in some form of corruption on a much greater scale. It should be remembered that 300 gold sovereigns in 1914 would equate with £25,000 to £30,000 in modern currency.

Whitaker's appearance raised the matter to an entirely new level. Now there were dark mutterings of 'conspiracy', and although Colonel Whitaker had retired from active duty in 1906 he was the holder of the Royal Victorian Order as well as the Royal Humane Society's medal for life-saving. After thirty-eight years in the army, he had enjoyed an honourable retirement for eight years, and two of his three sons were currently gentlemen cadets at the Royal Military College, Sandhurst. Against this background, the monstrous nature of the scandal, and its effect on society, may be imagined.

The preliminary hearing lasted from mid-January till early April and then the defendants were committed for trial at the Central Criminal Court. The case opened at the Old Bailey five weeks later before Mr Justice Darling, a judge whose forensic skills were matched by his rapier-sharp wit. Lord Darling was one of those judges who played to the gallery and could always be guaranteed to provide good copy for the press. From Lipton's point of view, the choice of judge could not have been more unfortunate for the adverse publicity the case was likely to attract. Furthermore, Whitaker was defended by none other than Tim Healy, as well known in Irish Nationalist circles as he was at the Bar and destined to become the first Governor-General of the Irish Free State.[21]

Whitaker denied that he had received his annual payment in regard to concessions granted to Lipton's and said that the money was solely as commission for his good services in Crete and Cyprus on behalf of Style and Winch, and by way of supporting this contention he entered the letter from Colonel Fiennes as evidence. As the prosecution were unable to track down Morris there was no one in the witness-box to refute this. Moreover, Whitaker argued that he had been on leave when he earned this commission, implying that it had no bearing on his military duties in Malta. Furthermore, he claimed that he had had no prior knowledge of Morris before Colonel Fiennes had introduced them.

Leading for the prosecution, the Attorney-General Sir John Simon had a comparatively easy task. Did Colonel Whitaker expect the judge and jury to accept that he had received £300 a year for three years purely as commission for beer sold, on one occasion, in Cyprus. He dismissed the latter as 'a trifling service'. Sir John latched on to the fact that the money paid to Whitaker had come from Lipton's and not Style and Winch. Savage tried to wriggle out of this awkward matter with a vague assertion that Morris was a muddle-headed fellow who confused his accounts. The story was paper-thin and fooled nobody. Healy knew the case was lost, but he decided to fling a few mud pies before he was finished. He concentrated on the fact that Colonel Fiennes was now the eighteenth Baron Saye and Sele and Comptroller of the Royal Household no less. Healy made much of the fact that Saye and Sele, as a peer of the realm, could not be tried at the Central Criminal Court but only the bar of the House of Lords. 'Colonel Whitaker is in the dock,' he thundered, 'but Lord Saye and Sele is in the Palace.'

Healy could, of course, have subpoenaed the noble lord as a

witness, but that would not have been helpful to his client. So, instead, he played on the fact that the scion of one of the oldest aristocratic families in the land had been soiling his hands with tradesmen. This gave Lord Darling his cue, and his summing-up was a devastating commentary on how far standards had fallen. He deplored that fact that 'a nobleman whose ancestor had set his hand to Magna Carta' should have induced the colonel of a regiment to act as a sort of envoy on behalf of a brewery firm, to smooth down an angry colonel and get him to think better of a certain beer. 'It shows a sad decadence from the tradition of a great family. It was better for such a man as Lord Saye and Sele to starve than get his living by cadging orders for beer.' The judge was merely expressing what was still a common attitude through all ranks of British society at the time: that there should be a clear demarcation between what was fit and unfit for a nobleman. This attitude goes far to explain why Lipton found such an impenetrable barrier when he tried to win entry to the Royal Yacht Club.

These strictures on Lord Saye and Sele were merely a sideshow. Judge Darling aimed his most devastating barbs at the hapless Whitaker. He had brought dishonour on his rank and his regiment by engaging in such a sordid pecuniary business and by accepting money as an inducement to show favour to a commercial firm. On the penultimate day of the trial all sixteen defendents changed their plea to guilty. Lord Darling had no hesitation therefore in sentencing Whitaker to six months' imprisonment, which was regarded as extremely lenient owing to the mitigating circumstances of the defendant's age and the fact that he had forfeited his army pension as a consequence. The civilian defendants, convicted on lesser charges, got off with heavy fines ranging from fifty pounds to £500. The eight NCOS were merely bound over. 'Among persons of their rank there was not the same horror of taking a bribe as there was among commissioned officers in the Army, and ought to be,' thundered *The Times* on 28 May. Three days later a letter from Lord Saye and Sele was published in *The Times*:

> In view of the attack that was made on my personal honour in the Central Criminal Court on Wednesday of last week, I have cancelled all public engagements pending the opportunity at an early date of vindicating my character in the only place open to me.[22]

When Parliament reopened a month later Lord Saye and Sele

rose to 'repudiate the mischievous and dangerous idea that the possession of an illustrious ancestry debars a man from earning an honest living'. His letter to Colonel Whitaker was 'nothing more than a request to a satisfied customer to speak to one who had once been a satisfied customer'. He hotly refuted the allegation that he had started the unfortunate Whitaker on the road that had brought him to his current predicament.

Lord Newton, a soldier, diplomat and Conservative MP for thirteen years before entering the Lords, rose at this juncture. He was a man of considerable distinction who should shortly go on to higher things, with a series of ministerial posts in the wartime government. Rather pointedly, Lord Newton asked Lord Saye and Sele why he had not given evidence in court. When Saye and Sele replied that he had been waiting anxiously to be called, Newton riposted, 'You have a will of your own, haven't you?' Newton then went off at a tangent to attack Lipton Limited in general and Sir Thomas Lipton in particular. It had now been shown to the world that it was the deliberate practice of Lipton's firm to engage in a campaign for the purpose of debauching a certain class of officers in the army. It was the deliberate policy of the board; Sir Thomas Lipton was chairman of the board and yet not one word of condemnation had fallen from this man who was really responsible. If he were chairman of a company which had been engaged for many years in practices of this kind he should be more inclined to seek temporary seclusion than to advertise himself in every conceivable way. He wanted to know whether Lipton's was still on the list of contractors to the War Office or had it been removed.[23]

At this point Lord Crewe intervened. He did not think it desirable or that the House should wish this discussion to be prolonged. He accepted Lord Saye and Sele's statement and made the comment that the defence had not been sufficiently careful to avoid casting blame upon persons such as his noble friend who were not directly concerned with the case. The following day *The Times* carried an announcement that Lord Newton proposed to table a question in the House of Lords whether Lipton's was still on the War Office list of contractors. His speech constitutes the gravest attack ever made on Lipton:

> It must be perfectly plain to everybody that the employees of Lipton Limited were associated in a flagrant conspiracy with government functionaries and that large sums of money were actually expended in bribing those officials – money which presumably came out of the pockets of the shareholders. The head of this engaging

enterprise – not the ornamental head but the chairman and managing director – is Sir Thomas Lipton, and in view of the well-established facts, it might have been reasonably expected that some adverse comment on their proceedings would have appeared in the press and that there would have been some condemnation expressed. On the contrary, we are invited daily, I might almost say hourly, to admire this gentleman as a sort of national hero, a magnificent sportsman of the true British type, a compendium of all the British and all the other Christian virtues, and I frequently see it suggested that his transcendent merits can only be recognised by making him a member of this House.[24]

Lord Newton went on to sympathise with the victims and criticise the system. Lipton's might say that they had been unfortunate in having been found out and that it was the practice of other firms as well as their own. That might be the case, but it seemed to him that an example should be made. If it was announced that in future the War Office and other bodies concerned would have nothing more to do with Lipton Limited, he felt convinced that that decision would meet with greater approval from the public generally than many actions with which the government had been recently associated. Lord Lucas replied that Lipton's had not held any War Office contract since 1912. Their name had been removed from the lists of firms eligible to hold War Office contracts and instruction had been issued that no new contracts were under any circumstances to be entered into with Lipton Limited, and that steps should be taken that all contracts with canteens now held by that firm be terminated as soon as possible.

A few days later the annual general meeting of the shareholders of Lipton Limited took place at Winchester House, Old Broad Street. In describing the meeting as 'animated' *The Times* made an understatement. Despite the year's comfortable trading profit of almost £200,000 and a half-yearly dividend of six per cent, the shareholders were in a mean, belligerent mood. Lipton, for his part, was in no mood to mollify them with homespun philosophy or humorous anecdotes as in previous years. He touched on the canteen scandal in an offhand, perfunctory manner. It was unfortunate, he said, that an old story had been brought up, but the practice had been abandoned many years before the case was brought. He regretted the loss of the canteen contract, but it was a very small and unimportant branch of their activities, yielding an annual profit of only £4,000. 'The thing is a pity,' he concluded, 'but there it was.' And

243

he passed cheerfully to the next item on the agenda.

The shareholders, however, were not so easily satisfied and Lipton's report was frequently interrupted by hecklers. When he touched upon the reorganisation of the company and appointment of new directors, there were shouts of 'We want them. We need them!' As he sat down half-a-dozen angry shareholders leapt to their feet. There were searching questions about the legal costs involved in the case. Why should the shareholders shell out £4,000 for the defence of a man who had been fined as a criminal at the Old Bailey? The unkindest cut of all was the jibe, 'Attend to your business and leave yachting alone', but this provoked the sympathetic rejoinder, 'Never mind about dividends, bring back the Cup!'

Once more Lipton's allies in the daily press closed ranks, and the meeting received far less publicity than might have been anticipated. The *Daily Mail* devoted an entire column to a verbatim report of Lipton's speech, without mentioning the protests and interruptions, and concluded by stating that the meeting had ended with a unanimous acceptance of the report and cheers for Sir Thomas and the *Shamrock*.

Needless to say, there is not a single word about the canteen scandal or its aftermath anywhere in Lipton's autobiography – nor, indeed, were any cuttings filed in the relevant scrapbook. We can only guess at his feelings. For an Honorary Colonel of the Highland Light Infantry to be struck off the War Office list of contractors, and for this to be declared for all to see, must have been humiliating in the extreme. He had been criticised in court, vilified in the House of Lords and ridiculed at the shareholders' meeting. He felt the sting of Lord Newton's attack, unaware of the fact that the noble lord, as a career Tory politician, welcomed the canteen scandal as an opportunity to attack the Liberal government machine (of which Lord Saye and Sele was a relatively minor cog). A standing joke in the gentlemen's clubs of St James's that summer was that old Tommy Lipton was down at the Solent with *Erin*'s steam up, ready to flee into exile if and when further revelations were made.

He was in a very sombre mood when he did indeed board his steam yacht at Portsmouth in July, to escort *Shamrock IV* to New York for the impending contest for the America's Cup.

10. WAR WORK
1914–19

What did you do in the Great War, Daddy?
Little girl to her father, in a recruiting poster of 1915

Shamrock IV and her escort *Erin* were in the mid-Atlantic when they picked up wireless signals from a German cruiser that Britain and Germany were at war. The yachts immediately altered course and headed for Bermuda. A few days later they sailed northwards, hugging the coast of the neutral United States. After *Shamrock* was laid up in Brooklyn, *Erin* recrossed the Atlantic, a voyage made hazardous by the presence of German commerce raiders and submarines.

Still smarting from the humiliation of the canteen scandal, Lipton watched the warlike preparations in Britain and witnessed 'the first flower of our young British manhood' setting out to fight the enemy. His one regret was that he could not roll back the years, don khaki and march with them *en route* for Flanders. Now sixty-six but still very fit and as mentally alert as ever, he fretted over the fact that there was no move on the part of officialdom to harness his formidable talents to the war effort. Well, if War Office contracts were still to be denied him, he would take the initative and convert *Erin* for use as a hospital ship. Actually, the idea seems to have been put to him by the Duchess of Westminster, one of the glamorous society ladies who was to have been a guest aboard *Erin* at Sandy Hook for the America's Cup races that autumn. Why should she not have her trip in *Erin* after all? Within weeks of the outbreak of hostilities Lipton and the Duchess were busy conveying an entire field hospital of ten doctors, twenty nursing sisters, sixty-two orderlies and a vast quantity of medical equipment to France under the auspices of the Red Cross. Delayed at Southampton by the activities of German submarines in the Channel, Lipton joked with the Duchess: 'I suppose the Kaiser wants back the cups he presented to the *Shamrock*.'[1]

While he was waiting at Southampton, Lipton received a telegram from the *Chicago Examiner* suggesting that he and the armaments king, Hiram Maxim, should form a committee to decide how the war could be brought to the speediest conclusion. Lipton considered the cable carefully before drafting a suitably diplomatic reply. Soon, he hoped, the United States would be presiding, in terms of its neutrality and history, over a peace conference. Thus he neatly deflected the proposal without giving offence.[2]

Lipton's first essay in war work was well publicised but, on the whole, it did not get the favourable reaction for which he had hoped. Lord Kitchener had no time for amateurs and gave no encouragement to private hospitals. Nor did the well-meaning Duchess have the press, certainly not the American press, on her side. There were several snide, malicious comments in the papers about the favourite wolfhound and the volume of Longfellow's poetry with which she was invariably photographed. They even dragged up the embarrassing tale of how the Duke of Westminster, during the Boer War, had become infatuated with a nurse of mature years but undeniable charms. The Duke had been detached unwillingly from these charms, under orders from King Edward himself, and sent back to England and the fiancée who was waiting for him there.[3]

Lipton's second attempt was much more successful. Early in January 1915 he transported a field hospital comprising seven surgeons, seven nurses and three orderlies to the Balkans under the joint auspices of the Order of St John of Jerusalem and the British Red Cross. The prospect of a Mediterranean cruise, coupled with the romance and glamour of working in faraway Serbia and Montenegro, attracted a large number of applicants for positions in this unit. It was at this time that Lipton received the letter from David Sinclair of Tillie and Henderson asking him to show special consideration to a female member of his staff. *Erin*, with a fresh coat of gleaming white paint and a broad red band above the waterline with red crosses at the bows and amidships, set sail from England in December and spent Christmas at Marseilles where medical supplies were taken on board. The hospital staff for the expedition were selected personally by Sir Frederick Treves, and were under the command of Captain Edward N. Bennett, a veteran of the Sudan campaign and the Boer War who had also been the Liberal Member for the Woodstock constituency of Oxfordshire in 1906–10. Lipton, who bore the entire costs of the expedition, was also on board, along with three of his powerful motor cars which he had generously donated. It was planned to drop off four doctors and some nurses as Antivari, three at Cetinje – the Montenegrin capital – and then deliver the remaining eight doctors and a number of nurses to Salonika. The first stop was Monte Carlo. Though the Casino Gardens thronged with men in uniform the war seemed very remote. The Red Cross staff were highly indignant at not being allowed into the Casino itself, and had to be content with strolling in the sunshine along the palm-lined promenades.[4]

From Monte Carlo they sailed through the Straits of Messina and passed through the Ionian Islands. There are some stunning pictures of *Erin* sailing through the steep-sided Corinth Canal, before crossing the Gulf of Aegina to dock at Piraeus during carnival. Their first view of Athens, capital of still-neutral Greece, was the colourful sight of everyone in fancy dress, scattering confetti. The ships in the harbour were also in festive mood, gaily dressed all-over and firing salutes. That night everyone was invited to a masked ball organised by the King and Queen of the Hellenes. The following day Lipton returned the compliment by entertaining Their Majesties to lunch aboard *Erin*. After lunch the royal party posed on the sun deck for photographs which Lipton would soon be sending off to all the newspapers. In due course the appropriate scrapbook would be replete with cuttings from more than a hundred papers which reproduced the picture showing King Constantine and Queen Sophia (sister of the Kaiser) along with the Grand Duke George of Russia, Prince George and Prince Alexander of Greece, and Prince Henry of Battenberg. There in front, seated cross-legged side by side, were King Constantine and Tommy Lipton.[5] This photograph, the last glimpse at a vanishing world, would be rendered all the more poignant a few short years later when the pro-German Constantine (a field-marshal in the Prussian army) was deposed and exiled, to be succeeded by King Alexander (1917–20) before briefly regaining the throne (1920–22). His elder son, as George II, would have an even more turbulent reign, being deposed in 1924 when Greece became a republic, restored in 1935, forced into exile during the German ocupation (1941) and restored again in September 1946 before dying a few months later. But back in the spring of 1915 Athens was a haven of tranquillity, untouched by the conflict raging a few hundred miles away.

Erin's passengers were still in holiday mood as the ship weighed anchor and sailed northwards into the Aegean Sea, their destination the seaport of Salonika where *Erin* berthed alongside the *Grianaig*. Formerly the property of the Duchess of Westminster, she was now owned and operated as a hospital ship by none other than Lord Dunraven whose temper at seeing Lipton was not improved by a bad attack of gout.[6] Salonika was an important seaport in north-eastern Greece and until two years previously it had been a Turkish city, the capital of the vilayet of Macedonia. From the sea, it presented a picturesque appearance, with its white walls and red-tiled roofs, but closer at hand it presented a tawdry spectacle of dereliction and decay, and the stench from the open sewers was indescribable. In the Second Balkan War, however, it had surrendered to the Greeks on the feast-day of its patron saint, Demetrios. King George proceeded to what was now, after Athens, the largest city in his kingdom and was assassinated there on 18 March 1913 by a Greek named Schinasi; it was assigned to Greece by the Treaty of London two months later. Its largely Turkish and Bulgar population were driven out and by the spring of 1915 this ethnic cleansing had been carried out so thoroughly that Salonika was now completely Hellenised. Following the collapse of Serbia in October 1915 it would become the base for a large Anglo–French expedition under Marshal Sarrail and General Sir Bryan Mahon, but as early as December 1914 it was being used surreptitiously by the British and French to supply guns, ammunition, supplies and 'military observers' to their hard-pressed Serb allies.

From Salonika, Lipton and his team of helpers journeyed by the Lipton Hospital Train through the Vardar Ravine to Serbian Macedonia. At the little frontier town of Ghevgeli, on 14 February, Lipton ran into Dr James Donnelly, whom he had last encountered in New York. As they greeted each other delightedly at this remote wayside station neither of them had any idea of how tragic was to be the sequel to their second meeting under such changed circumstances.

The redoubtable Dr James Donnelly had relinquished a comfortable position as Medical Officer for the Port of New York to head a Turkish field hospital during the recent Balkan Wars and was, in fact, immortalised (under the pseudonym of Dr Dilly) in *Harper of Heaven*, the second of Robert Service's autobiographical volumes.[7] Donnelly was something of a swashbuckler in medical circles, having worked in many of the world's trouble spots, from the Far East and Africa to Haiti before settling down as superintendent of the Lower Bay Quarantine Station. The outbreak of the First Balkan War however, provided him with the pretext to get back into action, but he was now facing the toughest crisis of his career. The dead and the dying were surreptitiously dumped on the steps of the hospital during the night. All day long the unpaved streets were filled with ox-carts hauling the corpses of the latest victims off to the overflowing cemeteries.

Donnelly explained that he was in charge of the hospital, a converted tobacco warehouse which had once been the personal property of the Sultan Abdul Hamid. It was located near the railway station and housed 2,000 typhus patients. Donnelly asked Lipton to come along and inspect the hospital before proceeding farther up-country. Lipton assented, and brought along as many medical comforts as he could spare. In his autobiography he graphically sketched the horrific sight:

> Almost too dreadful to describe were the scenes I saw that day! The bedding accommodation being wholly inadequate, many of the patients had to be placed two, three, and more in one bed. Here and there the dead were stretched alongside the living. Many of the patients were lying on the ground, with straw their only mattress. Dr Donnelly's difficulties were further increased through the fact that, of the twelve American nurses he had brought with him to this hospital, no fewer than nine had contracted typhus, and he had consequently to rely upon Austrian prisoners for practically the whole of his nursing help. I could not resist the temptation to talk with them in their miserable quarters. Thoughts of possible infection never occurred to me; it was an honour to mix with young girls of such high courage and lofty devotion to the cause of sick and suffering humanity.[8]

And Donnelly himself left an account of his meeting with Lipton, in his diary:

> Sir Thomas Lipton remembered that we had met at the Lotos Club ... It was a great sight to see how everyone looked at him, and how good and kind he was to all our doctors and nurses. He gave me a gold four-leafed shamrock, which I shall keep for my wife. He also gave me his picture, and is going to send me an American flag and an Irish flag.[9]

The heat, the stench and the swarms of flies can be imagined. It was a sickening baptism for worse horrors to come, when the Lipton expedition went on its way. At Ghevgeli station Donnelly, accompanied by Nurses Tetrault and Fry, took a few minutes off from their incessant toil to wave goodbye to the good samaritans. Ghevgeli was also close to the Bulgarian frontier and although the Bulgarians were still technically neutral, they were bitterly resentful of the fact that Serbia had seized parts of Macedonia which they themselves coveted. Consequently they were in the habit of lobbing shells into the town from their artillery positions on the nearby heights. Donnelly thought that it would be a wise precaution to fly the American flag over his makeshift hospital and asked Lipton if, by any chance, he had such a thing. Lipton obligingly telegraphed his captain at Salonika and shortly afterwards the flag was on its way by the next train. The flag was that very Stars and Stripes which had been presented to Lipton by the Sons of the American Revolution after his gesture of solidarity during the Spanish–American War almost two decades earlier.

From Ghevgeli the Lipton Train headed north into Serbia. Going by Uskub (modern Skopje) and Nish, they reached Belgrade where the hospital contingent was entertained by Prince Paul, younger son of King Peter of Serbia. Twenty years later he would become Regent of Yugoslavia following the murder of his brother, King Alexander, at Marseilles by a Croat terrorist. From the balcony of the royal palace on 18 February, Lipton and his host watched grimly as the Austrians bombarded the city. The first shots of the Great War had been fired across the Danube from the Austrian artillery batteries at Semlin. In August, September and November 1914 the Austrians had mounted major invasions of Serbia and eventually succeeded in capturing Belgrade, but the Serbian army, battle-hardened by the Balkan Wars and possessing better artillery than their enemy, drove the Austrians back and liberated Belgrade on 16 December. For several months there was a lull in the fighting, the Austrians keeping up a desultory barrage on the Serb capital, and it was this daily ritual, hitherto ignored, that excited so much comment in the world's press thanks to Lipton's presence there.

The next day the British and American papers carried the story with the stirring headline 'Lipton Under Fire'.[10] The nearest shell exploded 150 yards away – which would seem a pretty wide berth to those unfortunate enough to be on the receiving end of a Zeppelin air raid, or a later generation that endured the horrors of the Blitz – but back in 1915 there was still something of a novelty factor in the notion of the great magnate being within shelling range. Lipton himself described how he happened to be caught in the thick of an Austrian bombardment 'and how I escaped injury or death I am not very clear to this day'.[11]

From Belgrade Lipton and his companions travelled south again to Nish. The provincial capital of Macedonia was small and backward, aptly described by the Daily Sketch of 27

February as 'a miry, semi-Oriental place, ill-adapted for use as the seat of Government' sweltering at the base of a mountain. In pre-war times it had a population of about 25,000, but after the fall of Belgrade to the Austrians in late November 1914 the population of Nish was swollen four-fold with refugees. It was now the headquarters of the aged King Peter, Prince Alexander (regent and commander-in-chief) and the elderly Voivode Putnik, chief-of-staff of the Serb army. Every house of any size had been commandeered by the government for the temporary accommodation of its ministries, and even the meanest café had been suddenly upgraded to the status of a first-class hotel – in price at any rate. Chaos reigned. Austrian prisoners of war moved freely about the town and mingled with the ragged, barefoot Serbian infantry sent down from the battlefront for rest and recuperation. The British medical team arrived not a moment too soon, as a typhus epidemic was raging. The only effective treatment was being offered by a British unit under Lady Muriel Paget, a frequent pre-war guest on *Erin* and one of those beautiful amateurs that Kitchener so detested, together with an American Red Cross unit under Dr Edward W. Ryan.

Lipton played a major role in the battle against this dread disease. Not only had he conveyed from England a well-trained Red Cross unit and a vast quantity of medical supplies and equipment, but his very presence in Nish ensured that the plight of Serbia was well publicised in the world's press. Over the ensuing three weeks he made frequent forays into the surrounding countryside. Everywhere he went his footsteps were dogged by reporters and photographers who scented a good story as the elderly millionaire traipsed around Macedonia. And they got it, as the acres of newsprint in the British and American papers testified. Typical of the headlines in America was 'Cup Challenger Using Yacht for British Red Cross'. Vivid reports were accompanied by pictures of the familiar figure with the yachting cap and polka-dot bow tie, posing against a background of fever hospitals, field dressing-stations, derelict railway stations, fortifications and artillery emplacements. He was photographed on foot, on horseback and in army transport, in the company of princes, generals, foot soldiers, prisoners and the wounded. What the hard-pressed Serb infantrymen made of this tall stranger on his smartly groomed pony is not known. Perhaps they observed cynically: 'Well, he picked a nice day for it', as they watched his retreating figure, knowing that in a few days he would be back aboard his luxurious yacht while they would still be here in the trenches facing enemy shelling. Lipton's mission was hardly a dangerous affair by any stretch of the imagination, but it was a considerable undertaking for a man of his age and it certainly served a useful purpose.

The *Erin* weighed anchor and returned to Marseilles, from where Lipton travelled to Paris on 30 March to attend an international conference on the plight of Serbia. At this meeting he spoke passionately about the little country which was being destroyed not so much by Austrian guns as by disease. Serbia, he claimed, had lost a sixth of her population as a result of typhus, and no fewer than 192 doctors had lost their lives in the struggle. From Paris Lipton journeyed to London bringing with him Black 'Enry, an exotic waif whom he had picked up in Belgrade. Black 'Enry claimed to be seventeen, but if so he was remarkably small for his age. Latterly he had been a Red Cross orderly with the American mission in Belgrade, but this native of Sierra Leone had previously been a ship's boy, a lift boy in a Salonika hotel, batman to a Serb officer in Belgrade, a hospital attendant and even a bomb-thrower during the last retreat of the Serb Army. He spoke Senegalese, Greek, Italian, French, German, Serbo-Croat and English, but he could make nothing of the strange lingo spoken by Lipton's Sinhalese houseboys. Enrolled as Lipton's latest pet, he was brought back to England where he was, for the newspapers, a two-day wonder before vanishing into limbo again.

On his return to Britain Lipton sent an open letter to the press calling the public's attention to Serbia's plight. This letter was published by virtually every newspaper early in April and undoubtedly focused much-needed attention on a forgotten corner of the war. Although this article was generally well received, it incurred the displeasure of the *Baptist Times* of 16 April which criticised the severe penalties imposed on journalists for breaches of censorship – yet here was the Great Lipton getting away with it in his much-publicised letter. However, this worthy paper reserved most of its vitriol for the Press Bureau and its absurdities.

Lipton now organised a relief fund and with the proceeds took *Erin* out for a second expedition to Serbia. On this trip he was accompanied by Madame Slavko Gruitch, wife of the permanent under-secretary in the Serb Ministry of War, who served as his guide and interpreter. His arrival was greeted ecstatically by the Serbs and his triumphant progress through the war-torn country was a tremendous boost to their morale. Everywhere he was greeted as *Chika Toma* (Uncle Tom) and by midsummer the worst of the typhus epidemic was over, in large measure due to his efforts. He was given the freedom of the city of Nish, an honour accorded to no other foreigner, and on 31 May a grateful Prince Alexander invested him with the insignia of a Grand Commander of the Order of St Sava. Working for the Serbs appealed to Lipton's innate sympathies for underdogs. They were 'the little fellows in the big fight'.

On this expedition he brought much-needed supplies to the overcrowded hospital run by Mrs Hankin Hardy in what had formerly been the prison at Kragujevac. The Serbs not only decorated this gallant lady, but chivalrously bestowed an appropriate decoration on Mr Hardy for having agreed to let his wife go to Serbia. Accompanying Lipton on this trip was a hospital unit sent out by the Scottish branch of the National Union of Women's Suffrage Societies. Two of this party would die of typhus – Sister Louisa Jordan and Miss Margaret Neil Fraser who in happier times had been well known as captain of the Scottish ladies' golf team. Lipton's ultimate destination was the field hospital run by Dr Berry at Vrnyetska Banja, a mountain health-resort about a hundred miles from Nish. A photograph of Lipton posing on the steps of this hospital shows him with Dr Berry in khaki service dress, alongside a Serb surgeon and the British matron. On the left of the picture sit stiffly to attention two rows of Austrian prisoners with white bands round their service caps to indicate their status as medical orderlies. On the other side of the picture stand or sit a group of Serbs recovering from their war wounds. This vividly captures the bizarre nature of this all-but-forgotten campaign, a mere sideshow compared with the mighty conflict then raging on the Western Front.

A few weeks later when the relief expedition was preparing for the return journey, Lipton cabled Donnelly letting him know the hour at which his train would be passing through Ghevgeli, in the hope that he would have the opportunity to meet him and his nurses briefly before heading for Salonika. When the train reached Ghevgeli, however, there were no nurses, and no Dr Donnelly. Instead there was Dr Samuel Hodge, a young assistant from Knoxville, Tennessee, who stepped forward and said, 'We had your telegram, Sir Thomas, but Sisters Tetrault and Fry are down with typhus. And Dr Donnelly' – he turned away for a moment, recovered his composure, and added slowly, 'Dr Donnelly died of typhus yesterday.' Lipton, who had some premonition of tragedy, shook Hodge's hand wordlessly. Hodge himself was in the early stages of the dread disease, and it would be Lipton who would nurse him back to health aboard *Erin* over the ensuing three weeks.

Later, Hodge told him how Donnelly, when seized with the dread illness, dictated nine letters, including one for his wife in the United States. He said that if he recovered he would look after the letters himself, but if he died they were to be given to Lipton to despatch to his friends. Shortly before he expired, Donnelly made one last request, that his body should be wrapped in the American flag sent up from the *Erin*, and that the dear emblem of his country should be consigned to the grave with his remains.

Lipton carried out these instructions to the letter and on a subsequent visit to Ghevgeli that year took a photograph of Donnelly's grave, at the head of which a large tombstone had been erected. This picture he sent to Donnelly's widow in New York. Four years later, in March 1919, when Lipton paid his first post-war visit to New York, the first people to greet him as he disembarked from the *Aquitania* were Mrs Donnelly and her six-year-old son who had come down to the Cunard wharf especially to thank him. Lipton was exceedingly touched by this gesture. Later he arranged to pay for the boy's education and took a close interest in his subsequent career.

Lipton's exploits in Serbia were very much in keeping with the man – enterprising, successful and highly publicised. Here again, as at all other points of his career, his unerring sense of timing and gesture counselled him as to which course would most effectively combine the useful with the spectacular. He was doing what no one else was. Celebrities touring the rest areas well to the rear of the battlefront were ten a penny in Flanders and France, and only exceptionally was an individual considered newsworthy. But the photographs of Lipton's Serbian campaign filled no fewer than five pages of a *New York Times* midweek pictorial supplement. The sixth page, ironically (for America, of course, was still neutral), was taken up with studio portraits of four titled Hungarian ladies residing in America who had sold their jewellery for the benefit of the opposing side. Countess Joseph Potocki had given $100,000 to the Austrian War Office to purchase heavy artillery, Baroness Reitzes had sold a pearl necklace for $85,000 on behalf of the Viennese Free Bread Fund, Countess Sierstorff had donated a ton of tobacco for the soldiers at the front, and Countess Manon von Dumreicher had supplied 5,000 cork legs for maimed soldiers.[12]

By the time he returned to Athens after his very strenuous second tour of Serbia and Montenegro Lipton was in a state of collapse and spent several days in bed aboard *Erin* recuperating. King Constantine was also gravely ill at this time, and Lipton despatched Dr Richard Strong from the yacht to minister to the stricken monarch after his German physicians hastily left town. Dr Strong had previously stamped out cholera in the Philippines and was now head of the American Sanitary Commission in Serbia. By the end of June Lipton was well enough to travel and set off for Marseilles again. In England he continued to bombard the press with articles with such emotive titles as 'A Valley of Death' or 'The Terrible Truth about Serbia'. He paid a heartfelt tribute to Dr Donnelly and all the other American doctors and nurses he had met, and this fulsome praise was well reported in the American papers.

In midsummer Dr Armgaard Karl Graves, the German master spy, published his memoirs which were eagerly translated into English and released as *The Red Secrets of the Hohenzollerns*. About one particular Hohenzollern, the Kaiser Wilhelm, Dr Graves supplied a curious anecdote:

> During Cowes Week in 1904 the Kaiser and King Edward were the guests of honour on Sir Thomas Lipton's yacht. Among those present was a well-known lady. The talk naturally turned on the events of the day, and the Kaiser, much elated over the victory of his yacht *Meteor*, bragged a great deal. The lady, taking up the cudgels of one of her relations who was interested in one of the defeated vessels, incurred the displeasure of the Emperor by her able witticisms.
>
> The Kaiser made a hasty, ill-judged rejoinder, which reduced the lady to tears. The lady rose with characteristic English dignity and withdrew. King Edward . . . had noticed that something displeasing had occurred. On being told the circumstances he called over his nephew into the chart room and evidently spoke his mind.
>
> The Kaiser next morning left in a huff. This incident was the cause of the widened breach between King Edward and William II. The lady had a great deal of influence with King Edward and his Court. She became the implacable enemy of the Kaiser. The result of her animosity was far-reaching.[13]

The absurd inference drawn from this was that the root cause of the Great War could be traced back to Lipton's yacht a decade before hostilities actually broke out.

Lipton continued to make trips to Salonika, bringing much-needed medical supplies, but this work ended abruptly early in October with the collapse of Serbia and the landing of the Allied expedition at Salonika. Until the spring of 1915 he was still determined to go across the United States as usual, and he accepted numerous speaking engagements, including the Panama–Pacific Exposition in San Francisco, but his commitments in the Balkans, rather than any fear of German submarines in the Atlantic, forced him to cancel. Even as late as November 1915 he continued to entertain the hope that he might go to America, but the superhuman exertions of the spring and summer caught up with him. He caught a cold which threatened to develop into pneumonia. He was utterly exhausted and as he slowly recovered his doctors prescribed a prolonged period of rest. On 25 October he went down to Cornwall and spent the next three months taking things easy, with occasional motoring jaunts across the moors.

On his return to England after his last trip Lipton surrendered his steam yacht to the Admiralty for patrol work under her original name of *Aegusa*, to avoid confusion with HMS *Erin*. She remained in the Mediterranean, with her pre-war crew but under the command of a retired Vice-Admiral who had returned to active service at a reduced rank. Captain T.P. Walker was sixty-two – only four years younger than Lipton professed to be, and the old boy bitterly regretted that he was regarded as well beyond the age at which he could have gone to sea. He kept in touch with the crew and was greatly heartened to learn that the *Aegusa*, on Wednesday, 19 April 1916, had sunk an enemy submarine, with well-directed gunfire. His elation was short-lived. Only nine days later the armed yacht *Aegusa* went to the rescue of the mine-laying sloop *Nasturtium* after she had hit a mine and began to sink. The survivors were only just settling down to mugs of tea when the *Aegusa* herself struck a mine. The rescued sailors were blown up twice in as many hours. 'My beautiful and historic yacht went to the bottom of the sea, carrying with her, alas! six members of my crew. For the life of any one of these I would gladly have given the ship.'[14] These few words conceal the anguish he felt at the loss of the vessel whose decks had rung with the feet of royalty. Eventually he would have another *Erin*, larger and even more palatial than her namesake, but she never had quite the same place in his affections. The tragic loss of crew-members who had been for so many years in his personal service was a bitter blow. These boys for whom he had genuine affection were like the sons he never had, and he felt their deaths as if it were a family bereavement. From this time onward, Lipton increasingly felt a sense of loneliness which he had never before experienced, not even when his beloved mother had died in 1889.

Lipton's autobiography passes immediately from the sinking of his beloved *Erin* to his arrival in New York in 1919. Waugh writes of the intervening three and a half years as a period of hibernation. From time to time Lipton toyed with the idea of crossing the Atlantic to promote the British point of view. Certainly no one was better qualified to act as a vigorous propagandist for the Allied cause, and he had an encouraging response from Big Bill Thompson, the flamboyant Mayor of Chicago who promised a big parade in his honour. But Lipton intuitively realised that such junketings in wartime would be misconstrued at home. The only respite he allowed himself was a trip to Glasgow, his first in nine years. On consecutive days (16–17 June 1916) the *Bulletin* had pictures of Lipton posing outside his original shop in Stobcross Street and with his headquarters staff. In the latter photograph, William Love appears on the extreme right. Now long retired from the business, William was still living at Johnston Villa and was a county councillor and magistrate for Lanarkshire. Together the two old men strolled arm in arm down the main street of Cambuslang and reminisced about the days when they were young men, full of ambition.

The one disagreeable note that confronted him that summer of 1916 was the subtle pressure brought to bear on him, as a large employer of labour in Ireland, to dismiss any of his employees suspected of involvement in the Easter Rising. The *Irish Standard* of 10 June announced flatly that all Sinn Féin sympathisers employed by Lipton's had been dismissed. Even those found in possession of subversive literature or a republican tricolour had been sacked. Given Lipton's sympathies for Irish nationalism, both then and later on, this seems out of character; but in the context of the grim times such ruthless action is more understandable. And it must be borne in mind that all companies and institutions in Ireland were being urged by the authorities to take similar action, perhaps were being lent upon if they showed signs of resisting the draconian edicts while the country was under martial law.

Instead, Lipton concentrated on his business. So many of his junior executives and managerial staff were now on active service and quite a few had already been killed in action, deepening the old man's gloom and sense of loss. Just as the deaths of his beloved parents had led him to redouble his energies in business, so too Lipton now found in work the necessary distraction to the grim news from the Somme and Gallipoli. In the wake of the canteen scandal he belatedly instituted a thorough investigation of corrupt practices which had been going on behind his back. The culprits were sacked and Lipton made good the losses incurred by their dishonesty out of his own pocket. At the shareholders' annual meeting on 24 July 1916 he repaid £247,812 'to make good losses in capital which the company had sustained'. When this failed to impress the War Office sufficiently to reconsider their decision to withhold contracts, Lipton threw himself into war work, providing food parcels for troops on active service, and he made sure that the crates that were soon on their way to the trenches were clearly stencilled with the name of the donor. He entertained nurses and servicemen on leave at Osidge, gave gold watches to employees who had been decorated for gallantry in action, presented cups and trophies to cadet battalions and kicked off at charity football matches. In 1917 the *Daily Mail*, under the heading of 'Things We Want to Know', enquired whether Lipton's noticeable increase in weight was due to his lately renewed devotion to business. The question was answered when, in 1918, Lipton's was again paying a dividend of twelve and a half per cent

There was still the intention of going to America, and he provisionally accepted an invitation to address the World Salesmanship Congress at Detroit in July 1916; but in the end both he and Gordon Selfridge cabled their apologies. Yachting was a thing of the past in Britain, but Lipton kept up with the numerous contests in Canada, the United States and Latin America for the various Lipton cups he had instituted, and he was particularly pleased to hear that the Pacific yacht race had been won that year by a Seattle vessel named *Sir Tom*. There were rumours in the American press that he planned to go into partnership with the Herreshoff family (builder of the America's Cup defenders and other fine yachts), but what they had in mind was submarines and torpedo-boats, rather than racing yachts. And every Christmas he was a major contributor to William Randolph Hearst's fund for the poor of New York.

With no relatives of his own involved in the fighting, the war took on a rather detached character so far as he was concerned. Only once was he deeply affected by the casualty lists, and that was when on New Year's Eve he heard that Captain John C. Lauder, the only son of his close friend Harry, had been killed in action on 28 December 1916.[15] Only a week previously, Lipton had gone to the first night of Lauder's Christmas revue *Three Cheers* at the Shaftesbury Theatre and engaged in pawky Scottish banter with the comedian from his stage box, to the delight of the audience. Harry Lauder was staying at the Bonnington Hotel in Southampton Way, his wife having remained at home in Dunoon. On New Year's Eve, a Sunday, Lauder was feeling unaccountably low in spirits and telephoned his brother-in-law, Tom Vallance, who invited him out to Clapham for a Hogmanay party. On returning to his hotel around midnight, he was told by the porter that Sir Thomas Lipton had telephoned, asking him to call back. Wondering what was so urgent, he phoned Osidge.

Lipton's immediate reaction on hearing the news had been to telephone his old friend and offer his condolences. When Lauder returned his call, to his horror he realised, from the sound of Lauder's cheery voice, that the father had not yet been told. Lipton had not the heart to tell him; he could not rob his friend of those few extra hours over Christmas in which he could build dreams and hope. Thinking quickly and forcing jollity into his voice, he offered a New Year's greeting instead and rang off. A few hours later, the porter brought the dreaded telegram to Lauder's bedroom. It had been sent to Dunoon, opened by Mrs Lauder, and redirected to London. The grief-stricken comic took the first train north to comfort his wife, who had been taken ill on receipt of the news. Lipton was a tremendous comfort to Harry Lauder over the ensuing painful days. When Lauder wanted to cancel the show, it was Lipton who pleaded with him to carry on: the livelihood of 200 people connected with the revue was at stake. On 5 January 1917 Lauder returned to the stage, and his staunch friend was there, in his stage box, to give him moral support. Only once did Harry falter during the show. After the curtain came down and the lights went up, he addressed the house from the footlights. It was an extremely emotional scene, and Lipton was not the only man to weep uncontrollably that night.[16]

As the war entered its final year, Lipton was back to the routine of twenty years previously, putting in an eighteen-hour day at the office, and often returning to Osidge in the wee small hours. He would have a brief working lunch in his office, and would sit up late over reports. Sometimes he would bring back two or three colleagues for dinner at Osidge followed by conferences that lasted half the night. The only variation to this arduous routine was the occasional foray into the provinces to make a snap inspection of stores. The country was booming with plenty of war work available and more and more women taking up full-time employment while their menfolk were in the services. This new-found affluence was reflected in the volume of business in the Lipton stores which rose to record levels. He became an ardent champion of the new War Loan and tramped around the country making speeches on behalf of the Tank Bank, a mammoth fund-raising campaign in which the newfangled 'land-ships' were paraded. He was back in Glasgow late in 1917 drumming up support for the Tank Bank, and was immensely gratified to learn that Glasgow had raised £14,171,760 – five and a quarter million pounds of it in a single day, of which he personally had contributed £50,000. This was more than twice the total for Birmingham and an average of fourteen pounds per head for every man, woman and child in Glasgow.[17]

For relaxation he busied himself with his enormous scrapbooks – there were now more than fifty of them. There were new cuttings to be pasted in, but increasingly he found himself idly turning the pages of the earlier volumes, especially those that so exhaustively chronicled his valiant attempts on the America's Cup. Technically he might have been the loser, but somehow he always seemed to enjoy a far better press than the winners, and the saga of the *Shamrocks* was a tremendous achievement. Soon, he hoped, this wretched war would be at an end, and he could then pick up the gauntlet again.

11. DECLINE AND FALL
1919–27

Ah, fill the Cup: – what boots it to repeat
How Time is slipping underneath our Feet:
Unborn TOMORROW, and dead YESTERDAY,
Why fret about them if TODAY be sweet!
　　　Edward Fitzgerald, *Omar Khayyam*, ed. 1, xxxvi

As the *Aquitania* docked in New York Lipton's thoughts inevitably went back to that time, more than half a century earlier, when he had first stepped ashore at Castle Garden with no more than thirty shillings in his pocket.

Soon it would be business as usual and, besides, there was now more time to devote to the great passion of his declining years, yachting. The challenge with *Shamrock IV* had been deferred for six years, but now races for the Cup were scheduled to take place in July 1920. In the spring of 1919 he returned to the Brooklyn boatyard where his beautiful racing yacht was laid up. She was taken out of her shrouds and carefully inspected before going into the water, Lipton's personal standard, a green shamrock on a gold field, proudly fluttering from her mast.

When the *Daily Telegraph* launched a fund to purchase Sulgrave Manor, ancestral home of George Washington's family, as a monument to Anglo–American friendship, King George V contributed £100, but Lipton cabled $1,000 from New York. Lipton spent most of that year in America with much of his time being taken up with the negotiations to secure new premises for his American operation. His office block in Franklin Street, in downtown Manhattan, had burned down the previous winter but by midsummer he had concluded a deal with the Hoboken Land and Improvement Company to take a twenty-year lease on Unit D of the Terminal Building on the Hudson waterfront where the Lackawanna Ferry tied up. The twelve-storey building had previously been occupied by the Remington Arms Company whose lease expired on 15 May 1919. This deal gave Thomas J. Lipton Inc. 275,000 square feet of space on one of the best sites in the New York area. Soon he would be looking across the

Hudson at the Hoboken waterfront and his brand-new premises, with LIPTON'S TEA in gigantic letters for all to see, to reassure himself of how far he had come. This huge building was the administrative centre of his many enterprises in North America, quite separate from the British business and still wholly owned by himself. It was unaffected by the tiresome red tape which, increasingly, was making life so difficult for such a free-wheeling entrepreneur as himself. Here he had no shareholders snapping at his heels, and remarkably little intervention from state or federal authorities.

Lipton had returned to America not a moment too soon. Over the preceding two years he had done more than his share to promote Anglo–American relations, entertaining American nurses and servicemen at Osidge; but post-war America was in an ugly mood over the British behaviour in Ireland. Now Lipton's Irish nationalism was played to the hilt. There was an ugly scene at the St Regis Hotel on 26 June 1919 when the British financier Sir Charles Allan accosted two girls soliciting funds for the Irish Republic in the hotel lobby. He accused them of treason and bellowed for the manager to throw them out. Instead the manager summoned three of his burly Irish–American porters and summarily ejected Sir Charles who promptly moved, bag and baggage, to the Ritz–Carlton. As Sir Charles had announced his intentions of challenging for the America's Cup if Lipton stood down, the New York newspapers had some trenchant comments to make. This unfortunate fracas came hard on the heels of intemperate remarks by Harry Hawker, one of the aviators then attempting to fly the Atlantic but who had been forced to ditch his aircraft. The American Navy had mounted a crossing by flying-boats, supported by a fleet of destroyers spread out like a chain across the ocean. The NC-4 flying-boats had just arrived safely in the Azores, having flown the Atlantic in leisurely stages, and Hawker had made some caustic remarks about doing it the easy way. For this reason he was roundly condemned as a poor loser.

The genial Lipton, however, was getting as good a press as ever. He was photographed at the Battery examining with approval the fine schooner *Sir Thomas J. Lipton* named in his honour. When Mayor Hylan led the parade of New York's policemen, Honorary Commissioner Lipton was on the saluting dais alongside Governor Alfred Smith. When Lipton and the Prince of Wales attended the New York Horse Show in November, the American press was unanimous that these two goodwill ambassadors had done a great deal to restore harmony between the English-speaking peoples. On 30 November Lipton boarded the *Adriatic* for the voyage home, but in thick fog she collided with the freighter *St Michael* near the Statue of Liberty and her departure was delayed. By the time Lipton landed at Southampton on 12 December he regaled waiting pressmen with an endless stream of anecdotes and jokes about Prohibition. When the Revd William Lipton, Rector of the Episcopal Church of the Ascension in Bloomfield, New Jersey and reported to have come from Canada 'of Irish parents', died of cancer on 27 December at the age of forty-six, his titled namesake was quizzed closely by some reporters. Were they, by any chance related? Lipton, uncharacteristically tight-lipped, released a one-line statement: 'I have neither chick nor child, kith nor kin.'[1]

Lipton was back in Glasgow in February 1920, and when he took time out to visit Cambuslang the local newspaper mentioned that the present occupant of Johnston Villa was Sir Thomas's first manager, County Councillor William Love, JP. 'The bond of affection between these two enterprising and successful businessmen has strengthened with the passing years.'[2]

In America the previous summer he had attended the premiere of *Broken Blossoms* at the George M. Cohan Theater, and afterwards had dined with the film's director, David Wark Griffith. He had also attended the dinner at the Canadian Club of New York in honour of the film actress, Marie Dressler. In 1920 he put his Ceylon estates at the disposal of a film company producing an epic entitled *The Life of Buddha*. It was even rumoured that Lipton himself would take one of the key roles in the film, but his involvement with the cinema was strictly behind the camera. It later transpired that he was a backer of J. Stuart Blackton, a movie mogul and fellow yachtsman, who came from the United States in 1920 to put fresh life into the British film industry. The result of this collaboration was *The Glorious Adventure* with Lady Diana Duff-Cooper as Lady Beatrice Fair and Sir William Luff as King Charles II, released in July 1921. Later, Lipton would back the production of *The Virgin Queen*, a lavish costume drama with Lady Diana as Queen Elizabeth.

The world of 1920 was vastly different from the world of 1914. Four great empires had broken up, emperors, kings and princes had lost their thrones, and even the victorious Allies were still recovering slowly from the social and economic upheavals of the war. Revolution had swept across Russia and affected many other countries. At home, the Labour Party had supplanted the Liberals as the radical alternative and within three years would even form a government. Increased taxation and government controls on business practice were beginning to dent the impregnability of great business empires like Lipton's. Similarly the moral climate was subtly changing. In Edwardian times it was perfectly acceptable, indeed rather expected, that rich tycoons would enjoy an extravagant lifestyle. The size and luxurious condition of their motor cars, yachts and mansions were the very stuff of the gossip columns – Mammon was worshipped without reservation. Now such extravagance was coming to be questioned and criticised and the notion was developing that opulence was somehow a bad thing. This did not come overnight, and for a time the millionaires went back to enjoying themselves as uproariously and as royally as they had done before the war. Thus the atmosphere in which the 1920 series of America's Cup races was staged recaptured something of those earlier halcyon days at the turn of the century. The women no longer wore such huge hats or voluminous skirts, but otherwise things appeared to have changed very little. At Sandy Hook it was almost as if time had stood still. The millionaires with their fast yachts and pretty women were out in force. And there, in their midst, was Sir Thomas Lipton with his goatee beard, his blue polka-dot tie, his jaunty yachting cap. Admittedly, the beard was now pure white and the face more lined, but Lipton was still the same, with his boyish charm and genial smile. The *Erin* had gone, but here was the *Victoria* to take her place.

The newspapers on both sides of the Atlantic gave as much prominence to the forthcoming races and the respective boats as they had ever done. In 1914 Lipton had described his new yacht as a 'hit-or-miss' proposition. She was a big boat, built to carry an enormous sail, and she was definitely not the most elegant thing afloat, with a snub nose, straight stem, body squeezed in at the bulwarks, rounding outwards to the waistline, going in almost flat, then tapering towards the keel and expanding outwards at the foot. In silhouette she looked like a giant wineglass rather than a yacht. The racing commentator Francis B. Cooke described her as a freak, but although she was unusual she was certainly tough. She would, however, have to face a time allowance of six and a half minutes.

In view of this the defending crew hoped for a moderate breeze. Designed by Nathaniel Herreshoff, who had died in the interim, the defending yacht *Resolute* was Boston-owned and Boston-manned. Chris Christensen, who had been mate under the late Charlie Barr, was the skipper, with Charles Francis Adams at the helm and George Nichols, son-in-law of J. Pierpont

Morgan, as navigator. John Parkinson, the celebrated Harvard centre, was the strong man of the after-deck. The majority of the deck-hands were Scandinavian by birth. *Shamrock*, on the other hand, was skippered by Sir William P. Burton, one of Britain's most celebrated amateur yachtsmen, and his crew was composed of Essex fishermen with one notable exception, Sir William's wife Thora (a formidable yachtswoman in her own right). Seamen tend to be more superstitious than most and during the course of the races there was a widespread rumour that the fishermen resented the presence of the glamorous Lady Burton. It was even rumoured that Lipton was less than satisfied with his skipper and intended to replace him. But mindful of the old adage about not changing horses in midstream, Lipton persevered with the temperamental Burton, though undoubtedly these problems did not make for an equable atmosphere.

As it happens, despite the freakishness of the yacht and the bizarre choice of crew, the challenge mounted by *Shamrock IV* was the one which came closest to victory. The series began auspiciously when *Shamrock* won the first race by sheer luck, after making a poor start and being well astern in a drifting match, only pulling ahead when *Resolute*'s throat halyards parted. It was a victory that gave Lipton little pleasure; he did not wish to win by a fluke and sportingly offered to call off the race. It might be perfectly in order according to the rules but it was not his way, and although his friends overruled him he felt no confidence for the rest of the series from the clumsy manner in which *Shamrock* had been handled. His worst fears were justified when *Resolute* easily outsailed *Shamrock* in a light breeze but was unable to finish the course in time. It was at this critical point that Lipton seriously contemplated sacking the Burtons, but at the last moment he relented. Twenty-four hours later he had every reason for thanking his lucky stars that he had not made any change; for this time he had the satisfaction of seeing his yacht cross the finishing line ahead of *Resolute*. This win was greeted by the most incredible cacophony of ships' sirens, hooters and whistles imaginable as every vessel acknowledged the victory of the underdog. Nevertheless, it was not as convincing a victory as Lipton would have liked. In another drifting match, with intermittent puffs of wind, *Resolute* had the misfortune to become becalmed. *Shamrock* herself only just crossed the line within the time set.

Now *Shamrock* was two up. At this juncture Lipton ordered a special case to be made in which to take the Cup back to England in triumph. The experts, however, were not convinced that the series was lost, for so far there had not been a proper race. On the other hand, there were many pundits who opined that *Shamrock* would pull it off if she caught the defender on a broad reach in a strong breeze. Lipton and his supporters prayed for a wind of fifteen to twenty-five knots, the optimum conditions for their yacht to perform at its best. On the day, however, there was only a steady but light breeze which was favourable to the defender. In fact, *Shamrock*'s crew pulled out every stop and by dint of good seamanship actually crossed the finishing line ahead of *Resolute*, but it was not sufficient to offset that time allowance of six and a half minutes.

Spirits were still high aboard the *Victoria* that evening and everyone fervently hoped that the wind strength would continue to improve. On the fourth race, however, the wind averaged only five knots, conditions which enabled *Resolute* to complete the course three minutes ahead of *Shamrock*, even without the time allowance. On the morning of the fifth and final race, with the score at two all, Lipton awoke to find what he had been praying for all those years, grey skies and a stiff breeze of at least twenty knots. Now here was a chance for the ocean-going *Shamrock* to show what she was really made of. The wind was still rising when the *Victoria* came up from Brooklyn to Sandy Hook. Lipton was relishing the situation, his confidence increasing as the wind strength approached the twenty-five-knot level. His heart leaped at the prospect of victory, and already he could visualise the scenes of his greatest triumph as he brought the Cup back to Britain. After four attempts in twenty-one years, the greatest of all trophies would be his at long last.

One can imagine his feelings when he saw the 'No Race' signal being hoisted. In a white-hot fury he hurried over to *Shamrock* to find out what was happening, only to be told that the judges, feeling that the weather was too rough, had asked the boats whether they would agree to cancelling the races. Both *Resolute* and *Shamrock* had agreed. No record has survived of the exchange of words between Lipton and Burton but one may imagine that the air was blue. Lipton was beside himself with rage at the decision having been taken without consulting him. On his return to the *Victoria* he glowered furiously and said: '*Shamrock* had much worse weather than this coming over. She had her ocean rig and not her racing rig. But there was no more protection for the crew then than now.' These words were spoken in the heat of the moment, and later, when he had calmed down, he was forced to concede that the judges' decision had been correct. It would have been the height of folly, with men's lives at risk, had he countermanded the decision and forced the race to go on. Lipton formally retracted those hasty words, but even as he retracted it was plain to everyone that he still disagreed with the decision.

Inevitably his original comment, as well as the retraction, occasioned considerable coverage in the world's press which tended to side with Lipton. Even the American papers were unusually acerbic in their criticisms. The American yachting commentator John C. Spears talked of these 'paper-napkin sailboats' and described the day's non-event trenchantly:

> The wind-shy regatta committee and the skippers of the blown-glass *Resolute* and *Shamrock* were rewarded yesterday by weather exactly suited to their capacities. There was absolutely no danger at any time of losing top-hamper or of throwing spray over the well-polished shoes of the racing crews.[3]

Another American critic wrote forcibly, arguing that the time had come to change the rules of construction in order to ensure that the boats would be able to withstand a twenty-five-knot wind with racing rig. On the British side a typical comment was:

> Sandy Hook is sheltered on three sides by the land, and the Yankees have the frankness to ask the sporting world to be fooled by the calling-off of the race because their cockleshell was unable to stand up against a summer squall in a sheltered bay, while the sturdy British challenger that had stoutly weathered Atlantic storms was not allowed to sail the course.[4]

Had Sir William Burton refused to agree, the race would have had to go on. That much is clear, and it explains why the decision rankled so deeply with Lipton. On the other hand, he might nominally be the challenger but in the final analysis he was not the man in the boat. Had he been in a position to veto the decision to cancel he would have been ordering his crew to do something that he could not do himself, to undergo dangers which he could not share. It was a responsibility which he could not take. He had to accept his skipper's judgement, particularly in view of their earlier disagreement. Nevertheless Lipton's indignation was understandable. There is an element of danger in every sport, and yachting is more dangerous than most. The press comments about the inequalities between the yacht which had crossed the Atlantic and the defender were fully justified. *Shamrock* could have raced that day; it would have been unpleasant, but not impossible. On the other hand, relative lack of skill and experience were now beginning to tell in the *Shamrock* crew and dissension between crew-members and between the crew as a whole and the Burtons meant that there was precious little team spirit.

A few hours later the wind had blown itself out and *Resolute* won the inevitable drifting match. *Shamrock IV* would have been very lucky if she had taken the Cup, but at the same time she came pretty close to doing just that. Lipton's own comment on the 1920 series showed true sportsmanship:

> So far as pure sailing was concerned, it was virtually a dead-heat. And in one at least of the defender's two other victories rather baffling weather seemed to like us less than it did our opponent. But I did not grumble. It is all in the game. We had had a series of splendid races, and I had, at any rate, the melancholy satisfaction of knowing that in the final result the better boat had won.[5]

Lipton returned to England without the Cup but with his popularity higher than ever before. Now seventy-four, he was more in tune with the times than he had been in the preceding decade. Business was as brisk as ever, and although he had to tell the annual shareholders' meeting in 1921 that profits were dented by a huge increase in wage bills and freight charges he was still able to declare a dividend of twelve and a half per cent. There was now no longer the old nit-picking about his yachting pursuits. Instead he was warmly congratulated on his near miss. A narrow defeat was, in effect, almost a victory, and if Lipton's standing in the public eye was anything to go by, then his latest and most valiant attempt to prise away the 'mug' was a howling success. On his departure from America he had given the stock answer to the reporters clamouring to ask whether he would try again, that he would go home and consider the matter. He did think about it seriously, but it seemed as if he would now call it a day. Remarkably, a decade later, he would mount his fifth and final challenge.

In the summer of 1922, when the negotiations between the British government and the Irish delegation were at a crucial stage Lipton's opinions were canvassed by both sides. One day he would be dining with Churchill and Lord Birkenhead, and the next entertaining Michael Collins and Arthur Griffith. Lipton makes no mention of this diplomatic activity in his autobiography but his high standing with the leading figures in the Irish Free State government throughout the 1920s suggests that his innate tact and good sense must have played some part in smoothing the way towards a resolution of the differences between Ireland and Britain at that crucial period. When President Cosgrave paid his first state visit to London in November 1926 Lipton was with the Londonderrys and the Laverys, George Bernard Shaw and Lord Birkenhead at Claridge's for the official Irish reception. Interestingly, Lipton's old *bête noir* the Earl of Dunraven, who had drawn much closer to him since their hospital work during the war, was now in the curious position of being both a member of the House of Lords and a Senator in the new Irish Dáil.

The Roaring Twenties were, for Lipton at any rate, a much more tranquil time than the preceding decade. One of the most perceptive descriptions of him belongs to this period. Beverley Nichols, at that time a reporter with the *Weekly Despatch*, went out to Southgate and interviewed him at home. Subsequently the interview, in an expanded version, appeared in his book *Twenty-Five*, published by Jonathan Cape in 1925. The four pages provide the most vivid pen-portrait of Lipton ever written. It was one of the few interviews recorded in the book which were entirely respectful. The chapter in which it appeared was entitled 'Two Big Men and One Medium' – the other big man being Rudyard Kipling. The interview followed the usual line which Lipton must by that time have known by heart. He recounted the fanciful story of his early life and reprised the anecdotes about the Orphans, the banknotes and the Jumbo cheeses. He gossiped about royalty and concluded, as always, with a reverential reference to his mother: 'You stick to your mother, laddie, as you would stick to life. As long as you do that, you won't go far wrong.' Nichols was astonished at Lipton's idiosyncratic tastes in interior decor:

> As soon as one entered the hall the fun began. There were black china negresses, nice bright wallpapers, heads of healthy animals and at every turn photographs of some royalty in a large silver frame. One object in the billiard room I particularly admired. This was a sofa covered with cushions of really inspiring colours. One cushion which was placed between a blue and orange stripe and a white and black check had for its main design the star-spangled banner worked in blue and crimson wools . . . I could not help smiling a little at all the silver-framed photographs with the signatures written in that curious scrawl which denotes either a royal origin, success behind the footlights or *delirium tremens*.[6]

Despite this faintly patronising approach, Nichols was clearly impressed by Lipton. 'He was simple and charming. His pride was so naïve one could not possibly object to it.' Lipton's constant name-dropping with anecdotes sprinkled with 'The Kaiser said to me', 'Her Majesty remarked', or 'The Prince of Wales' were 'all only little pats on the back of the ex-factory boy'.

Lipton was now well beyond his allotted time span, but there was no let-up in his business activities. In particular, his Hoboken headquarters, which many had regarded in 1919 as the height of folly and extravagance, was now beginning to pay off handsomely. With the passage of the Volstead Act and the ban on alcoholic liquor, consumption of beverages like tea, coffee and cocoa soared, and Lipton profited accordingly. There was further expansion in the Ceylon tea estates as well as his Mexican coffee plantations. The number of Lipton shops had now passed the 600 mark and rising profits in America were matched by steadily increasing dividends at home. More and more, however, Lipton preferred to live in America and he continued to cut a flamboyant figure in the picture papers. In August 1920, on the eve of the *Shamrock IV* challenge, and accompanied by his friend Jimmy Stuart-FitzJames (heir of the Duke of Alva who had died twenty years earlier), he had visited the notorious Sing Sing Prison where, exceptionally, he was allowed to chat with some of the inmates on Death Row. Before leaving, he addressed the prisoners in the dining-hall, saying: 'There was never a man born who did not make a mistake. I've made them, and I guess you have.' He got an illuminated testimonial from the convicts, and repaid the compliment the following year by donating a three-foot-high silver loving-cup for the prison baseball competition. Thereafter Lipton, sporting a baseball cap, made a point of visiting Sing Sing each summer for the big ball game.

Even well into his seventies, Lipton's name was still being linked romantically with this or that prominent socialite, actress or celebrity. Roszicka (Rose) Dolly, one half of the famous Dolly Sisters, wrote an amusingly perceptive article about a weekend spent with Sir Thomas and revealed for the first time that he had never married 'because the woman I loved ran off and married another man because he had more of this world's goods than I had'.[7] A few hours later he calmly announced his engagement to Rose's twin, Jenny. Jenny Dolly herself wrote an article that showed the old charmer had lost none of his winning ways with the fair sex.[8]

On one return voyage from New York, when he was strolling

on the deck of the liner in his yachting cap, he was mistaken by a passenger for the steward, and when he obligingly fetched a deck chair at the passenger's bidding, he cheerfully pocketed the shilling tip.[9] Despite his immense fortune, Lipton lived as frugally as ever. His favourite pastime these days was his ever-growing collection of scrapbooks. One significant change in his lifestyle was his discovery of the pleasures of theatregoing. Up to the age of fifty he had never been inside a theatre, but now he became an avid first-nighter. Although he was no longer the intimate of the reigning sovereign, he was on friendly terms with royalty. He was photographed talking to King George at Richmond House and when the Duke of York (later King George VI) visited Glasgow in January 1923 Lipton lunched with him at Blythswood House and accompanied him to Hampden Park to see Queen's Park play Bathgate. Lipton had very few intimate friends, but they were for the most part drawn from big business: men like Tom Dewar the whisky magnate; Gordon Selfridge; Andrew Weir, Lord Inverforth, the shipping tycoon. For the first time in his life Lipton was mixing on easy terms with other self-made men, not commercial rivals of course, but men with whom he had a very great deal in common.

In particular Dewar and Lipton were extremely close. People spoke affectionately of the two millionaires as Tea Tom and Whisky Tom. They were very much on the same wavelength; each knew what the other was about. Dewar was also a confirmed bachelor and the press affectionately likened the two Toms to David and Jonathan. They could converse in a form of verbal shorthand, virtually unintelligible to outsiders. Everyone who saw them together remarked on their happiness in each other's company, always laughing and fooling about like a couple of schoolboys. Dewar was world-famous for his one-liners, but among his many accomplishments he was also a talented artist. He would sketch a portrait of his friend, complete with yachting cap, on one side of a postcard and send it off from England to America, or from the Continent to England, confident in the abilities of the appropriate postal administrations to see that the card thus addressed reached its destination. Lipton and Dewar had been close friends for fifteen years and for the rest of Dewar's life they would be well-nigh inseparable. When Sir Harry Lauder spied them in the stage box on the first night of his new revue at the Palace Theatre, he cried out 'Ah, there ye are, ye rascals!' and cracked jokes with the two Toms who gave as good as they got. The audience loved it.[10]

Lipton may not have been much of a music lover himself, but

he warmly supported the Lipton Choral Society, recruited from the City Road staff, which gave many fine public performances in the nearby Leysian Halls. He had for many years been one of the most generous supporters of William Randolph Hearst's Christmas fund and when Hearst and his wife visited London in June 1922 Lipton dined with them at the Savoy, along with D.W. Griffith. That year, Lipton had given a nostalgic interview to *The Bulletin*, the Glasgow picture paper, and reminisced about his boyhood exploits with model boats on Glasgow Green. Arising out of this, on 29 July he presented the Lipton Trophy to the Scottish Model Yacht Association and in subsequent years attended the annual races whenever he could. His interests in aviation were in no way diminished by the passing years; he was photographed with Jimmy James, winner of the Aerial Derby, in July 1921 and closely followed each stage of the Round Britain Air Race in September 1922. Always interested in the latest technology, he took part in the first attempt to broadcast across the Atlantic. On 2 October 1922 he was at radio station WOR in Newark, New Jersey, and went on the air at midnight, Eastern Standard Time, to speak to his old chum Gordon Selfridge. Although music was audible, the voices were unintelligible to each other. Five days later the experiment was repeated, this time linking Bamberger's department store in New York with Selfridge's in Oxford Street. On this occasion Lipton conversed with Selfridge in London and the store proprietor's son Harry in San Francisco, but father and son were unable to converse direct. On 14 January 1927 he picked up his telephone to find Captain Terence A. Brady of Yonkers, New York, on the line. 'It was as clear as if from the next street,' he told reporters later that day. If not the first transatlantic telephone call, it was certainly one of them, and was headline news on both sides of the ocean.

Post-war unemployment was running high as Christmas 1922 approached. Lipton contributed £25,000 from his own pocket to provide 120,000 food parcels, and was in Glasgow's City Chambers on Friday 22 December to help distribute 7,020 parcels to the unemployed of his native city. The pattern was repeated throughout the British Isles; even Dublin; which had recently become the capital of the Irish Free State, was not left out. The Boy Scouts rallied round to do the voluntary distribution.

Lipton was back in Glasgow in the autumn of 1923 to have the freedom of the city conferred on him: 2 October was undoubtedly the proudest day of his life and the honour meant much more to him than any of his orders and decorations. The ceremony took place in St Andrew's Hall, a stone's throw from the site of Lipton's first shop in Stobcross Street. Sir James Bell, a prominent civic administrator, sat alongside to receive the same honour; in the words of Lord Provost Paxton, they were both 'worthy citizens of Glasgow'.

In an extraordinarily long sentence the citation stated that the honour was being conferred on Lipton

> in acknowledgment of the exemplary and patriotic services which he had rendered to the country, particularly during the Great War, and to the corporation and the community by his repeated and generous gifts for the benefit of his poorer fellow citizens in time of hardship during unemployment, and in recognition of the credit and renown which from far and near he had brought to his native city by his devotion to and success in trade and commerce to the great advantage of the people, and to the promotion of British–American friendship and his determination as a sportsman to regain for this country the America's Cup and also an expression of the respect and admiration in which he was universally held.

In his speech Lord Provost Paxton spoke of Lipton as one who had never been ashamed of his background, who had never ceased to declare that he owed all he was or had been to his early training in Glasgow. In his response, Lipton recalled his days as an office boy earning half a crown a week and how he had promised his mother that one day she should have a carriage of her own. He told this story because he wanted every ambitious lad of Glasgow to feel that the way was open for him to succeed in life if only he would take his mother for his guiding star. He touched on his exploits in Serbia combating the typhus epidemic and finished by expressing the hope that 'auld Glesca' would enjoy continuing success. When discussing his mother Sir Thomas was seen to be close to tears. It was an extremely emotional performance and although the anecdotes were highly polished from repeated telling, it was a strangely subdued Lipton who brought his peroration to a close. It was not that he was overwhelmed by the large gathering assembled to do him honour; after all, as the *Glasgow Herald* put it, 'he was here amang his ain folk'. Perhaps the occasion focused his mind on his early days in Glasgow, of his brother John who might have become an eminent surgeon had his life not been snuffed out in his teens. Perhaps he was thinking of poor Margaret McAuslan and the wee unsought-for bairn on whom he had bestowed his name . . . Where was she now, he might have wondered, and

273

what of the boy that lived, the one he had named William, for the real love of his life?

He had recovered his composure and his easy manner after the civic lunch that followed and he was called upon to address a few words to the assembled company. He recounted some of his adventures in America as a boy and told a story which had only happened that very morning. Riding in the carriage on his way to being made a burgess he had passed the University and had remarked to his companion: 'How well I remember passing through these buildings daily when I was a lad.' When his companion looked surprised and incredulous Lipton had explained: 'Surely you, of all people, have not forgotten that I passed through Glasgow University? Regularly as clockwork every morning for three years I passed through it on my way to deliver groceries at the door of the kitchens which then used to be at the top of the building.' To a reporter afterwards he said of his freedom casket, 'I am prouder of this than I would be of a peerage, and indeed, I have refused a peerage.' In due course the paper printed the interview alongside a large cartoon of Lipton in nautical garb holding his burgess casket and casting aside the coronet and ermine robes of a peer of the realm. The cartoon was boldly captioned LIFE HAS NOTHING MORE TO OFFER.

In many ways that was true, and everything that came afterwards was an anticlimax. But for several years more Lipton was a name that was seldom absent from the social columns of the newspapers. When Sir Andrew Bonar Law died in November 1923 Lipton was strongly tipped as the Liberal candidate for the Glasgow Central Division, but once more he declined. He was a guest at the luncheon party given by Colonel and Mrs Knowles Stansfield for the exiled King George II of Greece and Queen Elisabeth, and he attended the party for the American humorist Will Rogers in the Pinafore Room at the Savoy. In 1924 the community of Lipton, Saskatchewan (population 400) was named in his honour. The following year in the United States, he planned a huge advertising campaign to popularise tea-drinking. He purchased a second *Erin* that year and brought back from America his twenty-three-metre *Shamrock* which he had taken over there four years earlier to race against *Shamrock IV*. He was a familiar sight at Cowes Week, the Clyde Fortnight and all the other big regattas round the coast. He donated the mast of *Shamrock IV* to the campus of New York University as a flagpole and attended the inaugural hoisting of the Stars and Stripes on 28 February 1925. In May he attended the funeral of Viscount Leverhulme. He donated a Lipton Cup for a great Pacific yacht race between San Francisco and Tahiti, and sold his steam yacht *Victoria* to James Shewan who renamed her *Patricia*. The yacht was subsequently raided by US Customs who impounded 400 cases of spirits on their way from Britain to thirsty Americans. Needless to say the American papers had a field-day with headlines proclaiming that the Millionaire's Yacht was now a Rum Runner. That was bad enough, but a year later it transpired that *Shamrock II* had been purchased by the Nassau, Bahamas liquor firm of Pinder, Collins and Brown and renamed *Isosceles*. She made a number of trips to the United States laden with bootleg booze, but sank at her anchorage during the great hurricane of July 1926.

In October 1925 Lipton was in Glasgow to present a silver trophy to the Boys' Brigade and to hand over Johnston Villa to the local nursing association. 'Up to last year it was occupied by that faithful henchman and friend of the baronet, ex-County Councillor William Love,' reported the *Cambuslang Advertiser*, 'but when Mr Love moved to another part of the city the house became tenantless.' The truth of the matter is that, in the autumn of 1924, William Love did the unpardonable: at the age of seventy he took a wife. Lipton's reaction to this is nowhere recorded, so we can only speculate that it was unfavourable. At any rate, the upshot was that William and his bride were obliged to vacate Johnston Villa forthwith. Love resigned as a Lanarkshire County Councillor in December and received a testimonial dinner from the Cambuslang Voters' Association. He and his wife moved back into the city, to a humble tenement flat in Greenhead Street opposite Glasgow Green, and there they lived very modestly until the end of their days. Lipton gave the house as a nurses' home in memory of his dear mother, with the sole condition that he might be permitted to visit it any time he was in Glasgow. He also donated fifty pounds of tea to the nurses and promised to keep them in free tea as long as he lived. In a very moving speech at the handover ceremony he extolled the merits of his late mother, and touched on his wartime experiences in Serbia, saying that it had been his sad duty to bring back the personal effects of 11 nurses who had died of typhus there.

In 1926 the celebrated cookery writer Elizabeth Craig visited Osidge and subsequently published an account of it. She described the dining-room with the set of dessert silver presented by the people of the United States, the bronze and marble statuary, the gold brocade curtains, the red damask wallpaper and the oak chair upholstered in red morocco leather, so that the room, 'seen through half-shut eyes, presented a mellow picture of black and brown, relieved by gold and red'. She wrote of the billiard room with its white marble bust of King Edward VII, of the snake poised on top of the piano as if ready to strike. She related that the cushions which had so impressed Beverley Nichols had been worked by the sisters of St Bridget's Convent in Ceylon. By now Osidge was filled to overflowing with furniture, bric-a-brac, souvenirs of foreign travel and presentation pieces from every corner of the globe. He was continually receiving presents. A friend who was there once for his birthday described him as no more than opening, glancing at, then closing the boxes.

His secretary, John Westwood, would go through them afterwards to organise the letters of acknowledgment and thanks, but the large safe was always piled high with partially opened packages. Only a small proportion of the presents graduated from the safe to mantelpieces, cabinets and occasional tables, but each successive birthday and Christmas would add to the general accumulation of geegaws and nick-nacks. Many of the most cherished possessions, which had graced the staterooms of the original *Erin*, but which had fortunately been removed before she was converted for war service, were now installed at Osidge, and included the great gold loving cup of 1899 and Lipton's collection of Nelson memorabilia. There was a vast profusion of silver-framed photographs, but the one which caught Miss Craig's attention was a cross formed by four silver hearts, each of which contained the signed photograph of a royal lady. The cross had been fitted with a ring for suspension by a ribbon round Lipton's neck. It was the Order of the Four Hearts and the portraits it contained were those of the Duchess of Hesse, Princess Hohenlohe-Langenburg, Princess Beatrice of Saxe-Coburg and Princess Ena of Battenberg. And – appropriately– Elizabeth Craig, alone of all his many interviewers, revealed Lipton's recipe for rice pudding.[11]

With Lord Dewar Lipton maintained a friendly rivalry over whose name was the better known globally. Nothing pleased Whisky Tom more than finding his product on sale in some exotic part of the world where Lipton's Tea was unknown. On one occasion Dewar cabled from Africa that 'Out here three pounds of your tea will buy me six wives'. Lipton immediately wired back, 'Am sending three parcel samples of best tea. Please arrange for samples of wives'. With Sir Harry Lauder the rivalry consisted in seeing which of them, for public consumption, could best exemplify the traditional Scottish virtue of canniness. In his autobiography Lipton tells a story to illustrate his friend's thrifty habits. Whenever he was performing in London, Sir Harry usually stayed at Osidge, saying that he got better attention there than at any hotel. 'And besides,' he would add with that little twinkle in his eye, 'it's much cheaper!' Sir Harry was driven to and from London by Lipton's chauffeur, Baker, but on one occasion Lipton played a trick on his friend.

> Usually he had one of my cars to drive him to and from the London theatres where he was working because, as he himself explained, it was not worth while bringing his own Rolls-Royce from Scotland for a week or two only! So one evening I arranged that instead of the usual limousine one of the factory delivery vans would be waiting for him when he finished his last show. I made certain that he would refuse to come home in it and hire a taxi. But no, home to Osidge he came in the van! When he arrived I chaffed him about not taking a taxi.
>
> 'A taxi from Stratford to New Southgate, Lipton!' he exclaimed. 'Why the cost would have been proheebitive!'
>
> The van incident, however, rankled a bit in Lauder's memory for a long while, but it gave him a chance to cause great laughter among his friends, 'for', he said, 'the smell of ham which he carried about with him for weeks made all the dogs in the country follow him!'[12]

Another anecdote concerns the only bet which Lipton ever made in all his life. It was with Harry Lauder.

> We were both going to America, he in the *Mauretania* and I on the *Baltic* and to please Harry I staked 9d against his 4d that I would be in America first. Harry beat me but it gave him some terribly anxious moments. The *Mauretania* ran into thick fog for about three days and Harry got so excited that he went down into the engine-room to urge on the stokers. Then he discovered that he had lost a 6d piece and all the stokers stopped to help him look for the coin. Harry finally found it in his shoe. Anyway I lost and weeks afterwards I got a postcard from Honolulu asking me to let him have the 9d and the accrued interest. I wrote back to say that I had invested it for him and that he would get it and the dividends when I returned.[13]

This anecdote was widely reported. Harry Lauder, then at the height of his fame, and one of the most highly paid entertainers of the period, cultivated a stage persona of extreme meanness, which, of course, provided him with endless material for his comic routines. The notion that Lipton, the man who had given away countless thousands, could match Harry Lauder in the meanness game was hilarious.

In reality, Lipton was a generous host, although increasingly eccentric and rather set in his ways. He had an all-male staff including Baker his chauffeur, Louis his English valet and John his Sinhalese butler. Three Sinhalese house-boys padded silently round the well-ordered house in long white skirts with combs holding their long black hair in place. Guests who wished to go into London for the evening were always provided with a car. No matter how late you returned, Louis would appear on the landing with a little book and a questionnaire: When did you wish to be called? When would you like your bath? Would you prefer to be shaved or to shave yourself? Where and when would you like your breakfast, upstairs or downstairs? Which papers would you like? What kind of fruit? Fruit was something of a speciality, thanks to the magnificent hothouses at Osidge. Even in the depths of winter there would be pears and strawberries, grapes and cantaloupe melons. Then would come Louis's final warning: Don't touch the window! Lipton kept the central heating on all year round and it was at a level which his Scottish friends (who did not share his American habit of lightweight clothing and silk underwear) found oppressive. The injunction not to touch the windows arose not so much for the even control of the central heating but because they were all wired up to the alarm system, in itself something of a novelty for the 1920s. Lipton in old age was excessively nervous, to the point of paranoia, about burglars and maintained a night watchman whose constant duty was to patrol the grounds and the perimeter of the house.

Lipton never appeared in the morning, preferring to breakfast alone in his bedroom. Then he would send for his doctor to give him his daily medical examination. He had seldom had a day's illness in all his life, apart from some eye trouble as a boy, and he was in remarkably good shape for a man of his age, but he regarded his body as a piece of machinery which required the constant care one would give a motor car. His doctor should give him a thorough inspection, just as Baker maintained his cars, and he wanted to be absolutely certain that nothing could go wrong during the day.

He left for his office in the City Road soon after nine o'clock and he would not return to Osidge until late afternoon at the earliest. On arrival, he would retire immediately to his study. In addition to Westwood who was described as his principal private secretary, 'a faithful, brainy, cultured Scotsman who has been at my right hand every hour and every day for something like thirty years',[14] Lipton had two business secretaries, both male of course. He had a ticker-tape machine at home and would work for about two hours, constantly watching the progress of the New York stock market. Unlike others of his class, he did not always observe the ritual of changing for dinner. Although he often had guests he never entertained formally, although his one concession to formality was the spray of orchids at each lady's plate, which she would be expected to pin to her dress. Lipton set immense store by fruit and had a huge bowl of it placed in front of him. 'He would munch grapes between mouthfuls as a Frenchman munches bread, and he would personally select the fruit for each guest in turn.'[15] Rice was served at every meal, and one way of ingratiating yourself with Lipton was to demand a second helping. After dinner, the party would go to the billiard room. Sometimes Lipton would join in the fun and though he had the reputation of being the world's best loser, he preferred to win at billiards, a fact which his senior executives ignored at their peril. Waugh recounted a story which he had from a man who stayed in the same hotel as Lipton in the south of France before the First World War:

> For three or four evenings he had watched Lipton playing with one of his secretaries and had noticed that Lipton always won by a few points. On the fourth night Lipton had been invited out and his secretary suggested to his fellow guest that they play a 250 up. The man in question was a very reasonable club player, who was accustomed to making breaks of thirty; he was surprised to find himself beaten by 100 points.[16]

Now in his seventies Lipton was content to play a single 100 up, watch for an hour or so, and then go back to his study for two or three hours' work. His guests had all retired for the night before he left his desk.

As a rule, at least one of his guests would be a business colleague. When there was business to be discussed, however, Lipton lost all sense of time. One of his principal executives in the 1920s was H.A. Snelling, who lived in Brighton. Anxious to get home that night, Snelling would remind his boss that the last train left Waterloo at midnight. 'So it does, so it does,' Lipton would say. 'Now be sure and ring me up when you are safe back home.' Lipton was always there to take the call. Snelling never knew whether Lipton was concerned over an employee's welfare or was merely making sure that he really had gone home and not to a West End nightclub. He did not spare himself, and he did not spare his staff.

Upon his guests, he made only one demand: if they were staying at Osidge over the weekend he insisted that they accompany him after Sunday lunch on his regular outing to North Mimms. The cavalcade would be loaded up with chocolates and sweets which Lipton lavished on the children of the village. This weekly habit had been going on for many years, ever since the day, long before the war, that his car had broken down at Cooper's Green and the children had shown such friendliness and concern that he had promised to return there on the following Sunday. And now even the children of those children were on the receiving end of this largesse. As many as five cars, laden with house guests, would make this pilgrimage. Louis would appear with a great stack of fur coats and every guest would find one to fit him. Lipton led the way, perched high in his 1910 Mercedes open tourer, in his fur coat and goggles, driving at a terrifying pace.

The chocolates were stored in hampers and he would distribute them himself, deploying all his old skills of showmanship, opening the top box, taking out a chocolate, examining it critically with cocked head, then tentatively taking a bite out of it, closing his eyes thoughtfully, and nodding approvingly as he handed the remaining portion to the nearest child. Then he would form them into a queue; there would be as many as 300 kids in line, and the guests would be amused at the antics of parents of the first children as they smuggled them to the rear of the queue to get a second box. This ritual became so popular in the district that a local minister complained that he could no longer get a congregation for Sunday school, and implored Lipton to complete his tour well before three o'clock. These Sunday expeditions continued right up until Lipton's death.

In the 1920s Lipton visited Glasgow at least once a year, and another ritual soon developed. He would stand outside his offices in Lancefield Street and distribute boxes of chocolates to the children of Anderston. Over 2,000 boxes were distributed in August 1926, but the following year at least 7,000 boys and girls got boxes. This event drew huge crowds and, of course, lavish press coverage.[17]

Though a teetotaller and now virtually a non-smoker, Lipton always ensured that wines, cigarettes and cigars were available for those guests who wanted them. He kept a good cellar with a fine range of wines, but spirits were banned – not even Dewar's whisky was available to Whisky Tom when he came to dinner. Lipton had few close friends but plenty of acquaintances and the latter were generally those who tolerated the fact that, at Osidge, their host must always be in the limelight, centre stage. Of course, there were also the inevitable hangers-on but Westwood kept a sharp look out for them, and no one was allowed to become a nuisance. As he got older, Lipton became more and more set in his ways. So long as he could do everything in just the way he wanted, all was well, and he could be the most charming and genial of hosts, full of good humour and ready with a fund of well-rehearsed anecdotes (many of which found a place in his autobiography). Those who got to know him well knew that he was at heart a very kind and very simple man. On the surface his life appeared to be drawing to a close in a warm sunset glow, but beneath the surface a situation was developing which would eventually spoil many of his last days.

In 1924 there had been a slight dip in profits, from £337,056 to £292,244, and a dividend of ten per cent was declared in place of the customary twelve per cent, but Lipton had explained this situation by the general reduction in prices and the cost of living. Future prospects were promising, and he was maintaining his policy of expansion by opening a number of new stores. Six months later all seemed quite well, when the interim dividend was passed. Few people took note of the perceptive comments of the economist Emil Davies in the *New Statesman* who painted a rather gloomy picture of the retail grocery trade and speculated whether the day would come when Lipton's would amalgamate with Maypole and Home and Colonial. Six months later, however, the true nature of the situation emerged at the shareholder's meeting of 1925. Profits were well down and no dividend would be paid. Lipton lamely explained that this startling development was due to a sharp fall in commodity values and the poor location of many of the branches. *The Times* commented on this explanation:

> These have doubtless been important handicaps, though as an explanation of the bad report they would sound more convincing had the very unfavourable trading results obtained by this company not been accompanied by the enjoyment of continued prosperity on the part of other concerns of a similar character. [18]

Not surprisingly, the shareholders were indignant and asked some very searching questions, but so strong was the faith of the general public and the loyalty of the press that Lipton was able to turn the occasion to his advantage. For example, one shareholder complained that Lipton was overtaxing his strength, that instead of knocking off work at 5 p. m. he went on till 3 a. m. The point the shareholder was making was that Lipton should delegate some of his workload to younger men. The press, however, concentrated on the first part of the comment, and several papers carried stories of the peculiar complaint of the Lipton shareholders that their chairman overworked, while one paper carried a cartoon of Lipton in nautical rig overtaxing his strength by dancing a hornpipe.

There were no such whimsicalities the following year. By 1926 it had become abundantly clear that the failure of 1925 was not due to a temporary setback but to a basic fault. The presence of Sir John Ferguson, munitions minister during the war, as the company's newly appointed deputy chairman, testified to the gravity of the situation. This was a black day for Lipton, as *The Times* reported:

> Dissatisfaction with the poor report of Lipton Ltd was made very apparent yesterday by the crowded and critical meeting assembled at Winchester House. Sir John Ferguson, the new deputy chairman, who was given a good reception, was unable to give the shareholders much comfort. He said the ramifications of the company were so widely spread and of such a huge and interdependent character that it would take a much longer time than he had yet at his disposal to submit well-considered proposals to his colleagues.
>
> Some of the speakers at the meeting met with considerable interruption and many of those present made no attempt to conceal their desire for the resignation of the old members of the board. Protests of the kind when companies are doing badly are not always justified, though in this case it is to be hoped that the very natural restiveness shown by the spectators will enable a most searching investigation to be made and thoroughgoing reforms introduced. Industrial depression scarcely affords an explanation of the company's misfortunes, for in spite of the same depression the company's competitors continue to flourish.[19]

Lipton's opening speech had, in fact, been little more than an introduction of Sir John Ferguson, and although he rose afterwards to move the adoption of the report, his assertion that the business was basically sound was greeted with impatience. Lipton had never been good with shareholders, or rather he was never a man to take criticism well. On this momentous occasion he made a singularly bad impression. It was his last confrontation with the company's shareholders.

The ensuing year was a very difficult and trying time for Lipton. Now he no longer had to contend merely with petulant shareholders but a management committee which had been established to investigate every aspect of the company. Lipton found himself on the receiving end of a very searching inquisition and one may imagine his barely concealed anger at being forced to explain past decisions, even his fundamental policies. It did not help that the men on the committee were all friends and colleagues of long standing who only had the best interests of the company – and Lipton himself – at heart. But, in the end, the best interests of the company dictated that he would have to stand down. William Blackwood said of Lipton at this time that, 'he was like a child from whom a beloved toy had been taken roughly and cruelly. He did not realise that what had been done was in his own best interests. He was full of pathetic regrets and rather stupid resentments.'[20]

In 1927, when the shareholders met, Lipton was no longer in the chair. His place had been taken by Sir John Ferguson whose name now appeared on the prospectus as executive chairman. In his opening speech Sir John announced:

> Sir Thomas Lipton, the founder of the business, whose whole life has been spent in the service of the business, expressed a desire to be relieved of all active management of the business, but he accepted the office of life president and chairman, a position which we hope he will fill for many years. The duties of this office will only entail his attendance at City Road for board meetings.

This face-saving appointment fooled no one, least of all Lipton himself. He had been ousted in a boardroom coup, and thereafter he took virtually no interest in the company he had created. It is doubtful whether he crossed the threshold of the City Road headquarters after that time. Within a couple of months rumours were circulating that a consortium headed by the Van den Bergh interests and the Meadow Dairy Company had virtually acquired control by purchase of Lipton's holdings. This boosted the value of the one pound shares to eighteen shillings and ninepence, a rise of five shillings in a week. On 9 September 1927 the rumour was confirmed, with the appointment of Lipton as honorary life chairman, 'which is obviously a tribute to his work as creator of the business', as *The Times* duly noted the following day. The sum paid to Lipton by the new syndicate is reputed to have been

£750,000. The deal, effectively Lipton's abdication, was allegedly signed in the stateroom of the *Shamrock*.

It is highly significant that those voluminous scrapbooks, now numbering eighty-four, came to a sudden halt at this time.[21] Lipton had lived for his work, and now that it had been wrenched away from him, there seemed to be nothing left to live for. Lipton's resentment at the way he had been treated was understandable, but sooner or later he would have had to step down and make way for younger men more in tune with the modern times.

As he himself had said at that last shareholders' meeting, the business was fundamentally sound. And indeed, after some relatively minor changes of policy, it was restored to an even keel and began declaring dividends again. The trouble in the mid-1920s, however, had been largely due to the fact that Lipton ran it as a one-man business. Sir John Ferguson, at the 1927 meeting, explained that: 'Under the old regime no attempt had been made even in prosperous years to strengthen the financial position of the company by writing down the goodwill.' In 1923 a revaluation upwards of certain of the company's freehold and leasehold properties, plant and machinery had increased, and would continue to keep high for several years, the annual charges of depreciation. It was also obvious that the business had been milked in order to pay the dividends of 1923 and 1924.

Lipton had a double standard where money was concerned, a not uncommon trait in millionaires who have started life with absolutely nothing. The man who could calmly write out a cheque for £25,000 for the Princess of Wales, or ten times that sum for a new racing yacht, would cavil at spending a fiver on himself. He would also find difficulty in laying out money on new plant and machinery, costing hundreds rather than thousands of pounds. This was certainly a fault in the later years; Lipton failed to realise that much of his early success had come from the boldness of his vision and his ability to spend relatively large sums on capital projects. This was coupled with the fact that the management structure in the chain of stores left much to be desired – Lipton had continued to operate with 600 stores much as he had done with six. A business of such vast ramifications was too much for a man in his seventies who was no longer devoting all his energies to his business, who was increasingly absorbed by another passion, yacht racing. Lipton never sought advice and resented it when it was offered. He was impatient, quick-tempered and ruthless where his business was concerned. He could not tolerate slackness or inefficiency and had absolutely no compunction about sacking men on the spot if one of his snap inspections revealed some shortcoming. He would walk briskly round a store or depot making mental notes, then as he left issue his instructions: 'Fire so-and-so,' and on his return he would make sure that so-and-so had been sacked. With his New York empire he was even more ruthless and dictatorial, and the staff in Hoboken would dread his departure. Within 48 hours a flood of cablegrams would come from the liner bound for England: 'Fire this one. Sack that one.' Sometimes it was possible for the American business to conceal and retain the victims of his disapproval but in England it was impossible. In July 1925 Emil Davies, in the *New Statesman,* drew attention to the fact that since the end of the war only one man besides the chairman had stayed on the board throughout the entire period, seven gentlemen having left after, in many cases, a very brief tenure of office. Davies went on to state that 'heads of departments and managers of tea-rooms were changed with the same frequency'.

In the hiring and firing of staff, Lipton's judgement was often unsound. Much of the trouble which arose in the 1920s was caused by the fact that he still thought as he had done in the 1890s, failing to realise that the world, especially since the war, had changed quite drastically. He looked for the same characteristics in his branch managers that he had demanded thirty years earlier, but the men who possessed these characteristics were not the best examples of the modern type. Lipton was easily taken in by the noisy, aggressive, brash type who talked big and promised a lot, but beneath the bluster and braggadocio was lazy and often dishonest. At the end of his career he made all too many such unfortunate appointments.

An unattractive trait which developed in the 1920s, amounting almost to paranoia, was a profound distrust of fellow directors, company executives and even quite minor functionaries. Not only did he have his house wired against burglars, but he had installed a number of listening devices. Even the sofas in the lounge were bugged so that he could eavesdrop on the conversations of company executives when he deliberately left them alone in the room. He learned a great deal this way but he also overheard much that would have been better unheard, and this merely fuelled his distrust. He also instituted a system of reports by staff home on leave from India or Ceylon; effectively he expected his overseas managers and executives to spy on each other. Inevitably this got around and the morale of the overseas staff dropped sharply. By the time Sir John Ferguson took over, the company's *esprit de corps* was at a low ebb.

Reforms were not achieved overnight. At the July 1928 meeting Sir John informed the shareholders that there had been a severe rationalisation of the headquarters staff. In May 1929 he announced that the capital would have to be reduced by £250,000 as the years would have to elapse before the heavy arrears of preference dividends were paid off. They were assured, however, that if this sum were written off and ordinary shares were issued to the preference holders, there would be a benefit to them of almost eighty per cent of the profits available for ordinary shares. Sir John got a rough ride from the shareholders that year, but in the end his unpalatable recommendations were grudgingly accepted. This drastic surgery paid off more quickly than anticipated and by 1930 Lipton shareholders were again beginning to receive dividends.

Today, the once-familiar Lipton grocery stores are a thing of the past, although some survived as late as the 1960s. Over the intervening years the Lipton chain was merged with Maypole and Home and Colonial under the banner of Allied Suppliers whose premises, shops and international stores were taken over by Unilever in 1972. Lipton, as a brand name, has disappeared off the shelves in British supermarkets, but it survives elsewhere and is arguably better known from Thailand to Timbuktu than it is in its home country these days. Today, Lipton is the world's biggest brand in tea, the product of 120 factories and sold in as many countries. The great Lipton tea estates in Ceylon (now Sri Lanka) were nationalised in the 1960s and nowadays the tea has to be purchased at auction for subsequent processing, blending and packaging. One wonders what Sir Thomas would have made of the modern fashion for dispensing tea in small individual sachets. Doubtless, had he lived long enough, he would have been in the forefront of this startling innovation of the late 1930s which has since become universal.

12. THE FINAL CHALLENGE
1927–31

Life's race well run,
Life's work well done,
Life's victory won,
Now cometh rest.
    Edward Hazen Parker

If Lipton was no longer at the helm of the British business, he was still very much in control in America and it must have been a considerable comfort to him to know that the empire ruled from the waterfront building in Hoboken was in such a flourishing condition. The time and money spent on challenging for the America's Cup had been amply repaid in promoting the image of the Lipton enterprise in the United States where the races had always enjoyed far greater coverage anyway. After Lipton's death the company found that it had to undertake very expensive advertising campaigns to make good the loss of publicity which had always attended his visits to New York. It was estimated that $500,000 spent on the challenge for the Cup was worth at least half as much again on an advertising campaign. Perhaps Lipton's English business had suffered as a consequence of his time devoted to yacht racing, but his American business most assuredly profited handsomely from it. It is significant that, shortly after the coup of 1927, Lipton characteristically bounced back by letting it be known that he intended having one more crack at the Cup. From time to time, of course, there had been rumours to this effect. Interestingly, at the age of eighty-five, Lord Dunraven had announced his intentions of co-operating with Lipton in another challenge, but the noble Earl had died in June 1926 with this ambition unresolved.

At home Lipton was inclined to vegetate. The only bright spots in an otherwise humdrum week would be the occasional jaunt to a theatre with Tom Dewar and the regular outing to Cooper's Green, after which he would pop round to Lord Inverforth's mansion at Arnos Grove for an evening of hymn singing. For a man who had never been much of a churchgoer, this may seem a rather strange occupation, but in his declining years it was a simple ritual which brought the old man immense comfort and pleasure.

In New York, however, Lipton led a very different life. There he was as much in the limelight as he had been in London at the turn of the century. To be sure, the Roaring Twenties, the era of speakeasies and gangsters, passed him by completely, but he still had a prominent part to play. He was constantly in the limelight and very much an ornament of the social scene. When, in November 1927, he was asked to comment on the flappers, he quipped that if a girl spent thirty shillings on a pair of silk stockings she had a perfect right to show twenty-nine shillings and sixpence worth, but added with a twinkle, that if she paid only thirty shillings and displayed thirty-two shillings ninepence worth 'She comes down a ways'. The following January he was enrolled in the exclusive Breakfast Club of Los Angeles and posed with fellow member Jack Dempsey. In New York Lipton was a bosom pal of Mayor Jimmy Walker and Grover Whalen, the charismatic commissioner of police, who invariably laid on a police escort complete with motorcycle cops to escort the great tycoon from the dockside to the Biltmore Hotel. He would drive slowly in his open car, and as they approached Fifth Avenue he would whip off his broad-brimmed fedora and put on his yachting cap. 'They'd hate to see me without this,' he would say, and he would tell his chauffeur to drive even more slowly. Children on the sidewalk would wave to him and their fathers would call out, 'When are you going to take that cup home, Tommy?' Lipton was in his element, and the old exhilaration, the zestful exuberance, would return as he drove past the skyscrapers of downtown Manhattan. When he drove down to the riverside to take the Lackawanna ferry across to Hoboken, his escort invariably drove him straight to the head of the queue; it was his boast that he was the only man in New York who could drive straight from his hotel to his office floor. The elevator in the Hoboken premises was so vast that he could drive his limousine straight into it and be taken up to the twelfth storey, right to his office door. When he departed at the end of his annual trip, there would be a ten pounds canister of tea for every member of the police escort, and for special people like Grover Whalen and his captains there would be a gold and green enamel pin with the *Shamrock* on it.

Lipton travelled with his valet, two stenographers and the indispensable John Westwood. Harsh things were often said about

Westwood – 'the head mogul of an invisible government' was one of the more complimentary comments.[1] But in fairness to Westwood, he was utterly devoted to his boss and smoothed the way for him in countless matters, often anticipating Lipton's whims and caprices. This was no easy matter in view of Lipton's quirkiness. He might leave his hotel for a short drive and then, on the spur of the moment, order the chauffeur to drive on to Toronto to see a local manager. Lipton rarely, if ever, carried cash and it was Westwood who had to deal with such mundane matters.

In his Hoboken office Lipton was every bit as autocratic as he had been in his heyday in City Road and things had to be done exactly as he ordered. He refused to have his office modernised and his New York attorney, Willard Taylor, was almost dismissed on the spot for having the temerity to suggest that it was time to have it redecorated. Here, as in City Road, Lipton insisted on glass partitions everywhere, so that he could see what everyone was doing. The sole exception, of course, was for himself – a stout oak partition screened him from the staff. On this wall hung a painting of Osidge and pictures of his yachts. He had his own dining-room where he would occasionally invite senior members of staff to lunches which were essentially business conferences. Executives dreaded these working lunches, at which plain water and ginger ale were the only beverages, and huge piles of rice laced with mango chutney formed the staple fare. From the moment he entered the office until at least two days after his departure the Hoboken staff were constantly on tenterhooks, dreading a summons from the great man. Lipton was now more alert than ever to the possible shortcomings of his executives. All his troubles, from the canteen scandal to the boardroom coup, had been the fault of corrupt or inefficient underlings. He had all the suspicious watchfulness of the absentee landlord returning to his estate and increasingly he was obsessed with the fear that the American staff were plotting behind his back. He began playing one man off against another, creating an atmosphere of corporate unease and distrust which could not have made for efficient business. When Waugh interviewed staff members who had been with the organisation in the 1920s he could get no more than grudging platitudes: 'He was all right if you took him in the right way,' was a general verdict, or they would smile wryly and comment, 'After all, there was no one like him.'

> He was quick-tempered, he was irascible, he was incalculable, impatient of criticism and of opposition: but at the same time there

was nothing trivial about him, nothing petty. He had that immense gusto, that zest for living. There was about him the glamour of the past. He had done so much and he had come so far. He had crowded seven lives into the space of one. You had that sense when you were in his company of looking upon innumerable other worlds and ways of living that time had integrated into his career and person. He was all that. And yet at heart he was a very simple person. Everyone who knew him has said that same thing of him.[2]

That trip to America in the autumn and winter of 1927–28 was his longest and most ambitious yet. He travelled all over the country, and was interviewed everywhere. In Los Angeles he addressed the Breakfast Club and told his appreciative audience that although he had the largest and costliest collection of silver cups in the world he would gladly trade the lot for 'that mug'. And he quipped that his only blood relatives were 'some New Jersey mosquitoes who welcomed me sixty years ago'. In February 1928 the Atlantic Yacht Club entertained him to dinner at the Ritz and in the course of the evening he offered a trophy to be held by the club and raced at Gravesend Bay, New York, for yachts of international class. In his speech of acceptance the Fleet Captain, A.V. Guidet, presented Lipton with a silk burgee for his next *Shamrock*. When he boarded the *Leviathan* in March, Lipton was seen off by the president of the New York Athletic Club, William Kennelly.

Six months later he was back in New York. Aboard the *Leviathan* on this momentous occasion was Frank Kellogg, bringing with him the famous Paris Pact which was intended to renounce war. Lipton generously gave up his special suite to the ambassador, joking, 'First time I crossed I travelled steerage. I'm used to discomfort.' Kellogg, utterly drained by his superhuman diplomatic efforts, passed the time on the voyage devouring detective stories, and asked Lipton if he had any he could borrow.

In October 1928, when the New York stock market was attaining record levels almost daily, a select band of millionaires treated themselves to a dinner at the Astor. Lipton was the oldest, the tallest and most erect. By May 1929 he was back again, offering a silver trophy for the annual regatta of the Philadelphia Outboard Motor Boat Association, to be staged at the end of June in the Schuylkill River. That month he learned that the New York Yacht Club had at long last accepted his fifth challenge for the Cup. Lipton was reported to be delighted; not only had his challenge been accepted, but on his own terms. There would be no time allowances and no handicaps. All boats were to be similar in design and specification, all would start together and the yacht that crossed the line first would be the winner. It was what he had been battling to achieve for three decades. While preparations were afoot for his fifth challenge, Lipton purchased the steam yacht *Albion* and renamed her *Erin* after his beloved pre-war yacht. This fine vessel had a gross tonnage of 1,346 and had been built by Swan Hunter in 1905. Soon she would be stripped down and virtually rebuilt to Lipton's exacting specifications. In September 1929 he attended the Sixth Annual Radio World's Fair at Madison Square Garden and made a broadcast. Radio, he said, was one of the wonders of the world; it brought practically all the civilised world into close contact. But when he began to tell his listeners that the *Erin* was the first vessel to have a private installation, nothing could stop him from passing from the *Erin* to the *Shamrock*. 'If any of my listeners have been away from their native land for over seventy years, they will well understand how eager that cup must be to get back home even for a week.' There was a chuckle in his voice. He sounded like a young man on the brink of a great adventure. The old boy was dubbed the world's best sport, and virtually everyone in America hoped that, at long last, he was going to win.

The following month, when the New York Athletic Club held a dinner in his honour, with a thousand guests crammed into its gymnasium, Lipton accepted a bronze plaque from Major Kennelly with the words, 'At last I have a boat built entirely to my specifications.' Had the conditions been different he might have won in 1901 and would assuredly have won in 1920. Now he felt more confident than ever. The octogenarian felt that he would achieve his greatest ambition before time and life itself ran out. At 11.15 a. m. on 8 December 1929, shortly after his departure for England, Lipton made telecommunications history again when he made the first ship-to-shore call by radio-telephone, speaking from the *Leviathan* some two hundred miles out from New York to William N. Rankine of the New York advertising agency of that name. For five minutes they discussed preliminary plans for Lipton's 1930 advertising campaign to make tea-drinking even more popular in the United States. As Alec Waugh reported, this first ship-to-shore call was also to prove the loyalty of the Americans to Lipton and the high regard in which they held him, for not only did Lipton talk about tea he also received a coded message couched in a casual message of good wishes. No one knew what the message was, of course, or rather no one realised that the casual message of good wishes was, in fact coded. The word 'Goodrich' indicated that all was well and that there was nothing to worry about. On the other hand, had the word 'Goodyear' appeared instead, then Lipton would have been warned that a highly embarrassing story was about to break. This concerned a Russian princess with whom, it seems, Lipton had conducted a very compromising correspondence. The princess had threatened that, unless she received adequate compensation, financial or matrimonial, she would issue an injunction to prevent Lipton from sailing. He had avoided this injunction by having himself smuggled aboard ship a day earlier than the other passengers, so that while the lady and her detectives were keeping a close watch on the Biltmore Lipton was already safely ensconced in his stateroom. 'Goodrich' assured him that no story had broken after he had sailed. Later the princess was bought off with a cheque for £10,000. That seemed to be the end of the matter.

A year later, however, when the slump was at its depths in America following the Wall Street crash, the bank through which the cheque had passed had crashed. Its accounts were the subject of a public audit, in the course of which the huge payment from Lipton to the princess came to light. The *New York Mirror* got hold of the story and planned a front-page splash but Lipton's friends and business associates intervened. At first all their threats and entreaties got them nowhere. In the end, they went to the newspaper's proprietor; without hesitation he telephoned his editor-in-chief and ordered him to kill the Lipton story.

Two months later, the story reached the *New York News*. Once again Lipton's friends went from editor to editor, to be met each time with cynically shaken heads. Once again they went to the proprietor, Patterson. 'Listen,' they said. 'Lipton's eighty. There's a chance at last of his getting elected to the Royal Yacht Club. If you print this story you may ruin it.' Patterson took no longer to decide than his rival had. 'The old boy's too good a sport to have that done to him by an American,' and he raised the telephone. The fact that two proprietors of sensational tabloids should have been so ready to suppress a good story out of regard for Lipton was really greater proof than the gold loving cup of the regard in which Lipton stood in America's esteem.[3] Waugh did not reveal the lady's identity, but the presence of cuttings relating to Countess Ganna Walska in the Lipton scrapbooks, seemingly unrelated to himself in any way, may be a clue. This Russian-born aristocrat had been briefly married to an Austrian, Baron Arcadie d'Eingorn, who was killed in the First

World War. Later she was briefly married in Paris to Alexander Smith Cochran, New York's wealthiest bachelor. Cochran had two yachts at Kiel Week in the summer of 1914 and it may have been there, if not later, that Lipton first made the acquaintance of this *femme fatale*. In the 1920s she had a desultory career as an actress in America, playing heavily accented European roles.

Even in Britain interest in the forthcoming contest revived. Although he was fêted and lionised in America which was now the centre of his existence, he was no less honoured and respected back home. The débâcle which led to his removal from the board had been largely confined to the financial pages of the broadsheets, and the man in the street knew little and cared less about the manner in which Lipton had been ousted. Lipton the millionaire yachtsman got infinitely more space in the press than Lipton the chairman of Lipton's. Now eighty-one, although only admitting to seventy-nine, he had acquired the status of a venerable national institution.

The new yacht was designed by Nicholson and constructed at Gosport. As he had done sixteen years before, Lipton organised a special train, gaily bedecked with bunting, to carry his guests and reporters down to the coast for the launching, on 14 April 1930. Lady Shaftesbury again did the honours, receiving a magnificent diamond brooch for her trouble. Then *Shamrock V* had her sea- trials and raced against her elder sister, the twenty-three-metre *Shamrock*, before taking on the best yachts in the country and beating them all. In May Lipton held a lavish party aboard the new *Erin* to celebrate his eightieth birthday. He was now at a time in his life when people boast rather than lie about their age, and he must often have regretted the vanity of forty years earlier when he had surreptitiously lopped two years off his age. Birthday greetings and tributes poured in from all over the world, coupled with good wishes for the Cup. On 8 July the Honourable Company of Master Mariners held a banquet in the Fishmongers' Hall in his honour. The American ambassador, Charles Gates Dawes, paid a warm tribute when he commented that Britain had the fastest aeroplane and the fastest car. 'If she produces the fastest yacht, American disappointment will be assuaged by her appreciation of the fine sportsmanship of this veteran now making his fifth attempt.' The Prince of Wales averred that even in the United States a victory for *Shamrock V* would be popular.

Then Lipton rose to respond to these glowing tributes and felicitations. Ramrod-straight as ever, he spoke without notes and addressed his audience in his customary forthright fashion, going through a routine which had been repeated many times before. For a few sentences his voice had all the old vigour and humour, but then he began to falter. He hesitated, paused, began a sentence, then stopped altogether. He put on his spectacles and hastily reached for his manuscript. Suddenly he appeared as he really was, a very old man near the end of his days. Haltingly he read the words he had recited by heart for thirty years.

Ten weeks later the *Leviathan* berthed in New York and a sprightly Lipton, his vigour fully restored, bounded down the gangplank to a tumultuous welcome. Almost twelve months had passed since the Wall Street crash but the market was now making a reasonable recovery and the bustling city was in buoyant mood the day Lipton landed, despite the thick fog and stiff breeze which marred his live broadcast from the quayside. Thousands thronged the Battery and the harbour was cluttered with excursion boats and pleasure craft which had turned out to greet the famous yachtsman. A special tug with a police escort came bustling out. 'Even when I came here as an emigrant I was never received by the police,' quipped Lipton, 'I'm certainly getting to be the devil of a fellow.' The old boy was in cracking form. In Boston, he laid a wreath on the memorial to the Boston Tea Party, and to Mary Curley, daughter of the mayor, he joked that he had always known that Boston had the most intelligent citizens in the country, since they had thrown the tea overboard when they discovered that it was not Lipton's. In New York, with the ferryboats blasting their horns and whistles and fireworks shooting up into the fog, he drove slowly from the waterfront to the Biltmore, escorted by the usual police cavalcade. When a man called out from the sidewalk, 'You've gotta win the cup – I've put so much money on you that I'll be in the workhouse if you don't,' Lipton riposted, 'Reserve a bed for me too.' He had never had such a genuinely rapturous welcome.

The races were scheduled to take place at Newport, Rhode Island, rather than Sandy Hook, because the weather was likely to be better and the crowds easier to manage. This playground of the super-rich had never known such wild excitement. The marina was crammed with yachts, and special excursion trains were running from all points of the compass, bringing thousands of spectators into the normally staid little resort town. The narrow streets were choked with traffic while airships roared overhead. The ferryboats were put back on their summer timetable, the hotels were booked out and the restaurants, bars and cafés were doing record business. The neighbouring town of

Lowell laid on an orchestral concert to celebrate the occasion. Back in England, the Gosport shipyard was brightly lit with electric signs to illustrate the progress of the races. In spite of the huge crowd, estimated at over three hundred, of excursion steamers and pleasure boats which followed the races, there were no problems about fouling the course. The races were conducted in ideal weather conditions. Everything was perfect.

The defender on this historic occasion was the aptly named *Enterprise* skippered by Howard Vanderbilt. American yachting was at its acme in 1930, and Vanderbilt was the finest yachtsman of his generation. To meet this latest challenge, however, a consortium of millionaires had constructed no fewer than four boats and then pitted them against each other to select the champion that would take on *Shamrock V*. In *Enterprise* the Americans had the finest yacht afloat, representing state-of-the-art technology. The huge mast was made of duralumin, a light but extremely strong alloy which had recently been developed for aircraft construction, while an innovation in the boom enabled the mainsail to slide from one side to another and take in more breeze. The mast, designed by W. Starling Burgess whose father had beaten the British challengers of the 1880s, was justly described as the greatest engineering feat in the development of racing yachts. It was at least 1,500 pounds lighter than *Shamrock*'s mast, and therefore enabled the American yacht to be much more lightly ballasted. Another innovation was the set of drum- winches which accelerated the trimming of sheets and halyards, leading one critic to observe sourly that *Enterprise* did not need yachtsmen but 'hurdy-gurdy grinders from the Bronx'.

Lipton's autobiography ended on a high note, quietly confident of victory and, at the same time, paying a warm tribute to Duncan Neill, the man who had done so much over the past thirty years to make the challenges viable:

> What then of my latest challenger? I can truthfully say that Mr Nicholson has turned out a fine boat, and one that has . . . given evidence of being a fast mover under varying conditions. Her skipper is Edward Heard, of Tollesbury, and we are all hopeful that the struggle will see him at the top of his form. With my old friend and trusty yachting advisor, Colonel Duncan Neil [*sic*], to lend him the benefit of his shrewd and lengthy experience, I am more than hopeful that Captain Heard will distinguish himself.
>
> Of Duncan Neil I would like to say this – he is one of the truest-hearted Scots it has ever been my good fortune to be associated with. He and I have been shipmates and 'cronies' for a very long

number of years. He has been my guide, philosopher, and friend in all my yachting challenges and adventures and, in addition, my delightful colleague and friend in many trips to different parts of the world. I always say that if I have one regret at all in connection with my *Shamrocks*, it is that I never have had one quite good enough to win the America's Cup; had I possessed one, Duncan Neil would have sailed her to victory with skill equal to that of the best yachtsman who ever trod a deck or squinted aloft at the lie of a sail in a stiffening breeze. Quiet, honest, straightforward and manly in all things and in every way, Duncan Neil has meant a great deal to me in my full and extended life.[4]

The races themselves were something of an anticlimax. *Enterprise* won the first, a straight there-and-back race with no windward leg owing to a shift in the breeze. Afterwards Vanderbilt said that it was a good race and conceded that the challenger was a fast boat; but Lipton commented, 'If I were not disappointed I should be in a mental home.' The second race was run in thick fog, and Lipton and his entourage aboard *Erin* had to follow it on the ship's radio. The first leg of the race was the first trial to windward, and the superiority of the *Enterprise* was now clearly demonstrated as she was the clear winner this time. Lipton, who had laid on a big party aboard his steam yacht in anticipation of victory, tried to put a brave face on things. The showgirl Evelyn Law had promised to dance a hornpipe if *Shamrock* won, and when the result came through he joked with his guests, 'There'll be a big change after tonight. I'm going to put the ladies in full charge.' Then he turned to one of the prettiest girls and said, 'How would you like to be the captain?' Promptly she responded, 'I'd like to be your captain any time, Sir Thomas.' But when the party dispersed a gloom thick as the fog which had blotted out the race descended on *Erin*. 'It's a great disappointment,' Lipton told reporters. 'Something apparently is wrong.'

With a sinking heart Lipton realised that his latest yacht was no match for the defender, but the show had to go on. With a superhuman effort he was as charming and genial a host as ever aboard *Erin*. Only for a split second did the mask of geniality slip. On the morning of the third race a party of sailors from the British warship *Heliotrope* were invited on board. The seamen were ill at ease and stood rigidly to attention when he greeted them. Their lack of response irritated him and he barked, 'What's the matter with you? Don't you speak English?' But just as quickly he apologised profusely and led them over to the buffet, making sure that they were having a good time. To bystanders, however, it was obvious that Sir Thomas was under immense strain.

Afterwards he settled himself into his favourite cane-backed chair on the main deck to watch the race, knowing in his heart of hearts that nothing short of a miracle could save the day. He sat bolt upright when *Shamrock* outmanoeuvred her opponent at the start. Oh, if only she could hold her own to the windward mark, there was just the ghost of a chance that she might win on the run home. With manic intensity he peered through his binoculars. Fifteen minutes passed; half an hour – *Shamrock* was still in the lead. His heart beat faster at the prospect of a win at last. Then, in a second, it was all over. The mast had snapped. Lipton leaped to his feet and bounded over to the rail. His beautiful *Shamrock* which had been doing so well a moment ago, was now a helpless wreck wallowing in a shroud of tumbled canvas.

The last race was run two days later, but the outcome was a foregone conclusion and public interest was waning. Nevertheless Lipton was determined to bow out in style and laid on a huge party on *Erin*. Lipton remained below, breakfasting late and alone, and did not come up on deck until the yachts were manoeuvring at the start line. *Shamrock* got off to a good start, but soon fell to leeward and from then onward lagged well behind. Long before the halfway mark *Enterprise* was leading by a mile and a half. Lipton followed the progress of the race from the bridge. He was alone and glad to be. This was the end, not of a race, not of a series, not of a thirty-year saga, but of his life. The ultimate goal, which had become such a magnificent obsession, had eluded him. Now there seemed little point in living. He was eighty-two and suddenly he felt it.

As the *Enterprise* crossed the finishing line Lipton gathered the reporters round him at the after rail. 'It's no good,' he said with sad finality. 'I can't win. I can't win.' He shook hands with them one by one. The following day the newspapers agreed that Sir Thomas had lost his bounce. He looked tired and worn, the sparkle gone from his eye. He moved dispiritedly among his guests, no longer feeling the need to put on a brave face, to muster that forced gaiety which had covered his previous defeats. The press had long praised his sportsmanship and in this hour of final defeat it was more than generous. The editorial in the *New York Times* neatly summed up the general feeling: 'If sentiment could have gained the victory, the America's Cup would be in the hands of Sir Thomas Lipton.' Its tribute to Harold Vanderbilt was tempered by the comment that it was 'almost a thankless task to defend the America's Cup when thousands of his fellow countrymen were almost clamouring for failure'.[5]

The sense of anticlimax and disappointment which pervaded the American press was matched by a general resentment in the British papers, that the challenge had been defeated not by superior seamanship but by the use of gadgetry. Both attitudes were immensely unfair to Harold Vanderbilt who had, in fact, put up one of the finest performances in the annals of the New York Yacht Club. This aspect of the aftermath, however, was rapidly dispelled by Will Rogers whose letter appeared in the *New York Times* on the same day as the editorial:

> What do you say to this? Let everyone send a dollar apiece for a fund to buy a loving cup for Sir Thomas Lipton bigger than the one he would have got if he had won, contributed to by everybody that really admires a fine sportsman. Send it to, I would suggest, a Lipton Cup Fund in care of Mayor Walker in New York. Let Jimmy buy it and present it on behalf of everybody with an inscription along this line: 'To possibly the world's worst yacht builder but absolutely the world's most cheerful loser'. You have been a benefit to mankind, Sir Thomas, you have made losing worth while.

Jimmy Walker responded enthusiastically and endorsed the suggestion with 'There might be some doubt about his ability to win the cup, but no doubt about his ability to capture our hearts'. Letters of approval came flooding in from all over the United States. Edward E. Spafford spoke for many when he wrote, 'Mr Lipton has come to this country on several occasions for the purpose of lifting the cup. He has lifted the hearts of the people of the country, who are anxious for him to lift a cup filled with the admiration of the people.' Patrick Quinlan of the Associated Silk Manufacturers suggested a peerage because of his efforts in cementing international goodwill – 'Earl Lipton of Tyrone' (reflecting the widespread fallacy that Lipton hailed from that county). Within ten days $16,000 had been subscribed in single dollar bills, and in due course the accompanying letters were bound into a Donors' Book which would accompany the loving cup. When Lipton sailed home on 27 September his spirit was as jaunty as ever, and he even promised the pressmen that he would make yet another challenge for the cup.

Two months later Lipton recrossed the Atlantic to collect the loving cup. Designed by Tiffany, it was made of eighteen-carat gold and stood eighteen inches high. Its plinth of sterling silver had been contributed by a consortium of Utah mine owners. It was finished in a dull burnished colour and darkly oxidised. Shamrocks clustered on the lid, while its sides were embellished with a model of the America's Cup in high relief; the great seal of the United States; Lipton's arms and the insignia of the Royal Ulster Yacht Club in bright enamels. It was engraved: 'In the name of the hundreds and thousands of Americans and well-wishers of Sir Thomas Johnstone Lipton, Bart., K.C.V.O.' In the aldermanic chamber of City Hall the loving cup was presented to Lipton by Mayor Walker, flanked by his old friends John 'Honey Fitz' Fitzgerald of Boston and Barron Collier. This was a proud moment for the old man, perhaps even prouder than that occasion seven years earlier when he had received the freedom of his native city.

It was an event which would long be remembered in New York City. The dais and balcony were draped with flags and bunting, the police band played rousing Sousa marches and a battery of microphones enabled commentators to broadcast the ceremony live to every corner of the nation. Mayor Walker was in splendid form, betraying no hint of the trouble which had just appeared on the horizon. The Seabury investigations into graft and corruption in the city administration had just begun and only a few days previously Franklin D. Roosevelt, then Governor of New York State, had warned the free-wheeling mayor that he would not be able to duck the investigation by the special grand jury. Brushing these concerns aside, Mayor Walker called upon the English-born Hector Fuller to read out the telegram just received from Will Rogers:

> I am sorry I can't be with you, Sir Thomas, but if you ever tried earning a living under a Republican administration you would know you haven't got any time to go gadding around. You think this is a fine cup. Say, this is nothing to the one we are going to give you when you lose next time. I am already starting on it. I love you, Sir Thomas, but I don't drink that damned tea. Come West, young man.

For some reason, best known to himself, Fuller omitted the crack about tea and thus lost a good laugh, but the newspapers printed the cable in full the following day. Then Jimmy Walker turned to his guest and said:

> You are the gamest loser in the world of sport. It is not simply a good-will cup from America. It could not have carried a more

widespread affection and admiration if it had come to you from the
League of Nations. Take it to your native land where there will be
no constitutional impediment to your full enjoyment of it.

With a hand on the cup, Lipton rose slowly and faced the
cheering crowd. 'Although I have lost, you make me feel that I
have won. But I will try again. Yes, I will try again.' He paused,
faltered, then suddenly sat down. With great presence of mind
Mayor Walker grabbed the microphone and said, 'I'm not
surprised that Sir Thomas finds it hard to speak. I sometimes do
myself, although for other reasons. I think his speech will sound
very well, read in Mr Fuller's very English accent'; then he passed
the script to Hector Fuller. By the time Fuller had delivered the
oration, Lipton had more or less regained his composure. He
staggered to his feet when the band struck up 'The Star-spangled
Banner' but Jimmy Walker, sensing that the old man was unwell,
gently put his hand on his arm and restrained him. Lipton
insisted, however, on getting up unsteadily for the closing bars of
'God Save the King'. Outside in the sharp winter sunshine, there
was a vast throng waiting to cheer him. Mustering all his
strength, he smiled and waved back. It was a very moving
occasion.

A few days later he left New York. His parting shot was that
he would challenge again, in the autumn of 1931 and would race
in 1932. Westwood, however, knew that this would definitely be
Lipton's last voyage. Mentally he was as alert as ever. Only the
day before he left New York he had gone over to Hoboken for
the last time. There he encountered a young English tea-taster
named Slater and not only remembered his name but could recall
the circumstances in which Slater had come to America instead
of going to Calcutta as originally intended. He was to have
replaced an employee who had changed his mind about resigning
at the last moment. When Lipton enquired whether the change of
plan had turned out happily, Slater smiled and said that he was
getting married the following month. A man in Calcutta changes
his mind, and a girl in New Jersey, of whose existence he will
never know, has her whole way of life altered. Did Lipton pause
to reflect on the fickleness of fate? Suppose he had never had that
unfortunate affair with Margaret McAuslan. Suppose he had
been able to settle down with a woman whom he could love, and
by whom he could have been loved in return. Suppose he had met
a girl in America on that first visit all those years ago . . . How
might his life and career have been different? But as he gazed
from the rail of the *Leviathan* on the day of his departure across

the Hudson and saw his name writ large on the Hoboken waterfront, and considered that gold loving cup and the bound volume of letters now lying in the ship's strongroom, he must have smiled to himself. No, he would not have lived his life any differently.

Later William Blackwood, Lipton's ghost-writer, commented to John Westwood, that the old boy was good for at least a couple more cracks at the Cup; but Westwood, who knew his boss more intimately than anyone else, shook his head and said quietly, 'Sir Thomas will NEVER cross the Atlantic to challenge again.' On the homeward voyage he attended to his Christmas cards and mailed them a few days after docking at Southampton. Appropriately the picture on the card that year showed the *Leviathan*. To his American friends he added a personal note, 'Very soon this dear old ship will bring me back among you'. Christmas was a very quiet, sombre affair, made the more poignant by the absence of his very dear friend Tom Dewar who had died recently. Close friends of long standing, such as 'Tay Pay' O'Connor and Captain Sycamore, had also passed away. Lipton must have felt that he was living on borrowed time. Dr Fairweather examined him every morning as usual, but also joined him most evenings for dinner and a brief game of billiards. Duncan Neill was a frequent visitor, discussing the plans for *Shamrock VI*, but Lipton's main companion over the ensuing months was William Blackwood. Together they worked on the manuscript of *Leaves from the Lipton Logs*, Lipton's own alliterative choice reflecting the nautical aspects of his later years.

In January 1931 he gave £10,000 for the poor of Glasgow in memory of his mother, his 'guiding star' as he referred to her in the deed of gift. When Lord Provost Kelly and Sir John Samuel reported to him in April that the money had been converted into vouchers entitling the poor to food and coal he was so delighted that he promptly donated a further £10,000. In the same month he was saddened by the news from Spain that the King and Queen of Spain had gone into exile: dear Alfonso and his charming wife, whom he had driven to and from Southampton in his Daimler and entertained so many times on *Erin* . Of all the royals he had known, Queen Ena was his favourite. This granddaughter of Queen Victoria was a real Scottish princess, having been born at Balmoral to Prince Henry and Princess Beatrice of Battenberg.

In May Lipton celebrated his eighty-third birthday. Among the many presents was one which he must have regarded with mixed feelings. His friends Lord Shaftesbury and Sir Philip Hunloke had finally persuaded the members of the Royal Yacht Club to elect Sir Thomas to the Squadron. What he made of this belated gesture is not known, for he never alluded to it in his auto-biography, and his only comment to the press was that it was very gratifying. 'I am sure it will interest my many friends in the USA,' he added cryptically. In June he announced plans to hold a grand reunion of expatriate Scots in Glasgow in 1932. In August he was at Cowes, the white ensign now fluttering from the jackstaff of *Shamrock V* for the first time. Membership of the Royal Yacht Club entitled him to take part in the King's Cup race. As Lipton's yachts had beaten all-comers in other races for two decades, this race had lost much of its significance; whoever won it could never be really certain that his was the best boat. Ironically, in the year that Lipton was at long last eligible to enter, the organisers threw it open to anyone, member or not, who had a British yacht with a sixty-foot-load water-line. In the end, it was a runaway victory for *Shamrock*. Lipton accepted the cup and the congratulations with his boyish smile, but pointedly did not attend the Squadron's dinner afterwards, and it is doubtful whether he ever set foot within the Club's hallowed portals. In the ensuing weeks *Shamrock* won the big J Class race and at Weymouth beat the King's yacht *Britannia*. *Shamrock* may have been beaten by the *Enterprise* at Newport, but in her own waters she was unassailable.

Meanwhile Lipton was negotiating with the New York Yacht Club over his impending challenge which was expected to be formally entered in September. The *New York Times* pointed out that the challenge would be coming not from Ulster this time but from the Royal Yacht Club which had not made a challenge since 1894, and that *Erin* would be flying the white ensign instead of the 'red duster' of the merchant navy. A subsequent announce-ment intimated that Lipton and the New York Yacht Club had agreed to ban below-deck drum-winches and duralumin masts. Instead, cabin accommodation was required. Even King George V had had *Britannia* altered and rerigged to meet the new requirements. Commenting on some of the extremely complex specifications which had been laid down, the newspaper joked: 'To the non-mathematically versed, the new rule is worse than a Chinese puzzle or Professor Einstein's theory of relativity.'

The Wall Street crash of 1929 had severely shaken the financial world but economic recovery was well under way when, in the summer of 1931 the Credit Anstalt, Austria's largest bank, collapsed. This sent shock waves through the banks of Europe and America, triggering off the Depression. In Britain,

Ramsay Macdonald's Labour government was forced on 25 August to form a coalition with its Conservative and Liberal opponents in a vain bid to save sterling, and three weeks later the Gold Standard was abandoned. In the current economic climate a challenge for the America's Cup seemed highly inappropriate. It was announced that the challenge was postponed for the time being.

Lipton was out motoring on Tuesday 22 September and caught a chill. For several days he nursed a severe cold, Dr G.A. Sutherland calling several times a day to check on his progress. By 1 October there was a slight improvement and Lipton got dressed, worked throughout the morning and in the evening had a few friends in for dinner. He was cheerful and animated and, afterwards, played a game of billiards. But later that night he was found in his room unconscious. He died the following evening, at 7.15 p. m. on 2 October. He had known little sickness in his life, and he died quickly and peacefully. Four doctors and two or three old friends were with him at the end. To the best of his knowledge, he had not a single living relative.

The following day the world's newspapers carried the obituaries and the encomiums with the familiar portrait of the tall figure in the yachting cap and polka-dot tie. The papers were unanimous in stressing the part which he had played in cementing good relations between Britain and America. In thirty years he never did or said anything that might have been misconstrued. Given the sensitivities of both countries and the intensity of the love–hate relationship between them, this was an astonishing feat, and illustrates what an uncanny grasp Lipton had for the mood of the moment or the feelings of the people he was among. It was his greatest asset. It was the quality which brought him early success as a shopkeeper in one of Glasgow's poorer districts, and it was a characteristic which, with his impeccable sense of timing, he never lost to the end of his days.

Lipton had been born in Glasgow, and it was to Glasgow that he would return. The coffin was brought north and on Wednesday, 7 October, the funeral service, conducted by the Revd Dr Cameron Reid, took place in St George's Church. Earlier that morning thousands had filed past the coffin before the altar to pay their last respects. Outside, the streets in the immediate vicinity were choked with people and all traffic was at a standstill. After the service, fully fifteen minutes elapsed before the congregation could follow the coffin from the church. The cortege slowly wound its way down Buchanan Street, along the

Trongate and the Saltmarket, then across the river and into Crown Street. All along the route the pavements were crowded with the ordinary men, women and children of the city, some of them old employees, most of them customers of long standing. From the windows of the tenements people gazed down on the procession led by a lone piper. It was a dull, dank, dreich day which fitted the sombre mood of the occasion. Just before Dixon's Blazes, the funeral procession turned left into Caledonia Street and presently entered the gateway of the Southern Necropolis where, eighty-odd years earlier, Thomas Lipton Senior had purchased a lair for thirty shillings on the death of little Frances. Over the ensuing decades Thomas and his wife Frances were to stand at that graveside watching the interment of two other children. In the fullness of time they too would be laid to rest there with their offspring. They could never have imagined that over forty years later, that grave would be piled-high with floral tributes from all over the world. Simultaneously in London, a memorial service at St Columba's in Pont Street was attended by over 500. There, as in Glasgow, the organ played 'Flowers o' the Forest'. The Revd Dr Fleming spoke of Lipton's filial devotion, 'his desire to save his mother from all want, his zest in living, his human largeness of heart'.

The house, policies and estate at Osidge were to be preserved as the Sir Thomas Lipton Memorial Home for Retired Nurses in memory of Frances Lipton. Osidge lay empty for several years and the cost of eradicating dry rot and remedying structural defects could only be met by selling off a substantial part of the surrounding estate. In the year after Lipton's death, however, the Piccadilly Line was extended out to Cockfosters and Southgate was transformed virtually overnight by a rash of speculative house-building. Today, The Chase is like any other suburban street in North London, but Osidge remains much the same: shamrocks adorn the gates and there is a blue plaque on the wall, with a bronze plaque to Lipton's mother in the hallway. Today it is a nursing home for elderly, retired nurses, but a small room contains Lipton memorabilia, including the paintings of Lipton's parents, flanked by large sepia photographs of Lipton himself and William Love. In the 1960s much of the remaining estate was sold off to developers and the money used to build an annexe, Shamrock House. While Johnston Villa in Cambuslang has now ceased to be a nurses' home (it is now the centre for the local medical practice), it is heartening to see that Osidge, even if shorn of its vast policies, is still much as it was in Lipton's day, and that the memory of this essentially good man is still fondly treasured.

With this exception, and a handful of small personal bequests to his servants and closest associates, the great bulk of his fortune, was bequeathed to the city of Glasgow, to be applied to 'the endowment and/or enfranchisement from existing debt of infirmaries and/or hospitals for the relief of the sick and poor and/or individually or collectively to the endowment or relief of the poor and destitute within the city of Glasgow and/or Cambuslang'. Lord Inverforth, H.A. Snelling, Duncan Neill, Colonel Spens and James Brooks were named as trustees. By the time Lipton's various interests had been settled and a very substantial sum had been paid in death duties, almost a million pounds came to Glasgow.

To the city he also bequeathed his collection of yachting trophies, with the notable exception of the first loving cup, which the Americans had presented to him in 1899. This he bequeathed to the New York Yacht Club. For many years the cups and trophies, the freedom caskets, the medals and decorations were on display in a special Lipton room of the People's Palace on Glasgow Green, barely a stone's throw from the spot where the Crown Street Clan had sailed their home-made yachts. The display was enlivened by photographs of the various *Shamrocks* and the royalty he had entertained aboard the *Erin*, together with an astonishing array of mementoes from all over the world – from the Jubilee pin given by a grateful Princess of Wales to the testimonial from the citizens of Nish. In 1951, however, the Lipton trophies and memorabilia were removed to the Museum and Art Galleries at Kelvingrove, and it is a matter of regret that the museum authorities have seen fit to consign them to storage facilities in various parts of Glasgow, out of sight and out of mind, when they could form a very important attraction for visitors, British and American alike.

To the Mitchell Library were consigned the eighty-four folio scrapbooks, together with photograph albums and other volumes. In recent years they have been refurbished and provided material for the wonderful exhibition at Glasgow's Royal Concert Hall in the winter of 1995.

Lipton's story is in these volumes, or rather they contain the newspaper record of his career from 1878 to 1926, and rather fragmentarily thereafter. There is much within these pages that was less than complimentary to him, but if his name was so much as mentioned in an article or news item it automatically found a place in the appropriate scrapbook. Fewer than a dozen scrapbooks chronicle Lipton's business and social life, the vast majority being devoted to the thirty-year saga of the challenges for the America's Cup. If 500 papers reported a race, then cuttings from every one of them would be dutifully pasted in. Waugh, who spent a week in the Mitchell Library poring over this vast archive, summed up Lipton's career in a few simplistic platitudes:

> It is astonishing, indeed, how little he introduced, how little new he brought into commerce; he initiated hardly anything. Each new Lipton's market had as its model that first shop in Stobcross Street, and that first shop had in its turn been modelled on his parents'. What his parents had done on a minute scale he did on an immense scale. That is the Lipton story in a line. He had no impulse to alter the existing fabric. He accepted Crown Street. Let Crown Street stay the way it was. He would root himself in a thousand Crown Streets.[6]

A closer examination of the scrapbooks, particularly the earlier volumes, would have told quite a different story. To be sure, Lipton's experiences in New York in the late 1860s had given him sufficient grounding for him to realise that he was only going to make headway if he rejected the principles on which his father and mother ran their little corner shop; but in so much else he was an innovator, and a brilliant, bold and imaginative one at that. Single-handedly, he revolutionised the retail provision trade. After Lipton it would never be the same again.

NOTES

Prologue

1. *Leaves from the Lipton Logs*, hereafter referred to as *Leaves*, p.24
2. William Blackwood, 'Sir Thomas Lipton', in *Post Victorians* (1933), p.341
3. *ibid*, p.332
4. *Leaves*, pp.21–2
5. Blackwood, *op. cit.*, p.333
6. *ibid*, p.341
7. *ibid*
8. Alec Waugh, *The Lipton Story* (London, 1950), hereafter referred to as Waugh, p.154

1. Boyhood, 1848–63

1. Quoted by Frank Biggar in *History of the Ulster Land War of 1760*
2. Dr Denis Carolan Rushe, *History of Monaghan for 200 Years* (Dundalk, 1921), p.69
3. *ibid* pp.73–4
4. Register House, Edinburgh, deaths register, parish of Cambuslang, 1889
5. Dates of death for Mary Ann and Frances Lipton are taken from the family tombstone in the Southern Necropolis, Glasgow, and were presumably supplied from a family source, perhaps the family bible. Dates of birth were not given, only their ages at the time of death
6. *Leaves*, p.25
7. Bob Crampsey, *The King's Grocer* (Glasgow, 1995), hereafter referred to as Crampsey, p.14
8. *Leaves*, pp.25–6
9. No record of Margaret's birth exists, as the parish registers of Downpatrick were lost in the destruction of the Four Courts, Dublin in 1922, but in the census returns of 1861 and 1871 her place of birth was given as Downpatrick. In the census of 1851 her age was given as ten and she was alleged to have been born in Lanarkshire
10. The 1841 census, for example, shows that a high proportion of the people then living in the Gorbals district of Glasgow were born in Ireland, or were the children of Irish immigrants
11. The Mormon International Genealogical Index for births in Glasgow contains an entry for Thomas Johnstone [*sic*] Lipton, 10 May 1850, under Hutchesontown, Gorbals; but this is a retrospective entry made from non-parochial sources, betrayed by the fact that the mother's name is not given, and especially by the misspelling of the middle name
12. *Leaves*, p.24
13. 1851 Census, Milton district, Barony parish
14. 1871 Census, Hutchesontown district, Gorbals parish
15. *Leaves*, p.26
16. Crampsey, p.15
17. cf Andrew Carnegie's *Autobiography* (1920) where there is a similar reticence
18. Death registers, Gorbals parish, 1857, entry 713
19. *Leaves*, pp.32–3
20. *ibid*, p.34
21. *ibid*, pp.34–5
22. James Mackay, *Kilmarnock* (1992), p.192; Thomas Chalmers, *Hundred Years of Gutta Percha* (R. and J. Dick, Glasgow, 1946)
23. *Leaves*, pp.35–36
24. *Leaves*, p.36
25. Glasgow directories, 1856–8; Matriculation album, Glasgow University; death certificate of John Lipton, Register House, Edinburgh
26. *Leaves*, p.37
27. Death register, Cambuslang parish, 1878
28. *Leaves*, p.38
29. Quoted by Rushe, *op. cit.*, pp.74–5
30. *Leaves*, pp.38–9
31. *ibid*, p.42
32. Article signed R.F.M., in the *Glasgow Evening Times*, 26 September 1911
33. *ibid*, p.39; no entry in 1858-9 Glasgow directories

34. *Leaves*, pp.42–3
35. *ibid*, pp.43–4
36. *ibid*, p.46
37. *ibid*, p.48
38. *ibid*,
39. *ibid*, p.49
40. *ibid*, p.50. The quotation is from Carnegie's *Autobiography*, p.13
41. *Leaves*, p.51

2. Early Employment, 1863–70
1. *Leaves*, p.39
2. *ibid*, p.52
3. 1871 Census, Hutchesontown district, Gorbals parish
4. *Leaves*, p.39
5. *ibid*, p.41
6. *ibid*, p.53
7. *ibid*, p.54
8. *ibid*, p.55
9. *ibid*, pp.57–8
10. *ibid*, p.59
11. *ibid*, pp.57–8
12. *ibid*, p.62
13. *ibid*, p.63
14. *ibid*, p.64
15. *New York Evening Post*, 27 August 1930
16. *Encyclopaedia Britannica* (1875), vol. XVII, p.460
17. *Leaves*, pp.64–5
18. See, for example, *Boys' Realm*, 1 July 1902
19. *Leaves*, p.66
20. *ibid*. According to the *Richmond News Leader*, 14 February 1906, TL was trying to trace old inhabitants of Dinwiddie County who might have remembered him, but apparently without success
21. *Leaves*, pp.68–9
22. *ibid*
23. G.G. Johnson, *A Social History of the Sea Islands* (Chapel Hill, NC, 1930). The *Charleston News*, 19 July 1931, has an article about the *Chisolm* plantation where TL laboured
24. *Leaves*, pp.71–2
25. *ibid*
26. *ibid*, pp.74–5
27. Mrs St Julien Ravenal, *Charleston, the Place and the People* (Charleston, 1925), pp.496–97
28. *Leaves*, p.77
29. *ibid*, p.78
30. *ibid*, p.79
31. *New York Sun*, 21 September 1926
32. *Chicago Sunday Tribune*, 25 July 1897

33. *Chicago Chronicle*, 28 November 1900
34. *Newark Advertiser*, 9 February 1907
35. *Leaves*, p.80
36. Tom Mahoney and Leonard Sloan, *The Great Merchants* (Harper and Row, New York, 1966), p.10
37. *Leaves*, p.80
38. *ibid*, pp.80–1
39. Previous biographers agree that TL spent four years in America. Waugh (pp.12, 21) has this period running from the spring of 1865 to the spring of 1869, though providing no explanation for either date. By implication the first date was calculated on the assumption of TL having been born in 1850, and accepting TL's statement that he celebrated his fifteenth birthday soon after he reached New York. Crampsey (p.25) merely repeats 1869 from Waugh
40. Robert B. Smallwood, *Sir Thomas Lipton, England's Great Merchant Sportsman*, an address to the Newcomen Society, New York on 8 January 1953

3. On His Own Account, 1870–78
1. *Leaves*, p.82
2. *ibid*, p.84
3. *ibid*, pp.85–6
4. Glasgow directories show James Alison in occupation up to 1864, but thereafter the premises were vacant
5. *Leaves*, p.87
6. *ibid*, p.88
7. *ibid*, p.89
8. *ibid*, p.90
9. Register of marriages, Hutchesontown district, Gorbals parish
10. Waugh, p.129
11. Glasgow, death registers
12. Glasgow, birth registers
13. *Leaves*, pp.91–2
14. *ibid*, pp.92–3
15. Dr Arthur Shenkin, in conversation with the author, January 1997
16. *Leaves*, p.95
17. *ibid*, pp.103–04, where TL persistently misspells it Lisnaske
18. *ibid*, p.105
19. Glasgow Directories, 1873-77
20. Unsigned article 'Enterprise in the Provision Trade', in *Larkhall Press*, 11 May 1878
21. *Leaves*, pp.110–11
22. *ibid*, p.118
23. *North British Daily Mail*, 29 May 1877
24. The *Scotsman*, 26 April 1877

4. Cambuslang, 1879–86

1. *Leaves*, pp.106–7
2. *ibid*, pp.108–9
3. *ibid*, p.109
4. *Dundee Courier and Argus*, 14 April 1879
5. *Glasgow Evening News*, 11 April 1879
6. *Paisley Daily Express*, 30 June 1879
7. *The Bailie*, 19 November 1879
8. *Leaves*, p.112
9. *Freeman's Journal*, 25 July 1879
10. As an example of late Victorian humour, it was reproduced by Waugh as an appendix, pp.275-77
11. *Glasgow Herald*, 22 October 1886
12. *Leaves*, pp.142–43
13. *Port Packing in Chicago*, season of 1885–86
14. *Leaves*, p.145
15. *ibid*, p.146
16. *ibid*, p.149–50
17. *ibid*, p.159–61
18. *ibid*, p.122
19. *ibid*, pp.122–23
20. *ibid*, p.113
21. *Newcastle Citizen*, undated press cutting but late December 1886
22. *Leaves*, pp.129–30
23. See, for example, *Aberdeen Evening Express* of 4 December 1884
24. *Scottish News*, 29 March 1886

5. A New Store Every Week, 1886–89

1. *The Magpie*, 13 March 1886
2. *American Dairyman*, 27 May 1886
3. *Omaha Daily World*, 10 November 1886
4. *South Wales Daily News*, 11 April 1887
5. *Glasgow Herald*, 4 February 1878, under heading 'Alleged Slander of a Provision Merchant'
6. *Liverpool Echo*, 9 April 1887
7. *Liverpool Review*, 12 March 1887
8. *Leaves*, p.121
9. *Glasgow Evening Times*, 19 June 1888
10. *The Bailie*, 15 August 1888
11. *Leaves*, pp.173–74
12. *ibid*, p.130
13. *Glasgow Herald*, 28 June 1889
14. *Leaves*, p.132
15. *ibid*, p.163
16. *Glasgow and Lanarkshire Illustrated* (Glasgow, 1903), p.49
17. Walter Freer, *My Life and Memories* (Glasgow Civic Press, 1929), p.59
18. *Leaves*, p.194–95
19. Death registers, Cambuslang parish, 1889

20. Waugh, p.48; Crampsey, p.53
21. *Leaves*, p.196
22. Death registers, Cambuslang parish, 1890
23. Quoted by Freer, *op. cit.*, p.60

6. Tea Tom, 1889–97

1. Quoted in *Essay on the Nature, Use and Abuse of Tea* (London, 1722)
2. Dr John Lettsom, *Natural History of the Tea Trade* (London, 1756)
3. *Literary Magazine*, vol. II (London, 1757), no. 13
4. *Leaves*, p.165
5. *ibid*, pp.132–34
6. Filed in scrapbook without comment!
7. *Alyth Guardian*, 20 June 1890
8. *Leaves*, pp.175–76
9. *Aberdeen Journal*, 10 October 1890
10. *Ceylon Observer*, 28 April 1892
11. *The Grocer*, 5 December 1891
12. *Hansard*
13. Lord Cromer, *Modern Egypt* (London, 1908)
14. *Leaves*, p.196
15. *Sporting Review*, 18 July 1890
16. *North British Grocer*, 20 February 1892
17. Originally published in the *Ceylon Times* and reprinted in the *Madras Times*, 16 June 1892
18. *Leaves*, p.198
19. *ibid*, p.135. The grounding of the *Orotava* was widely reported in the press, May 1897
20. *Glasgow Herald*, 1 and 8 August 1896
21. *Ceylon Observer*, 28 April 1892
22. Quoted in *Leaves*, p.197
23. *ibid*, p.188
24. Tom Mason, *The Story of Southgate* (nd) and Alan Dumayne, *Southgate* (1987)
25. *Scottish Sports*, 19 January 1892
26. *Ilustrated Sporting and Dramatic News, Moonshine, Fun, Black and White* and *The Lady*, issues of July-August 1895 and July 1896
27. *Pall Mall Gazette*, 11 March 1895
28. *Leaves*, p.202
29. William Blackwood, 'A Lovable and Unique Personality', the final chapter of *Leaves* written shortly after TL's death, pp.270–71
30. *Woman's Life*, 30 May 1896
31. *Glasgow Herald*, 14 June 1895
32. 'Notabilities of North London: Mr Thomas J. Lipton, the Napoleon of the

Provision Trade', in the *Fiction Press*, 17 August 1895

7. Sir Thomas, 1897–98
1. *Sheffield Telegraph*, 1 May 1897
2. *Pall Mall Gazette*, 8 June 1895
3. *Edinburgh Evening Dispatch*, 9 November 1892
4. *Birmingham Argus*, 18 May 1897
5. *The Star*, 26 May 1897
6. *Weekly Register*, 22 May 1897
7. Waugh, pp.150–52. This unlikely story was based on an interview with Catherine McLeod (Mrs Stewart) in Duluth, Minnesota. See 'Long-lost Sweetheart of Sir Thomas Lipton's Youth Found at Last' by Sara Roberts, in *Good Housekeeping*, October 1932
8. *The Sun*, 28 January 1898
9. Incredibly, in the 1881 Census for Cambuslang, William Love was described merely as a general servant
10. *The Sun*, 22 July 1898
11. *Times of Ceylon*, 11 May 1897
12. *Planters' Gazette* (India), 25 April 1894

8. The America's Cup, 1898–1914
1. *Moonshine*, 30 September 1898
2. *The Field*, December 1895
3. Lord Dunraven, *Past Times and Pastimes* (London, 1922), vol. I, p.63
4. *Leaves*, p.222
5. Cowes weekly newspaper [details to be supplied]
6. *Westminster Budget*, August 1898
7. *Leaves*, p.243
8. *Bristol Mercury*, 29 September 1899
9. See James Mackay, *Little Boss* (Edinburgh, 1997), pp.221–22
10. *Leaves*, pp.245–46
11. Quoted by Crampsey, p.85
12. *Leaves*, p.246
13. *The Times*, 2 October 1899
14. *New York Herald*, 8 October 1900
15. *Tatler*, 14 August 1901
16. *Leaves*, p.249
17. *Daily Express*, 1 October 1901
18. *New York Herald*, 16 October 1901
19. Many American reports, 31 October 1901
20. *New York Journal*, 8 February 1902 under headline 'Tea King introduced Steel King to the King'
21. *New York Herald*, 22 April 1902
22. *Philadelphia American*, 4 May 1902; *Providence Bulletin*, 18 May 1902
23. Quoted by Waugh, p.140

24. *The Sportsman*, 18 April 1903
25. Waugh, p.141
26. *New York Herald*, 4 September 1903
27. Waugh, p.144
28. *Town Topics*, 27 April 1903

9. The Golden Years, 1900–1914
1. *New York Daily News* and many other papers, 8 October 1900
2. *Pall Mall Gazette*, 20 October 1900
3. *New York Sun*, 9 December 1900
4. *Home Journal*, 10 January 1901
5. *Girls' Realm*, July 1900
6. The best accounts appeared in the *Standard* and *Daily Telegraph*, 22 August 1900
7. Tyne-Tees Television, in association witn Waterman/Arlon films, *The Story of the First World Cup* (1986)
8. *Leaves*, pp.230–31
9. *Hampshire Observer*, 29 November 1902
10. *Chicago American*, 8 September 1901
11. *Brooklyn Eagle*, 25 August 1918
12. *Indianapolis News*, 26 March 1907; *Albany Argus*, 22 November 1910; *Ontario Reporter*, 20 April 1916
13. Leopold Wolfling, *My Life Story, from Archduke to Grocer* (London, 1930), quoted in the *Daily Express*, 25 April 1930
14. *Court Journal*, 11 August 1900
15. *Ceylon Standard*, 3 March 1905
17. *Daily Mirror*, 2 September 1905; *Daily Chronicle*, 8 September 1905
16. *The Star*, 31 May 1906
18. *Weekend*, July 1910
19. W.D. Hornaday, in *Los Angeles Illustrated Weekly*, 12 May 1917
20. Text from the transcript of the trial at the Central Criminal Court. To protect men who were probably still alive in 1950, Waugh changed the names of the principals from Whitaker to Savage, and from Sawyer to Evans. Crampsey followed suit, although there seems no good reason for maintaining such a pretence at this remove in time
21. For an account of Healy's curious role as a British double agent see James Mackay, *Michael Collins* (Edinburgh, 1996), pp.276-7
22. *The Times* law reports, May 1914, *passim*
23. *Proceedings of the House of Lords*, debate on the Canteen scandal
24. *ibid*, speech by Lord Newton, 20 May 1914

10. War Work, 1914–19

1. *New York American*, 2 October 1914; *Glasgow Weekly Herald*, 10 October 1914; *Nursing Times*, 10 October 1914
2. *Chicago Examiner*, 14 August 1914
3. *Cleveland Leader*, 6 December 1914; *Tatler*, 16 December 1914
4. *Le Petit-Monegasque*, 32 January 1915; *Daily Mail*, 4 February 1915; *Daily Chronicle* and *Gentlewoman*, 9 January 1915
5. *Evening Standard*, 9 February 1915; *Daily Mail* 9 February 1915
6. Lord Dunraven, *op. cit.*, vol. I, p.242
7. James Mackay, *Vagabond of Verse* (Edinburgh 1995), p.207
8. *Leaves*, pp.252–54
9. Dr Donnelly's diary, quoted in the *New York Times*, 11 May 1915
10. *Pall Mall Gazette*, 19 February 1915; *Boston Post*, 20 February 1915; *Daily News* and other papers, 9 March 1915
11. *Leaves*, p.255
12. *New York Times*, mid-week Pictorial Supplement, 1 April 1915
13. *Daily Express*, 28 July 1915
14. *Leaves*, p.259
15. The present writer was told, in 1948, by Captain James Thom, ISO (allegedly an eye-witness) that Captain Lauder was shot by his own men
16. *Pittsburgh Sun*, 1 July 1918, for a very full account of this sad episode, written by Harry Lauder himself
17. *The Observer*, 20 January 1918

11. Decline and Fall, 1919–27

1. *Hudson Observer*, 28 December 1919; *Marine Journal*, 24 January 1920
2. *Cambuslang Pilot*, 21 and 28 February 1920
3. *New York Herald*, 26 July 1920
4. *Daily Telegraph*, 26 July 1920
5. *Leaves*, p.260
6. Beverley Nichols, *Twenty-Five* (London, 1925)
7. *Milwaukee Journal*, 28 December 1924
8. Jenny Dolly, 'Our Adventures in Society', in *Tit-Bits*, 31 January 1925
9. *Daily Telegraph*, 6 April 1921
10. *Pall Mall Gazette*, 1 February 1921
11. Quoted by Waugh, pp.207–8
12. *Leaves*, pp.217–18
13. *Liverpool Courier*, 18 September 1922. Many other Lipton anecdotes illustrating Harry Lauder's legendary meanness were reproduced in the newspapers of the 1920s
14. *Leaves*, p.264
15. Waugh, p.210
16. *ibid*, pp.210–11
17. *Glasgow Herald*, 28 September 1927
18. *The Times*, 13 July 1925 and many other papers of the same date
19. *The Times*, 24 July 1926 and *Sunday Chronicle*, 25 July 1926
20. William Blackwood, 'A Lovable and Unique Personality', postscript to *Leaves*, p.274
21. In fact, the collection in the Mitchell Library, Glasgow runs to 108 volumes. Cuttings covering later years (vols. 98–100 and 104) were probably arranged and mounted posthumously by TL's trustees

12. The Final Challenge, 1927–31

1. John H. Hickey, *The Life and Times of the Late Sir Thomas Lipton* (Hickey Publishing Company, New York, 1932)
2. Waugh, p.230
3. *ibid*, pp.256–57
4. *Leaves*, pp.261–62
5. *New York Times*, 19 September 1930
6. Waugh, p.261

SELECT BIBLIOGRAPHY

Bateman, C.T., *Sir Thomas J. Lipton and the America's Cup* (London, 1901)

Blackwood, William, 'Sir Thomas Lipton', in *Post Victorians* (London, 1933)

Crampsey, Bob, *The King's Grocer: the Life of Sir Thomas Lipton* (Glasgow, 1995)

Dunlap, G.D. *America's Cup Defenders*, (New York)

Dunraven, Earl of, *Past Times and Pastimes* (2 vols. London, 1922)

Heaton, Peter, *A History of Yachting in Pictures* (London 1972)

Hickey, John J., *The Life and Times of the Late Sir Thomas J. Lipton* (New York, 1932)

Lipton, Sir Thomas J., *Leaves from the Lipton Logs* (London, 1931)

Nichols, Beverley, *Twenty-Five* (London, 1925)

Smallwood, Robert B., *Sir Thomas Lipton, England's Great Merchant Sportsman, 1850–1931* (New York, 1953)

Waugh, Alec, *The Lipton Story* (London, 1950)

INDEX